Logic, Language, and the World
Volume 1

The Internal Structure of Predicates and Names

Richard L. Epstein

Advanced Reasoning Forum

COPYRIGHT © 2016 by Richard L. Epstein

ALL RIGHTS RESERVED. No part of this work covered by the copyright hereon may be reproduced or used in any form or by any means—graphic, electronic, or mechanical, including photocopying, recording, taping, Web distribution, information storage and retrieval systems, or in any other manner—without the written permission of the author.

The moral rights of the author have been asserted.

Names, characters, and incidents relating to any of the characters in this text are used fictitiously, and any resemblance to actual persons, living or dead, is entirely coincidental. *Honi soit qui mal y pense*.

For more information visit our website:
   www.ARFbooks.org
Or contact us:
   Advanced Reasoning Forum
   P. O. Box 635
   Socorro, NM 87801 USA
   rle@AdvancedReasoningForum.org

ISBN 978-1-938421-31-0 paperback

ISBN 978-1-938421-34-1 e-book

The Internal Structure of Predicates and Names

INTRODUCTION

BACKGROUND

    1   Formal Logic 1
    2   Classical Propositional Logic 5
    3   Formal Theories of Reasoning Well and Limitations of Propositional Logic 11
    4   The Language of Predicate Logic 13
    5   Semantics for Classical Predicate Logic 20
    6   An Axiomatization of Classical Predicate Logic 28
    7   Classical Predicate Logic with Equality 29
    8   Formalizing in Classical Predicate Logic 31

THE INTERNAL STRUCTURE OF PREDICATES

RESTRICTORS of UNARY PREDICATES

    9   Adverbs as Predicate Restrictors 38
   10   Adjectives as Predicate Restrictors 41
   11   A Formal Logic of Simple Predicate Restrictors for Unary Predicates 44
   12   Examples of Formalizing 47
   13   Are Predicate Restrictors Extensional? 57
   14   Multiple Predicate Restrictors 61
   15   Variable Predicate Restrictors 63
   16   A Formal Theory of Classical Predicate Logic with Predicate Restrictors
         of Unary Predicates 66
   17   Examples of Formalizing 69

OTHER PREDICATE MODIFIERS

   18   Predicate Negators 76
   19   Other Kinds of Predicate Modifiers? 78
   20   Modifiers of Modifiers 79
   21   The Pure Negator "Not" 84
   22   Examples of Formalizing 88

INTERNAL CONJUNCTIONS and DISJUNCTIONS

   23   "And" Joining Terms 94
   24   "And" Joining Predicates 102
   25   "And" Joining Modifiers 107
   26   "Or" Joining Predicates 113
   27   Examples of Formalizing 115

RELATIONS

   28   Modifiers of Relations 124
   29   Internal Conjunctions and Disjunctions with Relations 128
   30   Examples of Formalizing 129

A FORMAL THEORY of CLASSICAL PREDICATE LOGIC with PREDICATE MODIFIERS,
INTERNAL CONJUNCTIONS and INTERNAL DISJUNCTIONS
    31   A Formal Theory 138

PREDICATES USED AS RESTRICTORS
    32   Predicates Restricting Predicates 150
    33   Examples of Formalizing 154

SUMMARY 159

THE INTERNAL STRUCTURE OF NAMES

FUNCTIONS and DESCRIPTIVE FUNCTIONS
    34   Functions 164
    35   Classical Predicate Logic with Function Names 167
    36   Functions and Descriptive Names 171
    37   The Syntax of Descriptive Names and Descriptive Functions 174
    38   Semantics for Classical Predicate Logic with Descriptive Names
          and Descriptive Functions 177
    39   An Axiomatization of Classical Predicate Logic with Descriptive Names
          and Descriptive Functions 182
    40   Examples of Formalizing 184

NON-REFERRING SIMPLE NAMES
    41   Names that Don't Refer 192
    42   Classical Predicate Logic with Non-Referring Simple Names 194
    43   Examples of Formalizing 199
    44   Non-Referring Simple Names in Mathematics 204
    45   Classical Predicate Logic with Non-Referring Simple Names and
          Names for Partial Functions 206
    46   Examples of Formalizing Mathematics 210
    47   Classical Predicate Logic with Non-Referring Simple Names,
          Descriptive Names, and Descriptive Functions 213

SUMMARY 221

APPENDICES
    1   Minimal Metaphysics 224
    2   Events in the Metaphysics of Predicate Logic 227
    3   The Dynamic and the Static 231
    4   Propositional Operators 233
    5   A Mathematical Abstraction of the Semantics 235
    6   Parts of Things 240

	7	Completeness Proofs	242
		Classical Propositional Logic (PC)	243
		Classical Predicate Logic	246
		Classical Predicate Logic with Equality	251
		Classical Predicate Logic with Function Names	253
		Classical Predicate Logic with Descriptive Names and Descriptive Functions	254
		Classical Predicate Logic with Non-Referring Simple Names	258
		Classical Predicate Logic with Non-Referring Simple Names and Names for Partial Functions	263
		Classical Predicate Logic with Non-Referring Simple Names, Descriptive Names, and Descriptive Functions	265

Bibliography 270

Index of Notation 275

Index of Examples 276

Index 281

Acknowledgements

I am grateful to Fred Kroon and Juan Francisco Rizzo for many helpful discussions and criticisms of this work.

Appendix 2, "Events in the Metaphysics of Predicate Logic", was previously published in my *Reasoning and Formal Logic*.

Much of Chapter 43 on non-referring simple names appeared in Chapter XVI of my *Classical Mathematical Logic*.

Introduction

Modern formal logic surpasses in rigor, depth, and scope all that had previously been done in logic, it's said now.

But the limitations of modern formal logic are considerable and give the lie to that evaluation. The analysis of arguments, explanations, causal reasoning, and prescriptive reasoning—all part of the traditional scope of logic—depend on evaluating the strength of inferences, which is beyond modern formal methods that are concerned with only validity. Analyses of reasoning that depends on talk about mass or process lie outside the scope of modern formal logic, which is based on the assumption that the world is made up of things.

Even within the limits of the metaphysics and focus of modern formal logic, there is much that lies outside the formal methods that have been developed. This series of volumes is meant to extend the scope of what we can formalize, and in doing so see the real limitations of what can be done. Logic is presented as a tool to investigate the world through the medium and limitations of our language.

In the first section here I set out the standard of modern formal logic: classical predicate logic with equality. This is only a sketch, drawing on the full development in *An Introduction to Formal Logic*, which I refer to as Volume 0 of this series. Those familiar with that book need read only Chapter 3, the aside on the language of predicate logic on p. 19, and Chapter 8.

In the second section I show how we can extend classical predicate logic to formalize reasoning that involves adverbs and relative adjectives by viewing those as modifiers of simpler predicates. What we previously took to be atomic predicates, such as "barking loudly", can then have internal structure. Reasoning that involves conjunctions of terms, as in "Tom and Dick lifted the table", conjunctions of modifiers, conjunctions of predicates, and disjunctions of predicates can also be formalized by viewing them as part of the internal structure of atomic predicates.

The internal structure of names is the topic of the third and last section. Names for functions are used in classical predicate logic to form complex names, such as "sin (x^2)", which is what I present first. In our ordinary reasoning we use descriptions to form functions, such as "the wife of", and we use descriptions to form names, such as "the cat that scratched Zoe". To reason with those we need to take account of their internal structure, which we can do if we drop the assumption, basic to classical predicate logic, that every name must refer to a specific thing. Then we can devise formal logics as a guide to reasoning with simple, atomic names that do not refer.

The formal systems that are developed here are not just formalisms but are meant to help us understand how to reason well. Many worked examples show how we can use them. They also uncover limitations of the formal work. The analyses in the examples are tentative, presented with the hope of stimulating you to deeper and clearer analyses.

The work here proceeds by abstracting and creating formal models to formalize reasoning. By paying attention to the process of abstracting we gain insight into why we consider some reasoning to be good and some reasoning bad, and insight also into the deeper assumptions we make about the world on which our judgments rely. Questions about the metaphysics we assume for modern formal logic and the nature of formalizing have to be faced, most particularly the assumption that the world is made up of objects that we can name. Again, I can present only tentative answers, and often I can only pose a question about the relation of logic to language and how we use both to investigate the world. Some discussions are supplemented by my other work, and books and papers that I cite without attribution are mine. In the end I cannot tell you what is a thing. I cannot tell you what pointing and naming are. But by trying to clarify my ideas about things and naming I hope to lead you to clarify your ideas, to help us find a common basis on which to build and use modern formal logic.

The second volume of this series, *Time and Space*, is about how to extend modern formal logic to formalize reasoning that takes account of time and space; an overview of it is presented in my "Reflections on Temporal and Modal Logic". That volume shows in example after example that reasoning about process, mass, and change is outside the scope of modern formal logic not because of our lack of inventiveness in devising better formal systems but because the metaphysics of viewing the world as made up of things cannot encompass a conception of the world as made up of mass or process. The third volume, *The World as Process*, shows how we can talk and reason about the world as process, not just informally but with a rigorous formal system; an overview of that is presented in my "The World as Process".

Others use logic as a bulwark against the mysteries. They build a wall within which reason reigns and live within the cities built of logic. I use logic as a way into the mysteries, using reason where I can to lead me to the boundary beyond which reason has no sway if we are to enter. Logic is the path, not the end. There is no end but only a continual beginning.

Background

1 Propositions, Inferences, and Formal Logic

We would like rules to guide us in finding truths and, when that is not straightforward, to determine what follows from given assumptions: if this were true, then that would follow. To do this, we must agree on what it is that is true or false.

Proposition A *proposition* is a written or uttered part of speech used in such a way that it is true or false, but not both.

By "uttered" I include silent uttering to oneself, what we might call thinking of the sentence.[1]

Some say that propositions are abstract objects or thoughts that can be shared by all people and that what I have defined here are physical linguistic representatives of propositions. But those who hold such views reason using linguistic propositions, which can serve as a common basis on which to begin our work, as I discuss in Appendix 1.

Typically, we identify equiform words for our reasoning, where what we deem to be equiform depends on the uses we are making of the words. Similarly, we identify equiform propositions, though for those it is more difficult to be clear about what is or is not important for reasoning.

Words and propositions are types Throughout any particular discussion equiform words can be treated as the same for our reasoning. We identify them and treat them as if they were the same word. Equiform propositions, too, will be identified and treated as the same for our reasoning. Briefly, *a word or a proposition is a type*.

---

[1] In my previous work I defined a proposition to be a written or uttered declarative sentence that we agree to view as true or false, explaining that agreements need not be explicit (see *Propositional Logics* and *Predicate Logic*). I now think it is better to talk about how we use parts of speech. Also, to define "proposition" in terms of the notion of a declarative sentence is bad for two reasons. First, it is circular, for we typically define a declarative sentence to be one that is a proposition or is true or false. For example, Edward Sapir says:

> The sentence has, like the word, a psychological as well as a merely logical or abstracted existence. Its definition is not difficult. It is the linguistic expression of a proposition.
> *Language*, Chapter 2, paragraph 12

Second, we will consider parts of speech in artificial languages that we will want to treat as true or false, and, though they may formalize declarative sentences, they are not what we could normally call declarative sentences. Compare what Jean Buridan says in his *Summulae de Dialectica*, 9.6, Third Sophism:

> Even a barrel hoop hanging in front of a tavern is a proposition, "for it is equivalent in its signification to the conventionally signficative utterance that someone might yell at the entrance of the tavern: 'Wine is sold here!'"

Some say that types are abstract objects, in accord with their belief that propositions are abstract. In that case the assumption that words and propositions are types concerns which inscriptions and utterances (which is what we actually use in our reasoning) represent or express or point to the same abstract thing.

A proposition is true or false. But what does that mean? That is a big question which will occupy us throughout this book. For now, I will assume only that we have enough idea of what it means for a proposition to be true for us to begin our studies.

Propositions are true or false. An inference is what we use to say that one proposition follows from one or more others.

Inference An *inference* is a collection of two or more propositions—one of which is designated the *conclusion* and the others the *premises*—that is intended by the person who sets it out as either showing that the conclusion follows from the premises or investigating whether that is the case.

Some say that inferences, too, are abstract things. But all who reason use linguistic inferences, and it is those we can study whether or not we consider them to be representatives of abstract entities.[2]

When does an inference show that the conclusion follows from the premises? That depends in part on what kind of reasoning we are analyzing. Different conditions apply depending on whether we are concerned with arguments, explanations, mathematical reasoning, reasoning about cause and effect, or conditionals.[3] In our work here, we will consider an inference good only if it is valid.

Valid inferences An inference is *valid* means that there is no way the world could be in which the premises are true and conclusion false at the same time.

For example, the following is valid:

(1) Ralph is a dog.
     All dogs bark.
     Therefore, Ralph barks.

I can't prove that to you. At best I rephrase it in other words. If you understand English, it's clear that it's valid.

Similar inferences are also valid:

---

[2] Intent is crucial in determining whether what has been uttered is an inference, as can be seen in hundreds of examples in *Critical Thinking*. The examples of inferences in this book should be understood as prefaced by "imagine that someone has put forward the following inference".

[3] See *Reasoning in Science and Mathematics*, *The Fundamentals of Argument Analysis*, and *Cause and Effect, Conditionals, Explanations*.

Dick is a student.
All students study hard.
Therefore, Dick studies hard.

Suzy is a cheerleader.
All cheerleaders have a liver.
Therefore, Suzy has a liver.

It would facilitate our reasoning if we could clarify in what way these inferences are similar, for we have the intuition that we don't need to know anything about cheerleaders, or students, or dogs to see that they are valid. Somehow, it is the forms of the propositions in these inferences that matter.

Formal logic *Formal logic* is the analysis of inferences for validity in terms of the structure of the propositions appearing in the inference and the analysis of propositions for truth in terms of their structure.

Now consider:

Fido is a dog
Therefore, Fido barks.

To show that this is not valid, we show that there is a way the world could be in which the premise is true and conclusion false: Fido could be a basenji, a kind of dog that can't bark.

To invoke a way the world could be, a *possibility*, in the evaluation of an inference, we use a description when we wish to reason together. A description of the world is a collection of claims: we suppose that this, and that, and this are true. We do not require that we give a complete description of the world, for no one is capable of presenting such a description nor would anyone be capable of understanding one if presented. By using collections of claims to describe or to stand in for possibilities, we need not commit ourselves to a possibility being something real, such as a world in which I am not bald.

But what qualifies some collections of claims as describing a possibility and others not? Regardless of how we conceive of possibilities, we always seem to agree that a description of a way the world could be must be consistent. That is, it cannot have or entail a contradiction. It must be *logically possible*. So there is no way the world could be in which there is a square circle. But there seems to be no contradiction inherent in postulating that a dog could give birth to a donkey: it is logically possible.[4]

---

[4] Some logicians have formulated how to reason when the information we have is or might be inconsistent. A few have argued that contradictions, such as there being square circles, are possible. But such an assumption is not needed for reasoning around contradictions, as I show in "Paraconsistent Logics with Simple Semantics", and it would leave us with no semantic basis from which to start our analysis of possibilities, as I discuss in "Truth and Reasoning".

So a collection of claims describes a way the world could be if it neither contains nor entails a contradiction. Yet that requires knowing what it means for a collection of claims to entail another claim, which is what we are trying to understand. We find ourselves in a circle.

One way to extricate ourselves from this circle is to investigate parts of our reasoning, picking out just this or that kind of reasoning relative to restricted semantic and syntactic assumptions that allow for clarity of analysis, developing a formal logic. Then we can have a clearer notion of possibility and of valid inference for that kind of reasoning. As we extend our investigations to allow for more kinds of reasoning, we will have fuller analyses of logical possibilities and valid inferences.

2   Classical Propositional Logic

The simplest formal logics are *propositional logics* in which the only structure of propositions we consider is how they are formed by combination from other propositions. Traditionally, we confine our interest to four ways of combining or making propositions from others using the *connectives* "and", "or", "not", and "if ... then ...". We adopt symbols for our abstractions of the ordinary language connectives:

$\neg$ *negation* for "not"

$\vee$ *disjunction* for "or"

$\wedge$ *conjunction* for "and"

$\rightarrow$ *the conditional* for "if ... then ..."

These are *formal connectives*. So we might write "Juney is a dog $\wedge$ Juney barks" in place of "Juney is a dog and Juney barks". We might write "Tom sang $\rightarrow$ Dick played the piano" in place of "If Tom sang, then Dick played the piano". These phrases with formal connectives are not propositions until we say how we will understand these symbols.

To start, we need to set out how we can form new propositions from given ones using formal connectives. By defining a *formal language* we can give the structure of all the propositions we can form from any propositions we start with. First we take *propositional symbols* or *variables*, $p_0, p_1, \ldots$ that can stand for any propositions, though the intention is that they'll stand for ones that don't contain a formal connective or word that we would formalize as a formal connective. We then need *metavariables* to stand for any of the propositional symbols or complex expressions we'll form from those; we'll use $A, B, C, A_0, A_1, A_2, \ldots$. The analogue of a sentence in English is a *well-formed formula* (*wff*), which we define inductively.

Wffs and the formal language $L(p_0, p_1, \ldots, \neg, \rightarrow, \wedge, \vee)$

Vocabulary
   propositional variables p_0 p_1 ...
   connectives $\neg$ $\rightarrow$ $\wedge$ $\vee$
   parentheses) (

Well-formed formulas (wffs)

   Each of (p_0), (p_1), (p_2), (p_3), ... is a wff of *length* 1.

   If A is a wff of length n, then $(\neg A)$ is a wff of length $n+1$.

   If A and B are wffs and the maximum of their lengths is n, then $(A \rightarrow B)$, $(A \wedge B)$, and $(A \vee B)$ are wffs of length $n+1$.

A concatenation of symbols of the vocabulary is a *wff* just in case it is a wff of length n for some $n \geq 1$.

Wffs of length 1 are *atomic*; all others are *compound*.

No formal wff such as "$p_0 \wedge \neg p_1$" is a proposition. Only when we agree on how we understand the formal connectives and then assign propositions to the variables, such as "p_0" stands for "Ralph is a dog" and "p_1" stands for "Four cats are sitting in a tree," do we have a formula "Ralph is a dog $\wedge \neg$ (four cats are sitting in a tree)" that can be true or false.

Realizations and semi-formal languages A *realization* is an assignment of propositions to some or all of the propositional symbols. The *realization of a formal wff* is the formula we get when we replace the propositional symbols appearing in the formal wff with the propositions assigned to them; it is a *semi-formal wff*. The *semi-formal language* given by a realization is the collection of realizations of the formal wffs.

I'll use the same metavariables A, B, C, $A_0, A_1, A_2, \ldots$ to stand for semi-formal wffs, too, and p, q to stand for *atomic propositions* that realize the propositional symbols. We abbreviate "A if and only if B" as "A iff B", which means "if A, then B; and if B then A", and we write "A $\leftrightarrow$ B" for "(A$\rightarrow$ B) $\wedge$ (B$\rightarrow$ A)".

I've been using quotation marks around parts of speech or formal symbols to show that I'm talking about the linguistic item or symbol and not using it in the ordinary way. For example, I write "Dick" to indicate that I'm talking about the word and not using the word to refer to someone as when I write: Dick is a student. In what follows I'll often write formal symbols without quotation marks when it's clear I'm talking about the formal symbol, as when I say that $\wedge$ is a connective.

We've described the linguistic forms we'll study. This is the *syntax* of the theory of reasoning we're developing. We did so without any talk of what the formal symbols mean, other than knowing that they will be abstractions of certain English words or phrases, and also without any talk of the meanings or truth or falsity of the formulas of a semi-formal language, that is, the *semantics* of semi-formal languages. We have separated syntax from semantics, and this is what we must do if we want a simple inductive definition of the formal language that we can use in proofs about the language and semi-formal languages. Explicitly, we make the following assumption.

Form and meaningfulness What is grammatical and meaningful is determined solely by form and what primitive parts of speech are taken as meaningful. For a given semi-formal language every wff is a proposition.

There is an additional way we want to make the semantics independent of the syntax. Given a semi-formal wff, once the semantic values of the whole are determined, then any other proposition that has the same semantic values can be substituted for it in any logical analysis. That is, semantically it does not matter that "∧" appears in a formula such as "Ralph is a dog ∧ dogs bark" except for how that determines the semantic values of the whole. Explicitly, we make the following assumption.

Division of form and content If two propositions have the same semantic values, they are indistinguishable in any semantic analysis regardless of their form.

What are the semantic values? We've agreed to view each proposition as having a *truth-value*, that is, as being true or false. Often we want to take into account in our reasoning other semantic values such as subject matter, or the ways in which a proposition could be known to be true, or the likelihood of a proposition being true or false, or what things a proposition refers to, or what time it is meant to be about. But here, we'll make an assumption that will lead to the simplest formal system of propositional logic.

The classical abstraction for propositional logic The only semantic aspect of a proposition that matters to our reasoning is its truth-value.

The only question then is in what way, if any, the truth-value of the whole depends on its form and the semantic values of its parts. We might abstract very little from ordinary English and say that "and" has so many different kinds of uses that there is no regular relation between the truth-values of "Ralph is a dog" and "Ralph barks" that determines the truth-value of "Ralph is a dog ∧ Ralph barks". If we do that, we'll have a poor guide for how to reason. Rather, we abstract considerably by making the following assumption.

Compositionality The semantic values of the whole are determined by its form and the semantic values of its parts.

So with the classical abstraction, the truth-value of the whole is a function of the truth-values of its parts and of nothing else. Of the various ways we could interpret the formal symbols in accord with these assumptions, we adopt the following:

¬A is true iff A is false.

A ∧ B is true iff both A is true and B is true.

A ∨ B is true iff A is true or B is true or both are true.

A → B is true iff A is false or B is true.

Note that I've used "and", "or", "not", and "if . . . then" to explain the evaluations of the formal connectives. This is not circular. We are not defining or giving meaning to "and", "or", "not", "if . . . then . . ." but to $\land$, $\lor$, $\neg$, $\rightarrow$. I must assume you understand English.

Suppose now that we have a realization. We agree that the sentences assigned to the propositional variables, for example, "Ralph is a dog" for p_0, are propositions, that is, each has a truth-value. It is a further agreement to say which truth-value each has. Whether an atomic proposition is true or false is not for us as logicians to decide. We assign truth-values to the atomic propositions of the formal language by any method. Then we extend those to the compound propositions of the semi-formal language by the definitions above, where I use T to stand for "true" and F for "false"

Models A *model* is a semi-formal language, a *valuation* ν that assigns truth-values to the atomic propositions, and the extension of that assignment to all formulas of the semi-formal language via the classical truth-tables. If $\nu(A) = T$, A is *true in the model*, and we write $\nu \vDash A$, read as "ν validates A". If $\nu(A) = F$, A is *false* in the model, and we write $\nu \nvDash A$, read as "ν does not validate A".

Models, then, are the possibilities that classical propositional logic recognizes. For those possibilities to characterize validity, there have to be enough of them.

Sufficiency of the collection of models For any realization, any assignment of truth-values to the atomic propositions defines a model.

Valid inferences For a collection of formal wffs Γ and a formal wff A, the inference Γ *therefore* A is *valid* means that there is no model in which all the wffs in Γ are true and A is false. In that case we say that A is a *semantic consequence* of Γ, or that the pair Γ, A is a *semantic consequence*.

A semi-formal inference is valid if it is the realization of a formal inference that is valid. An inference in ordinary English is valid if there is a formalization of it on which we feel certain we'd all agree is valid.

We write $\Gamma \vDash A$ for "A is a semantic consequence of Γ", which we also read as "Γ validates A". We write $\Gamma \nvDash A$ when it's not the case that $\Gamma \vDash A$.

We can formalize "Ralph is a dog or Ralph isn't a dog" as "Ralph is a dog $\lor$ $\neg$ (Ralph is a dog)". This is true regardless of whether "Ralph is a dog" is true or "Ralph is a dog" is false. Indeed, any semi-formal proposition of the form $A \lor (\neg A)$ is true, as you can check. The form of such propositions, relative to the assumptions of classical propositional logic, guarantees their truth.

Tautologies A formal wff is a *tautology* or *valid* iff in every model its realization is evaluated as true. In that case we write $\vDash A$.

A semi-formal proposition is a tautology iff it is the realization of a wff that is a classical tautology.

A proposition in ordinary English is a tautology if there is a good formalization of it that is a tautology.

Classical propositional logic The formal language, the definitions of realization, models, tautology, and semantic consequence together comprise *classical propositional logic*.

Another way to characterize classical propositional logic is syntactically with an axiom system. Briefly, letting Γ, Σ, Δ, and subscripted versions of those stand for collections of wffs, semi-formal propositions, or ordinary language propositions, according to context, we have the following definition.

Proofs Given a collection of wffs, called the *axioms*, that are taken to be self-evidently true due to their form, a *proof* or *derivation of* B is a sequence $A_1, \ldots, A_n$ such that A_n is B and each A_i is either an axiom or is a result of applying a rule of the system to one or more of the preceding A_j's. If there is a proof of B, we say that B is a *theorem*, and we notate that as $\vdash B$.

A *proof of a proposition* B *from some wffs* Γ is a sequence $A_1, \ldots, A_n$ such that A_n is B and each A_i is an axiom, or is a wff from Γ, or is a result of applying a rule of the system to one or more of the preceding A_j's. In there is a proof of B from Γ, then we say that B is a *syntactic consequence of* Γ, which we notate as $\Gamma \vdash B$. If B is not a syntactic consequenceof A, we write $\Gamma \nvdash B$.

We can write $\dfrac{A_1, \ldots, A_n}{B}$ to mean that $A_1, \ldots, A_n \vdash B$.

Consistency, completeness, and theories

Γ is *consistent* iff for every A either $\Gamma \nvdash A$ or $\Gamma \nvdash \neg A$.

Γ is *complete* iff for every A, either $\Gamma \vdash A$ or $\Gamma \vdash \neg A$.

Γ is *a theory* iff for every A, if $\Gamma \vdash A$, then A is in Γ.

Soundness and completeness of an axiomatization

Given a syntax, a semantics, and an axiom system:

The axiomatization is *sound* means for every A, if $\vdash A$ then $\vDash A$.

The axiomatization is *complete* means for every A, $\vdash A$ iff $\vDash A$.

The axiomatization is *strongly complete* means for every Γ and A, $\Gamma \vDash A$ iff $\Gamma \vdash A$.

Here is an axiom system for classical propositional logic, where A, B, C stand for any wffs of the formal language.

Classical Propositional Logic

1. $\neg A \to (A \to B)$
2. $B \to (A \to B)$
3. $(A \to B) \to ((\neg A \to B) \to B)$
4. $(A \to (B \to C)) \to ((A \to B) \to (A \to C))$
5. $A \to (B \to (A \wedge B))$
6. $(A \wedge B) \to A$
7. $(A \wedge B) \to B$
8. $A \to (A \vee B)$
9. $B \to (A \vee B)$
10. $(A \to C) \to ((B \to C) \to ((A \vee B) \to C))$

rule $\quad \dfrac{A,\ A \to B}{B} \quad$ *modus ponens*

In Appendix 7, I prove the following.

Strong completeness of the axiomatization of classical predicate logic
For any wffs Γ and any wff A, $\Gamma \vdash A$ iff $\Gamma \vDash A$.

3 Formal Theories of Reasoning Well and Limitations of Propositional Logic

Classical propositional logic is meant to serve as a guide to us in our reasoning. We begin by considering the use of certain ordinary language sentence connectives and various examples of inferences. We try to describe, by formalizing, what we see as correct ways to evaluate inferences. Then we say that these are indeed the correct ways to evaluate inferences *relative to the assumptions we have made*. If the theory disagrees with an intuition of ours about what is true or what follows from what, we either give up that intuition in the belief that the assumptions on which we based our theory are correct and that the theory formalizes those well, or we show in what way the formal theory is inadequate to deal with that kind of reasoning due to other aspects of form or meaning of propositions that are crucial in that reasoning.

Creating and evaluating models or theories of reasoning or indeed any human activity or any science can be done well only by restricting our attention to some aspects of our experience and ignoring others.[5] It is beyond our ability to take account at one time of all of experience—if that phrase even makes sense. We cannot pay attention to all we encounter in the world at any one time, nor would we wish to. We cannot pay attention even to all aspects of what we and others say. It is nonsense when Donald Davidson proclaims his more than Leibnizian dream of a perfect calculus of meaning:

> I dream of a theory that makes the transition from ordinary idiom to canonical notation purely mechanical, and a canonical notation rich enough to capture, in its dull and explicit way, every difference and connection legitimately considered the business of a theory of meaning.[6]

These issues become clearer when we consider the limitations of propositional logic. I'll discuss only classical propositional logic, though similar remarks apply to other propositional logics. Consider the inference:

(1) Ralph is a dog.
     All dogs bark.
     Therefore, Ralph barks.

This is valid. There are no propositional connectives in it. So each proposition in the inference is atomic for propositional logic. Hence, the form of it in propositional logic is: p_1, p_2, therefore p_3. In a model we can assign truth or falsity to each atomic proposition independently of all others, and hence we can have a model in which

---

[5] See "On Models and Theories" and "Prescriptive Theories?". See particularly the section "The method of reflective equilibrium" in the latter article for a case study of what goes wrong when formal theories are evaluated solely by their consequences.

[6] "The Logical Form of Action Sentences", p. 115.

"Ralph is a dog" is true, "All dogs bark" is true, and "Ralph barks" is false. The inference is not valid in classical propositional logic.

Yet we all know that such an assignment of truth-values cannot be. It is not possible for the premises of (1) to be true and its conclusion false. So we cannot formalize the inference in classical propositional logic, for an informally valid inference should be formalized as a valid formal inference according to our criteria of formalization. There must be some aspect of these propositions that is not accounted for in classical propositional logic.

It might be just the meaning of the words in this inference. But then we think of the other inferences we looked at in Chapter 1:

> Dick is a student.
> All students study hard.
> Therefore, Dick studies hard.

> Suzy is a cheerleader.
> All cheerleaders have a liver.
> Therefore, Suzy has a liver.

We see a pattern. We note that the repetition of certain words in certain places in the inference matters to the evaluation of whether it is valid. In the second example it matters that the name "Suzy" appears in the first premise and the conclusion. It matters that the words "cheerleader" and "liver" appear in certain places. And the word "all" is crucial to the reasoning. The internal structure of the propositions in these inferences is significant for our reasoning, and hence the semantic aspects of parts of propositions matter, too.

4 The Language of Predicate Logic

We want to parse the internal structure of what we took to be atomic propositions in order to give structural analyses of examples of reasoning like those we saw in the last chapter. We have to relate parts of propositions—words and phrases—to our experience in order to attribute semantic values to them. But what parts and what experience?

The examples we saw in the last chapter are notably about things: dogs, Ralph, students, Dick, cheerleaders, Suzy. We have lots of words for things: chairs, tables, rocks, people, trees, . . . and lots of names for particular things. We organize our experience through our language in terms of things. Not all of our experience is in terms of things, for we also talk about water and mud, about the burning of a flame in a fireplace and the push of the wind, which don't seem to be things. But enough of our talk and our reasoning can be understood as about things for us to make the one big assumption on which modern formal logic is based.

Things, the world, and propositions The world is made up at least in part of things. The only propositions we will be interested in are those that are about things.

What do we mean by "thing"? We seem to be able to agree that rocks, people, dogs, tables, chairs, and trees are things. What we consider most basic about them is not what they're made of nor whether we happen to be looking at them, but only that they are individuals: this rock, that person, this dog, that tree. A thing—whatever it is—is individual and distinct from all else in the world. Yes, a thing may be composed of other things or masses, but what makes it a thing is that it is a whole, a distinct individual. How odd that sounds, for we seem to be saying over and over what we have no way to say except by saying "a thing" or "an individual".

Since each thing is distinct from all else, each is in some way distinguishable from all else. What we mean by saying that we can distinguish each thing we are talking about from all others will be determined in part by the kind of things we are talking about. Equally, it will determine what we consider to be a thing. There is no fixed answer to our question of what we mean by "distinguishable" that we can agree on for all things. Nonetheless, this is where we will start, refining and comparing our notions of things and distinguishability as we proceed in our work.

Consider now the proposition "Spot is a dog". This is about Spot. What we're saying about him is just the rest of the proposition: "is a dog". Generally, if a proposition has one or more names in it, we can take the names out and label that as the "about", what we'll call a "predicate". For example, we can parse the proposition "Spot loves Dick" as composed of two names "Spot" and "Dick" and a predicate "— loves —", or we can take just one of the names out and get a predicate "Spot loves —" or "— loves Dick".

14   Chapter 4

Names and predicates   A *name* is a word (or phrase) that we intend to use to pick out a single thing. A *predicate* is any incomplete phrase with specified gaps such that when the gaps are filled with names the phrase becomes a proposition.

Some people think that predicates, like propositions, are abstract. But in their reasoning they use what we have defined as predicates, though they consider those to be only representatives or expressions of abstract predicates.

What further structure of propositions will we recognize? Since we continue to take propositions as fundamental in our reasoning, we can continue to use the ways of forming new propositions from old ones with the formal connectives of propositional logic. We'll formalize "Ralph is a dog and Ralph barks" as "Ralph is a dog ∧ Ralph barks", and so we have a predicate "— is a dog ∧ — barks".

We talk not only of specific things but of things in general. Doing so, we say how many: seventeen, at least one, no more than forty-seven, many, almost all, each and every. To begin, as is traditional, let's restrict ourselves to considering just two ways: those that can be assimilated to talk about some thing or things, and those that can be assimilated to talk about all things.

These, then, are the parts we will use to parse propositions: names, predicates, propositional connectives, and ways to say "some" or "all". This is enough to begin. To make clear how we will parse propositions, we need to set out a formal language that will specify the structures we'll consider.

We start with symbols for names: $c_0, c_1, \ldots$. But we don't have names for everything we want to talk about, nor is it worth our time to name each thing prior to reasoning about it, even if that were possible. Rather, as in ordinary English, we can use temporary names. We say "that" and point, and if in the context of our conversation it's clear we mean to pick out the lamp on my table, then "that" functions as a temporary name to pick out the lamp. Formally, we can use the symbols $x_0, x_1, \ldots$ as *variables* to play the role of temporary names.

For our formalizations of "all" and "every", we'll use "∀", and for our formalizations of "some" or "there is" or "there exists", we'll use "∃". These are the *universal* and *existential quantifiers*. Then to formalize "Something barks" we can use variables to write "∃x_0 (x_0 barks)", where the predicate is "— barks" and the first use of x_0 is for the "thing" in "something" and the second is for the pronoun when we rewrite the informal proposition as "There is something such that it barks". Similarly, we can write "Everything breathes" as "∀ x_{17} (x_{17} breathes)".

Variables also serve to allow for cross-referencing. For example, if we wish to formalize "Everyone loves itself", we'd use the predicate "— loves —" intending for both blanks to be filled with a name of the same thing, as in "∀x_1 (x_1 loves x_1)".

Predicates can differ depending on how many blanks they have. If there is one blank, as in "—barks", we say the predicate is *unary*; if there are two blanks, as in "—loves —", we say the predicate is *binary*; if there are three blanks, as in

"— and — are the parents of —", we say the predicate is *ternary*; if there are n blanks, we say the predicate is *n-ary*, or its *arity* is n. It might seem we don't normally use predicates that are even 4-ary, but we do, as in "Spot chased Puff towards Dick and away from Suzy". It's hard, though, to think of an example where we would use a 47-ary predicate. But mathematicians do. It's a harmless generalization to allow for predicates of any arity in our formal work, a generalization that allows us not to worry in the middle of our reasoning whether we've got all the tools we need. So we'll take as formal symbols for predicates $P_0^1, P_0^2, P_0^3, \ldots, P_1^1, P_1^2, P_1^3, \ldots$, where the superscript tells us the arity of the predicate symbol, and the subscript tells us which predicate symbol it is in the list. Since it's usually clear what the arity of a predicate symbol is when we use it, I'll normally not write the superscript.

We need to be able to talk about parts of the formal language:

i, j, k, n, and subscripted versions of those stand for counting numbers;

x as well as y, z, w, and subscripted versions of the latter stand for variables;

u, v, and subscripted versions of those stand for *terms* (names or variables);

A, B, C, and subscripted versions of those stand for variables;

P, Q, and subscripted versions of Q stand for atomic predicates.

Wffs and the formal language[7] $L(\neg, \rightarrow, \wedge, \vee, \forall, \exists, P_0, P_1, \ldots, c_0, c_1, \ldots)$

Vocabulary   *predicate symbols* P_i^n for $n \geq 0$ and $i \geq 1$, where i is the arity

name symbols $c_0, c_1, \ldots$ ⎫
                                  ⎬ terms
variables $x_0, x_1, \ldots$ ⎭

propositional connectives $\neg, \rightarrow, \wedge, \vee$

quantifiers $\forall, \exists$

Punctuation   *parentheses* ( )   *comma* ,   *blank* —

Well-formed formulas (wffs)

i. If P is a k-ary predicate symbol and $u_1, \ldots, u_k$ are terms, then

$(P(-, \ldots, -)(u_1, \ldots, u_k))$

is a wff of length 1. The term u_i *fills the ith blank* in P (reading from the left).

If u_i is a variable, it is *free* in the wff; if it is a name symbol, it is not free.

ii. If A is a wff of length n, then $(\neg A)$ is a wff of length $n + 1$.

An occurrence of a variable in $(\neg A)$ is free iff it is free in A.[8]

---

[7] I explain the unusual parts of this particular definition in an aside on p. 19.
[8] This is an abbreviated statement which in full should read:

The ith occurrence of a variable in $(\neg A)$ reading from the left is free in $(\neg A)$ iff the ith occurrence of a variable in A reading from the left is free.

The succeeding steps of the definition can be made more precise in the same way.

iii. If A and B are wffs and the maximum of the lengths of A and B is n, then each of (A→B) and (A∧B) and (A∨B) is a wff of length $n + 1$.

An occurrence of a variable in (A→B) is free iff the corresponding occurrence of the variable in A or in B is free, and similarly for (A∧B) and (A∨B).

iv. If A is a wff of length n and some occurrence of x is free in A, then each of ($\forall x$ A) and ($\exists x$ A) is a wff of length $n + 1$.

An occurrence of a variable in either ($\forall x$ A) or ($\exists x$ A) is free iff the variable is not x and the corresponding occurrence in A is free.

A concatenation of symbols of the vocabulary is a *wff* iff it is a wff of length n for some $n \geq 1$.

A wff of length 1 is *atomic*. All other wffs are *compound*.

In ($\forall x$ A) the initial $\forall x$ has *scope* A and *binds* each free occurrence of x in A, and similarly for ($\exists x$ A).

A wff is *closed* if there is no occurrence of a variable free in it; otherwise it is *open*.

We adopt a convention on informally deleting parentheses:
- The parentheses around atomic wffs and the outer parentheses around the entire wff can be deleted.
- Parentheses between successive quantifiers at the beginning of a wff may be deleted.
- ¬ binds more strongly than ∧ and ∨, which bind more strongly than → . And $\forall x, \exists x$ bind more strongly than any of those.
- A conjunction or disjunction without parentheses is understood as associating the conjuncts or disjuncts to the left.
- Square brackets may be used in place of parentheses.

A term is free for a variable

A(x) means x occurs free in A (other variables may also be free in A).

A(u/x) is the formula that results by replacing every free occurrence of x in A by the term u (unless we say that it replaces only some). We say that A(u/x) is the result of *substituting u for x*.

The variable y is *free for an occurrence of x in* A if that occurrence of x is free and does not lie within the scope of an occurrence of $\forall y$ or $\exists y$. It is *free for x in* A if y is free for every free occurrence of x in A.

A formula of the formal language is not a proposition; it is the form of a proposition. Only when we assign predicates to the predicate symbols in it and names to the name symbols in it can we have a proposition. For example, consider:

$$P_0^1(-)(c_2) \land \forall x_3 \, (P_0^1(-) \, (x_3) \rightarrow P_2^1(-) \, (x_3))$$

We can assign "— is a dog" to $P_0^1(-)$, "— barks" to $P_2^1(-)$, "Ralph" to c_2, and get:

$$(- \text{ is a dog}) \, (\text{Ralph}) \land \forall x_3 \, ((- \text{is a dog}) \, (x_3) \rightarrow (- \text{ barks}) \, (x_3))$$

This is a proposition when we fix on a particular interpretation of the formal connectives, as we did in Chapter 2, and fix on a way to understand the quantifiers and variables, which we'll do in the next chapter.

___

Realizations and semi-formal languages An ordinary language name or predicate is *simple* iff it contains no part we could formalize as a name, predicate, propositional connective, variable, or quantifier, or combination of those.

A *realization* of the formal language is an assignment of simple names to none, some, or all of the name symbols and simple predicates to at least one of the predicate symbols. The *realization of a formal wff* is what we get when we replace the formal symbols in it with the parts of ordinary language that are assigned to them; it is a *semi-formal wff*. The *semi-formal language* for a realization is the realizations of all formal wffs.

___

The realization of a predicate symbol is the simplest predicate we can have in our semi-formal language. It has no structure relative to our other vocabulary except for the placement of blanks.

I'll use the same metavariables for parts of a semi-formal language; for example, $A, B, C, A_0, A_1, \ldots$ can stand for semi-formal wffs. The terminology of the formal language will be understood to apply to semi-formal formulas, so we can say that the formula "$((- \text{ barks}) \, (x_1))$" is open, and a simple predicate realizing a predicate symbol is *atomic*.

In a semi-formal language we divide the vocabulary into three parts.

___

Categorematic vocabulary, logical vocabulary, and punctuation

The *categorematic* vocabulary of a semi-formal language consists of the predicates that realize the predicate symbols and the names that realize the name symbols.

The *syncategorematic* or *logical* vocabulary of a semi-formal language consists of the formal symbols $\forall, \exists, \neg, \rightarrow, \land, \lor, x_0, x_1, \ldots$.

Punctuation is that part of the vocabulary that is not meant to formalize anything but is used only to facilitate reading wffs: blanks, commas, and parentheses.

Categorematic parts of the formal language joined by logical vocabulary and punctuation are categorematic.

___

We would like to formalize much of our reasoning in our system. That includes reasoning we do about the system, which involves predicates such as "— is a wff", "— is a proposition", "— is true", and names for parts of the language.

However, serious problems arise if we allow for these to be in a semi-formal language. If we realize the predicate symbol $P_0^1(-)$ as "— is true" and the name symbol "c_0" as a name for the semi-formal wff "$\neg$ (— is true) (c_0)", we'll have a version of the *liar paradox*: "This sentence is not true". Resolving whether or if that is true or false is a tortuous issue.[9] We can avoid that problem by imposing a sharp distinction between reasoning in our system, that is, our logic, and reasoning about our system, that is, our *metalogic*.

Metalogic vs. logic No name symbol can be realized as a name of any wff or part of a wff of the semi-formal language. No predicate symbol can be realized as a predicate that can apply to wffs or parts of wffs of the semi-formal language.

With the quantifier "$\exists$" we can formalize "there is" or "there exists" but only by treating those phrases as stipulating how many: at least one. However, in English we also use "exists" as a predicate, as in "Ralph exists". Should we allow that "— exists" can realize a predicate? If we do, then we can have a formalization of "There is something that doesn't exist" as "$\exists x\, (\neg\, (- \text{ exists})\, (x))$". Resolving how to evaluate such sentences will require choices that do not seem essential to our basic work. We'll defer such issues to the last section of this book, adopting the following.

Existence and $\exists$ Assertions about existence can be formalized only by using the quantifier $\exists$. The phrase "— exists" and other predicates informally equivalent to it are excluded from our realizations.

Unlike propositional logic, in predicate logic not every formula of a semi-formal language is a proposition. Consider, for example:

(1) $(-\text{barks})\,(x_1) \to (-\text{is a cat})\,(x_2)$

This is not a proposition even if we've settled on how to understand the connectives, variables, and quantifiers. It's a proposition only when we say what "x_1" and "x_2" stand for, which cannot be done within the formal language. So it is only when we add quantifiers to (1), making it a closed formula, that we have a proposition. For example, we could have $\forall x_1 \exists x_2 ((-\text{barks})(x_1) \to (-\text{is a cat})(x_2))$. Once we've fixed on how we'll understand the formal symbols, this is a proposition. *Only closed formulas of the semi-formal language are propositions.*

Some mathematicians and logicians view open formulas, such as $x < y \to \neg\, (y < x)$, as propositions, understanding the free occurrences of variables to be universally quantified. This is confusing because we're never sure whether someone is talking about an open formula or a proposition. Here we'll be explicit, writing, for example, $\forall x\, \forall y\, (x < y \to \neg\, (y < x))$. We can transform any open formula into a proposition in this way.

---

[9] See Chapters IV and XXII of *Classical Mathematical Logic*.

The universal closure of a wff Let $x_{i_1}, \ldots, x_{i_n}$ be a list of all the variables that occur free in A in *alphabetical order*, that is, $i_1 < \cdots < i_n$. The *universal closure* of A is: $\forall \ldots A \equiv_{\text{Def}} \forall x_{i_1} \cdots \forall x_{i_n} A$.

Aside: Unusual features of this formal language
This definition of the formal language differs from most in two respects. The first concerns the use of variables. Variables typically have three roles in a formal language of predicate logic: (i) they indicate what is being quantified, (ii) they serve as temporary names, and (iii) they index blanks in a predicate. The first two roles work together in our semantic analysis of quantification, as we'll see in the next chapter. But the third role creates two problems.

First, if we say that "x_1 is a dog" is or stands for a predicate, then so does "x_2 is a dog", and something must be said about why those are or stand for the same predicate. We can't say that it's because the variable is just a placeholder, because that isn't clear, and why can two different placeholders give the same predicate? After all, in "x_1 is a dog $\wedge$ x_2 is a dog" we don't say that these are the same predicate. Nor can we say that "it doesn't matter what variable we use" until we've explained variables, and that depends on already knowing what predicates are. A second problem, which will become clear later in the text, is that the use of variables without blanks makes it difficult to distinguish a predicate modifier from a propositional operator. So in the formal language here, the blanks are retained in the predicates. Though in English, blanks can appear in various places in a predicate, for the formal language I write the blanks following the predicate symbol, separated by commas, as in $P_2^3(-, -, -)$. Blanks are retained in semi-formal wffs, too, as in "($-$ is a dog) (Ralph)".

The second difference is that the usual definition of a formal language allows for superfluous quantifications such as $\forall x_3 (P_0^1(c_0))$. The rationale for including such formulas is that to do so simplifies the definition of the formal language, allowing a definition of bound and free variables to be made after the definition of the language. But the disadvantage is that semi-formal languages then contain formulas such as "$\forall x_3$ (Ralph is a dog)" that would correspond to the nonsensical "For everything, Ralph is a dog". The semantics for such uses of superfluous quantifiers simply ignore the quantifier, treating that wff as equivalent to "Ralph is a dog". That is not consonant with our normally treating nonsense as false, as I discuss in "Truth and Reasoning". The advantages of not allowing superfluous quantification, beyond ridding our semi-formal languages of nonsense, are significant:

We need no axiom schemes for superfluous quantification.

Many proofs about the language are simplified by no longer having to treat cases of superfluous quantification separately.

All variable-binding operators can be treated uniformly.

So in this formal language and in others that follow, no superfluous quantifiers are allowed. This requires that the definition of what it means for a variable to be bound or free has to be incorporated into the definition of the formal language.

5   Semantics for Classical Predicate Logic

In classical propositional logic the only aspects of a proposition we consider are its truth-value and form. So for an atomic proposition the only aspect we consider is its truth-value. Now an atomic proposition has form: a predicate and name(s). What semantic values will we ascribe to those parts and how will those values affect the truth-value of a complex proposition?

Names, naming, and the universe of a realization
When we use a name, we intend to *designate*, *pick out*, or *refer* to a particular thing. We're not always successful. But to simplify our first analyses, let's restrict ourselves to reasoning in which whenever we use a name, we do pick out a particular thing. There are other semantic values we could ascribe to a name besides what it picks out, but again to simplify, we'll consider just this one.

Names refer (***the classical abstraction of names***) If we use a phrase or a word as a name, we assume that we pick out exactly one thing with it, and that is all we assume about it.

We'd like to use our logic to talk about all things, anything at all. But to talk of all things, we need to have a conception of what it means to use a name or variable to pick out an object, and we have no general account of what it means to name or pick out any object whatsoever. We have only specific methods we can agree to adopt for particular kinds of things. So in any analysis of reasoning, we need to specify what kinds of things we are talking about and what methods we will use to distinguish (pick out, refer) to particular ones of those.

The universe of a semi-formal language Given a semi-formal language, we restrict our attention to some things to reason about; those comprise the *universe* of the semi-formal language. With the universe we specify what ways we can refer to those things using names and variables.

We require that there be at least one object in the universe, and for every name in the semi-formal language there is exactly one object in the universe that it names.

For a particular semi-formal language we can specify various universes. For example, consider the semi-formal language:

(1)   L ($\neg, \rightarrow, \wedge, \vee, \forall, \exists$; — is a dog, — is a cat, — eats grass, — is a wombat, — is the father of —; Bon Bon, Dusty, Howie, Juney, Anubis, Dick, Ralph)

We could take as universe all animals, living or toy. Or we could take as universe all animals, living or toy, that are in the U.S. and aren't in a zoo. Or we could take as universe all animals that have ever lived, all toys, and all tables.

To talk about the ways we can assign reference to names and variables, I'll use the metavariables σ, τ, γ, and subscripted versions of those. We need not (be able to) enumerate those, but we can be clear enough to be able to decide what counts as a way of giving reference and what does not.

Our assumption of the distinguishability of things demands that we be able (at least in theory) to distinguish any one object of the universe from any other. So given any object ɑ of the universe and any variable x, we should have some way of naming, σ, that assigns that object to that variable, which we can write as $\sigma(x) =$ ɑ. Since we'll be evaluating formulas in which lots of variables appear, it's convenient to assume that each variable $x_0, x_1, \ldots$ is or can be assigned a reference by each assignment of references. And since we've agreed that we'll use a name to pick out one thing only from the universe, all the methods of assigning reference should assign that same thing to that name. We codify these assumptions with the following.

Completeness of the collection of assignments of references There is at least one assignment of references. For every assignment of references σ, and every variable x, and every object of the universe, either σ assigns that object to x or there is an assignment τ that differs from σ only in that it assigns that object to x. Given any name c of the semi-formal language, all assignments of references assign the same object to c.

We write $\tau \sim_x \sigma$ to mean that the assignment of references τ differs from σ at most in what it assigns x.

Predicates
The definition of "predicate" requires that when the blanks in a predicate are filled with (temporary) names, we have a proposition, that is, a piece of language that is (or represents what is) true or false. But suppose we take as universe for the semi-formal language (1) all animals living or toy, and we add to the language the predicate "— is a prime number". Is "(— is a prime number) (Juney)" true or false? Juney is (was) a dog, and that sentence seems not only odd but a mistake, certainly not something we'd want to reason with. Perhaps with a judicious choice of universe and judicious choice of predicates such anomalies won't arise.

But this is not the only anomaly. Suppose we take as universe for the semi-formal language (1) all animals that have ever lived. Is "(— eats grass) (Juney)" true or false? That sentence is too vague: Juney, who is (was) a dog would on occasion eat grass, but it wasn't part of her normal diet; she wasn't an herbivore. In this case we could agree to make "— eats grass" more precise so we wouldn't have an atomic wff that is too vague to be a proposition. But it's not just this predicate. The name "Anubis" refers to an animal that is a wolf-dog hybrid I had that eludes classification as either a dog or not a dog, so "Anubis is a dog" is also too vague to be a proposition. Making every predicate sufficiently precise is a scientist's dream. We'd have to spend all our time doing that instead of analyzing our reasoning. And then we still would have no guide for how to reason well in our ordinary lives, for it is not the precise predicates we use but the imprecise ones.

Why don't we just excise such problematic sentences from our semi-formal language? If we were to do so, then what counts as a well-formed-formula will depend not only on form but on the meanings of its parts. We'd have no inductive definition of the semi-formal language and no way to prove anything about our formalizations of reasoning using induction on the length of formulas. Worse, it isn't clear that we could mix syntax and semantics without falling into circularity, contradiction, or incoherence. In any case, often it is only by reasoning with a sentence such as "Anubis is a dog" that we find that it is too vague. Are we then to say that all the reasoning that led us to that conclusion is no reasoning at all?

Much simpler and consonant with much of modern logic is to deal with such anomalies by treating any atomic formula that is odd, or nonsense, or too vague as false. We identify, for sentences, the not-true with the false: *falsity is the default truth-value*.[10] So, for example, we'll classify "(— is a dog) (Anubis)" as false, and "¬ (— is a dog) (Anubis)" as true. We adopt the following.

Form and meaningfulness What is grammatical and meaningful is determined solely by form and what primitive parts of speech are taken as meaningful. For a given semi-formal language with universe, every closed well-formed-formula is a proposition.

Remember that when we assign an object to a variable x, "(— is a dog) (x)" is a proposition, an atomic proposition. For example, if I point to my donkey and say, "That's what x is to stand for", then "(— is a dog) (x)" is false. Now we can state more formally our assumptions about the meaning of predicates.

---

[10] See *Propositional Logics* for the use of falsity as a default truth-value in many formal logics. Even adopting a 3-valued logic with values "true", "false", and "nonsense" amounts to taking falsity as the default truth-value, since "false" and "nonsense" are joined together as undesignated values. Alan R. White in *Truth*, Chapter 2, contrasts taking falsity as the default truth-value with the view that such sentences have no truth-value. For a discussion of vagueness in reasoning see "Truth and Reasoning" in *Reasoning and Formal Logic*.

In contrast, P. F. Strawson, in *Individuals*, p. 99, says:

> The idea of a predicate is correlative with that of a *range* of distinguishable individuals of which the predicate can be significantly, though not necessarily truly, affirmed.

It seems to me we have an independent notion of any particular predicate, such as "is a dog" or "ran". We also have a collection of individuals we'd like to reason about. We understand what the predicate means, but we may be at a loss whether it can be attributed to a particular thing, such as a hybrid wolf-dog or a horse that is trotting.

Predicates apply to objects (*the classical abstraction of predicates*) If we use a phrase or a word as a simple n-ary predicate, we assume that for any object or sequence of objects $a_1, \ldots, a_n$ in the universe the proposition that results by filling the blanks in the predicate with names of those objects in that order reading from the left is true or is false. Such a proposition is called an (*atomic*) *predication*; it is an *atomic proposition*. If the resulting proposition is true, we say that P is *true of* or *applies to* the objects $a_1, \ldots, a_n$ (*in that order*) or that P *holds* for those objects, or that those objects *satisfy* P.

In propositional logic we take the truth or falsity of an atomic proposition to be given: unexplained but assumed. Here, too, we take the truth or falsity of each atomic predication as given. We do not try to answer the question of what it means for a proposition such as "(— is a dog) (Ralph)" to be true; all we say is that it is true or false, and that's as far as we go. And that's as far as we can go if we wish to make our theory of how to reason acceptable and useful to people with a wide variety of views of the world. The idealist, the realist, the platonist, the pragmatist, the physicist, the artist, the theologian, all have their own understandings of what it means to say an atomic proposition is true, and our theory is indifferent to those. We leave to them an explanation of the truth of atomic propositions.

There are many other semantic values we could ascribe to predicates. But to simplify our work here, we'll adopt the following.

The classical abstraction of predicates The only semantic value of a predicate is the truth-values of the predications that can be made with it.

Implicit in the statement of the assumption that predicates apply to objects is that the truth or falsity of a proposition does not depend on how we name objects. This is compatible with if not strictly forced on us by our decision to take into account nothing of a name beyond what it refers to.

Extensionality of predicates A predicate is *extensional* if given any terms $u_1, \ldots, u_n$ and $v_1, \ldots, v_n$ such that each term that is a variable is supplemented with an indication of what it is to refer to, and for each i, $1 \leq i \leq n$, t_i and u_i both refer to the same object, then $P(-, \ldots, -)(u_1, \ldots, u_n)$ has the same truth-value as $P(-, \ldots, -)(v_1, \ldots, v_n)$.

Only extensional predicates are allowed in a semi-formal language.

In this assumption, if a variable appears more than once, we assume that it is given the same reference each time, that is, *the variables are consistently supplemented with indications of what each variable is to refer to.*

Given an atomic wff of the semi-formal language $P(-,\ldots,-)(v_1,\ldots,v_n)$ and an assignment of references σ, we've agreed that $P(-,\ldots,-)(v_1,\ldots,v_n)$ is a proposition when each v_i is given reference $\sigma(v_i)$. Now we further agree on its truth-value. Or rather, we assign a truth-value to it, since we may not know whether that predication is true or is false but wish to investigate the consequences of one or the other possibility. A *valuation based on* σ, which we notate as v_σ, is the assignment of truth-values to all such atomic wffs relative to the assignment of references σ. Then $\mathsf{v}_\sigma(P(-,\ldots,-)(v_1,\ldots,v_n)) = \mathsf{T}$ means that the valuation takes the predication as true, and $\mathsf{v}_\sigma(P(-,\ldots,-)(v_1,\ldots,v_n)) = \mathsf{F}$ means that the valuation takes the predication as false. We write $\mathsf{v}_\sigma \vDash A$ for $\mathsf{v}_\sigma(A) = \mathsf{T}$, and we write $\mathsf{v}_\sigma \nvDash A$ for $\mathsf{v}_\sigma(A) = \mathsf{F}$. Using this notation, we can state more succinctly our assumption that atomic predications are extensional.

The extensionality condition for atomic predications Given any predicate P and terms $u_1, \ldots, u_n$ and $v_1, \ldots, v_n$ and assignments of references σ and τ, if for each i, $\sigma(u_i) = \tau(v_i)$, then:

$$\mathsf{v}_\sigma \vDash P(-,\ldots,-)(u_1,\ldots,u_n) \text{ iff } \mathsf{v}_\tau \vDash P(-,\ldots,-)(v_1,\ldots,v_n).$$

Extending valuations to all closed formulas
To extend the valuations for atomic wffs to all closed formulas, we have to explain how we'll interpret the propositional connectives and the quantifiers.

First, we adopt an assumption we made for propositional logic, modified to note that parts of speech other than propositions can have semantic values. This with the assumption of form and meaningfulness ensures a division of syntax from semantics.

The division of form and content If two categorematic parts of a semi-formal language have the same semantic values, they are indistinguishable in any semantic analysis regardless of their form.

Unlike propositional logic, however, we do not and cannot have that the semantic values of the whole are determined by the semantic values of the parts. We know the meaning of the categorematic part of "$\exists x\,(-\text{ is a platypus})(x)$", and we know that $\exists$ is meant to formalize "there exists", but whether the formula is true depends on what is in the universe of the semi-formal language. We adopt instead the following.

Compositionality relative to what there is The semantic values of a proposition are determined by its form, the semantic values of its parts, and what things we are talking about (the universe of the realization).

Now we can set out an inductive method to extend all valuations at once to all closed formulas of the semi-formal language, as explained more fully in Volume 0.

The inductive extension of all valuations to all wffs
For all σ, for every wff A of the semi-formal language:

$v_\sigma(\neg A) = T$ iff $v_\sigma(A) = F$

$v_\sigma(A \wedge B) = T$ iff $v_\sigma(A) = T$ and $v_\sigma(B) = T$

$v_\sigma(A \vee B) = T$ iff $v_\sigma(A) = T$ or $v_\sigma(B) = T$

$v_\sigma(A \rightarrow B) = T$ iff $v_\sigma(A) = F$ or $v_\sigma(B) = T$

$v_\sigma(\exists x\, A) = T$ iff   for some assignment of references τ such that
       $\tau \sim_x \sigma$, $v_\tau(A) = T$ *the classical evaluation of* $\exists$

$v_\sigma(\forall x\, A) = T$ iff   for every assignment of references τ such that
       $\tau \sim_x \sigma$, $v_\tau(A) = T$ *the classical evaluation of* $\forall$

If $v_\sigma(A) = T$, we say that σ *satisfies* or *validates* A, and we write $v_\sigma \vDash A$ or $\sigma \vDash A$. If $v_\sigma(A) = F$, we write $v_\sigma \nvDash A$ or $\sigma \nvDash A$.

Models A *model* is a realization, a universe for the realization, a complete collection of assignments of references, valuations for atomic wffs satisfying the consistency conditions, the extension of the valuations to all wffs by the inductive definition above, and the valuation on all closed wffs.

Truth in a model For a model M, the valuation v for all *closed* wffs is defined:

$v(A) = T$ iff for every assignment of references σ, $v_\sigma(A) = T$.

$v(A) = F$ otherwise.

A closed semi-formal wff A is *true in a model* M means that $v(A) = T$. In that case we say that A is *valid in* M, or that M *validates* A, and we write $M \vDash A$.

A closed semi-formal wff A is *false in the model* means that $v(A) = F$, which we write as $M \nvDash A$.

The model M is *a model for the collection of closed wffs* Γ of the semi-formal language iff every wff of Γ is true in the model; we write $M \vDash \Gamma$ to mean that for every A in Γ, $M \vDash A$. We say the same for formal wffs if their realizations are true in the model.

We use the letters M, N and subscripted versions of those to denote models.

Here is a schematic representation of a model.

$L(\neg, \rightarrow, \wedge, \vee, \forall, \exists, P_0, P_1, \ldots, c_0, c_1, \ldots)$

↓ realization

$L(\neg, \rightarrow, \wedge, \vee, \forall, \exists$, realizations of predicate symbols and name symbols)
universe: specified in some manner

assignments of references, $\sigma, \tau, \ldots$; assignments of truth-values to atomic predications, $\nu_\sigma, \nu_\tau, \ldots$; assignment of contents to wffs; classical evaluations of $\neg, \rightarrow, \wedge, \vee$; classical evaluations of the quantifiers

{T, F}

The extensionality of all predications Let $u_1, \ldots, u_n$ be a list of all names in A and variables free in A. Let $v_1, \ldots, v_n$ be any terms such that for each i, v_i is free for u_i in A. Let σ, τ be any assignments of references such that for each i, $\sigma(u_i) = \tau(v_i)$. Then $\nu_\sigma \vDash A(u_1, \ldots, u_n)$ iff $\nu_\tau \vDash A(v_1/u_1, \ldots, v_n/u_n)$.

Proof Suppose A has length 0. Then it is atomic, and we are done by the condition of extensionality for atomic predications. Suppose then that the theorem is true for all wffs of length $\leq m$ and A is of length $m + 1$. If A is $\neg B$, then:

$\nu_\sigma \vDash \neg B(u_1, \ldots, u_n)$ iff $\nu_\sigma \nvDash B(u_1, \ldots, u_n)$
   iff (by induction) $\nu_\tau \nvDash B(v_1/u_1, \ldots, v_n/u_n)$
   iff $\nu_\tau \vDash \neg B(v_1/u_1, \ldots, v_n/u_n)$.

I'll leave the cases when A is $B \wedge C$, $B \vee C$, or $B \rightarrow C$ to you.
Suppose that A is $\forall x\, B$. Then:

$\nu_\sigma \vDash \forall x\, B(x, u_1, \ldots, u_n)$
   iff for every $\gamma \sim_x \sigma$, $\nu_\gamma \vDash B(x, u_1, \ldots, u_n)$
   iff for every $\delta \sim_x \tau$, $\nu_\delta \vDash B(x, v_1/u_1, \ldots, v_n/u_n)$
      (by induction, since x does not appear in any of $v_1, \ldots, v_n$ as these are free for $u_1, \ldots, u_n$ in A, so for each i, $\delta(v_i) = \tau(v_i) = \sigma(u_i)$)
   iff $\nu_\tau \vDash \forall x\, B(x, v_1/u_1, \ldots, v_n/u_n)$

The case when A is $\exists x\, B$ is done similarly. Hence by induction the lemma is true for wffs of all lengths. ∎

We have reduced the notion of a way the world could be to that of a model. Relative to this theory and this notion of possibility, we can provide a formalization of the notion of validity

---

Tautologies and valid inferences A closed wff A of the formal language is a *formal tautology* iff in every model its realization is true, in which case we write $\vDash A$.

An inference "$A_1, A_2, \ldots$ therefore B" from the formal language is a *formal valid inference* iff in any model in which the realizations of each of the premises are true, the conclusion is also true. Using Γ to stand for $A_1, A_2, \ldots$, we write $\Gamma \vDash B$ to mean the inference is valid.

A proposition A of a semi-formal language is a tautology iff it is a realization of a formal tautology. An inference from the semi-formal language "$A_1, A_2, \ldots$ therefore B" is *valid* (*in classical predicate logic*) means that it is a realization of a formal valid inference.

For this definition to characterize validity with respect to our assumptions, there have to be enough models to allow for any possibility relative to what we are paying attention to in our syntax and semantics.

Sufficiency of the collection of models For any realization and any universe and complete collection of assignments of references, any assignment of truth-values to the atomic predications satisfying the extensionality condition defines a model.

The categorematic words and phrases of the semi-formal language can be given any meaning we wish in a model, where "meaning" here is restricted to be which object a name picks out and which atomic predications are true. Hence, if an inference is valid, it is due to its form in classical predicate logic, and a tautology is true due to its form in classical predicate logic.

The form of a proposition The *form of a semi-formal proposition* is what we get when we replace the simple predicates that appear in it with formal predicate symbols and replace names with formal name symbols, so long as the replacement is *uniform and distinct*: the same predicate (name) symbol replaces every occurrence of a particular simple predicate (name), and different simple predicates (names) are replaced with different predicate (name) symbols.

The *form of a semi-formal inference* is what we get when we replace the semi-formal propositions appearing in it with formal wffs that serve as their forms, so long as the replacement of predicates and names is uniform and distinct throughout the inference.

Classical predicate logic The formal language, realizations, models, tautologies, and semantic consequence defined here comprise *classical predicate logic*.

6 An Axiomatization of Classical Predicate Logic

We can characterize the tautologies and valid inferences of classical predicate logic syntactically. We use the same definition of "proof", "soundness", "completeness", "consistency", and "theory" as in Chapter 2 except that here *only closed wffs are allowed in a proof sequence and in a theory*.

We can build on the axiomatization of classical propositional logic because every closed wff of the language of predicate logic that has the form of a classical propositional logic tautology is valid here, too. The axiom system for classical predicate logic I give here is in terms of schemes in the formal language: any wff that is an instance of any of the schemes is an axiom.

I. Propositional axioms

The axiom schemes of classical propositional logic (p. 10), where A, B, C are replaced by wffs of L and the universal closure is taken.

(For example, $\forall \ldots \neg A \to (A \to B)$ is a propositional axiom scheme.)

II. Axioms governing $\forall$

1. a. $\forall \ldots (\forall x\,(A \to B) \to (\forall x\,A \to \forall x\,B))$ *distribution of $\forall$*
        if x is free in both A and B
    b. $\forall \ldots (\forall x\,(A \to B) \to (\forall x\,A \to B))$
        if x is free in A and not free in B
    c. $\forall \ldots (\forall x\,(A \to B) \to (A \to \forall x\,B))$
        if x is free in B and not free in A

2. $\forall \ldots (\forall x\,\forall y\,A \to \forall y\,\forall x\,A)$ *commutativity of $\forall$*

3. $\forall \ldots (\forall x\,A(x) \to A(u/x))$ *universal instantiation*
    where u is free for x in A

III. Axioms governing the relation between $\forall$ and $\exists$

4. a. $\forall \ldots (\exists x\,A \to \neg\forall x\,\neg A)$
    b. $\forall \ldots (\neg\forall x\,\neg A \to \exists x\,A)$

Rule $\dfrac{A,\ A \to B}{B}$ where A and B are closed formulas   *modus ponens*

In Appendix 7, I prove the following.

Strong completeness of the axiomatization of classical predicate logic
For any wffs Γ and any wff A, $\Gamma \vdash A$ iff $\Gamma \vDash A$.

7 Classical Predicate Logic with Equality

In our reasoning we often want to say that two terms do or do not refer to the same object. So we add a binary predicate to the formal vocabulary of predicate logic that is meant as an abstraction of "— is the same as —".

The equality predicate The equality predicate "$\equiv$" is part of the formal language, the definition of which now includes an additional clause:

$(-\equiv-)(u,v)$ is an *atomic wff* for any terms u and v.

I use "$\equiv$" for the equality predicate in order to avoid confusion with the use of "$=$" as a convenient abbreviation in our ordinary writing. Informally, we can write $u \equiv v$ for $(-\equiv-)(u,v)$ and $u \not\equiv v$ for $\neg((-\equiv-)(u,v))$.

The equality predicate is part of the formal language. Though it has meaning of its own, we classify it as part of the logical vocabulary because it is meant to be interpreted the same in every model, like the other parts of the logical vocabulary that do not change their interpretation from model to model.

Interpretation of the equality predicate For any assignment of references σ in a model, $\vDash_\sigma u \equiv v$ iff $\sigma(u)$ is the same object as $\sigma(v)$.

It might be argued that the interpretation of "$\equiv$" does vary, since the criterion of what counts as an object and hence what is the same object re-identified varies with the presentation of the universe. In one model the shoes in Zoe's closet count as eight things; in another model they are viewed as four things, four pairs of shoes. However, given a semi-formal language and universe, we do not allow the assignment of any value whatever to an atomic predication using "$\equiv$", as we do with "— is a walrus".

Note that we can now have closed formal wffs with no categorematic part, such as "$\forall x_1 \exists x_2 \neg (x_1 \equiv x_2)$". Hence, for a semi-formal language we need not realize any predicate symbol.

We can axiomatize classical predicate logic with equality by adding to the axiomatization of classical predicate logic the following.

Axioms for equality

5. $\forall x\,(x \equiv x)$ *identity*

6. $\forall \ldots \forall x\, \forall y\,(x \equiv y \rightarrow (A(x) \rightarrow A(y/x)))$ *extensionality*
    where A is atomic and y replaces some
    but not necessarily all free occurrences of x in A.

Axiom scheme 5 formalizes that every variable does not vary its interpretation under a given assignment of references. Axiom scheme 6 formalizes the principle of extensionality of predicates for atomic wffs.

In Appendix 7 I prove the following.

Strong completeness of the axiomatization of classical predicate logic with equality
For any wffs Γ and any wff A, $\Gamma \vdash A$ iff $\Gamma \vDash A$.

Without "$\equiv$" in the language we cannot ensure syntactically that our models satisfy the extensionality condition. So all the formal and semi-formal languages that we'll look at will now include the identity predicate.

8   Formalizing in Classical Predicate Logic

In order to formalize ordinary language propositions and inferences in classical predicate logic and to see what we cannot formalize, we need some standard for what counts as a good (acceptable) formalization. That, with many examples, is developed in Volume 0, *An Introduction to Formal Logic*, which I summarize here.

Criteria of formalization

1. The formalization respects the assumptions that govern our choice of syncategorematic vocabulary and definition of truth in a model. The constraints we work under when we adopt classical predicate logic must be observed.

2. If a proposition is informally true due to its form or false due to its form, then its formalization is a tautology or anti-tautology, respectively.

3. If one proposition follows informally from another or a collection of other propositions, then its formalization is a formal semantic consequence of the formalizations of the other(s).

4. The formalization contains the same categorematic words as the original, allowing for changes of grammar to satisfy the first criterion.

5. The use of previously agreed-upon words or phrases to replace grammatical constructions not recognized by predicate logic may appear in a formalization.

6. If we give an analysis of a particular predicate by formalizing it with a formal symbol whose meaning we stipulate either by semantic agreements or an axiomatization, we may choose in advance to recognize certain other predicates or grammatical variations as being formalizable by the same symbol.

7. The grammar of the original is preserved by the formalization. That is, the structure of the original proposition with respect to the grammatical categories we have assumed (names, predicates, connectives, quantifiers, variables, phrase markers) is respected by the formalization.

    7.a. A regular translation of certain words or parts of words into syncategorematic terms is observed. Further, formalizations are regular in the sense that each proceeds in analogy with agreed-upon formalizations of others. This is the requirement of *parity of form*.

7.b. A proposition containing no words governed by Criterion 7.a is taken as atomic.

7.c. The order of the categorematic words and parts of the original is respected.

These criteria are supplemented by a number of conventions we adopt to guide us absent contextual clues. For example, we generally formalize "All dogs bark" as "$\forall x\,((-\text{ is a dog})\,(x) \to (-\text{ barks})\,(x))$", though in context we might formalize it as "$(\forall x\,(-\text{ is a dog})\,(x) \to (-\text{ barks})\,(x)) \land \exists x\,(-\text{ is a dog})\,(x)$".

One limitation we encounter in formalizing in classical predicate logic is illustrated by:

(1)   Dick is a bachelor.
      Therefore, Dick is not married.

We recognize this as valid. But the form it has in classical predicate logic is just: "$P(c)$, therefore $\neg Q(c)$", which is not valid. The inference (1) is valid due not to its form but because part of the meaning of "bachelor" is "unmarried man". So perhaps we should formalize (1) as:

$(-\text{ is a man})\,(\text{Dick}) \land \neg((-\text{ is married})\,(\text{Dick}))$
Therefore, $\neg((-\text{ is married})\,(\text{Dick}))$

A *formalization* is a translation into a semi-formal language that sticks as closely as possible to the form and words of the original, as understood by our agreements establishing classical predicate logic. An *analysis* is an attempt to make explicit our understandings of the words in a proposition that are not covered by the agreements establishing classical predicate logic. Incorporating analyses of words into the process of formalization changes the project of logic from investigation of logical validity based on form to one based on the meaning of categorematic words. A formalization should contain the same categorematic words as the original. To the extent that an analysis can be captured by one or many semi-formal propositions, we can use those *meaning axioms* to supplement a formalization, saying that the formalization is adequate only relative to our formalized assumption(s). In this case, we could require that (1) be formalized only in models in which the following is true:

$\forall x\,(-\text{ is a bachelor})\,(x) \to \neg((-\text{ is married})\,(x))$

Meaning axioms A *meaning axiom* is a semi-formal proposition that is meant to formalize some part of the meaning of particular categorematic parts of a semi-formal language. A formalization is made *relative to a meaning axiom* means we consider the formalization only in those models in which the meaning axiom is true.

We distinguish between inferences that are valid due to their form and those that are valid due to the meaning of the words in them.

Formal and material consequences An ordinary language inference is *formally valid* or a *formal consequence* in classical predicate logic iff there is a good formalization of it which is valid in classical predicate logic.

An ordinary language inference is *materially valid* or a *material consequence* in classical predicate logic iff it is not formally valid but there is a good formalization of it which is valid in classical predicate logic relative to a meaning axiom.

Still, there are major limitations on what we can formalize in classical predicate logic. There are many other semantic values of propositions, names, and predicates that we often consider in our reasoning. Other predicate logics have been devised to take those into account.[11]

Reasoning that involves quantifying over predicates or qualities such as "Marilyn Monroe had all the qualities of a great actress" cannot be formalized in classical predicate logic. But there are extensions of classical predicate logic that allow for formalizing such propositions, though only by invoking substantial additional metaphysics about predicates and collections.[12]

Nor can reasoning about masses such as snow, gold, and mud be formalized in classical predicate logic, for masses are not things. Alternative logics based on different assumptions about the world have been proposed for formalizing propositions such as "Snow is white".[13]

Yet in none of these theories can we formalize the following:

(2) Juney is barking loudly.
    Therefore, Juney is barking.

We recognize this is valid. But the only choice we have for formalizing it in predicate logic is to take "— is barking" and "— is barking loudly" as atomic. In that case we could have a model in which the premise is true and conclusion false, since we can assign values to these atomic predications independently of each other.

We could formalize (2) using a meaning axiom:

$$\forall x \, (\, (\text{— is barking loudly}) \, (x) \rightarrow (\text{— is barking}) \, (x) \,)$$

Our justification for doing so would be that it is the meaning of the words that guarantees the validity of (2). But then we consider:

---

[11] See *Propositional Logic*, *Predicate Logic*, and Stanisław Krajewski's and my "Relatedness Predicate Logic". In this volume, I focus on classical predicate logic as the simplest in which to present ideas that can be used in other predicate logics, too.

[12] A brief presentation of second-order classical predicate logic is in Volume 0. A more extensive examination of the metaphysical assumptions involved is given in *Predicate Logic*, and a mathematical presentation is given in *Classical Mathematical Logic*.

[13] See, for example, Harry C. Bunt, *Mass Terms and Model Theoretic Semantics*.

> Dick is eating quickly.
> Therefore, Dick is eating.
>
> Suzy is getting dressed carefully.
> Therefore, Suzy is getting dressed.

These, too, are valid, and the meanings of the words in them seem irrelevant to our evaluation. These inferences are valid due to their form, we feel, so they should be formally valid inferences. Yet they have no form in predicate logic beyond "P(c) therefore Q(c)".

The internal structure of what we have taken in predicate logic to be atomic propositions can matter to our reasoning.[14]

---

[14] Some of the ideas for analyzing the internal structure of predicates that I propose are similar to or perhaps the same as those set out by others, notably: E. J. Borowski, "Adverbials in Action Sentences"; Romane Clark, "Concerning the Logic of Predicate Modifiers" and "Deeds, Doings and What Is Done: The Non-Extensionality of Modifiers"; Terence Parsons, "The Logic of Grammatical Modifiers"; Ingmar Porn, "On the Logic of Adverbs"; Thomas Schwarz, "The Logic of Modifiers"; Richmond Thomason, "Logic and Adverbs"; and Richmond Thomason and Robert Stalnaker, "A Semantic Theory of Adverbs". M. K. Rennie in *Some Uses of Type Theory in the Analysis of Language* also deals with many of these issues within a tradition, which he documents, of giving semantics for ordinary language.

In Appendix 2 I discuss the view that we could formalize sentences such as (2) in classical predicate logic by appealing to events as a foundation for predicate logic.

The Internal Structure of Predicates

Restrictors of Unary Predicates

9   Adverbs as Predicate Restrictors

In the last chapter we looked at:

(1)   Juney is barking loudly.
Therefore, Juney is barking.

Dick is eating quickly.
Therefore, Dick is eating.

It seemed that the form of these guarantees their validity. But what is that form? Perhaps it is:

(name) is (verb)ing (adverb).
Therefore, (name) is (verb)ing.

But we also have:

(2)   Tom ran fast.
Therefore, Tom ran.

That bridge collapsed in a hurry.
Therefore, that bridge collapsed.

A more general form is:

(name) (verb) (adverb or adverbial phrase).
Therefore, (name) (verb).

But not all inferences of this form are valid:

(3)   Suzy is nearly awake.
Therefore, Suzy is awake.

Manuel almost walked.
Therefore, Manuel walked.

It isn't just the form of the inferences at (1) and (2) that lets us conclude they are valid. The adverb "loudly" restricts the application of "—is barking" to just those things that are barking loudly. It says how the barking is done. The adverb "quickly" tells us how Dick is eating: it restricts the application of the predicate "— is eating" to just those things that are eating quickly. In (3), "nearly" does not tell us how Suzy is awake, nor does "almost" restrict the predicate "— walked" to just some of the things that walked.

Should the inferences at (1) and (2) be understood as formal or material consequences? We do not need any meaning axioms to ensure the validity of them in a formal system once we recognize this form. But to recognize the form we need to know something about the meaning of the adverbs.

Compare:

(4)   Ralph is a dog.
      Therefore, something is a dog.

We formalize this as a valid inference in classical predicate logic because we recognize the word "Ralph" as a name that is being used to pick out exactly one object. We don't use "Xopoquitl" as a name because we do not recognize it as one; we do not use "— snigs flabbist" as a predicate because we do not recognize it as a phrase that when supplemented with a name will give a proposition. It is our reasoning we are formalizing, and our reasoning supposes some ability to use our language. Part of that ability we are invoking here is that we can recognize what grammatical category a word or phrase is in. One grammatical category is that of adverb. Among adverbs, some are *predicate restrictors*: they restrict what the predicate can apply to.[16] So long as a word or phrase has that function, and we can tell if it does by knowing our ordinary language, the inference is valid. Just as (4) is a formal consequence, so are the inferences at (1) and (2).

We can notate the form of those inferences as:

(P(—)/R) (a)
Therefore, P(—) (a)

Here R stands for an adverb that is a restrictor, and P(—)/R is the unary predicate P restricted by R. An inference of this form is valid when R stands for an adverb or adverbial phrase that tells how. The use of the adverb yields a different predicate, since we previously said that, for example, "— is barking" and "— is barking loudly" are predicates, indeed atomic predicates in classical predicate logic. We continue to employ the convention that when symbolizing the use of a predicate, we put the variables and names that fill the blanks at the right-hand side of the predicate.

What is the status of "/" in a semi-formal language? It isn't categorematic, for it has no semantic value apart from its use with a predicate, adverb, and name. Is it, then, logical vocabulary like $\wedge, \vee, \neg, \rightarrow, \forall, \exists$ and the variables $x_1, x_2, \ldots$, or is it punctuation, like parentheses, commas, and blanks? Compare:

Tom is taller than Dick

We formalize this as:

(5)   (— is taller than —) (Tom, Dick)

The parentheses, blanks, and comma clarify how to read (5): they separate the categorematic parts of it. We do not think we have to give an account of the way in which they contribute to the semantic value of the whole. All that contributes to the semantic value of the whole are the semantic values of the parts: "Tom", "Dick", "(— is taller than —)". They are brought together to form a whole, an atomic

---

[16] Some call these "affirmatives"; see J. A. W. Kamp, "Two Theories about Adjectives", p. 125.

proposition, by asserting that the predicate applies to the objects named by the names: the parentheses, blanks, and comma are our way of showing that this is what we are doing. They do not formalize any part of the original proposition, as $\wedge$ formalizes "and". Similarly, consider a formal version of (1):

(6)   ((− is barking)/loudly) (Juney)

The slash does not formalize any part of the premise of (1). We need it only to clarify the reading of (6) by separating the categorematic parts; those parts alone are what give meaning to (6). The slash is punctuation, not logical.

Note that we don't write the premise of (1) as:

(− is barking) (Juney)/loudly.

That would take "loudly" to modify "Juney is barking", which is already a proposition. We aren't creating new propositions from old ones. Rather, *we are relating atomic predicates by parsing the internal structure of some of them.*

In classical predicate logic we take "− is barking loudly" as primitive, atomic semantically as well as syntactically. We continue that here, treating (6) as semantically primitive. We may give a story, an explanation of that: the restrictor "loudly" pares down the extension of "− is barking" to only those things that are barking loudly; the restrictor "loudly" signifies a concept that modifies the concept signified by "− is barking" to apply to only some of the objects to which "− is barking" applies; the restrictor "loudly" represents an abstract operator that functions on abstract predicates to create new abstract predicates such that the abstract predicate represented by "− is barking/loudly" subparticipates in the predicate represented by "− is barking"; .... But all we need to continue our semantic analysis using (6) is that it has a truth-value, one that is related to the truth-value of "(− is barking) (Juney)". We continue to take "(− is barking)/loudly" as an atomic predicate, but a complex one. Any application of it to an object is an atomic proposition, true or false, with no further explanation required in our logical analysis.

10 Adjectives as Predicate Restrictors

Adjectives, too, can be used as restrictors. Consider:

(1) Buster is a small elephant.
Therefore, Buster is an elephant.

Tom is a bright student.
Therefore, Tom is a student.

Suzy is a great cheerleader.
Therefore, Suzy is a cheerleader.

Manuel is a strong paraplegic.
Therefore, Manuel is a paraplegic.

These are all valid. In each the adjective is restricting the predicate to those things of a certain kind. Adjectives that tell us what kind are predicate restrictors, too. We can use such an adjective to replace "R" in the characteristic form for valid restrictor inferences:

(2) (P(—)/R) (a)
Therefore, P(—) (a)

Are there adverbs or adjectives that in some cases are used as predicate restrictors and in some cases not? We'll consider that possibility later. For now, we claim only that if an inference has the form (2) where R is replaced by an adverb or adjective that is always used as a predicate restrictor, then the inference is valid. We know that "small", for example, is a restrictor. So we write the first inference at (1) as:

(3) ((— is an elephant)/ small) (Buster)
Therefore, (— is an elephant) (Buster)

However, there seems to be a big difference between adverbs and adjectives. We can form the predicate "— is small", but there is no predicate "— is loudly". If we formalize (1) as (3), we will have a predicate restrictor "small" and a predicate "— is small" that are unrelated.

But consider this inference using "is small" as a predicate:

Buster is a small elephant.
Therefore, Buster is small.

It's invalid: a small elephant is still very large. That's why we can't formalize "Buster is a small elephant" as "Buster is an elephant ∧ Buster is small". But then what do we mean by "small"? Buster is a small elephant, but he's not small. Over there, that's a small skyscraper, but it's not small.

The sentence "Buster is small" is too vague to be a proposition. The word "small" is a *relative adjective*: a predicate has to be specified which the adjective is meant to restrict, either explicitly or by context, for otherwise a use of the adjective gives a sentence that is too vague to be a proposition.[17] The phrase "is small" is not a predicate, just as "loudly" is not a predicate. In Chapter 12 we'll consider in examples whether some adjectives are not relative.

Still, if we take (2) to be a scheme of valid wffs, what are we to make of:

(4) Juney is a dog loudly.
     Juney is barking small.

Are we to countenance adjectives modifying verbs, and adverbs modifying classifications? We have (at least) two choices.

a. Distinguish between process and classification predicates
We can divide all predicates into process predicates (verbs) and classification predicates. We can divide all restrictors into adverbs, which can modify only process predicates, and adjectives, which can modify only classification predicates.

b. Nonsense is false
We take all nonsensical formulas to be false, the default truth-value. We take the sentences at (4) to be propositions, false ones, in order to have a simple, uniform definition of the formal language that allows for what is grammatical and meaningful to be determined solely by form and what primitive parts of speech are taken as meaningful. A restrictor can restrict a predicate to nothing: there are no objects of which "— is a dog/loudly" is true.

It seems that (a) is more faithful to how we actually use English, though shortly we'll see examples of words that can be used as both adjectives and adverbs, and in colloquial speech it is common to hear adjectives used as adverbs, as in "He talks good".[18] But would the extra work in the complication of the formal language for

---

[17] Romane Clark, in "Concerning the Logic of Predicate Modifiers", p. 334, says:

> I suggest that for logical purposes attributive adjectives standing alone be viewed as tacitly qualifying a common noun. "This ball is red" unfolds into "this ball is a red ball"; "John is famous" into "John is a famous person".

Compare what Jean Buridan says, in his *Summulae de Dialectica* 4.2.6:

> ... as regards non-substantivated adjectives I hold that they cannot be the subject of a proposition in themselves, i.e., without a substantive name, for the proposition would be ungrammatical, unless the substantive were implied. But I am doubtful whether they can be predicated in themselves by virtue of the implied substantive, since in a conversion the subject should become the predicate and the predicate should become the subject, and an adjective cannot become the subject in itself, unless it gets substantivated. And on this question we should have recourse to grammar, if the truth cannot be determined in logic.

[18] In German, "gut" is used as both an adjective and an adverb.

(a) make any difference to our reasoning? That is, even if we could clearly distinguish between processes and classifications, is there any form of valid inferences we need to respect that distinguishes them?

We've seen none, so there seems to be no good motive to adopt (a) in formalizing our reasoning. If as we develop our theories we find that the difference between processes and classifications matters for what is a valid scheme of propositions or inferences, we'll have (a) as an option. In the meantime let's adopt (b) as part of a general rule for formalizing.

Parsimony of formalizing We do not take account of aspects of linguistic usage unless we see that they are needed to distinguish some informal scheme of tautologies or valid inferences.

When a restrictor restricts the application of a predicate to nothing, as in "(— is barking)/small) (Juney)", the wff is false.

Predicate restrictors A *predicate restrictor* is a word or phrase that can be used to modify any predicate to create a different predicate that applies to all or some of the things to which the original predicate applies and to nothing else or applies to nothing at all.

Generally, if a restrictor is an adjective (phrase), it says what kind, and if it is an adverb (phrase), it tells how, though we'll see other kinds of restrictors later.

In ordinary speech the following is valid:

Juney is barking loudly.
Therefore, something is barking loudly.

To formalize this, we have to be able to use our new forms in quantifications:

((— is barking)/loudly) (Juney)
Therefore, $\exists x$ (((— is barking)/loudly) (x))

A formal language and semantics will make this clearer.

11 A Formal Logic of Simple Predicate Restrictors for Unary Predicates

The formal language and realizations

Vocabulary
  predicate symbols $P_0, P_1, P_2, \ldots$
  predicate restrictor symbols $R_0, R_1, \ldots$
  name symbols $c_0, c_1, \ldots$ $\Big\}$ *terms*
  variables $x_0, x_1, \ldots$
  propositional connectives $\neg, \rightarrow, \wedge, \vee$
  quantifiers $\forall, \exists$
  equality predicate $\equiv$

Punctuation
  parentheses $)$ $($ comma $,$ blank $—$ slash $/$

Inductive definition of wff
The previous definition (p. 15) restricted to unary predicate symbols requires a change at the first stage only:

i. If P is a predicate symbol and u is a term, then $(P(-)(u))$ is a wff of length 1.

   If P is a predicate symbol, R a restrictor symbol, and u a term, then $((P(-)/R)(u))$ is a wff of length 1.

   In both cases we say that u *fills the blank in* the wff. If u is a variable, it is *free* in the wff and the wff is *open*; otherwise the wff is *closed*.

Every wff of length 1 is *atomic*. If an atomic wff contains a restrictor symbol, it is *modified atomic*.

In addition to our previous metavariables, I'll use $R, R', R_0, R_1, \ldots$ to range over predicate restrictor symbols

For realizations, we first say that a predicate restrictor of our ordinary language is *simple* if it contains no part we could formalize as a name, variable, propositional connective, quantifier, predicate, predicate restrictor, or combination of those. Then the definitions of a *realization* and of a *semi-formal language* are as before, adding only that a realization assigns simple predicate restrictors to some, none, or all predicate restrictor symbols. As before, the formulas of the semi-formal language inherit the terminology of the formal language. A realization of an atomic wff where the blank is filled with a name is an *atomic proposition*.

Semantics

We start with a semi-formal language. Then we take a universe for it along with a complete collection of assignments of references.

We then give a valuation for all formulas. As before, we take the truth-values of atomic predications as primitive. That is, for every assignment of references σ and every atomic wff $A(u)$, we assume a value of either T or F for $\vDash_\sigma(A(u))$, subject to the following condition.

Res_1 If P is a simple predicate and R is a predicate restrictor, then for any assignment of references σ and any variable x,

If $\vDash_\sigma \vDash ((P(-)/R)(x))$, then $\vDash_\sigma \vDash P(x)$.

Note that by universal instantiation, this will apply to any term u, not just variables. Then the inductive definition of truth in a model is as before.

Now it is clearer why we do not use variables to mark the blanks in a predicate. Suppose we notated the binary predicate "— barked" as "x barked". Then in evaluating "$\exists x ((x \text{ barked})/\text{loudly})$" we would have an assignment of references giving reference to x in "$(x \text{ barked})/\text{loudly}$". That would make "loudly" a propositional operator, not a predicate restrictor.[19]

These semantics are compositional because the semantic value of an atomic proposition depends only on the semantic values of the parts of it and on its form, where the form takes into account restrictors, and the semantic value of a restrictor is the restriction of each predicate it can modify.

An axiomatization

The only change we have made from classical predicate logic is to recognize more structure of some atomic wffs in the formal language. This allows us to see by their form that certain ones are related to others by the condition Res_1. Hence, we have a strongly complete axiomatization of this theory of predicate restrictors by adding the following axiom scheme to the axiomatization of classical first-order predicate logic:

Res_1 $\forall x ((P(-)/R)(x) \to (P(-))(x))$

By adding this axiom scheme to the usual axiomatization of classical predicate logic with equality, we can prove all the semantic consequences of Res_1. That does not mean we can prove all the consequences of our informal conception of how adverbs and adjectives function as restrictors of unary predicates in our ordinary reasoning. We can only axiomatize what we have assumed from our informal conception, and that's the single aspect of predicate restrictors that qualifies them as predicate restrictors, Res_1.

---

[19] See Appendix 4 for why the use of "propositional operators" is wrong.

Aside: The meaning of a predicate restrictor

A predicate restrictor takes any unary predicate and creates a new unary predicate from it. This is like a function that takes a name and creates a new name from it (Chapters 34 and 35). We do not need to say in classical predicate logic what a function is beyond giving its role in the theory. Here, we do not say what a predicate restrictor is beyond giving its role in the theory.

In classical predicate logic the only semantic value we give to an atomic predicate in a model is the determination of which objects it applies to and which objects it does not apply to. If you like, that is the meaning of a predicate in classical predicate logic for that model.

In classical predicate logic the only semantic value we give to a function in a model is the results we get from applying the function to objects. If you like, that is the meaning of a function in classical predicate logic for that model.

Here, the only semantic value we give to a predicate restrictor in a model is how it restricts each atomic predicate. If you like, that is the meaning of a predicate restrictor in classical predicate logic for that model.

One might object that this is a poor approach to the meaning of restrictors. After all, it is through our knowing the meaning of restrictors such as "small" and "loudly" that we can apply them correctly. But the same can be said of "is a dog". In any case, this analysis of meaning of predicate restrictors is closer to practice than the dictionary analysis. For example, consider the word "rotten". We classify ice that has thawed and refrozen and no longer will support weight as rotten in analogy with classifying fruit or meat as rotten, and in further analogies we classify people as rotten and luck as rotten. I do not know how to give a dictionary meaning for "rotten" that covers all these that are joined by analogy and historical practice. The meaning of "rotten", it could be said, can best be indicated by pointing to its use in simple predications as being true or false.

I discuss further the issue of meaning and formal semantics in Appendix 5.

12 Examples of Formalizing

Example 1 Zoe is blond.
   Therefore, *Zoe is a person*.

Analysis The adjective "blond" is relative; after all, we use "blond" differently for people and for wood. So "Zoe is blond" is too vague to be a proposition. But we all know that "Zoe" is used as a name for a person, so we understand "blond" to be relative to people. Hence, we formalize the example as:

$$\frac{(- \text{ is a person}/\text{blond})(\text{Zoe})}{(- \text{ is a person})(\text{Zoe})}$$

$$\frac{(P_1(-)/R_1)(c_0)}{(P_1(-))(c_0)}$$

But now the premise contains the categorematic word "person", which does not appear in the original. This seems to violate the criteria of formalization, being an analysis prior to formalization. But the analysis we do for "Zoe is blond" is not converting one proposition to another. It is eliminating vagueness in order to have a proposition to analyze. We do not violate the criteria of formalization, and the formalized inference is valid.

Example 2 Everything is blond.

Analysis The word "blond" is an adjective, used to restrict the application of a predicate. But we have no predicate here. The word "everything" in a formalization must mean every thing in the universe. Unless we have an atomic predicate in the semiformal language that is meant to pick out all things in the universe, we can't formalize the example, for we have no notion of "blond" that applies to all things.

Example 3 Ralph is purple.
   Therefore, *Ralph is not a dog*.

Analysis Is every adjective relative? What about colors? The inference is missing a premise "Anything that's purple isn't a dog", which is true, and with that it's a valid, good argument. But there doesn't seem to be any noun we could use to make "Ralph is purple" into a predicate with restrictor. He's purple. That's all there is to it. Any shade of purple will do.

Example 4 Spot is a male.

Analysis Some say that whether a thing is a male is independent of what kind of thing it is. They claim that a biological definition in terms of function and genes can be given. They view "— is a male" as a predicate, dividing up all things into

48   *Chapter 12*

two classes: those that are males and those that aren't. On that understanding, the example should be formalized as:

   (— is a male) (Spot)

But there are male dogs, male people, male chickens, male seahorses; many kinds of things can be divided into those that are male and those that are not. What it means to be a male seahorse is very different from what it means to be a male dog, though there is a continuity of meaning based on biological analogy. On this view "male" is an adjective, classifying relative to particular kinds of things, and the example is too vague to be a proposition: it elicits the question "Spot is a male what?" Since we know that Spot is Dick's dog, we can answer "Spot is a male dog", which we can formalize as:

   (— is a dog / male) (Spot)

Whether to treat a word or phrase as a predicate or as an adjective can depend on a close examination of the meaning of the word and how we use it to classify.

Example 5   Birta is a female. So Birta is not a male.

Analysis   If "is a female" is a predicate, we formalize the premise as:

   (— is a female) (Birta)

If "female" is an adjective, we first have to answer "Birta is a female what?" Since she's my dog, I answer "Birta is a female dog", which we formalize as:

   (— is a dog / female) (Birta)

In either case we need a meaning axiom relating "female" to "male". If "— is a female" is a predicate, we use:

   $\forall x \, (\, (— \text{ is a female}) \, (x) \to \neg \, (— \text{ is a male}) \, (x) \,)$

If "female" is an adjective, then we can relate it to "male" only relative to particular predicates. We can describe that with a scheme of meaning axioms:

   $\forall x \, (\, (P(—) / \text{male}) \, (x) \to \neg \, (P(—) / \text{female}) \, (x) \,)$

Example 6   Spot is afraid.

   ((— is a dog) / afraid) (Spot)

Analysis   Dick said this when he saw Spot run into the house and under the bed when a thunderstorm began. "Afraid" seems to be an adjective that is not relative. We don't use "afraid" differently for dogs and for people and for grasshoppers.

Actually, unless we are speaking very loosely, we don't say that a grasshopper is afraid. Grasshoppers are too different from us for us to feel confident that they feel anything like the emotions we do.

It's only because we feel confident that dogs feel as we do that we say they are afraid, or happy, or disgusted. To say that "afraid" is not relative, not a different classification for dogs than for people, is to build into our analyses the assumption that dogs and people are so similar that they feel as we do. That's a pretty big assumption, one that shouldn't be built into our formalizing. More carefully, we'll take "afraid" to be a relative adjective and formalize the example as above.

To assert "That grasshopper is afraid", we must make clear what "afraid" means for grasshoppers, relating it in some way to what we mean by "afraid" for people and dogs, and then, with an indication of what "x" is to refer to, formalize that sentence as "$((-$ is a grasshopper)/afraid) (x)".

Example 7 Dick is awake.

Analysis Surely "awake" is an adjective that is not relative. It doesn't matter what kind of thing we are talking about: awake is awake.

I won't dispute that, though I think a pretty good argument can be made that "awake" is relative: a bear coming out of hibernation is awake differently than a person. If "awake" and other adjectives are not relative, we can accommodate them in our theory by using them solely as predicates.

Example 8 Suzy is beautiful.

Analysis If adjectives are always relative, we should formalize this as:

$((-$ is a woman)/beautiful) (Suzy)

But I can tell you from personal experience that "You're beautiful for a woman" is not a good thing to say.

It seems in ordinary life we sometimes do take adjectives to be absolute, not relative. Platonists believe there is a single quality of being beautiful that is exemplified in many things. This sunset is beautiful because it participates in the beautiful; this dog is beautiful because it participates in the beautiful. But you do not need to be a platonist to think that "beautiful" is absolute: we call a particular sunset and a particular dog beautiful because of some idea we have of beauty, whether that be a platonic quality or simply a way we classify according to a physical or emotional response we have to an experience.

People who hold that view will then have two ways to formalize the word "beautiful", as in:

Suzy is beautiful.
($-$ is beautiful) (Suzy)

Birta is a beautiful dog.
($-$ is a dog/beautiful) (Birta)

In some cases "is beautiful" would be a predicate, in others a predicate restrictor. Those who say that "beautiful" can be a predicate need to tell us which if either of the following hold.

$\forall x \, ((-\text{is a dog}/\text{beautiful}) \, (x) \rightarrow (-\text{is beautiful}) \, (x))$

$\forall x \, ((-\text{is beautiful}) \, (x) \wedge (-\text{is a dog}) \, (x) \rightarrow (-\text{is a dog}/\text{beautiful}) \, (x))$

We need some relationship between the predicate restrictor and the predicate, as well as rules for formalizing, or else we have no idea whether to formalize "Birta is a beautiful dog" as "(—is a dog/beautiful) (Birta)" or "(—is a dog) (Birta) ∧ (—is beautiful) (Birta)". Such an explanation might be given for how to reason with "beautiful". And also for "ugly". And for "peculiar". And perhaps even for what seems the archetype of relative adjectives, "small". But we still have a right to ask someone who holds that view what more general understanding of qualities or adjectives lies behind their classifications, or else we have no more than an *ad hoc* methodology. Absent such a theory, I'll assume that the adjectives we're working with are relative adjectives: each requires a predicate to restrict, or more tendentiously, a class for comparison.

Aside: *Beauty is in the eye of the beholder*
Beauty, they say, is in the eye of the beholder. I do not have different notions of beauty for dogs and buildings and apples. You do not have different notions of beauty for dogs and buildings and apples. But you and I have different notions of what is beautiful. What is beautiful for me is what elicits in me a particular (kind of) feeling. What is beautiful for you is what elicits in you a particular (kind of) feeling. We communicate by comparing our classifications, hoping, thereby, to achieve some intersubjective notion of beauty.

On this view, "— is beautiful" is not a predicate, nor is "beautiful" a relative adjective. When Tom says, "Suzy is beautiful", we should understand that as "Suzy is beautiful to Tom". Each of the following is a distinct proposition, and the truth of one does not entail the truth of any of the others:

Suzy is beautiful to Tom.
Suzy is beautiful to Dick.
Suzy is beautiful to Harry.
Suzy is beautiful to Zoe.
Suzy is beautiful to Suzy.

To formalize these, we can use the predicate "— is beautiful to —". Then we would have, for example:

(— is beautiful to —) (Suzy, Tom)

We could either restrict the second blank to be filled only with terms that refer to humans or take "(— is beautiful —) (Suzy, x)" to be false when x refers to an object that is not a person.

Tom, however, might insist that Suzy really is beautiful, even though he knows that there's no absolute notion of beautiful. He means that (almost) everyone would classify Suzy as beautiful, or at least everyone in some particular group, say Western Europeans and Americans. We might try to formalize that intersubjective use of "beautiful" by:

$\forall x \, \forall a \, \forall b \, [(-\text{is beautiful to} -) \, (x, a) \rightarrow (-\text{is beautiful to} -) \, (x, b)]$

But that's too strict. The "almost" is crucial: our intersubjective agreement in the use of "beautiful" would be fulfilled if almost everyone agreed on its use. There are always people who have (for us) odd evaluations. To formalize that intersubjective standard, we'd need a formal abstraction of "almost all", which we do not have.

In our work here we have taken truth and falsity as fundamental in establishing our norms of reasoning well. But John M. Ellis in *Language, Thought, and Logic* holds that it is our evaluative adjectives such as "beautiful" and "ugly", "good" and "bad", "delicious" and "disgusting" that are the most fundamental classifications we use, more fundamental than truth and falsity. How and whether to use those as the basis for evaluating reasoning is a question I'll leave to others.

Example 9 Zoe: *Snakes are bad.*

Analysis The adjectives "bad" and "good" do seem to be non-relative—if we could agree on what they mean. Some people would say that this example has no truth-value: it is meant only as an expression of approval or disapproval by Zoe. Whatever difficulties there are in formalizing it are not due to the assumptions of our logic but to the controversy over the meaning of evaluative adjectives.

Example 10 *Wanda was fired.*

Analysis What is "fired" relative to? It's odd to say "Wanda was a fired person". That's because "fired" in "—was fired" is not an adjective but part of a passive form of a verb, which, in accord with the rules for formalizing developed in Volume 0, should be converted into an active form: "Someone fired Wanda".

Example 11 *Dick has two dogs.*

Analysis It makes no sense to say "Dick has two". Two what? Two dogs, two cars, two shoes, two pairs of shoes, . . . ? We can count only when we specify what kind of things we are counting. The word "two" is a relative adjective.[20]

We saw in Chapter 9 of Volume 0 that we can represent the counting of things by counting variables that refer to different things. For this example, we can view "has" as a binary predicate subscripted by "p" to show it's meant in the sense of "possesses", and then we have:

$$\exists x \, \exists y \, ((- \text{ has}_p -)(\text{Dick}, x) \land (- \text{ has}_p -)(\text{Dick}, y) \land \\ (- \text{ is a dog})(x) \land (- \text{ is a dog})(y) \land \neg (x \equiv y))$$

This, then, is an example of a relative adjective that is not formalized as a predicate restrictor.

Example 12 *Manuel's singing is emotional.*

Analysis The word "emotional" is a relative adjective. But what is it restricting here? The phrase "Manuel's singing" is used as a noun phrase, picking out a thing. But what thing?

---

[20] See "Mathematics as the Art of Abstraction" in *Reasoning in Science and Mathematics*.

If it's meant as his singing right now, it would seem to name an event, but using events is a bad way to do formalizations in predicate logic, as I discuss in Appendix 2. Instead, we can formalize the example as:

((— is singing)/emotionally) (Manuel)

On the other hand, if what's meant is Manuel's singing in general, not now, but today, yesterday, any time he sings in his usual way, then "Manuel's singing" would be a mass term, which is outside the scope of predicate logic (see Volume 0). Alternatively, we could respect the use of tenses with a habitual form for "is singing", as done in Volume 2, *Time and Space in Formal Logic*.

Example 13   Manuel is emotional.

(— is a person /emotional) (Manuel)

$(P_{23}(-)/R_8) (c_4)$

Analysis   The formalization follows as for Example 1 by supplying the predicate "— is a person". But what is the relation of "emotional" here and "emotionally" in the last example? We have lots of paired adjectives and adverbs: "loud"–"loudly", "quick"–"quickly", "large"–"largely". Though there seems to be some underlying meaning in common for each pair, I can see no general pattern of inferences we need to respect for adjective-adverb pairs, though in some cases we might have relations between them we want to formalize with meaning axioms.

Example 14   Juney is loud.

Analysis   The example is not a proposition because "loud" is relative. Is Juney loud in her barking, in her digging, in her running? Or does she make a lot of noise relative to other dogs? Until we are clear what is meant, we can't formalize this.

Example 15   Juney is barking loudly.
   Therefore, *Juney is not barking softly.*

$\dfrac{((- \text{ is barking})/\text{loudly}) (\text{Juney})}{\neg(((- \text{ is barking})/\text{softly}) (\text{Juney}))}$

$\dfrac{(P_1(-)/R_1) (c_0)}{\neg((P_1(-)/R_2) (c_0))}$

Analysis   The semi-formal inference is not valid: "loudly" and "softly" may be evaluated in a model so as to make the premise true and conclusion false. But we know from the meaning of the words "loudly" and "softly" that the informal inference is valid. So we formalize the inference relative to a scheme of meaning axioms: $\forall x_0 ((P/\text{loudly})(x_0) \rightarrow \neg (P/\text{softly}(x_0)))$.

We cannot relate "loudly" and "softly" apart from modifying predicates. To say that no matter what predicate "loudly" or "softly" modifies, the modified predicates will apply to different objects would require quantifying over predicates.

Example 16 Spot was doing something loudly.

Analysis The example is too vague to be a proposition. The restrictor "loudly" must restrict some particular predicate to be clear enough to formalize. You might think the example is clear enough were you to hear a lot of noise outside the house and recognize that it's made by Spot. But later you might find that Spot was trying to kill a cat that got in the yard and remark, "Gosh, he didn't make much noise at all for trying to kill a cat", so you were wrong. But then you reply, "Well, he was doing something loudly". But you couldn't say what he was doing that he was doing loudly. However, if we have only a finite number of simple predicates in the semi-formal language, $P_1, \ldots, P_n$, we could formalize the example as:

$(P_1 / \text{loudly}) (\text{Spot}) \vee \ldots \vee (P_n / \text{loudly}) (\text{Spot})$

Alternatively, we might interpret the sentence as "Spot was making a lot of noise", which is a proposition. But "noise" is a mass term, so we couldn't formalize that either.

Example 17 Everything that barks is a dog.
 Juney barks loudly.
  Therefore, Juney is a dog.

$\forall x \, (\, (- \text{ barks}) (x) \rightarrow (- \text{ is a dog}) (x) \,)$
$((- \text{ barks}) / \text{loudly}) (\text{Juney})$
─────────────────────────────
 $(- \text{ is a dog}) (\text{Juney})$

$\forall x_2 \, (\, (P_1(-)) (x_2) \rightarrow (P_3(-)) (x_2) \,)$
$(P_1(-)/R_1) (c_0)$
─────────────────────
 $(P_3(-)) (c_0)$

Analysis The example is valid. From the second premise, by Res_1 we can deduce "$(-$ barks$)$ (Juney)", and from that and the first premise by universal instantiation and *modus ponens* we can deduce the conclusion.

Example 18 All dogs are loyal.
  $\forall x \, (\, (-\text{is a dog}) (x) \rightarrow (-\text{is a dog}/\text{loyal}) (x) \,)$

Analysis We think of loyalty, of being loyal, as a quality that many creatures can have. It's not even clear whether we generalize from the loyalty of dogs to the idea that people can be loyal or vice versa. So it seems "loyal" is not a relative adjective. But the standards for a cat to be loyal are certainly different than for a dog, which are different still from a person being loyal. So "loyal" is a relative adjective. In this example it's clearly used as relative to dogs, so we invoke the convention on formalizing common nouns with "all" to get the formalization.

54   Chapter 12

Example 19   Some dogs are loyal.

$\exists x \, (\, (-\text{is a dog}/\text{loyal}) \, (x) \,)$

Analysis   The formalization is now straightforward.

These examples suggest a general convention for formalizing.

Relativizing quantifiers with adjectives   Given a common or collective noun α that we can convert into a predicate P_α, and an adjective β that is a restrictor, we formalize:

All α are β $\forall x \, (P_\alpha \, (-) \, (x) \rightarrow (P_\alpha/\beta) \, (-) \, (x))$

Some α are β $\exists x \, (P_\alpha/\beta) \, (-) \, (x)$

Example 20   (a) *Yoshikawa is a Japanese pilot.*
Therefore,   (b) *Yoshikawa is a pilot.*
       and   (c) *Yoshikawa is Japanese.*

Analysis   The example is from Romane Clark, who says that both of the inferences are valid.[21] But (c) is not a proposition. We accept it as one only because we take "Yoshikawa" to be the name of a person and implicitly understand "Japanese" to be restricting the predicate "— is a person". A formalization of (c) is:

(d) $(-\text{is a person}/\text{Japanese}) \, (\text{Yoshikawa})$

A formalization of (a) would then be:

(e) $(-\text{is a pilot}/\text{Japanese}) \, (\text{Yoshikawa}) \, \wedge \, (-\text{is a person}) \, (\text{Yoshikawa})$

The inference from (e) to (b) is valid because "Japanese" is a restrictor. But the inference from (e) to (d) is not valid. Still, every pilot is a person. We can make that assumption explicit:

(f) $\forall x \, (\, (-\text{is a pilot}) \, (x) \rightarrow (-\text{is a person}) \, (x) \,)$

Perhaps we can get (d) from (e) and (f) via the scheme:

$\forall x \, (P(x) \rightarrow Q(x)) \rightarrow \forall y \, (P/R(y) \rightarrow Q/R(y))$

But that is not a scheme of tautologies, as the following example shows:

$(-\text{is a pilot}/\text{old}) \, (\text{Yoshikawa}) \rightarrow (-\text{is a person}/\text{old}) \, (\text{Yoshikawa})$

A pilot over 55 is old, whereas we wouldn't normally classify someone who is 55 as an old person. To get (d) from (e) and (f) we have to add a meaning axiom:

$\forall x \, (\, (-\text{is a pilot}/\text{Japanese}) \, (x) \rightarrow (-\text{is a person})/\text{Japanese}) \, (x) \,)$

This is a proposition that's true because of the particular categorematic words in it.

---

[21] "Concerning the Logic of Predicate Modifiers", p. 324.

Example 21   (a) *Bidú is a large mammal.*

   (b) *Bidú is a dog.*

   (c) *Every dog is a mammal.*

Therefore,   (d) *Bidú is a large dog.*

$\quad$ ((— is a mammal)/large) (Bidú)
$\quad$ (— is a dog) (Bidú)
$\quad$ $\forall x$ ((— is a dog) (x) → (— is a mammal) (x))
$\quad$ ─────────────────────────────
$\quad\quad$ ((— is a dog)/large) (Bidú)

Analysis This seems to be the right direction for our reasoning. If something is large relative to a bigger collection of things, it's certainly large relative to a smaller collection that's contained in the bigger. The following, it seems, should be a scheme of tautologies:

$\quad$ $\forall x\, (P(x) \to Q(x)) \to \forall y\, (Q/R\,(y) \wedge P(y) \to P/R\,(y))$

But it isn't. Consider:

$\quad$ If every dog is a mammal, then every smart mammal that is a dog
$\quad$ is a smart dog.

The antecedent is true. But the conclusion is false, for Juney was a stupid dog but she was a smart mammal: compared to sheep and cows she was pretty near a genius.

To get from (a) and (b) to (d) we need a meaning axiom for these particular categorematic words:

$\forall x\, ((- \text{ is a mammal}/\text{large})\,(x) \wedge (- \text{ is a dog})\,(x) \to (- \text{ is a dog}/\text{large})\,(x)$

It's not the form of this or the previous example that ensures their validity but the meaning of the words in them.

Example 22 *Any person who is tall is not short.*

$\quad$ $\forall x\, (((- \text{ is a person})/\text{tall})\,(x) \to \neg ((- \text{ is a person})/\text{short})\,(x))$

$\quad$ $\forall x_1\, (P_2(-)/R_1)(x_1) \to \neg (P_2(-)/R_2)(x_1))$

Analysis All atomic sentences in our semi-formal languages that we consider too vague to be propositions are classified as false (p. 22). Nonetheless, we can continue to formalize assertions we know are true that involve words like "tall" and "short". With a universe of all living creatures, it may be that "((— is a person)/tall) (Lee)" is false because it is too vague. But the example is true, since the antecedent of it is false when x refers to that person. That is how we set up the conditional to be evaluated: it is true when the antecedent does not apply.

$\quad$ But what about the following?

$\quad$ Any person who is not short is tall.

This is false, and the formalization of it is, too:

$\forall x\, (\neg\, ((-\text{ is a person})/\text{short})\,(x) \rightarrow ((-\text{ is a person})/\text{tall})\,(x)\,)$

To assert "$\neg\, ((-\text{ is a person})/\text{short})\,(x)$" for some particular reference for x is just to assert that "$(-\text{ is a person})/\text{short})\,(x)$" is not true—for whatever reason, including the possibility that the sentence is too vague. It doesn't tell us that the person is therefore tall. What we do have is:

$\forall x\, (((-\text{ is a person})/\text{short})\,(x) \rightarrow \neg\,((-\text{ is a person})/\text{tall})\,(x)\,)$

Example 23 *Everything that breathes also senses, and vice versa.*
Tom breathes slowly.
Therefore, *Tom senses slowly.*

$\forall x\, (x \text{ breathes} \leftrightarrow x \text{ senses})$
$((-\text{ breathes})/\text{slowly})\,(\text{Tom})$
─────────────────────────
$\quad ((-\text{ senses})/\text{slowly})\,(\text{Tom})$

Analysis The inference is invalid. Even if two predicates are equivalent in the sense of being true or false of exactly the same objects, the restrictions of them might not be equivalent. Some say that this shows that the applications of predicate restrictors are not extensional.

13   Are Predicate Restrictors Extensional?

To answer this question, we have to agree on what we mean by "extensional".

Names
In classical predicate logic, the only semantic value of a name that we take into account is what object it refers to. No connotation or sense of a name enters into our semantic evaluation of a proposition, even though in our ordinary reasoning we often take account of how we name things.

It's sometimes said that the *extension* of a name is its reference. Any semantic value of a name other than reference is then called *intensional*.

Predicates
Given a predicate P and some object, we say that the *application of the predicate to that object is extensional* if P is true or false of that object independently of how it is named, and similarly for sequences of objects for non-unary predicates.

We adopt the assumption in classical predicate logic that all applications of predicates are extensional. We allow a predicate in a semi-formal language only if all applications of it to objects in the universe are extensional. If we should use a predicate in our reasoning in a way that is not extensional in this sense, we cannot use classical predicate logic to formalize that reasoning. We have to look to another logic in which some further semantic value of names is taken into account.

Alternatively, rather than assuming extensionality, we could first adopt the assumption of the *division of form and content*: if two categorematic parts of our semi-formal language have the same semantic values, then they are indistinguishable in any semantic analysis regardless of their form. Since the only semantic value of a term is its reference in classical predicate logic, all applications of predicates must be extensional.

People with very different views of the nature of predicates use classical predicate logic. Some think predicates are concrete linguistic items: utterances and inscriptions. Others think they are linguistic types: equivalences on utterances and inscriptions. Others think they are abstract linguistic types. Others think they are related to thoughts, which are somehow universal. Others think predicates are completely abstract and not linguistic at all, as, they say, propositions are. All these people can use classical predicate logic as a guide for reasoning because the only way in which a predicate is taken into account in any formalization is through a specific linguistic expression. We consider a sentence such as "Ralph is a dog" and take in our semi-formal language the linguistic expression "— is a dog" as a predicate, whether as a particular utterance or inscription, or as a representative of a type that needn't be more than equivalences we draw between different utterances and inscriptions, or as a representative of an abstract object. The reasons we give for why "(— is a dog) (Ralph)" or any other atomic predication is true or is false may depend on how we understand what predicates are, but for the semantics of classical predicate logic all that matters is that each atomic predication is true or is false.

Those who use classical predicate logic often make the abstraction to identify a predicate with its *extension*: those things (or sequences of things) of which it is true. Some say that the extension of a predicate is an abstract object: the collection of things or sequences of things of which the predicate is true, where a sequence is also said to be an abstract thing.[22] But that is not essential for us to talk together of the extension of a predicate.

Identifying a predicate with its extension assumes that there is no further semantic value of the predicate that is significant for reasoning we are formalizing. That assumption is rejected for non-classical predicate logics in which the sense or connotation of a linguistic expression taken as (referring to, or as the name of) a predicate matters to analyses of reasoning, even for predicates all of whose applications are extensional.[23]

But the abstraction to identify a predicate with its extension is incorrect even in classical predicate logic. We pay attention to more about predicates than just their extension. We consider their form.

Platonists deny that. They say that the following are different ways of referring to a single predicate, one which, in classical predicate logic, is or can be identified with the collection of all things of which any one of these formulas is true:

— is Marilyn Monroe

— is Norma Jeane Baker

$\forall x \, ((- \text{ is a dog}) (x) \lor \neg (- \text{ is a dog}) (x)) \land (- \text{ is Norma Jeane Mortenson})$

The platonist may ask whether they refer to the same predicate, while someone who views these expressions as distinct predicates asks whether they are equivalent.

Predicate restrictors
Frank Jackson in *Perception* says:

> The "predicate modifier" theorist must, however, see a certain *intensionality* in *all* adverbs. "*x* senses" and "*x* breathes" are (we may suppose) co-extensional. But John does not breathe slowly if and only if he senses slowly. p. 71

And Hans Kamp in "Two Theories about Adjectives" says,

> Clearly all predicative adjectives are extensional. Non-extensional adjectives are for example *affectionate* and *skillful*. Even if (in a given world) all and only cobblers are darts players, it may well be that not all and only skillful cobblers

---

[22] See the mathematical abstraction of the semantics presented in Volume 0 and here in Appendix 5.

[23] See "Relatedness Predicate Logic" by Stanisław Krajewski and me, where subject matter is attributed to each predicate.

Are Predicate Restrictors Extensional? 59

are skillful darts players; and even if all men were fathers, the set of affectionate fathers would not necessarily coincide with the set of affectionate men. p. 125

To conclude from these examples, as Jackson and Kamp do, that the application of a predicate restrictor like "slowly" or "skillful" is not extensional seems to assume a definition like:

> The application of a predicate restrictor to a predicate is *extensional* iff it gives the same value, that is, results in the same predicate, regardless of how the predicate is presented (named).

And that in turn assumes that predicates are not linguistic.

If we view predicates as linguistic, then "— senses" and "— breathes" are different predicates. Even if we assume that they have the same extension, there is no reason to suppose that restricting each with "slowly" will result in predicates with the same extension. Non-extensionality of applications of predicate restrictors would arise only by identifying a predicate with its extension.

But that is just what we do in classical predicate logic. What is non-extensional is that predicates with the same semantic values can be restricted in the same way to give predicates with different semantic values. That contradicts the division of form and content: if two predicates have the same extension, they should be indistinguishable in any semantic analysis. But in the examples, the restrictions result in predicates with different extensions.

We can abandon the principle of the division of form and content. This does not create problems for the definition of a formal language: for that we need only the principle of form and meaningfulness. The division of form and content is made in order to be explicit about what semantic assumptions we are making, that is, what semantic values we are ascribing to categorematic parts of the semi-formal language as opposed to their form. The form of a simple predicate is just the way we write it, with blanks, in English.

If we wish to view the forms of simple predicates as contributing to the semantic value of propositions in which they appear, then we could say that their form is a semantic value. Odd as that sounds, it is consistent with the view that "— breathes" and "— senses" have the same extension but have different intensions, for that is just to say they are different predicates. We can adopt a minimal notion of the intension of a predicate: it is the linguistic predicate itself (viewed as a type).

This is not the way people usually look at extensions and intensions of predicates. They take predicates to be something apart from linguistic expressions and take the intensions and extensions of those to be independent of the linguistic expressions, too. They say that "is a bachelor" and "is an unmarried man" are both names of the same predicate. But that seems to give no clarity for why we might assign different intensions to those. And if we do assign different intensions, then they are or name different predicates. What we have are linguistic expressions that we understand how to use in evaluating truth-values of atomic propositions in which they appear. In detailing how we assign distinct semantic values to those expressions, distinct in their intensions though they may coincide in their extensions, we are saying how we understand those linguistic expressions differently. The predicate as something beyond the linguistic expressions begins to have less and less substance: we have access to it only through the linguistic expressions, and we come to know its properties and nature only by investigating our use of those linguistic expressions. Certainly one can say that there is an abstract thing that is the predicate which is named or expressed by "breathes". But apart from how we ascribe semantic values to that linguistic expression, I don't know what that predicate is. We have the hard work of trying to be explicit about how we understand certain linguistic expressions; we do not need to add to our work a story of what abstract things those linguistic expressions "express" or "represent", though we may if we wish.

Intensions vs. extensions
Classical predicate logic is the simplest predicate logic because it ascribes to the primitive parts of the semi-formal language only the minimal semantic values they must have to function as parts of a semi-formal language: to a name we ascribe a reference, to a predicate we ascribe an extension. Any other semantic content ascribed to names or predicates that is not the reference or extension must perforce then not be extensional. Hence, any semantic value that is ascribed to a name beyond its reference must be (part of) its intension; any semantic value that is ascribed to a predicate beyond its extension must be (part of) its intension.

The standard notion of the intension of a name or predicate, then, is so broad as to be useless as a guide for constructing models of how to reason well. We can use in our formalizations of reasoning only particular semantic values we ascribe to names and predicates, such as subject matter or the way a name points to its reference. About these we can try to be explicit. About the intension of a name or predicate in quite general terms, the only useful thing we can say is that it is any or perhaps all semantic values of the expression other than reference and extension.

Are applications of predicate restrictors extensional in classical predicate logic?
It is still open whether in adding predicate restrictors to classical predicate logic we must understand each predicate to have an intension as well as an extension.

If the form of a simple predicate is not part of its intension, we have to abandon the principle of the division of form and content. That is what I will do here.[24] I accept the charge that doing so is an evasion of being explicit about what aspect of predicates we need to take into account in our use of predicate restrictors because I don't know what aspect that is. You can take the work I develop here as a challenge to formulate clearly such an aspect.

---

[24] Except in the mathematical abstraction of the semantics.

14 Multiple Predicate Restrictors

We often use more than one predicate restrictor:

(1)   Anubis is a big wild dog.

We know that "big" is a predicate restrictor; here it's restricting "— is a wild dog". The following is valid:

(2)   Anubis is a big wild dog.
       Therefore, Anubis is a wild dog.

Since "wild" is a predicate restrictor, too, we can conclude "Anubis is a dog" from the conclusion of (2). If we restrict and then restrict again, we are still restricting the original predicate.

In order to respect more valid inferences, we can and should allow for a predicate restrictor to be applied not only to simple atomic predicates but also to modified atomic wffs. We then can take the form of (1) to be:

   (((— is a dog)/wild)/big) (Anubis)

We need the parentheses to make it clear that "wild" restricts the predicate "— is a dog" and "big" restricts the predicate "(— is a dog)/wild".

Does the order of the restrictors matter? Consider

   Anubis is a wild big dog.
   (((— is a dog)/big)/wild) (Anubis)

This need not have the same truth-value as (1), since wild dogs are generally small, and a big wild dog may not be a big dog. Permuting restrictors is not a scheme of valid inferences.

And since a big wild dog might not be big, the following is invalid, too:

Anubis is a big wild dog.
Therefore, Anubis is a big dog.

$$\frac{(((- \text{ is a dog})/\text{wild})/\text{big}) (\text{Anubis})}{((- \text{ is a dog})/\text{big}) (\text{Anubis})}$$

Deleting one in a series of restrictors is not a scheme of valid inferences.

The only obvious semantic condition we have with multiple restrictors is the one we have for all restrictors, Res_1, but now for any atomic wff and not just simple predicates:

If A is an atomic wff and R is a predicate restrictor, then for any assignment of references σ and any term u,
If $\upsilon_\sigma \vDash (A(-)/R)(u)$, then $\upsilon_\sigma \vDash A(u)$

62   *Chapter 14*

Aside: *Why Venn diagrams don't work with predicate restrictors*
Why don't I use Venn diagrams to illustrate the examples? Venn diagrams are misleading and not illustrative. Normally we would draw:

Anubis is a big wild dog.

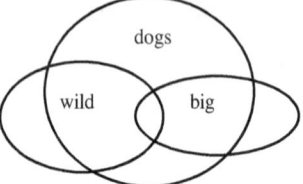

But this is to treat "wild" and "large" as predicates. They make no comparison except to the entire universe of the model. By this picture, something is a big wild dog iff it is a wild big dog, which we know is not right. Rather we should draw:

Anubis is a wild big dog.   Anubis is a big wild dog.

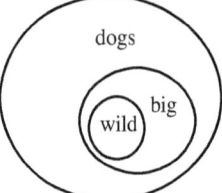   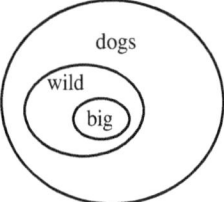

We are comparing, not predicating. The area for "big" in the left-hand diagram has to be completely within the area for "dogs". There might not even be overlap between the collection of wild big dogs and big wild dogs. Beyond that, these two diagrams don't illuminate any of the issues we have been discussing in this chapter.

Aside: Formalizing vs. semantics for natural languages
Frank Jackson and Hans Kamp in the works I quoted from in the previous chapter see their work as giving (recognizing? establishing?) semantics for natural languages. But they offer no experimental evidence that we use language or understand meanings in the ways they describe.

But aren't I doing the same, citing this example, that example, appealing to intuition? No. Here we are modeling, abstracting. If in these circumstances we can agree that these words play these roles—syntactic and semantic—we can trace their inferential relations with respect to validity and invalidity. I am investigating how we can better understand the world in part through our ordinary language and in part through new methods of analysis. It does not count against this theory that "a large red house" is grammatical while "a red large house" is at best peculiar if not ungrammatical, for we can distinguish how these can describe the world differently and take account of their distinct roles in inferences.

15 Variable Predicate Restrictors

The following informal inference is valid:

(1) Spot was barking at Suzy.
     Therefore, Spot was barking.

The prepositional phrase "at Suzy" in (1) acts as an adverb. It is a restrictor, telling us how Spot was barking.
   Similarly, the following are valid:

   Spot was barking at Tom.
   Therefore, Spot was barking.

   Spot was barking at Puff.
   Therefore, Spot was barking.

We can use any name after "at" and have a valid inference.
   Compare: "— was barking" is a proposition when the blank is filled with a name. Here "at —" is a predicate restrictor when the blank is filled with a name, a variable predicate restrictor. In (1) the predicate "— was barking at —" can be parsed as "(— was barking)/(at —)". We have an atomic predicate whose internal structure is noted in order to separate the categorematic parts.
   When we fill the blank in "at —" we get a predicate restrictor like "at Suzy". This we can use to restrict "— was barking". Then we can ask whether that new predicate applies to Spot. But we can't fill the blank in "— was barking" with the name "Spot" first, for we'd get "(Spot was barking)/(at —)". The phrase that is a predicate restrictor when the blank is filled with a name would be parsed as a modifier of a proposition. We have to fill in the blank in the predicate restrictor first.
   We can use more than one variable predicate restrictor in a sequence, too:

(2) Spot ran from Dick to Zoe.

Viewing "from —" and "to —" as variable predicate restrictors, we can formalize this as:

(3) (((— ran)/(from Dick))/(to Zoe)) (Spot)

   We do not write (2) as:

   (((— ran)/(from —))/(to —)) (Spot, Dick, Zoe)

If we did, it would not be clear that the blanks in the variable predicate restrictors have to be filled first. Rather, in (3) we first have a unary predicate "— ran" that is modified by the predicate restrictor "from —" with "Dick" filling the blank to get "(— ran)/(from Dick)". Then we restrict that unary predicate with the variable predicate restrictor "to —" with its blank filled with "Zoe" to get the unary predicate

"((−ran)/(from Dick))/(to Zoe)". Then we fill that predicate's blank with "Spot". This is the only way to read (2) that is compatible with taking these as predicate restrictors. In any case, it is (2) that determines the truth-value of (3).

But if we read (2) as (3), why bother to consider "from Dick" as anything more than a single unit, a predicate restrictor with no structure? If we do, then we can't respect valid inferences such as:

Spot was running from Dick.
Therefore, Spot was running from something.

Taking "from —" as a variable predicate restrictor we can formalize this as:

((− was running)/(from Dick)) (Spot)
Therefore, $\exists x$ ((− was running)/(from x)) (Spot)

This is an instance of *existential generalization*: if A(c), then $\exists x A(x)$.

Are there variable predicate restrictors that have more than one blank? Consider:

Tom is standing between Zoe and Suzy.
So Tom is standing.

Tom is standing between Dick and Suzy.
So Tom is standing.

These are valid. The phrase "between — and —" is a variable predicate restrictor. So we can formalize the first of these two as:

((− is standing)/between (Zoe, Suzy)) (Tom)
Therefore, (− is standing) (Tom)

Variable predicate restrictor A *variable predicate restrictor* is any incomplete phrase with specified gaps such that when the gaps are filled with names the phrase becomes a predicate restrictor.

To classify a phrase as a variable predicate restrictor requires that regardless of what name (possibly temporary) of an object in the universe fills the blank, a predicate restrictor results. We'll consider this assumption more later. For now, let's assume only that we can recognize some phrases, such as "at —", "to —", "from —", "near —", "between — and —", as variable predicate restrictors.

Are there semantic principles governing variable restrictors that we need to adopt besides a simple modification of Res_1 that allows for them to be treated as restrictors? Consider:

Spot barked loudly at Puff.
So Spot barked at Puff.

This is valid. But does its form guarantee that? Consider:

> Spot jumped carefully on Suzy.
> Therefore, Spot jumped on Suzy.

> Tom is singing slowly with Dick.
> So Tom is singing with Dick.

These, too, are valid. I cannot find any instance of the following that is not valid.

> *Deleting a restrictor before a variable restrictor*
> $((P(-)/R_1)/R_2(b))$ (c)
> *Therefore*, $(P(-)/R_2(b))$ (c)

Perhaps that's just my lack of imagination. But even if we investigate every restrictor and variable restrictor pair in English and conclude that the scheme is valid for each, we are not justified in taking a semantic condition that validates this scheme unless we can find something in the nature of the meaning of restrictors and variable restrictors that guarantees the validity of the scheme. The next ordinary language to which we try to apply our theory might have a restrictor and a variable restrictor for which the scheme is invalid. But even if we weren't concerned with tying our theory so closely to reasoning in English, generalizing from some examples, inducting on experience, is not enough.

Inducting on experience is not a justification for semantics We do not build a formal theory by inducting on examples, no matter how complete the collection of examples. Each syntactic principle must be justified by a semantic principle, and each semantic principle must be justified by our understanding of how the syntactical categories of the theory have meaning.

We look to examples to see a pattern of valid inferences. Finding a pattern, we look for some significance that makes the inferences valid. Finding none, we content ourselves with using meaning axioms to formalize any instance of the scheme that is valid. If we think we have found some pattern of meaning, we try to be explicit and state it as a semantic rule that justifies the validity of the scheme. This is what we did when we said that a restrictor either says how, or in what way, or what kind. We may later find an exception, a counterexample, in which case we must reflect more on the significance of the scheme to find a suitably narrower semantic principle or else abandon our attempt to account for the examples semantically.

One can build a descriptive theory of our use of ordinary language on the basis of inducting from examples. But we are trying to give a theory of how to reason well, which is prescriptive. A prescription is either basic or based on some prior principles; there is no reason to think that a generalization from experience is ever an adequate prior principle for a prescription.

16 A Formal Theory of Classical Predicate Logic with Predicate Restrictors of Unary Predicates

The definition of the formal language of classical predicate logic begins with the simplest formulas, what we call the "atomic wffs", and then builds complex wffs by joining those with a connective or adding a quantifier. The simplest wffs of classical predicate logic really are very simple: just a predicate symbol and terms. Now we can have atomic wffs that have structure with multiple restrictors, so we have to use an inductive definition for just the base level of wffs: first a predicate symbol and terms, then those modified by a restrictor, then those further modified by a restrictor, ... Once the base level of atomic wffs is defined, the definition proceeds exactly as for classical predicate logic, building more complex wffs using connectives and quantifiers. Since the interpretation of the quantifiers and connectives is the same as for classical predicate logic, the only change in the semantics is to relate the structure of some atomic wffs to others. So we need to add only axioms for those relations to the axioms of classical predicate logic to get a strong completeness theorem.

The formal language, realizations, and semi-formal languages

Vocabulary
  predicate symbols $P_0, P_1, P_2, \ldots$
  predicate restrictor symbols
    restrictor symbols $R_0, R_1, \ldots$
    variable restrictor symbols R_n^i for every $n \geq 0$ and $i \geq 1$
  name symbols $c_0, c_1, \ldots$ ⎫
  variables $x_0, x_1, \ldots$ ⎬ *terms*
  propositional connectives $\neg, \rightarrow, \wedge, \vee$
  quantifiers $\forall, \exists$
  equality predicate $\equiv$
Punctuation *parentheses* ( )   *comma* ,   *blank* —   *slash* /

Inductive definition of formal atomic predicates
  i. If P is a predicate symbol, then (P(—)) is a formal atomic predicate which is assigned degree 0.
  ii. If Q is a formal atomic predicate of degree k, and R is a restrictor symbol, then (Q/R) is a formal atomic predicate of degree $k + 1$.

iii. If Q is a formal atomic predicate of degree k, and R is an n-ary variable restrictor symbol, and $u_1, \ldots, u_n$ are terms, then $(Q/R(u_1, \ldots, u_n))$ is a formal atomic predicate of degree $k + 1$.

iv. A concatenation of symbols is an atomic predicate formula iff it is a formal atomic predicate of some degree $k \geq 0$.

Formal atomic predicates of degree ≥ 1 are *modified formal atomic predicates*.

Inductive definition of wff
Only the first stage of the definition for classical predicate logic (p. 20) is changed:
  i. If Q is a formal atomic predicate and u is a term, then $((Q)(u))$ is an atomic wff of length 1.

I'll use $Q, Q_1, Q_2, \ldots$ to stand for formal atomic predicates, while P stands for a predicate symbol, and $A, B, C, A_0, A_1, \ldots$ stand for atomic wffs as before.

Note that every atomic predicate is unary: there is only one blank in it, the blank in the predicate symbol. Any blank in a variable restrictor is filled with a term.

I'll let you prove that the degree of an atomic predicate formula is the number of appearances of the slash in it and that there is one and only one way to read each wff (compare the proof of the unique readability of wffs in Volume 0).

Realizations and semi-formal languages An ordinary language name, restrictor, or predicate is *simple* iff it contains no part we could formalize as a name, predicate, restrictor, propositional connective, variable, or quantifier, or combination of those.

A *realization* of the formal language is an assignment of:
- Simple names to none, some, or all of the name symbols;
- Simple non-variable restrictors to none, some, or all of the restrictor symbols;
- Simple variable restrictors to none, some, or all of the variable restrictor symbols;
- Simple predicates to none, some, or all of the predicate symbols.

The *realization of a formal wff* is what we get when we replace the formal symbols in it with the parts of ordinary language that are assigned to them; it is a *semi-formal wff*. The *semi-formal language* for a realization is the collection of all realizations of formal wffs.

We use the same terminology and conventions as for our previous formal and semi-formal languages. Now R and R´ stand for predicate restrictor symbols or simple predicate restrictors as the context determines.

68   Chapter 16

Semantics

First, we must recast the extensionality condition to apply to atomic wffs, not just simple predicates.

The extensionality condition for atomic predications Let A be any atomic wff and $u_1, \ldots, u_n$ all the terms appearing in A. Let B be A with terms $v_1, \ldots, v_n$ replacing $u_1, \ldots, u_n$. If σ and τ are assignments of references such that for each i, $\sigma(u_i) = \tau(v_i)$, then $\vDash_\sigma \vDash A$ iff $\vDash_\tau \vDash B$.

We also require a more general form for the semantic condition on restrictors.

RES_1   If Q is an atomic predicate and R is a simple predicate restrictor, then for any assignment of references σ,

   If $\vDash_\sigma \vDash (Q/R)(x)$, then $\vDash_\sigma \vDash Q(x)$.

If Q is an atomic predicate, R is an n-ary predicate restrictor symbol, then for any assignment of references σ,

   If $\vDash_\sigma \vDash (Q/R(y_1, \ldots, y_n))(x)$, then $\vDash_\sigma \vDash Q(x)$.

An axiomatization

All we've done is allow atomic wffs in the formal language to have more structure than previously in such a way that we can see by their form that certain ones are related to others by the condition RES_1. Hence the axiomatization of classical predicate logic is strongly complete for this system if we add to it the following axiom schemes.

RES_1

   $\forall \ldots \forall z ((Q/R)(x) \to Q(x))$

   where Q is a formal atomic predicate and R is a predicate restrictor symbol

   $\forall \ldots \forall z ((Q/R(y_1, \ldots, y_n))(x) \to Q(x))$

   where Q is a formal atomic predicate and R is an n-ary variable predicate restrictor symbol

---

17 Examples of Formalizing

Example 1 Peter left in a car.
  Therefore, *there is something Peter left in.*

$$\frac{\exists x\,((-\text{ is a car})\,(x) \wedge ((-\text{ left})/(\text{in } x))\,(\text{Peter}))}{\exists x\,(((-\text{ left})/(\text{in } x))\,(\text{Peter}))}$$

$$\frac{\exists x_0\,(P_{17}(-)(x) \wedge (P_{18}(-)/R_1(x_0))\,(c_0))}{\exists x_0\,((P_{18}(-)/R_1(x_0))\,(c_0))}$$

Analysis We formalize "a car" by the general method of converting nouns into predicates (Volume 0, p. 94) The informal inference is then valid. So, too, is the following:

  Peter left in a truck.
  Therefore, there is something Peter left in.

Cars and trucks are things. We can quantify over them in predicate logic. We can treat "in —" as a variable predicate restrictor, so the formalization is valid.

Example 2 Peter left in a huff.
  Therefore, *there is something Peter left in.*

$$\frac{((-\text{ left})/(\text{in a huff}))\,(\text{Peter}))}{\exists x\,(((-\text{ left})/(\text{in } x))\,(\text{Peter}))}$$

$$\frac{(P_{18}(-)/R_{88})\,(c_0))}{\exists x_0\,((P_{18}(-)/R_1(x_0))\,(c_0))}$$

Analysis This is not valid. Huffs are not things. We don't and, it seems, we can't quantify over them and reason with them as things. Hence, we cannot take "in" as a variable predicate restrictor here; the inference does not have the same form as the previous example. Rather, "in a huff" is a simple predicate restrictor.

Example 3 Tom is in Dick's house.

Analysis We can formalize "Dick's house" as "(— is a house)/of (Dick)". Then it seems we have the variable predicate restrictor "in —". But what predicate is it restricting? The only candidate here is "— is", and that won't do. We've agreed not to allow an existence predicate in our semi-formal languages.

  To formalize this example, we can take "— is in —" as an atomic predicate. Or we can try to recast the predicate to use "in —" as a predicate restrictor. That's easy in a language such as Portuguese where there's a verb for continuing to be, the sense used in the example, which differs from "to be" or "to exist".[25] But in

---

[25] In Portuguese we'd translate the example as "Tom fica na casa do Dick", using the verb "ficar" rather than "ser", or "estar", or "existir". In French we'd use the verb "rester".

English we have no such word. This shows an ambiguity in the use of "is" that we can rectify by coining a new usage, writing this example as "Tom is$_{remains}$ in Dick's house", and formalizing it as:

$\exists x\,(\,((-\text{ is a house})/\text{of (Dick)})\,(x) \wedge (-\text{ is}_{remains}/\text{in }(x))\,(\text{Tom})$

Example 4 Tom will telephone in a day.

Analysis This is a proposition, as is "Tom will telephone in a week", "Tom will telephone in a moment". But to allow for spans of time in our universe entails a great deal of analysis and substantial assumptions, as you can see in Volume 2, *Time and Space in Formal Logic*.

Example 5 Spot is Dick's dog.

$((-\text{ is a dog})/\text{of (Dick)})\,(\text{Spot})$

$(P_1(-)/R_2(c_2))\,(c_3))$

Analysis Considering the many uses of "of" in English, we might need to distinguish this use as one of possession, perhaps as "of$_{possesses}$".

Sometimes we mean to indicate uniqueness with the possessive form in English. We could add that here using the equality predicate:

(*) $((-\text{ is a dog})/\text{of}_{possesses}\,(\text{Dick}))\,(\text{Spot})$
       $\wedge\ \forall x_0\,((-\text{ is a dog})/\text{of}_{possesses}\,(x_0))\,(\text{Spot}) \rightarrow x_0 \equiv \text{Dick})\,)$

In classical logic without predicate modifiers we have no choice but to take the example as atomic, relative to a meaning axiom:

$\forall x_0\,\forall x_1\,((\,(-\text{ is a dog of }-)\,(x_0, x_1) \rightarrow (-\text{ is a dog})\,(x_0)\,)$

Example 6 Spot belongs only to Dick.
         Therefore, *Spot belongs only.*

Analysis This seems to be a counterexample to Res_1. But the premise is used elliptically for "Spot belongs to Dick and Spot belongs to no one else", which we can formalize as (*) in the last example.

Example 7 Spot was barking at 47.
         Therefore, *Spot was barking.*

$$\frac{((-\text{ was barking})/(\text{at }47)\,(\text{Spot})}{(-\text{ was barking})\,(\text{Spot})}$$

Analysis In Chapter 15 we remarked that the same inference with "Suzy" in place of "47" is valid. This inference is valid, too. That's because the premise is false, at least in any model in which we might want to formalize the inference. Falsity is the default truth-value we assign to any sentence we take as a proposition that we deem to be odd, or nonsense, or too vague.

We have the variable predicate restrictor "at —". When the blank is filled with "47", it gives us a restrictor that when applied to "— is barking" yields a new predicate that applies to no thing. Because we allow for a predicate restrictor to restrict a predicate to apply to no things, our theory of predicate restrictors can use falsity as the default truth-value.

If we should work in a model in which "47" names some person, then the premise could be true, and then the conclusion would be, too.

Example 8   Anubis is a big wild big dog.

$((((-\text{ is a dog})/\text{big})/\text{wild})/\text{big}) (\text{Anubis})$

$(((P_1(-)/R_8)/R_9)/R_8) (c_1)$

Analysis   In ordinary speech we do not repeat a predicate restrictor. But such repetitions are not necessarily superfluous: what is classified as a big wild big dog should be bigger than just a wild big dog.

Example 9   Spot is barking loudly rapidly.
            Spot is barking rapidly loudly.

Analysis   The formalizations of these are different:

(a) $((-\text{ is barking})/\text{rapidly})/\text{loudly}) (\text{Spot})$

(b) $((-\text{ is barking})/\text{loudly})/\text{rapidly}) (\text{Spot})$

But are their truth-values the same? It may be that in comparison to things that are barking rapidly, Spot is barking loudly, but in comparison to all things that are barking, he isn't barking loudly at all. That is, (a) could be true and (b) false. I'll let you convince yourself that (b) could be true and (a) false, too.

It seems more natural to me to read the examples as equivalent because we think of adverbs as not applied successively but each individually to the verb. That would be to read the first example as "Spot barked loudly and rapidly", the second as "Spot barked rapidly and loudly". In Example 16 of Chapter 27, we'll see how to formalize those as equivalent.

Example 10   Brutus stabbed with a knife with a knife.

$\exists x_0 ((-\text{ is a knife}) (x_0) \land (((-\text{ stabbed})/\text{with } (x_0))/(\text{with } (x_0))) (\text{Brutus}))$

Analysis   This example is similar to one by Romane Clark, who suggests that we can collapse the iterated use of a predicate restrictor:[26]

$\forall \ldots (\forall x (((P(-)/R)/R) (x) \leftrightarrow (P(-)/R) (x)))$

After all, we never use iterated restrictors. But we do:

---

[26] "Concerning the Logic of Predicate Modifiers", p. 333, where he discusses "Brutus stabbed Caesar with a knife with a knife". He does not use this notation.

72   Chapter 17

Exercise 17 is a hard, hard problem.

A hard, hard problem is a lot harder to solve than a hard problem. We can't collapse iterated restrictors generally, though in some cases we can add a meaning axiom that allows for that.[27]

Example 11   *Example 1 is an example of ordinary speech.*

Analysis Whatever speech is, it's not a thing we can point to or re-identify as we would need to be able to do for it to be in a universe of a model. Speech is akin to mud and snow: a mass. Though we speak of masses as being things, they are not the sort we can reason about in predicate logic. Nor can we treat "ordinary speech" as a predicate, "(— is speech/ordinary)", because for a thing to satisfy that, it would have to be speech. The example is true, but we cannot formalize it in our system.

Example 12   *Every rabid cat is killed.*

   Not formalizable.

Analysis We can't formalize this as:

(a) $\forall x_1 \, (\, (\, (\, (- \text{ is a cat})/\text{rabid}) \, (x_1) \to ((- \text{ is a cat})/\text{killed}) \, (x_1) \,)$

The example could be true, but if a cat is rabid, it's alive, so (a) would be false on the ordinary reading of the words. The example is meant as "Every cat that is rabid will be killed", and to formalize that, we need to take account of time through tenses.

Example 13   *Flo slid down a hill on the snow in a sled.*

   Not formalizable.

Analysis It seems we could formalize this as:

   $\exists x \, \exists y \, ((- \text{ is a hill}) \, (x) \wedge (- \text{ is a sled}) \, (y) \wedge$
   $\quad ((((- \text{ slid})/\text{ down } (x))/\text{ on the snow})/\text{in } (y)) \, (\text{Flo}))$

There is no problem taking the scope of the existential quantifiers to include the variable restrictors. The phrase "on the snow" is a simple modifier because we cannot take the mass term "snow" as either a predicate that applies to things or as the name of a thing. The problem, though, is that "down the hill in a sled" shouldn't be read as a succession of modifiers. We can see that with:

   Flo slid down a hill on the snow in a sled quickly.

Here "quickly" applies to the other two modifiers together, not in succession. We'll see how to formalize that reading of the example in Example 17 of Chapter 27.

---

[27] Repeated uses of modifiers is quite common in some pidgin English, as in "He has plenty, plenty money", which is not equivalent to "He has plenty money".

Example 14 Zoe is running from something.

$\exists x_1 (-\text{ is running}/\text{from}(x_1))$ (Zoe)

Analysis This is straightforward to formalize treating "from $(-)$" as a variable predicate restrictor.

But last week Dick and Tom were downtown and suddenly Zoe came running around a corner looking behind her. Dick said to Tom:

(a) Zoe is running from something.

Tom Dick ← Zoe

What could that something be? It might be an accident she's seen, a vicious cat, an hallucination, the sparking of a wire, water gushing from a fire hydrant, skunk odor. Many of the possibilities of what she is running from would not be things in the sense in which we reason in predicate logic, so to formalize (a) in predicate logic with a quantifier and variable for "something" would be wrong. More, Zoe could just be running from, with a generalized anxiety of there being a reason to run from without any idea of something she is running from.[28] In (a), "something" is as much a dummy as "it" is in "It's raining". Just as informatively and more accurately, Dick could have said:

(b) Zoe is running from.

It is not that (a) and (b) are equivalent: (a) is a bad way we are forced to talk because English demands subjects and objects; (b) is more accurate as a description Dick is trying to give of the world. But then what is the role of "from"?

It is a predicate restrictor, related to the variable predicate restrictor "from $(-)$" by the following valid inference pattern:

$(P/\text{from}(b))(a)$
Therefore, $(P/\text{from})(a)$

We might take "from" as a distinct predicate restrictor, or we might allow the predicate restrictor "from$(-)$" to be used with no term filling the blank. In that case we'd need to ask whether every variable predicate restrictor could be used with no term(s) filling the blank(s).

Our project is to learn how to reason about the world through our experience. We start with reasoning in English (or some other ordinary language). Much of our experience is shaped by our using that language. But not all. We can perceive outside its limits, as we do with "Zoe is running from", and if we can, we should try to incorporate such ways of experiencing the world into our analyses of how to reason well. But for this example we would need major modifications of our formal and informal analyses, ones which will seem more natural when we adopt a different view of the world as process rather than made up of things in Volume 3, *The World as Process*.

---

[28] Compare the discussion in "The Directedness of Emotions".

Other Predicate Modifiers

18 Predicate Negators

Not all adverbs are predicate restrictors. Consider this proposition about Manuel, whose legs are paralyzed:

(1)   Manuel almost walked.

The adverb "almost" modifies the predicate "— walked", but it does not restrict the predicate. We can't answer "How did Manuel walk?" by saying "almost". Anyone who almost walked did not walk.
   Consider, too:

(2)   Tom is nearly a college graduate.

The adjective "nearly" modifies the predicate "— is a college graduate", but it does not restrict it. We can't answer "What kind of college graduate is Tom?" by saying "nearly". Anyone who is nearly a college graduate is not a college graduate. Rather, the following inferences are valid:

> Manuel almost walked.
> Therefore, Manuel did not walk.

> Tom is nearly a college graduate.
> Therefore, Tom is not a college graduate.

> Zoe nearly closed the door.
> Therefore, Zoe did not close the door.

Predicate negator A *predicate negator* is a word or phrase that is used to modify a predicate such that anything the new predicate is true of does not satisfy the original predicate.[29]

> The following valid inference is characteristic of negators:
>
> $(P(-)/N)$ (a)
> Therefore, $\neg P(a)$

Note that the reverse inference is not valid: from "Zoe did not close the door" we cannot conclude "Zoe nearly closed the door".
   The words "almost" and "nearly" can serve as both adjectives and adverbs. In (1) we could have used "nearly" in place of "almost", and in (2) we could have used "almost" in place of "nearly". There is no clear division of negators according to whether they modify a classification predicate or a process predicate.

---

[29] Some call these "privatives"; see J. A. W. Kamp, "Two Theories about Adjectives", p. 125.

We'll see more predicate negators in the examples in Chapter 22. But I have not found any variable predicate negator. So extending our theory of predicate restrictors to allow for negators is not difficult. We add to the formal language:

predicate negator symbols $N_0, N_1, \ldots$

In the definition of formal atomic predicates and of the formal language we add new clauses identical with those for simple predicate restrictors except using predicate negator symbols. The definitions of the semi-formal language, realizations, and truth in a model follow as before, requiring that a *simple* part of ordinary language is one that also contains no part we could formalize as a negator, and we realize predicate negator symbols as simple predicate negators. I'll use $N, N', N_1, N_2, \ldots$ as metavariables for both predicate negator symbols and predicate negators, depending on context.

For the semantics, we add the following condition.

Neg If Q is an atomic predicate and N a predicate negator, then for any assignment of references σ:

If $\upsilon_\sigma \vDash (Q/N)(x)$, then $\upsilon_\sigma \nvDash Q(x)$.

Note that this allows for Q/N to apply to nothing.

We can give a strongly complete axiomatization of these semantics by adding to the axioms of the theory of predicate restrictors the following.

Neg If Q is a formal atomic predicate and N is a predicate negator symbol, then:

$\forall \ldots (Q/N)(x) \rightarrow \neg Q(x)$

We do not need to add that any object that satisfies Q does not satisfy Q/N. That is the contrapositive of Neg and is true in a model iff Neg is true in a model.[30]

---

[30] The medieval logician William of Sherwood compared negators and restrictors:

From a Modificational Whole. We argue from a modificational whole (*a toto in modo*) destructively only, and a modificational whole is a verb used without modification (*dictum simpliciter*)— e.g., "Socrates is not running; therefore he is not running well." Maxim: *What does not go together with [something] with respect to a modificational whole does not go together with [it] with respect to a part.* ...

From a modificational part—i.e., a modified (*determinatum*) verb—we argue constructively only, as follows: "Socrates is running well; therefore, Socrates is running." Maxim: *What goes together with [something] with respect to a modificational part goes together with [it] with respect to the whole.*

William of Sherwood's Introduction to Logic, pp. 83–84

19 Other Kinds of Predicate Modifiers?

Consider:

> Otto is an alleged thief.

The word "alleged" modifies the predicate "— is a thief". Some alleged thieves are not thieves; some alleged thieves are thieves. It's not just the meaning of the word that determines whether an object that satisfies the modified predicate also satisfies the original predicate but rather what is true in the world. New predicates formed with this modifier have no regular relation to the predicates that are being modified, or at least none that I can see.[31] So in accord with the principal of parsimony of formalizing, we won't add a category for such modifiers. If we want to reason with the example, we'll take "— is an alleged thief" as an atomic predicate.

Another kind of predicate modifier shows up in a story about the sheep I keep. They're called "Barbados", they have no wool, and they look a lot like goats. When people visit, they call them goats, and I say, "Those are really sheep". Words like "really", "actually", "real" (as in "It's a real sheep") are *emphasizers*.[32] They make no modification of the predicate at all. They are rhetorical flourishes. Just as we formalize "Believe me, those are sheep" in an argument as "Those are sheep", we can ignore emphasizers when we formalize as they do not contribute to our evaluation of our reasoning.[33]

Of more concern would be words that have a discernible though not complete regularity as modifiers, acting sometimes as negators and sometimes as restrictors. Perhaps there are such words or phrases in English; I have found none.

If we should find other kinds of predicate modifiers, ones for which some general semantic rule holds that we can take account of in our reasoning, I suspect we could accommodate those in the general method of modeling the internal structure of predicates we have here.[34]

---

[31] Such modifiers have been dubbed "neutralizers" by Romane Clark in "Concerning the Logic of Predicate Modifiers", p. 329.

[32] Emphasizers are often called *intensives* in English grammar.

[33] See *Critical Thinking* for a discussion of eliminating such phrases in argument analysis.

[34] Romane Clark in "Concerning the Logic of Predicate Modifiers", p. 329, says that some modifiers are "enlargers": they enlarge the extension of the predicate they modify. That is, they satisfy $\forall x \, (P(-)(x) \to (P(-)/E(x)))$. He gives the example "possible addict" in "John is a possible addict". This is philosophers' jargon. We say "It's possible that John is an addict" or "Possibly, John is an addict". We do not need to populate our universes with possible addicts. Another example he gives is "nearly", which we have seen is a negator. We could construe the inference "John closed the door, therefore, John nearly closed the door" as valid only if those propositions were indexed to different times.

20 Modifiers of Modifiers

In ordinary speech we use modifiers of modifiers, for example:

(1)   Juney barked almost loudly.

In our syntax we've allowed for modifiers of predicates only, so our only options to formalize (1) are:

　　(((− barked)/loudly)/almost) (Juney)

　　(((− barked)/almost)/loudly) (Juney)

But from (1) we can conclude "Juney barked", which we can't from either of these because "almost" is a negator.
　　To formalize (1) we need to recognize that "almost loudly" is itself a modifier. All we need do, it seems, is move the parentheses:

(2)   ((− barked)/(loudly/almost)) (Juney)

Then we have a compound modifier: a restrictor modified by a negator. But if we want to use the theory we've developed, we need to be able to classify a compound modifier as either a restrictor or a negator based solely on its form.
　　In (1), "almost loudly" is a compound modifier that tells how Juney was barking. So it is a predicate restrictor. But "almost" tells us that Juney wasn't barking loudly: it is a negator of "loudly". From (1) we can conclude:

　　Juney barked.

　　Juney didn't bark loudly.

So from (2) we should be able to conclude:

　　(− barked) (Juney)

　　¬ ((− barked)/loudly) (Juney)

We have the same pattern with:

(3)   Foo-Foo is a nearly purebred dog.

We can formalize this as:

(4)   ((− is a dog)/(purebred/nearly)) (Foo-Foo)

The negator "nearly" negates the restrictor "purebred", telling us what kind of dog Foo-Foo is: one that is not purebred. From (4) we should be able to conclude:

　　(− is a dog) (Foo-Foo)

　　¬ ((− is a dog)/purebred) (Foo-Foo)

We can modify a variable restrictor with a negator, too:

(5) (a) Dick is standing nearly next to Zoe.

(b) ((— is standing)/(next to (Zoe)/nearly)) (Dick)

From (5b) we should be able to conclude:

(— is standing) (Dick)

¬((— is standing)/next to (Zoe)) (Dick)

A restrictor tells what kind or how. When a predicate is modified by a negated restrictor, it also tells us what kind or how, namely not the kind or how of the original restrictor. So when we have a negator N modifying a restrictor R, the compound (R/N) is a restrictor that is disjoint in its application from the original restrictor. We can state this as two semantic conditions for our models:

If $v_\sigma \vDash (Q/(R/N))(x)$, then $v_\sigma \vDash Q(x)$.

RN If $v_\sigma \vDash (Q/(R/N))(x)$, then $v_\sigma \nvDash (Q/R)(x)$

We don't need to add the first condition, since it will follow from classifying (R/N) as a restrictor.

Let's look at the three other possibilities for compound modifiers.

A negator modifying a negator (N/N´)
Consider:

(6) This is a nearly counterfeit dollar bill.

From this we can conclude that the object is not a counterfeit dollar bill; perhaps it's one of those pieces of paper that are meant to stand for money in a board game. We also can't conclude that it is a dollar bill. That's to read (6) as:

((—is a dollar bill)/counterfeit)/nearly) (x)

Similarly, consider:

(7) Birta is almost barking fakily.

From this we can conclude that Birta is not barking fakily. But we cannot conclude that Birta is barking or that Birta is not barking. That's to read (7) as:

((—is barking)/fakily)/almost) (Birta)

In many cases where we have two negators in succession the more natural way to read the sentence is as ((Q/N)/N´) rather than Q/(N/N´). But consider:

(8) Birta is barking almost fakily.

Here "almost" is modifying "fakily". From (8) we can conclude:

Birta is not barking fakily.

Birta is barking.

If we formalize (8) as:

((− is barking)/(fakily/almost)) (Birta)

we want that we can conclude both:

¬((− is barking)/fakily) (Birta)

(− is barking) (Birta)

A negator cancels the predicate to which it is applied. A negator, similarly, cancels a modifier to which it is applied, as we saw with propositions of the form Q/(R/N). To assert Q/(N/N′) is to say that Q applies, rather than not applying as would be if it were modified by N: the negator cancels the negator. That is, (N/N′) is a restrictor that is disjoint in its application from the modifier N. We can state this as two semantic conditions for our models:

If $\upsilon_\sigma \vDash Q/(N/N')(x)$, then $\upsilon_\sigma \vDash Q(x)$.

NN′ If $\upsilon_\sigma \vDash Q/(N/N')(x)$, then $\upsilon_\sigma \nvDash (Q/N)(x)$.

We don't need to add the first condition because it will follow from classifying (N/N′) as a restrictor.

A restrictor modifying a restrictor (R/R′)
Consider:

Birta is a large cute dog.

From this we can conclude:

Birta is a dog.
Birta is a cute dog.

But this is exactly what we have from:

(((− is a dog)/cute)/large) (Birta)

Whatever satisfies a predicate Q/(R/R′) also satisfies Q/R, which makes the compound a restrictor, but one that has no reading I can find except what we have with (Q/R)/R′. Absent a different reading, one for which there are inferences that distinguish between (Q/R)/R′ and Q/(R/R′), there seems to be no reason to allow for a restrictor to modify a restrictor.

A restrictor modifying a negator (N/R)
Suppose we're looking at a sculpture and someone says:

(9)   That's an obviously fake Rodin.

It seems we have a compound "obviously fake", where "obviously" is a restrictor and "fake" is a negator. Now whatever is an obviously fake Rodin is also a fake Rodin. And whatever is a fake Rodin is not a Rodin. So using "b" as a name for the sculpture the person is pointing to, from (9) we can conclude:

82 *Chapter 20*

b is a fake Rodin.
b is not a Rodin.

But that is what we have with:

$((((-\text{ is a Rodin})/\text{fake})/\text{obviously})\ (b)$

Whatever satisfies a predicate Q/(N/R) also satisfies Q/N, which makes N/R a negator, but one that has no reading that differs in its consequences that I can find except what we have with (Q/N)/R. There seems to be no reason to allow for compound modifiers of the form N/R in our languages.

In sum, we need to allow for modifiers of modifiers to formalize some ordinary language inferences, but only those in which a negator modifies a modifier.

For a formal language of predicate modifiers, we have to set out the structure of modifiers that we can use in the inductive definition of atomic wffs of Chapter 16.

Formal modifiers

i. Every non-variable predicate restrictor symbol is a formal restrictor of degree 1.

Every predicate negator symbol is a formal negator of degree 1.

Every variable restrictor symbol each of whose blanks is filled with a term is a formal restrictor of degree 1.

ii. If R is a formal restrictor of degree k, and N is a formal negator, then (R/N) is a formal restrictor of degree $k + 1$.

iii. If N is a formal negator symbol, and N´ is a formal negator symbol, then (N/N´) is a formal restrictor of degree 2.

iv. A concatenation of symbols is a formal modifier iff it is a formal restrictor or formal negator of degree k for some k.

If the degree of a formal modifier is > 1, it is a *complex* formal modifier.

A formal modifier is *n*-ary iff it has exactly n blanks in it. If $n > 0$, it is a *variable formal modifier*.

Note that we don't have negators of degree greater than 1 since a negator modifying a negator is a restrictor. I'll let you prove the following:

- The degree of a formal modifier is the number of predicate restrictor and predicate negator symbols appearing in it, counting repetitions.
- There is one and only one way to read each formal modifier.
- Every complex formal modifier is a formal restrictor.

The definition of the formal language then follows as before using "formal restrictor" or "formal negator" in place of "restrictor symbol".

I'll use M, M′, $M_1, M_2, \ldots$ as metavariables for formal modifiers or modifiers in a semi-formal language, as context determines. Now R, R′ can stand for any predicate restrictor, whether simple or complex, and N, N′ can stand for any predicate negator.

The semantics for this theory add *RN* and *NN′* to our previous theory.

Negated modifiers For any atomic predicate Q, any restrictor R (possibly variable with its blanks filled), and any assignment of references σ:

RN   If $\upsilon_\sigma \vDash Q/(R/N)\,(x)$, then $\upsilon_\sigma \nvDash (Q/R)\,(x)$.

NN′   If $\upsilon_\sigma \vDash Q/(N/N')\,(x)$, then $\upsilon_\sigma \nvDash (Q/N)\,(x)$.

We can give a strongly complete axiomatization of this theory by adding the following schemes.

Negated modifiers

RN $\forall \ldots (Q/(R/N))(x) \rightarrow \neg((Q/R)(x))$

NN′ $\forall \ldots (Q/(N/N'))(x) \rightarrow \neg((Q/N)(x))$

21 The Pure Negator "Not"

Though not common in our ordinary speech, it's not unheard of for us to use "not" as a modifier. We use "not" as a negator of a restrictor, as in:

(1)   Juney is barking not-loudly.

(2)   Birta is a not-small dog.

These are clear, and the truth-conditions for them are straightforward:

>   (1) is true iff Juney is barking and Juney is not barking loudly.

>   (2) is true iff Birta is a dog and Birta is not a small dog.

So we can formalize (1) and (2) as:

> $(-$ is barking$)$ (Juney) $\wedge \neg((-$ is barking$)/$loudly$)$ (Juney)$)$

> $(-$ is a dog$)$ (Ralph) $\wedge \neg((-$ is a dog$)/$small$)$ (Ralph)$)$

But this works only for the present tense. Consider:

(3)   Juney was barking not-loudly.

We can't formalize this as:

(4) $(-$ was barking$)$ (Juney) $\wedge \neg(((-$ was barking$)/$loudly$)$ (Juney)$)$

The first conjunct of (4) could be true at a time when Juney was barking loudly, while the second could be true of another time when Juney wasn't barking at all. We have that (4) is a consequence of (3) but not vice versa. In Volume 2, *Time and Space in Formal Logic*, we'll see how to take account of time in our formal analyses of reasoning so that we can assert that each of the conjuncts of (4) are about the same time. Then we can get the equivalence of (3) and (4).

But that's not enough. Consider:

Tom was speaking carefully not clearly.

This isn't equivalent to "Tom was speaking carefully and Tom was speaking not clearly", even if we take account of time. For this to be true, Tom was being careful about speaking not clearly, perhaps because he didn't want to be understood. The restrictor "carefully" is modifying "not clearly". We need to allow "not" to modify a restrictor.

What about "not" modifying a negator? Consider:

Birta is a not-fake dog.

If this is true, then Birta is a dog. But she isn't a fake dog, which is a kind of non-dog. Conversely, if Birta is a dog, then she isn't a fake dog. We have:

Birta is a dog iff Birta is a not-fake dog

Modifying a negator with "not" does nothing more than negate the negator, which is a way or kind, but any way or kind, since the negator isn't a way or kind. That is, a negator modified by "not" is only an emphasizer. We said earlier that we have no need to formalize emphasizers in our system. Perhaps if predicates, names, and modifiers can have some content, such as subject matter, there will be a need to distinguish "Birta is a dog" and "Birta is a not-fake dog" as poets do. So though we need to allow "not" to modify a restrictor, we don't take it to modify a negator.

What about "not" modifying a predicate directly? Consider:

(5) Helio is not barking.

We've assumed that every name refers in the propositions we're studying. We did so not because it is essential for our work nor because it gives us a better guide for how to reason. We made that assumption in order to simplify our work, intending to extend our analyses later to accommodate reasoning with names that need not refer in the third part of this volume. If "Helio" does not refer, then there is a difference between (5) formalized as:

(6) $\neg\,(\,(-\text{ is barking})\,(\text{Helio})\,)$

and (5) formalized with "not" modifying the predicate:

(7) $(\text{not-}(-\text{ is barking}))\,(\text{Helio})$

That's because (6) could be true in a model and (7) false if "Helio" does not pick out any thing, for (6) is entirely negative, while (7) asserts something about Helio, namely, he is not-barking. He is doing something, even if it be only what we might characterize as refraining from barking.[35] Hence, "Helio" must refer for (7) to be true. From (7) we could infer "$\exists x\,(x \equiv \text{Helio})$", but not from (6). Because this is important for our later work, we should allow for "not" to negate a predicate directly.[36] In this part of the book, though, where all names are assumed to refer, we'll need to codify that (6) and (7) are equivalent.

Can we modify negated atomic predicates? Consider:

(8) Juney is not-barking loudly.

(9) Ralph is a small non-dog.

When we use "loudly" as a modifier, it must be relative to some predicate. We know

---

[35] The characterization of an action as refraining from doing something is important in the study of prescriptive claims; see "Reasoning with Prescriptive Claims" in *Prescriptive Reasoning*.

[36] The medievals recognized this distinction by the placement of "non" in the proposition: "Homo non est asinus" (Man is not a donkey) for the propositional negation, and "Homo est non asinus" (Man is a non-donkey) for the predicate modifier. There must be at least one man for the latter to be true, but not so for the former. See, for example, p. 15 of the Introduction to Buridan, *Summulae de Dialectica*.

what it means (sufficiently well) to say of something that it is barking loudly. But I have no idea what criteria we could use to determine whether something is not-barking loudly. If Juney is not-barking, she could be digging in the yard, chasing a rabbit, eating her dinner, sleeping, ... The criteria for any of those to be done loudly are very different. Similarly, I have no idea what criteria we could use to determine whether something is a small non-dog. If Ralph is a non-dog, he could be a mouse, or an elephant, or a skyscraper, or .... The criteria for any of those to be small are different. The sentences (8) and (9) are too vague to be taken as propositions. This is not the case with other negators: we know well enough what it means to say that Juney is nearly barking for us to use a modifier as in "Juney is nearly barking loudly". Hence, though we'll allow "not" to modify a simple atomic predicate, we won't allow that to be further modified.

To allow a way to formalize uses of "not" as a modifier, we'll add to the formal language a distinguished negator symbol ∼, the *pure negator*. We intend for this to have the same meaning in every model, so it will be part of the logical vocabulary. We'll call an application of a pure negator to a predicate a *pure negated predicate*. In what follows, I'll write ∼Q in place of Q/∼.

What is the relation of this pure negator to other predicate negators? Consider:

(10)   Juney is barking almost loudly.

From this we can conclude "Juney is barking not-loudly". If we formalize (10) as:

(11)   ((− is barking)/(loudly/almost)) (Juney)

we can conclude by Res_1:

(12)   (− is barking) (Juney)

And we can conclude from (11) by RN:

(13)   ¬ ((− is barking)/loudly) (Juney)

But without marking (11), (12), and (13) as about the same time, we can't conclude:

(14)   ((− is barking)/∼loudly) (Juney)

We need to adopt a principle that allows us to conclude (14) from (11).

In total, then, our semantic assumptions about the use of the pure negator will be codified in the following.

Pure negated predicates   For any atomic predicate Q,

$\quad \vDash_\sigma \sim Q(x)$ iff $\vDash_\sigma \neg Q(x)$

Pure negated restrictors   For any atomic predicate Q and restrictor R,

   If $\vDash_\sigma (Q/\sim R)(x)$, then $\vDash_\sigma Q(x)$ and $\nvDash_\sigma ((Q/R)(x))$.

Negators of restrictors and pure negated restrictors For any atomic predicate Q and restrictor R,

If $\upsilon_\sigma \vDash (Q/(R/N))(x)$, then $\upsilon_\sigma \vDash (Q/{\sim}R)(x)$.

We can axiomatize these by adding the following schemes.

Pure negated predicates For any atomic predicate Q,

$\forall \ldots {\sim}Q(x) \leftrightarrow \neg Q(x)$

Pure negated restrictors For any formal atomic predicate Q and formal restrictor R:

$\forall \ldots (Q/{\sim}R)(x) \rightarrow (Q(x) \wedge \neg((Q/R)(x)))$

Negators of restrictors and pure negated restrictors For any atomic predicate Q and restrictor R,

$\forall \ldots (Q/(R/N))(x) \rightarrow (Q/{\sim}R)(x)$

22 Examples of Formalizing

Example 1 Tom is almost a college graduate.
   Therefore, *someone is a college graduate*.

$$\frac{((-\text{ is a college graduate})/\text{almost})\,(\text{Tom})}{\exists x\,((-\text{ is a college graduate})\,(x))}$$

$$\frac{(P_{64}(-)/N_1)\,(c_6)}{\exists x_0\, P_{64}(-)(x_0)}$$

Analysis The inference is invalid. The existence of something that satisfies a predicate modified by a negator does not tell us what satisfies the predicate.

Example 2 Spot is nearly a cute dog.
   So *Spot is a dog, but not a cute dog*.

$$\frac{((-\text{ is a dog})/(\text{cute}/\text{nearly}))\,(\text{Spot})}{(-\text{ is a dog})\,(\text{Spot}) \wedge \neg\,(((-\text{ is a dog})/\text{cute})\,(\text{Spot}))}$$

$$\frac{(P_1(-)/(R_{11}/N_2))\,(c_3)}{P_1(-)\,(c_3) \wedge \neg\,(P_1(-)/(R_{11})\,(c_3))}$$

Analysis The example is valid by virtue of *RN*, as "(cute/nearly)" is a restrictor.

Example 3 Puff is not even a nearly cute cat.

$$((-\text{ is a cat})/\sim(\text{nearly}/\text{cute}))\,(\text{Puff}) \wedge ((-\text{ is a cat})/\sim\text{cute})\,(\text{Puff})$$

$$(P_{666}(-)/\sim(R_{11}/N_2))\,(c_5) \wedge (P_{666}(-)/\sim R_{11})\,(c_5)$$

Analysis We use our understanding of "not even" to formalize this using the second conjunct.
   Note that from this we can conclude "$(-$ is a cat) (Puff)", which we couldn't if we used "$\neg\,((-\text{ is a cat})/\sim(\text{nearly}/\text{cute}))\,(\text{Puff})$".

Example 4 Puff barely jumped.

Analysis The modifier "barely" is a restrictor, for from the example we can conclude that Puff jumped. But we can conclude more:

   Puff almost didn't jump.

We need a meaning axiom to derive this, for which we'd need to use:

   $(\sim(-\text{ jumped}))/\text{almost}$

But we don't allow a pure-negated predicate to be modified. Hence, I see no way to formalize this example.

Example 5 Tom is speaking almost clearly.

  ((− is speaking) / (clearly / almost)) (Tom)

Analysis From this example we can conclude that Tom is speaking. So, following the grammar of the example, we formalize it as above. Since "(clearly / almost)" is a restrictor, we can conclude "(− is speaking) (Tom)".

Example 6 Tom is almost speaking clearly.

Analysis In our ordinary speech it isn't clear whether "Tom is speaking" follows from this or whether the example could be true if Tom were humming and sort of garbling words. If we can conclude "Tom is speaking", we should formalize the example as we did Example 5. If we can't, we have two choices, and which to use would be clear in speech from where the emphasis is made:

  ((− is speaking) / clearly) / almost)) (Tom)

or ((− is speaking) / almost) / clearly)) (Tom)

Example 7 Birta barked very loudly.

Analysis The word "very" in English is used only as a modifier of a modifier. Should we have a separate category of modifiers that modify only other modifiers?

We wouldn't normally say "Birta is barking very". But we say something similar: "Birta is really barking". The word "very" means "a lot", "more than normal", "to a high degree", which is how "really" is used when spoken emphatically and not just as an emphasizer. Thinking of "very" in that way, we can use it as a modifier of a predicate:

  ((− is barking) / very [a lot]) (Birta)

  ((− is a cheerleader) / very [a lot]) (Suzy)

Example 8 Ralph is a very fake dog.

  (((− is a dog) / fake) / very) (Ralph)

  ($P_1(-) / N_3) / R_{18}$) (c_8)

Analysis From the ordinary language example we can conclude both:

  Ralph is a fake dog.
  Ralph is not a dog.

That is what we get with the example as formalized above. If we try to read it as "(((− is a dog) / (fake / very)) (Ralph)", we'd have to take "fake / very" as a negator, one which takes us first to fake dogs and then to ones that are very fake. But that's what we have with the formalization in the example. The only way I know how to give truth-conditions for a restrictor applied to a negator is by reading those as applied successively to the same predicate.

90   Chapter 22

Example 9   *Suzy is (a) too naive (person).*

Analysis   We wouldn't normally use "too" as a modifier of an unmodified predicate. But understanding "too" as "in excess", "overly", "more than enough" we can use it as a modifier of predicates also:

((— barked)/too [excessively]) (Birta)

((— was a supervisor)/too [more than enough]) (Jose)

There seems to be no need for a separate category of modifiers of modifiers. I'll leave the formalization to you.

Example 10   *Tom is speaking too loudly.*
  Therefore, *Tom is speaking loudly.*

$$\frac{(((-\text{ is speaking})/\text{loudly})/\text{too}) (\text{Tom})}{((-\text{ is speaking})/\text{loudly}) (\text{Tom})}$$

$$\frac{((P_5(-)/R_5)/R_{10}) (c_{11})}{(P_5(-)/R_5) (c_{11}))}$$

Analysis   This is valid, formalizing a restrictor of a restrictor as two restrictors applied in succession.
  It would seem that a more natural reading of the example is:

((— is speaking) (loudly/too)) (Tom)

But as discussed on p. 81, using a restrictor to modify a restrictor formalizes no new inferential relations that aren't accounted for by viewing the two restrictors as applied successively.

Example 11   *Tom is speaking, too.*

Analysis   In the previous example "too" means "in excess". In this example "too" means "also". It's used in ordinary speech to assert that a proposition is true in addition to other true propositions. Assuming those propositions have already been stated and formalized, we can formalize the example as "(— is speaking) (Tom)".

Example 12   *Puff is an unattractive cat.*

((— is a cat)/~ attractive) (Puff)

$(P_{666}(-)/\sim R_{33}) (c_{19})$

Analysis   So common is the use of negating restrictors in English that we use "un" as a standard prefix to mark that.

Example 13   *Spot is fearless.*

Analysis   It would seem that "less" used as a suffix plays the same role as "un", negating the restrictor. But if we rewrite the example to make explicit what "fearless" means, we get "Spot is without fear". We could have the variable restrictor "with (—)" negated by the pure negator ~, but "fear" in not the name of a thing, at least not in the sense of a thing we can reason about in predicate logic. The only formalization of this example that I can see is:

((— is a dog)/~fearful) (Spot)

I'll leave to you to contemplate whether this is analysis rather than formalization or whether this could be part of a convention for how to formalize adjectives with the suffix "-less" and adverbs that end with "-lessly", as in "Spot is barking fearlessly".

Internal Conjunctions and Disjunctions

23 "And" Joining Terms

Consider:

(1) Dick and Tom sang.

We can't formalize this as:

(2) (— sang) (Dick) ∧ (— sang) (Tom)

For (1) to be true, Dick and Tom sang together, while (2) could be true if Dick and Tom sang at different times, or in different locations, or each was singing quietly to himself in the same room. Though (1) and (2) are not equivalent, (2) does follow from (1): if Dick and Tom (together) sang, then each one sang.

We also talk of two objects together in a classification predicate:

(3) x and y are shoes

If this applies to two objects, then each is a shoe. But it's not enough that each is a shoe for two objects together to be a pair of shoes, as both could be left shoes. This is to construe "and" as meaning "and together" in whatever way that means for the particular predicate we're considering, in this case a pair of shoes.

For such uses of "and", our formalizations must respect the following inference pattern as valid:

(4) P(a and b)
Therefore, P(a) and P(b)

But the following pattern is not valid:

P(a) and P(b)
Therefore, P(a and b)

Using "and" in this manner, the order in which the objects are referred to does not matter. For example, the following is valid:

Dick and Tom sang.
Therefore, Tom and Dick sang.

So our formalizations need to validate the following inference pattern:

(5) P(a and b)
Therefore, P(b and a)

We might formalize such uses of "and" by adding to our universe pairs of things. For example, we could say that the unordered pair (Dick, Tom) satisfies "— sang", while if Suzy sang but not with Dick or Tom, then the unordered pair (Suzy, Tom) would not satisfy "— sang". We'd also need to add to our universe triplets to formalize "Dick and Tom and Harry sang". And for choral singing, we'd need to add ordered n-tuples to our universe for arbitrarily large n. This would be a major change to the foundations of our systems, even if we accept that pairs, triplets, and n-tuples are things. We would have two levels of things: the base universe and the amplification of that with other things, namely unordered n-tuples. Though we're all willing to say that a pair of shoes is a thing, we do not answer the question "How many things are in that drawer?" with "Twelve: eight shoes and four pairs of shoes". Naming things is different from naming pairs of things. Moreover, we do not want the wff "$\forall x$ (x breathes)" to be false when the universe is all mammals because a matched pair of horses does not breathe.

Alternatively, we could add n-ary versions of each simple unary predicate for each $n \geq 2$. For example, for "— sang" we'd add:

"—, — sang$_2$"   "—, —, — sang$_3$"   "—, —, —, — sang$_4$", ...

We'd then add as a semantic principle:

If $\mathsf{a}_1, \ldots, \mathsf{a}_n$ satisfy "sang$_n$", then each a_i satisfies "— sang".

This would reflect the idea that we have a different understanding of a predicate when applied to more than one thing. Still, it is the same predicate applied to more than one thing: that's why we'd use numerals to link the higher arity versions of the unary predicate.

Another alternative is to follow the grammar of the original propositions and use a symbol ∧ to join terms to formalize "and" in the sense of *together with* or *both together* relative to the particular predicate in which the terms appear. Then we can formalize (1) and (3) as:

(6)   (— sang) (Dick ∧ Tom)

(7)   (— is a shoe) (x ∧ y)

In classical predicate logic without modifiers, we take (1) and (3) as atomic. We can do the same here: each of (6) and (7) (when x and y are assigned reference) is true or false in a model, and we need go no further than that. It is part of the meaning of "sang" that determines whether it applies to Dick and Tom together; it is part of the meaning of "— is a shoe" that determines whether it applies to two objects together. In any wff P(u ∧ v), the connector ∧ joins the terms *relative to* P.

We have a choice. We can put into the syntax n-ary versions of every unary predicate for every $n \geq 1$, or we can follow the grammar of the original and use conjunctions of terms, taking as part of the meaning of a unary predicate when it applies to things taken together. The approach of conjoining terms seems better because adding just one new piece of vocabulary is better than multiplying every unary predicate and because when we deal with relations we'd have to multiply each of those too: "—, — lifted$_{3\text{ab-c}}$ —", and "— lifted$_{3\text{a-bc}}$ —, —", and "—, — lifted$_{4\text{ab-cd}}$ —, —", and "—, —, — lifted$_{4\text{abc-d}}$ —", and . . . . And, as we'll see, we'd have to have n-ary versions of every k-ary modifier for all $k > n$. Moreover, conjoining terms fits into a pattern of formalizations of other uses of "and" in atomic predicates that we'll see in the next two chapters.

So let's use the symbol ∧ to join terms to formalize uses of "and" in the sense of *both together with neither having precedence over the other*. What part of speech is ∧ ? It is not categorematic. Nor is it only punctuation: that would be what we'd have if we took *n*-ary versions of unary predicates with "and" acting as a comma. The symbol ∧ is logical. It formalizes a particular reading of "and". It has meaning only when joining two categorematic parts of the vocabulary, creating a new categorematic piece of our language. The conjunction "Tom ∧ Dick" is not a new term: that would be to have pairs in the universe. It is a conjunction of terms, with a well-defined role to play in the syntax and semantics, different from, though related to, the role of terms. It is a *conjunction* that is *internal to atomic wffs*.

We can modify predicates in which we have terms joined by "and". Consider, for example:

(8) Dick and Tom sang in harmony.

The phrase "in harmony" is a restrictor. So from (8) we can conclude "Dick and Tom sang" and hence "(— sang) (Dick)" and "(— sang) (Tom)". That is, Res_1 applies for a conjunction of terms as well as for a single term:

(Q/R) (a ∧ b)
Therefore, Q(a ∧ b)

But we can't conclude "Dick sang in harmony" from (8) because no one can sing in harmony by himself. Similarly, we have:

x and *y* (together) are expensive shoes

The word "expensive" is a restrictor, so we can conclude from this that the things referred to by *x* and *y* are a pair of shoes, and hence that each is a shoe. But we can't conclude that each is an expensive shoe, for one shoe by itself is of little value. The following inference pattern is not valid:

(P/R) (a ∧ b)
Therefore, (P/R) (a) ∧ (P/R) (b)

We also use "and" to join terms in a variable restrictor, as in:

(9) Dick was dancing with Suzy and Zoe.

We can formalize this as:

((— was dancing)/with (Suzy ∧ Zoe)) (Dick)

Just as with the use of conjunctions of terms in simple predicates, the order of the terms does not matter. We will need to respect (5) for complex atomic predicates.

From (9) can we conclude "Dick danced with Suzy and Dick danced with Zoe"? More generally, does the following hold for variable restrictors?

(10) (Q/R(a ∧ b)) (c)
Therefore, (Q/R(a)) (c) ∧ (Q/R(b)) (c)

Consider:

Spot ran towards Suzy and Zoe.
Therefore, Spot ran towards Suzy and Spot ran towards Zoe.

Spot barked at Puff and Suzy.
Therefore, Spot barked at Puff and Spot barked at Suzy.

It seems these are valid for the same reason that (2) follows from (1). But the following is more problematic:

Dick and Tom played tennis with Zoe and Suzy.

This is true only if all four were playing tennis together, what we call "doubles tennis". It doesn't seem correct to conclude from this "Dick played tennis with Zoe". Since this and the other examples are not clearly valid, let's not assume (10).

The variable restrictor need not be unary. We can use "and" to join terms as in:

Spot was lying between where Dick and Suzy are and where Zoe and Tom are.

We can formalize this as:

((— was lying)/between (Dick ∧ Suzy, Zoe ∧ Tom)) (Spot)

We can also join more than two terms in a description, as in:

(11) Dick and Tom and Harry sang.

This is true iff the three were singing together. Compare then:

(12) (Dick and Tom) and Harry sang.
Dick and (Tom and Harry) sang.

Perhaps there is some way in which one but not all of these would be true. But typically when we want to distinguish (12) from (11) we say in what way Dick and Tom were singing together separately but yet together with Harry. So I'm going to assume that when we conjoin terms, we mean for them to be all together, regardless of the pairing we might make. Hence, these will be taken to be equivalent:

(13) (— sang) ((Dick ∧ Tom) ∧ Harry)

(14) (— sang) (Dick ∧ (Tom ∧ Harry))

We'll adopt the general principle for any atomic wff A:

A(a ∧ (b ∧ c)) is semantically equivalent to A((a ∧ b) ∧ c)

So either of (13) or (14) will be suitable to formalize (11). When there is no indication in our informal reasoning, let's adopt the convention to associate to the left.

This is what we do when we formalize "Ralph barked and Spot barked and Dick barked" as "(Ralph barked ∧ Spot barked) ∧ Dick barked", which we ensure is equivalent to "Ralph barked ∧ (Spot barked ∧ Dick barked)".

But now consider:

Dick and Dick sang.
Zoe danced with Dick and Dick.

We recognize these as grammatical in English, but unless we think that the second occurrence of "Dick" in each is meant to refer to a different person than the first, we consider them to be nonsense. It isn't just the repetition of terms that creates this kind of problem, though. Consider:

Marilyn Monroe and Norma Jeane Baker sang.

This is good English, and it doesn't seem to be nonsense. But when we discover that "Marilyn Monroe" and "Norma Jeane Baker" refer to the same person, we think it's wrong: no one can sing with herself. Wrong, nonsense, these we classify as false in logical analyses. And it's not just conjoining two terms. Consider:

Dick and Tom and Dick sang.
Zoe danced with Dick and Tom and Dick.

These, too, are nonsense, and hence false. Generally, any atomic wff in which there is a conjunction of terms where two of the terms refer to the same thing we'll classify as false. To do that we need to be able to say that two terms refer to the same thing. We can state our semantic assumption as:

$\vDash_\sigma x \equiv y \rightarrow \neg A(d)$

where d is a conjunction of terms in which both x and y appear.

It's enough to adopt this for variables, because then this condition follows for all terms by universal instantiation.

Finally, as you can check, all the semantic principles governing modifiers that we adopted previously apply when they are formulated for a conjunction of terms in place of a single term.

Now we can incorporate conjunctions of terms in our formal theories.[37]

Syntax
I'll use the metavariables $d, d', d_1, d_2, \ldots$ to range over formal terms or conjunctions of terms as defined here.

Formal conjunctions of terms

  i. Every variable is a term of degree 1.
     Every name symbol is a term of degree 1.

---

[37] Adam Morton in "Complex Individuals and Multigrade Relations" formalizes such uses of "and" based on a particular metaphysics that he relates to the metaphysics of classical predicate logic.

ii. If d is a term or a formal conjunction of terms of degree n,
and d' is a term or formal conjunction of terms of degree m,
then $(d \wedge d')$ is a formal conjunction of terms of degree $n + m$.

iii. A concatenation of symbols is a formal conjunction of terms iff
it is a conjunction of terms of degree n for some $n \geq 2$.

I'll use $d, d', d_1, d_2, \ldots$ to range over realizations of terms or conjunctions of terms in a semi-formal language, too, depending on context. I'll leave to you to prove:

- There is only one way to read any formal conjunction of terms.[38]
- Every formal conjunction of terms is of the form $(d \wedge d')$.
- The degree of a formal conjunction of terms is the number of terms, counting repetitions, that appear in it.

I'll let you define what it means for a term to appear in a conjunction of terms. I'll adopt the informal convention of dropping outer parentheses around a conjunction of terms when it's clear what's meant.

Conjunctions of terms are not terms. The word *term* continues to be reserved for variables and names only. For example:

x_1	a formal term
c_0	a formal term
$(x_1 \wedge c_0)$	a formal conjunction of terms
$((c_0 \wedge c_1) \wedge c_2)$	a formal conjunction of terms
$(c_0 \wedge (x_1 \wedge c_2))$	a formal conjunction of terms
Dick	a term
(Dick $\wedge$ Tom)	a conjunction of terms
(Dick $\wedge$ x_1)	a conjunction of terms
((Dick $\wedge$ Tom) $\wedge$ Harry)	a conjunction of terms
(Dick $\wedge$ (x_1 $\wedge$ Harry))	a conjunction of terms

We make the following modification to the definition of *wff* :

The use of $\equiv$ is as before (involving only terms). In all other places in the definitions, where the word "term" appears we write "term or formal conjunction of terms". Where a metavariable for a term appears, a metavariable is used to range over both terms and formal conjunctions of terms.

---

[38] Compare the proof of the unique readability of terms in the language of predicate logic with functions in Chapter 35.

100   Chapter 23

I'll let you prove the unique readability of wffs and give a definition of "the term or conjunction of terms d appears in A", which we can notate as $A(d)$. Note that the use of conjunctions of terms does not depend on our having modifiers in the language but can be adopted for ordinary classical predicate logic with $\equiv$.

Semantics

We do not need to give an explanation of what it means for "(Tom ∧ Dick) sang" to be true; that is still atomic. The only issue is how a claim such as that relates to other predications. We require that our models satisfy the schemes discussed earlier, where A stands for any atomic predicate and P for a simple predicate.

Commutativity of ∧

$\mathsf{v}_\sigma \vDash A(d \wedge d')$ iff $\mathsf{v}_\sigma \vDash A(d' \wedge d)$

where $d \wedge d'$ appears in A and $d' \wedge d$ replaces some but not necessarily all of those appearances.

Associativity of ∧

$\mathsf{v}_\sigma \vDash A((d_1 \wedge d_2) \wedge d_3)$ iff $\mathsf{v}_\sigma \vDash A(d_1 \wedge (d_2 \wedge d_3))$

where $(d_1 \wedge d_2) \wedge d_3$ appears in A and $d_1 \wedge (d_2 \wedge d_3)$ replaces some but not necessarily all of those appearances.

∧ ***implies*** ∧

If $\mathsf{v}_\sigma \vDash P(d)$ and u is a term that appears in d, then $\mathsf{v}_\sigma \vDash P(u)$.

Duplicated reference in conjoined terms

If $\mathsf{v}_\sigma \vDash x \equiv y$, then $\mathsf{v}_\sigma \nvDash A(d)$

where d is a conjunction of terms in which both x and y appear.

We also take all of our previous semantic principles, such as *Res*, to apply with a conjunction of terms in place of a term.

We do not assume ∧ *implies* ∧ for all atomic wffs generally because of the discussion of (10).

It is enough to have the first two conditions and the last condition apply to atomic wffs, since that ensures they apply when A is any wff.[39]

Axiomatizing

All the axioms of our previous theories are now formulated in our expanded language where a conjunction of terms can appear in a scheme in place of a term, except for universal instantiation and the equality axioms which must continue to be formulated solely for terms. We now add the following axioms, where A stands for any formal atomic predicate and P for any predicate symbol.

---

[39] Compare the proof of the extensionality of all wffs on p. 26 here.

Commutativity of ∧
$\forall \ldots A(d \wedge d') \rightarrow A(d' \wedge d)$

where $d \wedge d'$ appears in A and $d' \wedge d$ replaces some but not necessarily all of those appearances.

Associativity of ∧
$\forall \ldots A((d_1 \wedge d_2) \wedge d_3) \leftrightarrow A(d_1 \wedge (d_2 \wedge d_3))$

where $(d_1 \wedge d_2) \wedge d_3$ appears in A and $d_1 \wedge (d_2 \wedge d_3)$ replaces some but not necessarily all of those appearances.

∧ implies ∧
$\forall \ldots P(d) \rightarrow P(u)$

where P is any predicate symbol and u is a term that appears in d.

Duplicated reference in conjoined terms
$\forall x \, \forall y \, (x \equiv y \rightarrow \neg A(d))$

where d is a conjunction of terms in which both x and y appear.

The completeness theorem for classical predicate logic with equality needs no changes to hold for this axiom system except to note that all the axioms hold in every model.

24 "And" Joining Predicates

We also use "and" to join predicates in our ordinary speech:

(1) Juney is running and barking.

In classical predicate logic we would formalize this as:

$\quad$ (— is running) (Juney) $\wedge$ (— is barking) (Juney)

But consider:

(2) Juney was running and barking.

We cannot formalize this as:

(3) (— was running) (Juney) $\wedge$ (— was barking) (Juney)

We could have (3) true yet (2) false: at one time Juney was running, at another time she was barking, but she never ran and barked at the same time.

$\quad$ If it's only time considerations that prevent (3) from being a good formalization of (2), we could replace $\wedge$ with a conjunction that takes time into consideration, as we'll see in Volume 2, *Time and Space in Formal Logic*. But we'd still have an issue with modifiers even in the present tense. Consider:

(4) Juney is running and barking loudly.

It wouldn't be right to formalize this as:

(5) ((— is running)/loudly) (Juney) $\wedge$ ((— is barking)/loudly) (Juney)

It could be that (4) is true while both conjuncts of (5) are false if only the combination of running and barking is done loudly. We have a different standard for what counts as loudly for running and barking together as opposed to each individually. We have a conception of running and barking together as different than just running simultaneously with barking.

$\quad$ Consider also this example provided by Fred Kroon:

(6) Dward is a good scholar and administrator.

(7) Dward is a good scholar and Dward is a good administrator.

It could be that (6) is true while each part of (7) is false: Dward is a mediocre scholar (compared to other scholars) and just a so-so administrator (compared to other administrators), but is good at the combination of the two jobs together. We think of the conjoined descriptions as meaning something different from just the two descriptions applying simultaneously. In writing we sometimes indicate this "together" idea with a hyphen, as in "Dward is a good scholar-administrator". Often we find out that this is what is meant only by context, or by quizzing the speaker, or by seeing a modifier applied to the combined description.

This "together" aspect of the conjoined predicates shows up especially with the use of negators. Consider:

Tom almost sang and danced.

This could be true when Tom both sang and Tom danced at the same time, but he didn't do the two in a together or combined way.

I do not know how to clarify what we mean by this idea of predicates applying together differently from applying simultaneously. The together-nature of the terms being joined is understood via the meaning of the predicate in which they appear. But here there is no further standard beyond our experience and our understanding of the words. Nonetheless, I think that the examples with modifiers show that we do have such a conception.

There are schemes of valid inferences that require us to formalize such uses of "and". We've already seen examples of one:

(P and Q) (a)
Therefore, $P(a) \wedge Q(a)$

On the reading of "and" in these examples as indicating no precedence or greater weight of the one description over the other, we also have:

(9) (P and Q) (a)
Therefore, (Q and P) (a)

We can also join more than two predicates for a description. Consider:

(10) Tom sang, danced, and mimed.

Tom (sang and danced) and mimed.

Tom sang and (danced and mimed).

Are these three equivalent? It may be that we have some idea of predicates applying together that would distinguish these. But I cannot find any clear understanding that would justify the propositions at (10) as not equivalent. I have only an idea of predicates applying together, all together, so that the first of (10) is basic, and the others are just ways we can reduce the ternary use of "and" joining predicates to a binary use. On this understanding of "and" joining predicates in the sense of *the predicates applying together with neither having greater weight or precedence over the other*, we have the valid scheme:

((Q_1 and Q_2) and Q_3) (a)
Therefore, (Q_1 and (Q_2 and Q_3)) (a)

We also join modified atomic predicates. For example,

(11) Dick was singing slowly and dancing quickly.

When we conjoin predicates that are already modified, it's because we want each modifier to apply to just one of the predicates. Then we can apply a modifier to the conjunction of the modified predicates, as in:

Dick was carefully singing slowly and dancing quickly.

From (11) we can conclude:

Dick was singing and dancing quickly.

Dick was singing and dancing.

I'll let you explain why the following are valid:

$(Q_1$ and $(Q_2/R))$ (c)
Therefore, $(Q_1$ and $Q_2)$ (c)

$((Q_1/R)$ and $Q_2)$ (c)
Therefore, $(Q_1$ and $Q_2)$ (c)

We only need adopt one of these in our semantics for the other will follow by (9).
But note that the following is not valid:

Dick is singing and dancing quickly.
Therefore, Dick is singing quickly and Dick is dancing quickly.

Dick could be singing and dancing quickly, though compared to someone who is only dancing he could be fairly slow. This scheme is not valid:

$((Q_1$ and $Q_2)/R)$ (c)
Therefore, (Q_1/R) (c) $\wedge$ (Q_2/R) (c)

But what if one of the atomic predicates is a pure negated predicate, that is, a simple predicate modified by "not"? Consider:

Spot was barking and not growling loudly.

It makes sense to apply "loudly" to "barking and not growling" because we can have a standard for applying "loudly" to "was barking". But it doesn't make sense to say:

Spot was not barking and not growling loudly.

If Spot was not barking and not growling, he could have been doing anything, even sleeping. We have no standard for the use of "loudly" for doing anything. So *we can join a pure negated predicate only with one that is not a pure negated predicate*.

Let's use the symbol + for our abstraction of joining atomic predicates, which we'll call the *predicate conjoiner*. When we join two unary predicates, they're meant to apply together to a single term or conjunction of terms as a *conjunction of predicates*.

from   "— was barking" and "— was running"
we get   "— was barking + was running"

from   "— is a scholar" and "— is an administrator"

we get "— is a scholar + is an administrator"

from   "(— is singing)/slowly" and "(— is dancing)/quickly"

we get "— is singing/slowly + is dancing/quickly"

From two unary predicates we get a new unary predicate.

This new symbol is part of the logical vocabulary. It formalizes a particular reading of certain uses of "and". From two pieces of categorematic vocabulary, we get a new categorematic piece of our language. Previously we had to take "Dick was singing and dancing" as an atomic proposition; here we are only noting that certain relations hold between that and other propositions by taking "— was singing + was dancing" as atomic. That is, "— was singing + was dancing" is an atomic predicate. The conjunction of atomic predicates is a new atomic predicate, a *conjunction* that is *internal to atomic wffs*.

Now we can set out a formal theory of conjunctions of predicates.

Syntax

We add to the formal language(s) the formal symbol "+". We add the following clause to the definition of *formal atomic predicate*:

> If $Q_1(-)$ and $Q_2(-)$ are formal atomic predicates of degrees n and m, respectively, and at least one of them is not a pure negated predicate, then $(Q_1 + Q_2)(-)$ is a formal atomic predicate of degree $n + m + 1$.

I'll let you show that there is only one way to read any formal atomic predicate. So I'll write $A(Q_1 + Q_2)$ to mean that the predicate $Q_1 + Q_2$ appears in the atomic wff A.

Semantics

Our models satisfy the following additional conditions, where A is an atomic wff and Q, Q_1, Q_2, Q_3 are atomic predicates.

Commutativity of +

> $\vDash_\sigma A(Q_1 + Q_2)$ iff $\vDash_\sigma A(Q_2 + Q_1)$
>
> where $(Q_1 + Q_2)$ appears in A, and $(Q_2 + Q_1)$ replaces some but not necessarily all of those appearances.

Associativity of +

> $\vDash_\sigma A((Q_1 + Q_2) + Q_3)$ iff $\vDash_\sigma A(Q_1 + (Q_2 + Q_3))$
>
> where $(Q_1 + Q_2) + Q_3$ appears in A, and $Q_1 + (Q_2 + Q_3)$ replaces some but not necessarily all of those appearances.

106   Chapter 24

Restrictors and +

If $\nu_\sigma \vDash (Q_1 + (Q_2/R))\,(d)$, then $\nu_\sigma \vDash (Q_1 + Q_2)\,(d)$.

+ implies ∧

If $\nu_\sigma \vDash (Q_1 + Q_2)\,(d)$, then $\nu_\sigma \vDash Q_1(d)$ and $\nu_\sigma \vDash Q_2(d)$

It is enough to have the first two semantic conditions apply to atomic wffs, since that ensures they apply when A is any wff.[40]

Axiomatizing

To obtain a strongly complete axiomatization of these semantics we add the following axiom schemes to our previous axiomatization(s), where A is an atomic wff and B, C, B_1, B_2, B_3 stand for formal atomic predicates.

Commutativity of +

$\forall\ldots\ A(Q_1 + Q_2) \leftrightarrow A(Q_2 + Q_1)$

where $Q_1 + Q_2$ appears in A and $Q_2 + Q_1$ replaces some but not necessarily all of those appearances.

Associativity of +

$\forall\ldots\ A((Q_1 + Q_2) + Q_3) \leftrightarrow A(Q_1 + (Q_2 + Q_3))$

where $(Q_1 + Q_2) + Q_3$ appears in A, and $Q_1 + (Q_2 + Q_3)$ replaces some but not necessarily all of those appearances.

Restrictors and +

$\forall\ldots\ (Q_1 + (Q_2/R))\,(d) \to (Q_1 + Q_2)\,(d)$

+ implies ∧

$\forall\ldots\ (Q_1 + Q_2)\,(d) \to (Q_1(d) \land Q_2(d))$

Aside: The use of variables and blanks

It might seem that the usual language of classical predicate logic allows for formalizing joinings of predicates, as in "x is running ∧ x is barking". But in any semantic analysis of that wff, x is assigned a reference and the wff becomes a proposition, which is what justifies our using ∧ as a propositional connective. So we cannot modify that phrase with "loudly" any more than we can modify "Juney is running ∧ Juney is barking" with "loudly". It is crucial here to distinguish the role of variables from that of blanks.

---

[40] Compare the proof of the extensionality of all wffs on p. 26 here.

25 "And" Joining Modifiers

Compare:

(1) Birta is a small and cute dog.

(2) Birta is a small dog and Birta is a cute dog

The truth-conditions for these are the same. We don't have a distinct notion of "small and cute" that isn't just being small and being cute.

But the equivalence breaks down when we don't have the present tense:

(3) Birta was a small and cute dog.

(4) Birta was a small dog and Birta was a cute dog.

We could have (4) true but (3) false if Birta was an ugly dog when she was small but grew up to be a cute big dog. The inference from (3) to (4) is valid, though, and so, since "small" and "cute" are restrictors, we can conclude "Birta was a dog" from (3).

Even in the present tense, though, (2) isn't a good formalization of (1) because we can modify "small and cute":

(5) Birta is a large small and cute dog.

This is not equivalent to:

(6) Birta is a large small dog and Birta is a large cute dog.

Birta might not be large in comparison to other small dogs, but only in comparison to other small dogs that are cute, so (6) does not follow from (5).

We can also have two adverb restrictors joined.

(7) Juney was barking loudly and fiercely.

From this follows:

(8) Juney was barking loudly and Juney was barking fiercely.

But the inference from (8) to (7) is invalid.

We have to respect the same sort of inferences with variable predicate modifiers. Consider:

(9) Spot was lying close to Dick and far from Zoe.

There is no precedence of one of these restrictors over the other: we're not first restricting "—is lying" to those objects close to Dick and then further restricting to objects that are far from Zoe. Here "close to —" and "far from —" are variable restrictors. From (9) we can conclude:

Spot was lying close to Dick and Spot was lying far from Zoe.

But the inference in the other direction is invalid. Further, we can modify the two variable restrictors that are joined as in:

Spot is lying relatively close to Dick and far from Zoe.

Should we also allow for a restrictor and a negator to be joined? Consider:

(10) Ralph is a small and toy dog.

If Ralph is a small and toy dog, then Ralph is a small dog and a toy dog. But that's contradictory. If Ralph is a small dog, he's a dog; if Ralph is a toy dog, he's not a dog. Applying any predicate modifier and any predicate negator jointly results in a predicate that applies to nothing, and there's no need to formalize that. The only reading of (10) that makes any sense is "Ralph is a small toy dog", and we already have the tools to formalize that.

I have not been able to find an example of two negators joined that makes sense. I cannot imagine using "Juney was almost and hardly barking" or "Ralph was a fake and toy dog" in any reasoning. Unless someone can provide a pattern of examples of such a combination whose internal structure needs to be taken into account by our formalizations, let's consider joining only two restrictors. We do need to recognize that informal structure in order to justify the pattern we saw above:

(11) $A/(R_1$ and $R_2)$
Therefore A/R_1 and A/R_2.

There is also a pattern of valid inferences we need to respect in which there is a use of negators as part of joined restrictors. Consider:

(12) Tom is speaking softly and almost clearly.
Therefore,
(13) Tom is speaking softly and not clearly.

From (12) by (11) we can conclude "Tom is speaking softly and Tom is speaking almost clearly". From that we can conclude "Tom is speaking not-clearly". But that doesn't give us (13). We need to respect the following pattern:

$A/(R_1$ and $(R_2/N))$
Therefore $A/(R_1$ and $\sim R_2)$

Let's use "&" to formalize uses of "and" joining predicate restrictors in the sense that *both restrictors are meant to apply simultaneously, without any precedence of one over the other*. As with ∧ and +, we take & to be logical vocabulary and require that it be associative and commutative.

Syntax

We add to our formal language(s) the symbol "&" with the clause:

If R_1 and R_2 are predicate restrictors, then $(R_1$ & $R_2)$ is a predicate restrictor.

I'll let you show that there is one and only one way to read any formal atomic predicate. So we can write A(R & R´) to mean that the restrictor R & R´ appears in the atomic wff A.

Semantics
Our models will satisfy the following conditions, where A is any atomic wff.

Commutativity of &
$\quad \nu_\sigma \models A(R_1 \,\&\, R_2)$ iff $\nu_\sigma \models A(R_2 \,\&\, R_1)$

where $R_1 \,\&\, R_2$ appears in A and $R_2 \,\&\, R_1$ replaces some but not necessarily all of those appearances.

Associativity of &
$\quad \nu_\sigma \models A((R_1 \,\&\, R_2) \,\&\, R_3)$ iff $\nu_\sigma \models A(R_1 \,\&\, (R_2 \,\&\, R_3))$

where $(R_1 \,\&\, R_2) \,\&\, R_3$ appears in A and $R_1 \,\&\, (R_2 \,\&\, R_3)$ replaces some but not necessarily all of those appearances.

& implies ∧
$\quad$ If $\nu_\sigma \models (A/(R_1 \,\&\, R_2))(d)$, then $\nu_\sigma \models (A/R_1)(d)$ and $\nu_\sigma \models (A/R_2)(d)$.

Negators and the pure negator in joined restrictors
$\quad$ If $\nu_\sigma \models (A/(R_1 \,\&\, (R_2/N)))(d)$, then $\nu_\sigma \models (A/(R_1 \,\&\, \sim R_2))(d)$

Note that A may contain a variable restrictor that contains one or more terms or conjunctions of terms. Again, it is enough to have the first two of these semantic conditions apply to atomic wffs, since that ensures they apply when A is any wff.

Axiomatizing
To obtain a strongly complete axiomatization of these semantics we add the following axiom schemes to our previous axiomatization(s), where A is a formal atomic wff.

Commutativity of &
$\quad \forall \ldots \; A(R_1 \,\&\, R_2) \to A(R_2 \,\&\, R_1)$

where $R_1 \,\&\, R_2$ appears in A and $R_2 \,\&\, R_1$ replaces some but not necessarily all of those appearances.

Associativity of &
$\quad \forall \ldots \; A((R_1 \,\&\, R_2) \,\&\, R_3) \leftrightarrow A(R_1 \,\&\, (R_2 \,\&\, R_3))$

where $(R_1 \,\&\, R_2) \,\&\, R_3$ appears in A and $R_1 \,\&\, (R_2 \,\&\, R_3)$ replaces some but not necessarily all of those appearances.

& implies ∧
$$\forall\ldots\ (A/(R_1\ \&\ R_2))\,(d) \to ((A/R_1)\,(d) \wedge (A/R_2)\,(d))$$

Negators and the pure negator in joined restrictors
$$\forall\ldots\ (A/(R_1\ \&\ (R_2/N)))\,(d) \to (A/(R_1\ \&\ \sim R_2))\,(d)$$

26 "Or" Joining Predicates

We use "or" in ordinary speech to form what seem to be compound terms and compound modifiers:

    Tom or Dick sang.

    Puff was a stupid or stubborn cat.

    Zoe carefully spoke loudly or clearly.

We can formalize these with the tools we already have. With the inclusive reading of "or", we have:

    $(—\text{ sang})(\text{Tom}) \vee (—\text{ sang})(\text{Dick})$

    $(—\text{ was a cat})/\text{stupid})(\text{Puff}) \vee (—\text{ was a cat})/\text{stubborn})(\text{Puff})$

    $(((—\text{ spoke})/\text{loudly})/\text{carefully})(\text{Zoe}) \vee$
        $(((—\text{ spoke})/\text{clearly})/\text{carefully})(\text{Zoe})$

Time considerations do not affect these equivalences. There doesn't appear to be a reason to add an internal disjunction for terms or modifiers.

Nor does it seem that we need to add an internal disjunction for predicates. For example:

    Helen is a man or woman iff Helen is a man or Helen is a woman.

But consider:

(1)   Helen is strong.

We might interpret this as:

(2)   Helen is a strong woman.

Or we might interpret it as:

    Helen is a strong animal.

Unless the speaker or the context makes it clear, there's no right way to make (1) into a proposition. Suppose the speaker says she meant:

(3)   Helen is a strong person.

It's a wider class for comparison than in (2): Helen is strong compared not just to women, but to all people. But "all people" amounts to men and women. So (3) is equivalent to:

(4)   Helen is a strong (man or woman).

In English we have a word "person" for "man or woman". But if we didn't, it wouldn't be right to use:

Helen is a strong man or Helen is a strong woman.

This could be true if Helen is strong compared to other women but not to men. The use of "or" joining predicates is a way to arrive at a larger class for comparison.

For example, when my dogs chased after something last week I said:

That is a big rabbit or hare.

Rabbits and hares are different, and to my knowledge we don't have a single word for both. But whichever it was the dogs were chasing, it was big compared to both rabbits and hares, which is a wider comparison than saying it was big for a rabbit or big for a hare.

We can also use "or" between modified atomic predicates:

(5) Helen is a strong (short man or healthy woman).

This establishes a wider comparison than just to short men or just to healthy women.

We have motive to formalize disjunctions of predicates in our systems. What schemes of valid inferences and tautologies do we need to respect? We already have:

$$(Q_1 \text{ or } Q_2)(c) \leftrightarrow (Q_1(c) \lor Q_2(c))$$

It might seem that if we're comparing to a larger class, then the modifier must apply to each part. But the following example shows that's not a valid rule of inference:

Helen is a strong (man or woman).
Therefore, Helen is a strong man and Helen is a strong woman.

Helen is not both a man and a woman. Rather:

Helen is a strong (man or woman).
Therefore, Helen is a strong man or Helen is a strong woman.

Helen is a strong (man or woman) and Helen is a woman.
Therefore, Helen is a strong woman.

We want to respect both:

$((Q_1 \text{ or } Q_2)/R)(c)$
Therefore, $(Q_1/R)(c) \lor (Q_2/R)(c)$

$((Q_1 \text{ or } Q_2)/R)(c) \land Q_2(c)$
Therefore, $(Q_2/R)(c)$

But this isn't possible if one of the atomic predicates is a pure negated one. For example, consider:

Helen is a big cheerleader or not-secretary.

There is a wider comparison here, but too wide: "not-secretary" could be anything, even an automobile. And we know that we can't use "Helen is a big not-secretary" as a proposition. So we don't allow for using "or" to join a pure negated predicate.

Finally, because neither predicate of the disjunction is meant to take precedence, commutativity and associativity of disjunctions of predicates hold.

Let's use the symbol $\cup$ for our abstraction of joining atomic predicates with "or" in the sense of one or (not exclusively) the other predicate applying with neither having greater weight or precedence over the other. We'll call this the *predicate disjoiner*. When we disjoin two unary predicates, they're meant to apply together to a single subject as a *disjunction of predicates*, a *disjunction that is internal to atomic wffs*. As with conjunctions of predicates, from two unary predicates we get a new unary predicate.

> from   "— is a man" and "— is a woman"
> we get   "— is a man $\cup$ is a woman"
>
> from   "(— is a man)/short" and "(— is a woman)/healthy"
> we get   "— is a man/short $\cup$ is a woman/healthy"

So for example, we can formalize (4) as:

> $((-$ is a man $\cup$ is a woman)/strong) (Helen)

Now we can set out a formal theory of disjunctions of predicates.

Syntax

We add to the formal language(s) the formal symbol $\cup$. We add the following clause to the definition of *formal atomic predicate*.

> If $Q_1(-)$ and $Q_2(-)$ are formal atomic predicates of degrees n and m respectively, and neither is a pure negated predicate, then $(Q_1 \cup Q_2)(-)$ is a formal atomic predicate formula of degree $n + m + 1$.

I'll let you show that there is only one way to read any formal atomic predicate.

Semantics

Our models satisfy the following additional conditions, where A is an atomic wff, and Q_1, Q_2, Q_3 are atomic predicates.

Commutativity of $\cup$

> $v_\sigma \vDash A(Q_1 \cup Q_2)$ iff $v_\sigma \vDash A(Q_2 \cup Q_1)$
>
> where $(Q_1 \cup Q_2)$ appears in A, and $(Q_2 \cup Q_1)$ replaces some but not necessarily all of those appearances.

Associativity of $\cup$

> $v_\sigma \vDash A((Q_1 \cup Q_2) \cup Q_3)$ iff $v_\sigma \vDash A(Q_1 \cup (Q_2 \cup Q_3))$
>
> where $(Q_1 \cup Q_2) \cup Q_3$ appears in A, and $Q_1 \cup (Q_2 \cup Q_3)$ replaces some but not necessarily all of those appearances.

Equivalence of $\cup$ and $\vee$

$\mathsf{v}_\sigma \vDash (Q_1 \cup Q_2)(d)$ iff $\mathsf{v}_\sigma \vDash Q_1(d)$ or $\mathsf{v}_\sigma \vDash Q_2(d)$

$\cup$ implies $\vee$ with restrictors

If $\mathsf{v}_\sigma \vDash ((Q_1 \cup Q_2)/R)(d)$, then $\mathsf{v}_\sigma \vDash (Q_1/R))(d)$ or $\mathsf{v}_\sigma \vDash (Q_2/R))(d)$

Restrictors and $\cup$

If $\mathsf{v}_\sigma \vDash ((Q_1 \cup Q_2)/R)(d)$ and $\mathsf{v}_\sigma \vDash Q_1(d)$, then $\mathsf{v}_\sigma \vDash (Q_1/R)(d)$

It is enough to have the first two semantic conditions apply to atomic wffs, since that ensures they apply when A is any wff.

Note that from the equivalence of $\cup$ and $\vee$, we have that:

$\mathsf{v}_\sigma \vDash (Q_1 \cup Q_1)(d)$ iff $\mathsf{v}_\sigma \vDash Q_1(d)$

Repetition of a predicate in a disjunction is superfluous, not nonsense.

Axiomatizing

To obtain a strongly complete axiomatization of these semantics we add the following axiom schemes to our previous axiomatization(s).

Commutativity of $\cup$

$\forall \ldots \ A(Q_1 \cup Q_2) \leftrightarrow A(Q_2 \cup Q_1)$

where $(Q_1 \cup Q_2)$ appears in A, and $(Q_2 \cup Q_1)$ replaces some but not necessarily all of those appearances.

Associativity of $\cup$

$\forall \ldots \ A((Q_1 \cup Q_2) \cup Q_3) \leftrightarrow A(Q_1 \cup (Q_2 \cup Q_3))$

where $(Q_1 \cup Q_2) \cup Q_3$ appears in A, and $Q_1 \cup (Q_2 \cup Q_3)$ replaces some but not necessarily all of those appearances.

Equivalence of $\cup$ and $\vee$

$\forall \ldots \ (Q_1 \cup Q_2)(d) \leftrightarrow (Q_1(d) \vee Q_2(d))$

$\cup$ implies $\vee$ with restrictors

$\forall \ldots \ ((Q_1 \cup Q_2)/R)(d) \rightarrow (Q_1/R))(d) \vee (Q_2/R))(d)$

Restrictors and $\cup$

$\forall \ldots \ ((Q_1 \cup Q_1)/R)(d) \wedge Q_1(d) \rightarrow (Q_1/R)(d)$

27 Examples of Formalizing

Example 1 Tom is walking from somewhere.

Analysis Let's assume that places can be treated as things. Do we then need a quantifier internal to the atomic predicate to formalize the example, as in:

   $((- \text{ is walking})/\exists x \,(\text{from } x))\,(\text{Tom}))$

The only way I see to evaluate this is as we evaluate:

   $\exists x \,(- \text{ is walking}/\text{from } (x))\,(\text{Tom})$

The conditions for this to be true in a model are:

   there is some assignment of references σ such that
   $\mathsf{v}_\sigma \vDash (- \text{ is walking}/\text{from } (x))\,(\text{Tom})$.

Still, there's a worry. The following is valid:

   Tom is walking from somewhere.
   Therefore, Tom is walking.

Yet it's not obvious that the following is valid:

   $\exists x \,((- \text{ is walking}/\text{from } (x))\,(\text{Tom}))$
   Therefore, $(- \text{ is walking})\,(\text{Tom})$

But it is.[41]

Similarly, we can use the following formalizations:

Juney barked at everyone.

   $\forall x \,((-\text{is a person})\,(x) \rightarrow (- \text{ barked}/\text{at } (x))\,(\text{Juney}))$

Dick danced with Suzy and someone.

   $\exists x \,((- \text{ danced}/\text{with } (\text{Suzy} \wedge x))\,(\text{Dick}))$

There's no apparent reason to allow for quantification within atomic predicates.

Example 2 Roger and Clara are happily married.

   $((- \text{ is married})/\text{happily})\,(\text{Roger} \wedge \text{Clara})$

   $(P_{71}(-)/R_{12})\,(c_{32} \wedge c_{32})$

---

[41] To see this, suppose that "$\exists x \,(- \text{ is walking}/\text{from } x)\,(\text{Tom})$" plus "$\neg$ (Tom is walking)" is consistent. Then expand the semi-formal language by a countable number of new name symbols and construct a model of those two wffs from the name symbols as in the usual completeness theorem for classical predicate logic (see Appendix 7) in which "$\exists x \,(- \text{ is walking}/\text{from } x)\,(\text{Tom})$" has a witness. In that model, "Tom is walking" is true by virtue of RES_1, which is a contradiction. So "$\exists x \,(- \text{ is walking}/\text{from } x)\,(\text{Tom})$" plus "$\neg$ (Tom is walking)" is inconsistent, and hence "Tom is walking" is a semantic consequence of "$\exists x \,(- \text{ is walking}/\text{from } x)\,(\text{Tom})$".

116   Chapter 27

Analysis Let's assume that what's meant by the example is that Roger and Clara are married to each other. From that we can conclude "Roger is married", and from the formalization we can conclude "(— is married) (Roger)" by using Res_1 to conclude "(— is married)/(Roger ∧ Clara)" and then invoking ∧ *implies* ∧ .

Example 3 Dick and Tom and Harry sang in three-part harmony.
Therefore, *Dick and Tom sang in three-part harmony.*

$$\frac{((- \text{ sang})/\text{in three-part harmony}) (\text{Dick} \wedge \text{Tom} \wedge \text{Harry})}{((- \text{ sang})/\text{in three-part harmony}) (\text{Dick} \wedge \text{Tom})}$$

$$\frac{(P_{31}(-)/R_{81}) (c_2 \wedge c_6 \wedge c_7)}{(P_{31}(-)/R_{81}) (c_2 \wedge c_6)}$$

Analysis The inference is invalid and is another example of why we take the semantic principle ∧ *implies* ∧ to hold only for simple predicates.

Example 4 If everything breathes, then Tom and Dick breathe.

$\forall x ((- \text{ breathes}) (x) \to ((- \text{ breathes}) (\text{Tom}) \wedge (- \text{ breathes}) (\text{Dick})))$

Analysis We don't formalize "and" in the example as ∧ because we don't think that the speaker means that Tom and Dick breathe together. The example is a tautology, but it wouldn't be if we used:

$\forall x ((- \text{ breathes}) (x) \to (- \text{ breathes}) (\text{Tom} \wedge \text{Dick}))$

This is another example of why in universal instantiation we do not allow for a conjunction of terms to be substituted for a variable.

Example 5 Tom is standing between Zoe and Suzy.

$((- \text{ is standing})/(\text{between Zoe and Suzy})) (\text{Tom})$

$(P_6(-)/R_{17}(c_{10}, c_1)) (c_2)$

Analysis We do not formalize "and" in the example with ∧ . There is no unary modifier "between —", so "and" must be taken as part of the binary structure of the modifier "between — and —".

Example 6 Dick danced with Suzy and Zoe.
Therefore, *Dick danced with Suzy.*

$$\frac{((- \text{ danced})/\text{with} (\text{Suzy} \wedge \text{Zoe})) (\text{Dick})}{((- \text{ danced})/\text{with} (\text{Suzy})) (\text{Dick})}$$

$$\frac{(P_7(-)/R_4(c_{10} \wedge c_1)) (c_2)}{(P7_1(-)/R_4(c_{10})) (c_2)}$$

Analysis The semi-formal inference is not valid. If we nonetheless think the conclusion follows from the premise, we'll have to adopt a meaning axiom:

(a) $\forall x \, \forall y \, \forall z \, [((-\text{ danced})/\text{with} \, (x \wedge y)) \, (z) \rightarrow ((-\text{ danced})/\text{with} \, (x)) \, (z)]$

But we also have that the inference "Dick danced with Suzy and Zoe and Maria, therefore, Dick danced with Suzy and Zoe" is valid. So we'll need a fuller scheme of meaning axioms:

$\forall \ldots \, ((-\text{ danced})/\text{with} \, (d \wedge d')) \, (x) \rightarrow ((-\text{ danced})/\text{with} \, (d)) \, (x)$

Example 7 Buddy and Birta barked loudly at a stranger.

$\exists x \, ((-\text{ is a stranger}) \, (x) \wedge (((-\text{ barked})/\text{loudly})/\text{at} \, (x)) \, (\text{Buddy} \wedge \text{Birta}))$

$\exists x_1 \, ([P_{22}(-)(x_1) \wedge ((P_8(-)/R_5)/R_3(x_1))] \, (c_{20} \wedge c_0))$

Analysis We need to conjoin the terms because the restrictor "loudly" is meant to restrict "— barking" applied to both Buddy and Birta.

We could give "loudly" wider scope modifying "barked at a stranger":

$\exists x \, ((-\text{ is a stranger}) \, (x) \wedge (((-\text{ barked})/\text{at} \, (x))/\text{loudly}) \, (\text{Buddy} \wedge \text{Birta}))$

Deciding which of these is best would depend on what the speaker intended. But it doesn't seem right to conjoin the two restrictors.

Example 8 Bon Bon and Gladys are matched donkeys.
     Therefore, *Bon Bon is one of a matched pair of donkeys.*

$$\frac{((-\text{ is a donkey})/\text{matched}) \, (\text{Bon Bon} \wedge \text{Gladys})}{\exists x \, (((-\text{ is a donkey})/\text{matched}) \, (\text{Bon Bon} \wedge x))}$$

Analysis The example is valid. But we cannot conclude "Bon Bon is a matched donkey" from the premise.

Example 9 This is a pair of shiny shoes. So that one is a shiny shoe.

Analysis If we were to name the shoes "a" and "b", a formalization of the example would be:

$$\frac{((-\text{ is a shoe})/\text{shiny}) \, (a \wedge b)}{((-\text{ is a shoe})/\text{shiny}) \, (a)}$$

Certainly if the premise is true the conclusion is true. But that's not because of the form of the inference. It's from the meaning of the word "shiny" that a pair of shoes is shiny iff each shoe is shiny. To formalize that understanding, we can take as a meaning axiom:

$\forall x \, \forall y \, ((-\text{ is a shoe})/\text{shiny}) \, (x \wedge y) \leftrightarrow$
    $(-\text{ is a shoe})/\text{shiny} \, (x) \wedge (-\text{ is a shoe})/\text{shiny} \, (y))$

Example 10 Three men conspired.

$\exists x \exists y \exists z ((-$ is a man$)(x) \wedge (-$ is a man$)(y) \wedge (-$ is a man$)(z)$
$\wedge (x \not\equiv y) \wedge (x \not\equiv z) \wedge (y \not\equiv z) \wedge (-$ conspired$)(x \wedge y \wedge z))$

Analysis Understanding the example as meaning that the men conspired together, we cannot formalize this as:

$\exists x \exists y \exists z ((-$ is a man$)(x) \wedge (-$ is a man$)(y) \wedge (-$ is a man$)(z)$
$\wedge (x \not\equiv y) \wedge (x \not\equiv z) \wedge (y \not\equiv z)$
$\wedge (-$ conspired$)(x) \wedge (-$ conspired$)(y) \wedge (-$ conspired$)(z))$

Example 11 All the men conspired.

Analysis If we know in advance that the number of men in the universe of the model is less than, say, 47, we could formalize this. Absent that assumption, we have no way to formalize the example.

Example 12 Juney is barking loudly and quietly.
    Therefore, Juney is barking.

$\dfrac{((-$ is barking$)/($loudly & quietly$))($Juney$)}{(-$ is barking$)($Juney$)}$

Analysis The phrase "loudly & quietly" is a restrictor, so the inference is valid. But in any model in which the words have their usual interpretation, the modifier "loudly & quietly" restricts a predicate to apply to nothing. We could ensure that by adopting a meaning axiom.

Example 13 Every faithful and obedient dog is house-trained.

$\forall x ((-$ is a dog$)/($faithful & obedient$)(x) \rightarrow$
$(-$ is a dog$)/$house-trained$)(x))$

$\forall x_1 ((P_1/(R_{13}$ & $R_{14})(x_1) \rightarrow ((P_1/R_{16}(x_1))$

Analysis Because the example is in the present tense it might seem we could formalize the antecedent of the conditional as:

$(-$ is a dog$)/$faithful $\wedge (-$ is a dog$)/$obedient$)(x)$

But that would be to ignore all the other inferences such a phrase could appear in for which we need to employ &, for example "Every faithful and obedient small dog is house-trained". We invoke the criterion of parity of form (p. 31).

Example 14 June is a gorgeous redheaded Christian woman.

$((-$ is a woman$)/($gorgeous & redheaded & Christian$))($June$)$

Analysis To formalize the example, we have to ask what reference classes are intended for the adjectives. I don't think the speaker is asserting that June is gorgeous and redheaded compared only to Christian women. Rather, all three adjectives together are meant to apply to June as a woman, so we use the formalization given in the example. We don't formalize the example as:

(— is a woman)/gorgeous) (June) ∧ (— is a woman)/redheaded) (June)
∧ (— is a woman)/Christian)) (June)

That follows from the formalization given in the example, but it would not allow for parity of form in formalizing "June is a previously gorgeous redheaded Christian woman" where "previously" applies to "gorgeous redheaded Christian woman". That might be true when June is old with white hair and is now a Buddhist.

Example 15 Juney is a not-ugly black-and-white dog.

(((— is a dog)/black-and-white)/~ugly) (Juney)

$(P_1(—)/(R_{14}/~R_{16}))$ (c_9)

Analysis The modifier "black-and-white" cannot be construed as "black & white" because what is black is not white, and what is white is not black. Rather, "black-and-white" is a simple restrictor, not related to the restrictors "white" and "black" in any regular way with the resources we have. Nor can we reverse the order of the words, for (it seems) a white-and-black dog is not a black-and-white dog.

Example 16 Spot is barking loudly rapidly.

((— is barking)/(loudly & rapidly)) (Spot)

Analysis We can now formalize the adverbs as applied together rather than successively, as we wished to do in Example 9 of Chapter 17.

Example 17 Flo slid down a hill on the snow in a sled.

∃x ∃y ((— is a hill) (x) ∧ (— is a sled) (y) ∧
((((— slid)/ (down (x) & on the snow)/in y) (Flo))

$\exists x_1 \exists x_2 ((P_{803}(—)(x_1) \land P_{65}(—)(x_2) \land$
$(((P_{66}(—)/R_7(x_1) \& R_{82})/R_1(x_2)) (c_{11})))$

Analysis We lacked the tools to formalize this when we considered it as Example 13 of Chapter 17.

Example 18 Spot is a not-fierce large and cute dog.

(((— is a dog)/(large & cute))/~fierce) (Spot)

$(P_1(—)/(R_{80} \& R_{11})/~R_{19})$ (c_3)

Analysis Here we are joining modifiers that are modified by a negated restrictor.

Example 19 Birta is a loveable large and not-cute dog.

$(((-$ is a dog)/(large & $\sim$ cute)/loveable)) (Birta)

$(P_1(-)/(R_{80}$ & $\sim R_{11}))/R_0)$ (c_0)

Analysis This is an example of a negated restrictor joined with a simple modifier. Alternatively, if we thought that "loveable" is not a relative adjective, we would formalize the example as:

$(-$ is a dog)/(large & $\sim$ cute) (Birta) $\wedge$ ($-$ is loveable) (Birta)

Or if "loveable" is meant for dogs generally, we could formalize the example as:

$(-$ is a dog)/(large & $\sim$ cute & loveable) (Birta)

Example 20 Suzy nonchalantly stood between Tom and Dick and next to Zoe.

$((-$ stood)/((between Tom and Dick & next to (Zoe))/nonchalantly)) (Suzy)

$(P_{33}(-)/(R_{17}(c_0, c_1)$ & $R_2(c_3))/R_8)$ (c_7)

Analysis No blanks appear in the variable restrictors; the only blank is in the simple atomic predicate. In "Tom and Dick" the word "and" does not conjoin terms because "between $-$" is not a modifier.

This reading takes "nonchalantly" to have widest scope. For it to have minimum scope, modifying only the predicate "$-$ stood", we'd say "Suzy stood nonchalantly between Tom and Dick and next to Zoe".

Example 21 Birta and Buddy are chasing and sniffing.

$(-$ is chasing $+$ is sniffing) (Birta $\wedge$ Buddy)

$(P_{37} + P_{38})$ $(-)$ $(c_0 \wedge c_{12})$

Analysis I said this when my dogs were running and sniffing the ground and running and sniffing, and running and sniffing, and . . . . It's an example of a conjunction of terms with a conjunction of predicates.

Example 22 Wanda and Suzy very loudly and merrily danced and sang with all of their friends.

$\forall x (((-$ is a friend)/of (Wanda $\wedge$ Suzy)) $(x) \to$
$((-$ danced $+$ sang)/((loudly & merrily)/very/with (x))) (Wanda $\wedge$ Suzy))

Analysis Here we have unary predicates conjoined, simple modifiers conjoined, and terms conjoined, as well as a modifier of a modifier.

Example 23 Wanda and Suzy very loudly and merrily danced and sang, though not with abandon, with all of their friends.

$\forall x (((-$ is a friend)/of (Wanda $\wedge$ Suzy)) $(x) \to$ $((-$ danced $+$ sang)/
(loudly & merrily)/very / $\sim$(with abandon)/with (x)) (Wanda $\wedge$ Suzy))

Analysis The only issue here is how to formalize "though not with abandon". We could take "though" as a connective, reading the phrase as elliptical for "and they did not dance very loudly and merrily with abandon". But it seems more natural to read "though" as indicating "and not" in the sense of one more modifier, a negated one. The word "with" is used as a variable restrictor in "with all of their friends", but "with abandon" is a simple modifier, for we do not recognize "abandon" as a thing.

Example 24 (In Portuguese) *Dick está esperando pacientemente.*

Analysis João, from Brazil, is in the mall talking on the phone to Tom, who is at home. João sees Dick in the mall. Tom says that Zoe will be there soon. João, whose native language is Portuguese, thinks to himself the phrase in the example and wants to translate it to Tom. But he's unsure whether to translate "esperando" as "waiting", "hoping", or "expecting". So he says:

Dick is waiting or expecting or hoping for Zoe patiently.

That is, Dick is being patient by the standard of waiting, of expecting, and of hoping. We can formalize this as:

(((— (is waiting ∪ is expecting) ∪ is hoping) / patiently) / for (Zoe)) (Dick)

Example 25 *A big man or dog is barking loudly.*

∃x (((— is a man ∪ — is a dog) / big) (x) ∧ (— is barking) / loudly) (x))

Analysis The English is ambiguous between "(big man) or dog" and "big (man or dog)"; that's usually resolved by emphasis in speech. I've chosen the latter, and then we need to use ∪ here to establish the wider comparison.

Example 26 *The one lecturing and disputing is a master or bachelor.*

∃! x ((— is lecturing ∩ is disputing) ∧ (— is a master ∪ is a bachelor) (x))

Analysis The idea of using conjunctions and disjunctions internal to atomic predicates is not new. The example comes from the 14th century logician Jean Buridan, whose analysis suggests the formalization I've used:

... the whole phrase 'the one lecturing and disputing' is a single subject, although hypothetical, namely, conjunctive, and the whole phrase 'master or bachelor' is similarly a single predicate, although disjunctive.[42]

---

[42] *Summulae de Dialectica*, 1.3.2 (p. 24).

Relations

28 Modifiers of Relations

Predicates that aren't unary are called *relations*. We want to extend our theory of modifiers to apply to those. Formally that's easy: we allow for simple relations and modify the semantic principles and their syntactic formalizations accordingly.

But a serious issue of formalization arises with process predicates. Every process verb in English is either intransitive (unary) or transitive (binary). Process predicates of higher arity arise by using conjunctions of terms in unary and binary ones, as in "Tom and Dick lifted the table and tablecloth". Now consider:

(1) Spot chased a ball.
    Therefore, Spot chased something.   formal consequence

(2) Tom ran a marathon.
    Therefore, Tom ran something.   formal consequence

(3) Spot chased.
    Therefore, Spot chased something.   valid

(4) Tom ran.
    Therefore, Tom ran something.   invalid

Is (3) a formal or material consequence? It can't be formal, since (4) is invalid. It is part of the meaning of "chased" in English that makes (3) valid, requiring a meaning axiom in order to be formalized correctly. In classical predicate logic without modifiers we could use:

$$\forall x \,((-\text{ chased})(x) \rightarrow \exists y \,(-\text{ chased }-)(x, y))$$

Whether a verb is transitive is part of its meaning.

You might argue that we can recognize whether a verb is transitive and so take that to be part of its form. After all, we said it's part of the meaning of "small" that it's a restrictor, and part of the meaning of "nearly" that it's a negator, and we assigned different forms to those.

But no restrictor is a negator, and no negator is a restrictor, yet there are process predicates we cannot classify as transitive or intransitive. We say "Dick cursed" but cannot conclude "Dick cursed something", yet "Dick cursed Puff" is a transitive use of "curse". We wouldn't necessarily consider a translation bad if it took a transitive verb in English to an intransitive one in another language. We don't want to elevate the distinction between transitive and intransitive verbs of English into a formal distinction, making (3) a formal consequence, since there would be too many exceptions—even one would be too many.

Besides, though we find it odd to say in English "Dick likes" or "Dick wants" or "Dick threw", the meaning is clear and those are propositions, not nonsense. Every transitive verb has a unary version.[43]

How, then, should we formalize (1)–(4)? Consider:

(5)   Spot chased Puff

We can view the term "Puff" as modifying "— chased". To evaluate whether (5) is true we consider those things that chased, restrict them to ones that chased Puff, and then verify whether Spot is one of those.

To view a word or phrase as a term in some contexts and as a restrictor in others can lead to confusion. We can mark the role of "Puff" as a restrictor in (5) by using a variable restrictor "obj(—)" to formalize the role of terms used as objects of verbs. Then we can formalize (5) as:

(6)   ((— chased)/obj(Puff)) (Spot)

We can formalize (1) as:

$\exists x\,(\,(-\text{ is a ball})\,(x) \land ((-\text{ chased})/\text{obj}(x))\,(\text{Spot})\,)$
Therefore, $\exists x\,(\,((-\text{ chased})/\text{obj}(x))\,(\text{Spot})\,)$

This is a formal consequence in our system.

We can formalize (3) as:

(— chased) (Spot)
Therefore, $\exists x\,(\,((-\text{ chased})/\text{obj}(x))\,(\text{Spot})\,)$

This is a material consequence if we take the formalization relative to a meaning axiom that states that "chased" is transitive:

$\exists x\,(\,(-\text{ chased})\,(x) \rightarrow \exists y\,((-\text{ chased})/\text{obj}(y))\,(x)\,)$

We can formalize (4) as:

(— ran) (Tom)
Therefore, $\exists x\,(\,(\,(-\text{ ran})/\text{obj}(x)\,)\,(\text{Tom})\,)$

This is invalid in our system, and no meaning axiom for "ran" that we might adopt will make it valid.

In English grammar we recognize a difference between (1) and (2). We say that the phrase "a ball" in (1) designates a direct object, while in (2) "a marathon" is used for a complementing object. To recognize that distinction by using two

---

[43] A Colombian visiting me who was learning English would regularly say "I like" and "I want" as complete sentences, since those translate exactly what she would say in Spanish. I had to explain that in English certain verbs have to have an object, though I could give no reason why. Compare: A linguist, Melissa Axelrod, told me that a native speaker of Koyukon with whom she was compiling a grammar for that language came into her office laughing and said, "Imagine, he wanted me to translate 'He swam'." In Koyukon that would have to be marked for duration and other aspects.

distinguished variable restrictors would be to reinstate the division between transitive and intransitive verbs as fundamental in our formalizations. However, I can find no inference that distinguishes between the role of a complementing object and a direct object except for those that depend on the meaning of a word.

Why not go further and use "obj(—)" for indirect objects, too? The differences there do matter. Compare:

Spot ran to Dick.
Spot ran with Dick.

We cannot formalize these both as "((— ran)/obj(Dick)) (Spot)" because the first could be true and the second false, and vice versa. We have many variable restrictors of process predicates corresponding to different prepositions in English.[44]

Now we have two issues to resolve. First, consider:

(6)   ((— is a dog)/obj(Dick)) (Spot)

This makes no sense. We need a preposition to indicate what relation Dick is meant to have to "— is a dog" beyond simply being used as an object. Should we say that (6) is not well-formed?

We could require that the variable modifier "obj(—)" is allowed to modify only process predicates. If we were to do that, we would have to distinguish between process and classification predicates in our formal language, using distinct symbols for each kind. This would elevate the distinction between process predicates and classification predicates to a fundamental role in our syntax and semantics. Yet the distinction does not have a clear semantic basis, as I point out in Appendix 3. So, as before, we take nonsense to be false, allowing the variable restrictor "obj(—)" to modify any predicate.

Are there any inferences that distinguish the role of "obj(—)" from that of any other variable restrictor? Without the distinction between transitive and intransitive verbs put into our formal language, I can find none that do not depend on the meaning of particular words. So we need not adopt any new semantic principles for this new restrictor. But "obj(—)" is different from other restrictors. The modifier "with(—)" has meaning on its own: it is categorematic. The modifier "obj(—)" has no meaning on its own: it only marks the role of the term as a restrictor. It is like a case marking in an ordinary language, though a case that makes no distinction between direct and complementing objects, if indeed that distinction has a semantic basis. The modifier "obj(—)" is part of the logical vocabulary.

In summary, the theory of modifiers with unary predicates is sufficient to formalize reasoning with process predicates so long as we add a new restrictor to our logical vocabulary. We make no distinction between process predicates and unary classification predicates.

---

[44] Some languages have only one preposition (see Peter Svenonius, "The Physiology of P"), so perhaps a single indirect object variable modifier would be useful to formalize reasoning in those.

In contrast, there are classification predicates that cannot be reduced in any obvious way to unary predicates. Consider:

— and — are twins
— is taller than —

We use modifiers with these predicates in ordinary speech:

Helga and Leopoldo are fraternal twins.
Tom is much taller than Dick.

Formalizing these is straightforward by allowing a modifier to apply to a relation:

((— and — are twins) / fraternal) (Helga, Leopoldo)
((— is taller than —) / much) (Tom, Dick)

In the usual formulation of classical predicate logic, people sometimes call "(— and Leopoldo are twins)" a predicate. But the following are all equivalent:

(— and — are twins) (Helga and Leopold)
(— and Leopold are twins) (Helga)
(Helga and — are twins) (Leopold)

And I can't figure out any reading of a modifier applied to a partially filled predicate. So I see no reason to allow them in our systems.

Aside: *Objects of verbs and our metaphysics*
As English speakers we conceive of some processes as directed. They are, in our conception, inherently intentional, even when the subject is not a creature. We say, "The wind delivered the leaf to our feet".

Part of our understanding of the world is ascribing intentions to other people. So basic is this that we ascribe intention to all kinds of things, even to cats and the stone we tripped over. We think we are modern and have gone beyond the primitive view that stones and the wind are intentional actors—until we curse the stone we tripped over.

Our language grew up in this mental milieu and reflects it.[45] Our language, therefore, encodes it, even when we feel that it is not an accurate representation of the world. To code it into our formal theory with a distinction between transitive and intransitive verbs seems to accord too great a metaphysical status to our uses of certain words as directed processes.

With our methods here we do code into our semi-formal languages a distinction between an actor and what is acted on (or what complements what the actor is doing).

---

[45] Dorothy L. Cheney and Robert M. Seyforth suggest in *Baboon Metaphysics* that there is an evolutionary basis for this.

29 Internal Conjunctions and Disjunctions with Relations

Conjunctions of terms
In the formalizations we give of process predicates, there are no process relations, only unary ones with modifiers. It is essential in formalizing those that we can use conjunctions of terms, as in:

> Dick and Tom lifted the table and tablecloth.
>
> $\exists x \exists y\,(\,(-\text{ is a table})\,(x) \wedge (-\text{ is a tablecloth})\,(y) \wedge$
> $\quad ((-\text{ lifted})/\text{obj}(x \wedge y))\,(\text{Dick} \wedge \text{Tom})\,)$

Do we need conjunctions of terms with classification relations? Consider:

> Tom and Dick are taller than Manuel.

It makes no sense to read this as asserting that Tom and Dick together are taller than Manuel. The only reading we can give of it is:

> $(-\text{ is taller than }-)\,(\text{Tom, Manuel}) \wedge (-\text{ taller than }-)\,(\text{Dick, Manuel})$

Consider, too:

> (Lou and Ethelbert) and Belinda are twins.
>
> $(-\text{ are twins})\,(\text{Lou} \wedge \text{Ethelbert, Belinda})$

This makes no sense at all. If they are twins, then there aren't three of them. It isn't just that we have a special word, "triplets", for three children born of the same mother at the same time. It's that "twins" means only two.

    I can find no example of a proposition we'd want to formalize as having a conjunction of terms in a classification relation. Until someone gives such an example, *we can restrict the use of conjunction of terms in predicates to appear in only unary predicates*.

Conjunctions and disjunctions of relations
Again, it is only classification predicates that are relations. So consider:

> Tom is a lot taller and stronger than Dick.

The question is whether this is equivalent to:

> Tom is a lot taller than Dick, and Tom is a lot stronger than Dick.

It seems to me they are, for I can find no other reading of the proposition.
    I can find no good example of a proposition that we'd want to formalize as conjoining two classification relations in order to modify the use of the relations together, which is one of the criteria for our using an internal conjunction. Nor can I find any example where we would want to use a disjunction of predicates. Until someone gives such examples, *we can restrict the use of the conjunctions and disjunctions of predicates to only unary predicates*.

30 Examples of Formalizing

Example 1 (a) *Dick is a brother of Jane.*
   Therefore, *Dick is a brother.*

$$\frac{((-\text{ is a brother})/\text{of}(\text{Jane}))\,(\text{Dick})}{(-\text{ is a brother})\,(\text{Dick})}$$

(b) *Dick is a brother.*
   Therefore, *Dick is a brother of someone.*

$$\frac{(-\text{ is a brother})\,(\text{Dick})}{\exists x\,((-\text{ is a brother})/\text{of}(x))\,(\text{Dick})}$$

Analysis Here we have to relate what appears to be a binary classification predicate to a unary version of it. We can do that by taking "of" as a unary restrictor (compare Example 3 of Chapter 17). The formalization of (a) is then a formal consequence. The formalization of (b) is a material consequence relative to:

$$\forall x\,((-\text{ is a brother})\,(x) \to \exists y\,(-\text{ is a brother})/\text{of}(y))\,(x))$$

Example 2 *Louis and Lorelei are neighbors of John and Sue.*
   Therefore, *Lorelei is a neighbor of John.*

$$\frac{(-\text{ is a neighbor})/\text{of}(\text{John} \wedge \text{Sue})\,(\text{Louis} \wedge \text{Lorelei})}{((-\text{ is a neighbor})/\text{of}(\text{John}))\,(\text{Lorelei})}$$

$$\frac{(P_{73}/R_2(c_{41} \wedge c_{42}))\,(c_{43} \wedge c_{44})}{(P_{73}/R_2(c_{41}))\,(c_{44})}$$

Analysis Just as "Dick threw" is meaningful though seemingly incomplete in English, so "Lorelei is a neighbor" is meaningful though seemingly incomplete. We can take "of" as a unary restrictor with a conjunction of terms filling the blank. Our system does not classify the inference as a formal consequence. But the informal inference is valid. To ensure that the formalization is also valid we need a meaning axiom, which I'll let you formulate.

Example 3 *Zoe packed a bag.*
   So *Zoe packed.*

$$\frac{\exists x\,((-\text{ is a bag})\,(x) \wedge (-\text{ packed})/\text{obj}(x)\,(\text{Zoe}, x))}{(-\text{ packed})\,(\text{Zoe})}$$

$$\frac{\exists x_1\,(P_{28}(x_1) \wedge (P_{23}/\text{obj}(x_1))\,(c_1))}{P_{23}(c_1)}$$

Analysis The example is valid. But is "packed" transitive or intransitive? We don't have to resolve that to formalize the example.

Example 4   Dick and Tom wheeled Manuel in a wheelchair up a ramp into a gym.

$\exists x \, \exists y \, \exists z \, (\, (- \text{ is a wheelchair}) \, (x) \wedge \, (- \text{ is a ramp}) \, (y) \wedge \, (- \text{ is a gym}) \, (z) \wedge$

$((- \text{ wheeled})/\text{obj}(\text{Manuel}))/(\text{in } (x) \ \& \text{ up } (y) \ \& \text{ into } (z) \,) \, (\text{Dick} \wedge \text{Tom}))$

Analysis   Though more complicated, the method here is the same as in the previous examples. From this formalization, "$(-$ wheeled) (Dick)", formalizing "Dick wheeled", follows. That sounds strange to us because in English "wheeled" is transitive. Nonetheless, it is true if the example is true: Dick did indeed do that.

Both of the following are consequences of the informal example:

Dick and Tom wheeled Manuel up a ramp.

Dick and Tom wheeled Manuel into a gym.

The formalizations of these follow from the formalization of the example, too. They would not follow if we chose to formalize the restrictors applying successively rather than conjoined.

Example 5   Socrates died Xantippe.

$((- \text{ died})/\text{obj}(\text{Xantippe})) \, (\text{Socrates})$

Analysis   Some verbs such as "die" cannot take a direct object or an indirect object, so the example is not grammatical. Or at least that's what English teachers might say. But, as we've seen, to say that it's not grammatical is to elevate the meaning of the word into the grammar. We treat the example not as ill-formed but false, formalizing it as above.

Example 6   Dick has a dog.

$\exists x \, [\, (- \text{ is a dog}) \, (x) \wedge \, (- \text{ has}_p)/\text{obj}(x) \, (\text{Dick}) \,]$

Analysis   Here "has" is meant as in the sense of "possesses", which we indicate with the subscript. But the formalization seems odd because "$(-$ has$_p$)" is true of every human: each of us has something. So "$(-$ has$_p$)" and "$(-$ is a human)" have the same extension in a universe of humans. Doesn't this show that we should take "has" here as a binary predicate?

That "$(-$ has$_p$)" and "$(-$ is a human)" have the same extension does not mean that all modifications of them have the same extension. The formalization of the example is true, but the following is false:

$\exists x \, [\, (- \text{ is a dog}) \, (x) \wedge \, (- \text{ is a human})/\text{obj}(x) \, (\text{Dick}) \,]$

In classical predicate logic with modifiers, the meaning of a predicate is not just its extension, but its extension and the extension of every modification of it.

Example 7   Tom and Suzy are lovers.

$(- \text{ is a lover}) \, (\text{Tom} \wedge \text{Suzy})$

Analysis It might seem that taking "— is a lover" as the predicate here is wrong, as that just means "— loves someone". But Rudolfo could be a lover though he's a gigolo and loves no one.

Example 8   Dick and Zoe are living together.

Analysis We could formalize this as:

   ((— lives)/together with (Zoe)) Dick)

But that does not reflect the grammar of the original, which takes Dick and Zoe together as the subject of the verb. Distinguishing "lives" not as "survives" but as "resides", we can have a formalization that better respects the grammar of the original:

   (— resides) (Dick ∧ Zoe)

Which of these formalizations we choose depends on which criterion of formalization we deem most important: respecting the grammar or not using a new categorematic word as part of an informal analysis.

Example 9   Suzy passionately loves Tom.
             Suzy loves Tom passionately.

Analysis Following the grammar of the originals we have two formalizations:

(a)   (((— loves)/passionately)/obj(Tom))) (Suzy)

(b)   (((— loves)/obj(Tom))/passionately) (Suzy)

These are not equivalent. For (a) to be true, Suzy has to be passionate compared to all those who love. But for (b) to be true, Suzy has to be passionate only compared to those who love Tom.

Nonetheless, we feel that the two sentences of the example are equivalent. If we read successive adverbs as applying together to the verb, we will have:

(c)   ((— loves)/(obj(Tom) & passionately)) (Suzy)

This is equivalent to "((— loves)/(passionately & obj(Tom))) (Suzy)". It is not equivalent to:

(d)   ((— loves)/obj(Tom)) (Suzy) ∧ ((— loves)/passionately) (Suzy)

That could be true because Suzy loves Ricardo passionately but loves Tom only as she would a brother.

Example 10   Slowly with Dick Spot stalked Puff.

Analysis The precision of our formal language reveals an ambiguity here:

   ((— stalked)/obj(Puff))/with (Dick))/slowly) (Spot)

   ((— stalked)/obj(Puff)/slowly)/with (Dick)) (Spot)

Until we resolve the ambiguity, we cannot formalize the example. Note that though we find it odd to say "Dick chased", it's O.K. to say "Dick stalked". There seems to be no clear semantic pattern of how we use verbs transitively or intransitively in English.

Example 11 Suzy carefully carried and petted Puff.

$\quad$ (((− carried + petted)/carefully)/obj(Puff)) (Suzy)

Analysis The formalization is routine using a conjunction of predicates.

Example 12 Slowly, Tom escorted Zoe and Dick pushed Manuel.

Analysis This was said when Tom, Zoe, Dick, and Manuel went to a dance where Dick was pushing Manuel in his wheelchair. The grammar suggests that "slowly" is a propositional modifier modifying "Tom escorted Zoe and Dick pushed Suzy". But "slowly" doesn't mean "it is slowly true that": we can talk of the time at which a proposition is true, but we don't talk of nor do we have any clear idea what it means to say how long it took for a proposition to become true. Rather, "slowly" is modifying both predicates "− escorted" and "− pushed".

$\quad$ We can't conjoin those predicates and modify the conjunction of them with "slowly" because the conjunction of two unary predicates is a unary predicate: "− escorted + pushed", while we need two different terms to fill the blanks.

$\quad$ Nor can we formalize the example as:

$\quad$ (((− escorted)/obj(Zoe))/slowly) (Tom) ∧
$\quad\quad$ (((− pushed)/obj(Manuel))/slowly) (Dick)

This could be true while the example is false if Tom escorted Zoe at one time and Dick pushed Manuel at another. To formalize this example we need a temporal conjunction, one that formalizes "and at the same time", which is given in Volume 2, *Time and Space in Formal Logic*.

Example 13 Dick was quickly irritated and chased Spot.

Analysis It seems we are conjoining two predicates here, but it would be odd if not wrong to use a single modifier for both. The example is better understood as:

(a) Dick, who was quickly irritated, chased Spot.

We can't formalize this as:

(b) Dick was quickly irritated ∧ Dick chased Spot.

For (a) to be true, both conjuncts of (b) have to be true at the same time. But this is the only reason that (b) fails to be a good formalization. Again, we need a formalization of "and then", which will allow us to formalize propositions involving relative clauses that require recognizing tense or a time element, as we'll see in Volume 2, *Time and Space in Formal Logic*.

Example 14 This towel is drier than that towel.

Analysis This is an example of a comparative. Letting "*a*" be a name for the first towel and "*b*" a name for the second, we could formalize this as:

(— is drier than —) (*a*, *b*)

But how does "— is drier than —" relate to the adjective "dry"?

The comparative "— is drier than —" could be construed as a degree-version of "dry", formalizing the example as:

((— is a towel/dry)/to degree (*c*)) (*a*)
∧ ((— is a towel/dry)/to degree (*d*)) (*b*) ∧ (— is greater than —) (*c*, *d*)

Though we could make degrees of dryness precise with a device that measures water content, specifying exactly what portion of a towel is measured, that would be to substitute a precise predicate for an imprecise one and leave us with no way to use the example in ordinary reasoning. All we can say is that there is some degree of dryness of *a* and degree of dryness of *b* that satisfy:

∃*x* ∃*y* (((— is a towel/dry)/to degree (*x*)) (*a*)
∧ ((— is a towel/dry)/to degree (*y*)) (*b*) ∧ (— is greater than —) (*x*, *y*))

Since we can't specify the exact degrees, we'd have to understand the existence operator to be non-constructive.

I think that's what we do in our ordinary speech and reasoning: we use implicit degrees and a non-constructive existence operator. We feel the two towels and say, "Yes this towel is drier than that one", though we can't say how much drier.

Should we incorporate such an understanding of comparatives into our formal logic? For each model we'd need a second universe of numbers that are used for degree measurements, whether of how dry or how tall or how smart. We'd have to have a non-constructive existence operator, at least when employed to quantify degrees. And for all that, we still wouldn't have anything more useful than taking "— is drier than —" as an atomic predicate, except perhaps a greater fidelity to ordinary speech. We might take as a meaning axiom:

∀*x* ((— is a towel/dry)/ to degree (1)) (*x*) ↔ (— is a towel/dry) (*x*)

But I suspect that's false: we'd classify a towel as dry even if it was dry to degree .96, or even to degree .95213. We don't use degrees with any precision, even at the extremes. So there doesn't seem to be any use for a degree version of "dry" instead of using the comparative in formalizing valid inferences.

Further, though what we classify as dry may depend on what kind of thing it is, one thing being drier than another is absolute, independent of what kind of things are being compared. We have the predicate modifier "dry" and the atomic predicate "— is drier than —". I see no better way to deal with this and other comparatives.

134   Chapter 30

Example 15   Tom walked faster than Wanda ran.[46]

Analysis Here we have a comparative "faster than". But what is it comparing? We could say it's comparing Tom's walking to Wanda's running, but that way of talking about actions as if they were things is a bad way to formalize in predicate logic, as I explain in Appendix 2. In any case, what we are comparing is the rate at which Tom walked to the rate at which Wanda ran. We seem to have no option here but to use degrees or a measure of some sort, as in:

$\exists \alpha \, \exists \beta \, (\, ((-\text{walked})/\text{at rate}(\alpha))\,(\text{Tom}) \land ((-\text{ran})/\text{at rate}(\beta))\,(\text{Wanda}) \land \alpha > \beta \,)$

Example 16   Helga and Leopoldo are twins.

Analysis In Chapter 28 we took "— and — are twins" as a binary relation. Could we instead view "twin" as an adjective? In this example it would be relative to people, but it could be relative to dogs or pieces of machinery. We might formalize the example:

   $((-\text{ is a person})/\text{twin})/(\text{Helga} \land \text{Leopoldo})$

But this seems too odd, an unnecessary attempt to reduce a binary relation to a unary one with a modifier, when the modifier doesn't have a clear unary meaning.

Example 17   Dick and Zoe are a happy couple.

   $((-\text{ and } - \text{ are a couple})/\text{happy})\,(\text{Dick}, \text{Zoe})$

   $P_{667}/R_{20}\,(c_2, c_1)$

Analysis We might think to formalize the example as:

(a) $((-\text{ is a person})/\text{happy})\,(\text{Dick} \land \text{Zoe})$

But that's to understand "couple" as a pair of people, whereas "are a couple" in English means the people are bound emotionally in some way more than friendship: romantically, or living together, or sexually. We could try to capture that meaning of "couple" using perhaps:

   $((-\text{ is a person})/\text{romantic})/\text{happy})\,(\text{Dick} \land \text{Zoe})$

But this isn't right either, and we would be violating the criteria of formalization by doing an analysis of the meaning of a word prior to formalizing and introducing a categorematic word into the formalization that is not found in the original. We need to take "— and — are a couple" as simple.

Example 18 (x_1, x_2) is between (x_3, x_4) and (x_5, x_6)

   $(-\text{ is between } - \text{ and } -)/(\,(x_1, x_2), (x_3, x_4), (x_5, x_6)\,)$

   $P_{1000}(-, -, -)(\,(x_1, x_2), (x_3, x_4), (x_5, x_6)\,)$

---

[46] The example comes from Thomas Schwartz, "The Logic of Modifiers", though I use names rather than pronouns. My analysis is different from his.

Analysis In formalizing two-dimensional Euclidean geometry in classical predicate logic, we take $B(x, y, z)$ as a primitive ternary predicate meant as an abstraction of "(— is between — and —)".[47] We could, however, take "is" here in the sense of "remains" as discussed in Example 4 of Chapter 20 and use "between" as a modifier:

$$(- \text{ is}_{\text{remains}}/\text{between}\,((x_3, x_4) \wedge (x_5, x_6)))\,((x_1, x_2))$$

This and the last example show that it is possible to formalize some propositions that involve relations by using wffs that involve only a unary predicate with conjunctions of terms and with modifiers. But even if we countenance analyses of the meanings of words as built into formalizations, as in the previous example, and are willing to forego considerable simplicity of expression, as in this example, there will still be relations which cannot be reduced to unary predicates with modifiers and conjunctions of terms, at least not in any straightforward way, as Example 18 shows.

Note that we can modify the ternary predicate of this example:

$$(- \text{ is between } - \text{ and } -)/\text{nearly}\,(\,(x_1, x_2), (x_3, x_4), (x_5, x_6)\,)$$

---

[47] See *Classical Mathematical Logic*.

A Formal Theory of Classical Predicate Logic with Predicate Modifiers, Internal Conjunctions, and Internal Disjunctions

31 A Formal Theory

The formal language
The definition of the formal language is now more complicated. As before, once we define the atomic wffs, we will use the usual definition for compound wffs formed with connectors or quantifiers.

For the atomic wffs, several steps are needed. First, to allow for conjunctions of terms, we need to give an inductive definition of "term". Then we can give an inductive definition of "formal modifier", where terms appear in the variable predicate restrictors and conjunctions of modifiers are allowed. Then an inductive definition is needed for the formal atomic wffs to allow for multiple modifiers and conjunctions and disjunctions of atomic wffs.

Vocabulary
    predicate symbols P_n^i for $n \geq 0$ and $i \geq 1$, where i is the arity
    equality predicate $- \equiv -$
    predicate modifier symbols
        restrictor symbols $R_0, R_1, \ldots$
        variable restrictor symbols R_n^i for $n \geq 0$ and $i \geq 1$, where i is the arity
        logical variable restrictor obj
        negator symbols $N_0, N_1, \ldots$
        logical negator ~
    name symbols $c_0, c_1, \ldots$ ⎫
    variables $x_0, x_1, \ldots$ ⎬ *terms*
    internal logical symbols
        term conjoiner ∧
        predicate conjoiner +
        modifier conjoiner &
        predicate disjoiner ∪
    external logical symbols
        propositional connectives ¬, →, ∧, ∨
        quantifiers ∀, ∃

Punctuation
    parentheses ( )   *comma* ,
    blank —   *slash* /

Terms and conjunctions of terms
  i. Each variable and each name symbol is a term of degree 1.
  ii. If d is a term or a formal conjunction of terms of degree n, and d' is a term or formal conjunction of terms of degree m, then $(d \wedge d')$ is a formal conjunction of terms of degree $n + m$.
  iii. A concatenation of symbols is a formal conjunction of terms iff it is a conjunction of terms of degree n for some $n \geq 2$.

Formal modifiers
  i. Every predicate restrictor symbol is a formal restrictor of degree 1.

  If R is a k-ary variable predicate restrictor symbol and $d_1, \ldots, d_k$ are terms or conjunction of terms, then $R(d_1, \ldots, d_k)$ is a formal restrictor of degree 1.

  If d is a term or conjunction of terms, then obj(d) is a formal restrictor of degree 1.

  Every predicate negator symbol is a formal negator of degree 1.

  The logical negator ~ is a formal negator of degree 1.

  ii. If R is a formal restrictor of degree n, then (~R) is a formal restrictor of degree $n + 1$.

  iii. If R is a formal restrictor of degree n and N is a formal negator, then (R/N) is a formal restrictor of degree $n + 1$.

  iv. If N and N´ are formal negators, then (N/N´) is a formal restrictor of degree 2.

  v. If R and R´ are formal restrictors of degree n and degree m respectively, then (R & R´) is a formal restrictor of degree $n + m$. It is a *conjunction of restrictors*.

  vi. A concatenation of symbols is a formal modifier iff it is a formal restrictor or formal negator of degree n for some $n \geq 1$.

  Formal modifiers of degree ≥ 2 are *complex*.

Formal atomic predicates
  i. If P is a k-ary predicate symbol, then $P(-, \ldots, -)$ with k blanks is a k-ary formal atomic predicate of degree 0. It is a *simple* formal atomic predicate.

  ii. If $Q(-, \ldots, -)$ is a k-ary formal atomic predicate of degree n, then $(Q/\sim)(-, \ldots, -)$ is a k-ary formal atomic predicate of degree $n + 1$. It is a *pure negated predicate*.

iii. If $Q(-, \ldots, -)$ is a k-ary formal atomic predicate of degree n, and M is a formal modifier other than $\sim$, and Q is not a pure negated predicate, then $(Q/M)(-, \ldots, -)$ is a k-ary formal atomic predicate of degree $n + 1$.

iv. If $Q_1(-)$ and $Q_2(-)$ are unary formal atomic predicates of degrees n and m, respectively, and at least one of them is not a pure negated predicate, then $(Q_1 + Q_2)(-)$ is a unary formal atomic predicate of degree $n + m + 1$. It is an *internally conjoined* formal atomic predicate.

v. If $Q_1(-)$ and $Q_2(-)$ are unary formal atomic predicates of degrees n and m, respectively, and neither is a pure negated predicate, then $(Q_1 \cup Q_2)(-)$ is a unary formal atomic predicate formula of degree $n + m + 1$. It is an *internally disjoined* formal atomic predicate.

vi. A concatenation of symbols is a formal atomic predicate iff it is a formal atomic predicate of degree n for some n.

Formal atomic predicates of degree ≥ 1 are *modified formal atomic predicates*.

Well-formed-formulas (Wffs)

i. If u and v are terms, then $((-\equiv -)(u,v))$ is a wff of length 1.

If Q is a k-ary formal atomic predicate and $u_1, \ldots, u_k$ are terms, then $(Q(u_1, \ldots, u_k))$ is a wff of length 1, where $u_1, \ldots, u_k$ fill the blanks in Q in that order, reading from the left.

If Q is a unary formal atomic predicate and d is a formal conjunction of terms, then $(Q(d))$ is a wff of length 1.

A wff of length 1 is *closed* if no variable appears in it; otherwise it is *open* and each occurrence of each variable in it is *free*.

ii. If A is a wff of length n, then $(\neg A)$ is a wff of length $n + 1$. An occurrence of a variable in $(\neg A)$ is free iff the corresponding occurence of the variable in A is free.

iii. If A and B are wffs and the maximum of the lengths of A and B is n, then each of $(A \rightarrow B)$ and $(A \wedge B)$ and $(A \vee B)$ is a wff of length $n + 1$. An occurrence of a variable in $(A \rightarrow B)$ is free iff the corresponding occurence of the variable in A or in B is free, and similarly for $(A \wedge B)$ and $(A \vee B)$.

iv. If A is a wff of length n and some occurrence of x is free in A, then each of $(\forall x A)$ and $(\exists x A)$ is a wff of length $n + 1$. An occurrence of a variable in $(\forall x A)$ and $(\exists x A)$ is free iff the variable is not x and the corresponding occurrence in A is free.

v. A concatenation of symbols is a *wff* iff it is a wff of length n, for some $n \geq 1$.

A wff of length 1 is *atomic*. All other wffs are *compound*.

A Formal Theory

In ($\forall x$ A), the initial $\forall x$ has *scope* A and *binds* each free occurrence of x in A, and similarly for ($\exists x$ A).

A wff is *closed* if there is no occurrence of a variable free in it; otherwise it is *open*.

I'll let you prove the following using the methods for proving the unique readability of wffs in Appendix 2 of Volume 0 and of terms in Chapter 35 here.

Lemma 1
a. The degree of a conjunction of terms is the number of terms appearing in it, counting repetitions.
b. The degree of a conjunction of terms minus 1 is the number of appearances of the symbol $\wedge$ in it.
c. There is a unique way to read each conjunction of terms.
d. The degree of a formal modifier is the number of modifiers appearing in it, counting repetitions.
e. There is a unique way to read each formal modifier.
f. There is a unique way to read each formal atomic predicate.
g. The degree of a wff minus 1 is the number of appearances of the following symbols in it, counting repetitions: $\wedge$ $\vee$ $\neg$ $\rightarrow$ $\forall$ $\exists$.
h. There is a unique way to read each wff.

I'll let you give a definition of "X appears in A", written A(X), where X is a term, conjunction of terms, formal predicate, modifier, or wff.

Informal conventions

The parentheses around atomic wffs and the outer parentheses around an entire wff may be deleted.

Parentheses between successive quantifiers at the beginning of a wff and the corresponding parentheses at the end of the wff may be deleted.

Formal symbols bind in the following order of strength, from strongest at the left to weakest, where two symbols one above the other bind equally strongly:

$$\wedge \quad \& \quad + \quad \sim \quad / \quad \begin{matrix}\forall x \\ \exists x\end{matrix} \quad \neg \quad \begin{matrix}\wedge \\ \vee\end{matrix} \quad \rightarrow$$

$(- \equiv -)(u, v)$ is written informally as $(u \equiv v)$, and $\neg((- \equiv -)(u, v))$ as $u \not\equiv v$. Informally, we write $\sim$Q for Q/$\sim$.

Realizations and semi-formal languages

An *ordinary language name*, *predicate*, *restrictor*, *variable restrictor*, or *negator* is *simple* iff it contains no part we could formalize as a name, variable, propositional connective, quantifier, internal conjunction, internal disjunction, predicate, predicate modifier, or a combination of those.

A *realization* of the formal language is an assignment of:

- Simple names to none, some, or all of the name symbols.
- Simple non-variable restrictors to none, some, or all of the formal non-variable restrictor symbols.
- Simple variable restrictors to none, some, or all of the variable restrictor symbols.
- Simple negators to none, some, or all of the negator symbols.
- Simple predicates to none, some, or all of the predicate symbols.

The *realization of a formal wff* is the formula we get when we replace the formal symbols with the parts of ordinary language that are assigned to them; it is a *semi-formal wff*. The *semi-formal language* for a realization is the collection of realizations of formal wffs. Parts of the semi-formal language inherit the terminology applied to parts of the formal language with the word "formal" deleted.

The simple names, predicates, and modifiers of the realization are *categorematic*. The rest of the vocabulary is *logical* or *syncategorematic*. Categorematic parts of the formal language joined by punctuation or logical vocabulary are categorematic.

Semantics

A *model* of the formal language consists of a *realization* plus:

- *A universe for the realization*

The universe is a collection consisting of at least one thing.

- *Assignments of references*

There is at least one assignment of references: a way to assign to each term of the semi-formal language an object of the universe. Given any name c of the semi-formal language, all assignments of reference assign the same object to c. The *assignments are complete*: for every assignment of references σ, and every variable x, and every object of the universe, either σ assigns that object to x or there is an assignment τ that differs from σ only in that it assigns that object to x.

We write $\tau \sim_x \sigma$ to mean that the assignment of references τ differs from σ at most in what it assigns x.

- *Satisfaction of atomic wffs*

For each assignment of references σ, there is a valuation υ_σ that assigns to each atomic wff a truth-value T or F. If A is an atomic wff and the terms appearing in A are $u_1, \ldots, u_n$ in order reading from the left (including repetitions), we write $\upsilon_\sigma(A) = T$ or $\upsilon_\sigma \vDash A$ to mean that A is (taken to be) *true of the objects*

$\sigma(u_1), \ldots, \sigma(u_n)$ in that order; we write $v_\sigma(A) = F$ or $v_\sigma \not\models A$ to mean that A is (taken to be) not true (false) of the objects $\sigma(u_1), \ldots, \sigma(u_n)$ in that order.

- *Semantic conditions on the satisfaction of atomic wffs*

The valuations of atomic wffs satisfy the following conditions, where R, R', R_1, R_2, R_3 are restrictors or variable restrictors; N, N' are negators; M is a modifier; u and v are terms; $d, d', d_1, \ldots, d_n$ are terms or conjunctions of terms; $\vec{d}$ and $\vec{e}$ are sequences of terms or sequences of conjunctions of terms of the appropriate length for the arity of the predicate or restrictor; P is a simple atomic predicate; $Q, Q_1, Q_2, \ldots$ are atomic predicates; $A, B, C, A_0, A_1, \ldots$ are atomic wffs; $A(X)$ means the part of language X appears in A; and σ, τ are assignments of references.

Note that some of these conditions differ from their first presentation in the text in order to allow for complex atomic wffs, modifiers, conjunctions of terms, or relations.

Equality
$v_\sigma \models (- \equiv -)(u, v)$ iff $\sigma(u) = \sigma(v)$.

Extensionality
If $\sigma(x) = \sigma(y)$ and $v_\sigma \models A(x)$, then $v_\sigma \models A(y/x)$.

RES If $v_\sigma \models (Q/R)(\vec{d})$, then $v_\sigma \models Q(\vec{d})$.

Neg If $v_\sigma \models (Q/N)(\vec{d})$, then $v_\sigma \not\models Q(\vec{d})$.

RN If $v_\sigma \models (Q/(R/N))(\vec{d})$, then $v_\sigma \not\models (Q/R)(\vec{d})$.

NN' If $v_\sigma \models (Q/(N/N'))(\vec{d})$, then $v_\sigma \not\models (Q/N)(\vec{d})$.

Pure negated restrictors
If $v_\sigma \models (Q/\sim R)(\vec{d})$, then $v_\sigma \models Q(\vec{d})$ and $v_\sigma \not\models (Q/R)(\vec{d})$.

Negators of restrictors and pure negated restrictors
If $v_\sigma \models (Q/(R/N))(\vec{d})$, then $v_\sigma \models (Q/\sim R)(\vec{d})$.

Commutativity of $\wedge$
If $v_\sigma \models A(d \wedge d')$, then $\models A(d' \wedge d)$
where $d \wedge d'$ appears in A and $d' \wedge d$ replaces some but not necessarily all of those appearances.

Associativity of $\wedge$
If $v_\sigma \models A((d_1 \wedge d_2) \wedge d_3)$, then $v_\sigma \models A(d_1 \wedge (d_2 \wedge d_3))$
where $(d_1 \wedge d_2) \wedge d_3$ appears in A and $d_1 \wedge (d_2 \wedge d_3)$ replaces some but not necessarily all of those appearances.

∧ implies ∧
If $\mathbf{v}_\sigma \vDash P(d)$ and u is a term that appears in d, then $\mathbf{v}_\sigma \vDash P(u)$.

Duplicated reference in conjoined terms
If $\mathbf{v}_\sigma \vDash x \equiv y$, then $\mathbf{v}_\sigma \nvDash A(d)$
where d is a conjunction of terms in which both x and y appear.

Commutativity of +
If $\mathbf{v}_\sigma \vDash A(Q_1 + Q_2)$, then $\mathbf{v}_\sigma \vDash A(Q_2 + Q_1)$
where $(Q_1 + Q_2)$ appears in A, and $(Q_2 + Q_1)$ replaces some but not necessarily all of those appearances.

Associativity of +
If $\mathbf{v}_\sigma \vDash A((Q_1 + Q_2) + Q_3)$, then $\mathbf{v}_\sigma \vDash A(Q_1 + (Q_2 + Q_3))$
where $(Q_1 + Q_2) + Q_3$ appears in A, and $Q_1 + (Q_2 + Q_3)$ replaces some but not necessarily all of those appearances.

- *Restrictors and +*
If $\mathbf{v}_\sigma \vDash (Q_1 + (Q_2/R))(d)$, then $\mathbf{v}_\sigma \vDash (Q_1 + Q_2)(d)$.

+ implies ∧
If $\mathbf{v}_\sigma \vDash (Q_1 + Q_2)(d)$, then $\mathbf{v}_\sigma \vDash Q_1(d)$ and $\mathbf{v}_\sigma \vDash Q_2(d)$

Commutativity of &
If $\mathbf{v}_\sigma \vDash A(R_1 \& R_2)$ iff $\mathbf{v}_\sigma \vDash A(R_2 \& R_1)$
where $R_1 \& R_2$ appears in A and $R_2 \& R_1$ replaces some but not necessarily all of those appearances.

Associativity of &
If $\mathbf{v}_\sigma \vDash A((R_1 \& R_2) \& R_3)$, then $\mathbf{v}_\sigma \vDash A(R_1 \& (R_2 \& R_3))$
where $(R_1 \& R_2) \& R_3$ appears in A and $R_1 \& (R_2 \& R_3)$ replaces some but not necessarily all of those appearances.

& implies ∧
If $\mathbf{v}_\sigma \vDash (A/(R_1 \& R_2))(d)$, then $\mathbf{v}_\sigma \vDash (A/R_1)(d)$ and $\mathbf{v}_\sigma \vDash (A/R_2)(d)$.

Negators and the pure negator in joined restrictors
If $\mathbf{v}_\sigma \vDash (A/(R_1 \& (R_2/N)))(d)$, then $\mathbf{v}_\sigma \vDash (A/(R_1 \& \sim R_2))(d)$

Commutativity of ∪
If $\mathbf{v}_\sigma \vDash A(Q_1 \cup Q_2)$, then $\mathbf{v}_\sigma \vDash A(Q_2 \cup Q_1)$
where $(Q_1 \cup Q_2)$ appears in A, and $(Q_2 \cup Q_1)$ replaces some but not necessarily all of those appearances.

Associativity of ∪

If $v_\sigma \vDash A((Q_1 \cup Q_2) \cup Q_3)$, then $v_\sigma \vDash A(Q_1 \cup (Q_2 \cup Q_3))$

   where $(Q_1 \cup Q_2) \cup Q_3$ appears in A, and $Q_1 \cup (Q_2 \cup Q_3)$ replaces some but not necessarily all of those appearances.

Equivalence of ∪ *and* ∨

$v_\sigma \vDash (Q_1 \cup Q_2)(d)$ iff $v_\sigma \vDash Q_1(d) \lor v_\sigma \vDash Q_2(d)$

∪ *implies* ∨ *with restrictors*

If $v_\sigma \vDash ((Q_1 \cup Q_2)/R)(d)$, then $v_\sigma \vDash (Q_1/R))(d) \lor (Q_2/R))(d)$

Restrictors and ∪

If $v_\sigma \vDash ((Q_1 \cup Q_2)/R)(d) \land Q_1(d)$, then $v_\sigma \vDash (Q_1/R)(d)$

- *Satisfaction of compound wffs*

The definition by simultanenous induction of the extension of all valuations from atomic wffs to all compound wffs is the standard one from classical predicate logic:

$v_\sigma(\neg A) = T$ iff $v_\sigma(A) = F$

$v_\sigma(A \land B) = T$ iff $v_\sigma(A) = T$ and $v_\sigma(B) = T$

$v_\sigma(A \lor B) = T$ iff $v_\sigma(A) = T$ or $v_\sigma(B) = T$

$v_\sigma(A \rightarrow B) = T$ iff $v_\sigma(A) = F$ or $v_\sigma(B) = T$

$v_\sigma(\exists x\, A) = T$ iff   for some assignment of references τ such that
$\tau \sim_x \sigma$, $v_\tau(A) = T$

$v_\sigma(\forall x\, A) = T$ iff   for every assignment of references τ such that
$\tau \sim_x \sigma$, $v_\tau(A) = T$

The valuation v for all closed wffs A is defined by:

$v(A) = T$ iff for every assignment of references σ, $v_\sigma(A) = T$;

$v(A) = F$ otherwise.

We write $v \vDash A$ for $v(A) = T$ and $v \nvDash A$ for $v(A) = F$.

- *Sufficiency of the collection of models*

   For any realization and any collection of things and complete collection of assignments of references, any assignment of truth-values to the atomic predications satisfying these semantic conditions serves to define a model.

   I'll let you prove the following two lemmas.

Lemma 2 For each wff A there is a unique value $v(A)$.

Lemma 3 Each of the following conditions holds for all wffs, not just atomic ones:

extensionality	*commutativity of* &
communtativity of ∧	*associativity of* &
associativity of ∧	*commutativity of* ∪
commutativity of +	*associativity of* ∪
associativity of +	

Axiomatization

The following axioms are added to the axiomatization of classical predicate logic (p. 28) with equality (p. 29), where R, R´ are formal predicate restrictors; N, N´ are formal negators; M is a formal modifier; $d_1, \ldots, d_n$ are formal terms or conjunctions of terms; $\vec{d}$ is a sequence of terms or formal conjunctions of terms of the appropriate length for the arity of the predicate or restrictor; P is a predicate symbol; Q, Q_1, Q_2, ... stand for formal atomic predicates; A, B, C stand for atomic wffs; and A(X) means the part of language X appears in A.

RES   ∀ ... (Q/R)($\vec{d}$) → Q($\vec{d}$)

Neg   ∀ ... (Q/N)($\vec{d}$) → ¬Q($\vec{d}$)

RN   ∀ ... (Q/(R/N))($\vec{d}$) → ¬(Q/R)($\vec{d}$)

NN´   ∀ ... (Q/(N/N´))($\vec{d}$) → ¬(Q/N)($\vec{d}$)

Pure negated restrictors
∀ ... (Q/~R)($\vec{d}$) → (Q($\vec{d}$) ∧ (Q/R)($\vec{d}$))

Negators of restrictors and pure negated restrictors
∀ ... (Q/(R/N)($\vec{d}$) → (Q/~R)($\vec{d}$)

Commutativity of ∧
∀ ... A(d ∧ d´) → A(d´ ∧ d)
> where d ∧ d´ appears in A and d´ ∧ d replaces some but not necessarily all of those appearances.

Associativity of ∧
∀ ... A((d_1 ∧ d_2) ∧ d_3) → A(d_1 ∧ (d_2 ∧ d_3))
> where (d_1 ∧ d_2) ∧ d_3 appears in A and d_1 ∧ (d_2 ∧ d_3) replaces some but not necessarily all of those appearances.

∧ implies ∧
∀ ... P(d) → P(u)
> where u is a term that appears in d.

Duplicated reference in conjoined terms

$\forall \ldots x \equiv y \rightarrow \neg A(d)$

where d is a conjunction of terms in which both x and y appear.

Commutativity of +

$\forall \ldots A(Q_1 + Q_2) \rightarrow A(Q_2 + Q_1)$

where $(Q_1 + Q_2)$ appears in A, and $(Q_2 + Q_1)$ replaces some but not necessarily all of those appearances.

Associativity of +

$\forall \ldots A((Q_1 + Q_2) + Q_3) \rightarrow A(Q_1 + (Q_2 + Q_3))$

where $(Q_1 + Q_2) + Q_3$ appears in A, and $Q_1 + (Q_2 + Q_3)$ replaces some but not necessarily all of those appearances.

Restrictors and +

$\forall \ldots (Q_1 + (Q_2/R))\,(d) \rightarrow (Q_1 + Q_2)\,(d)$

+ implies ∧

$\forall \ldots (Q_1 + Q_2)\,(d) \rightarrow (Q_1(d) \wedge Q_2(d))$

Commutativity of &

$\forall \ldots A(R_1 \,\&\, R_2) \rightarrow A(R_2 \,\&\, R_1)$

where $R_1 \,\&\, R_2$ appears in A and $R_2 \,\&\, R_1$ replaces some but not necessarily all of those appearances.

Associativity of &

$\forall \ldots A((R_1 \,\&\, R_2) \,\&\, R_3) \rightarrow A(R_1 \,\&\, (R_2 \,\&\, R_3))$

where $(R_1 \,\&\, R_2) \,\&\, R_3$ appears in A and $R_1 \,\&\, (R_2 \,\&\, R_3)$ replaces some but not necessarily all of those appearances.

& implies ∧

$\forall \ldots (Q/(R_1 \,\&\, R_2))\,(\vec{d}) \rightarrow ((Q/R_1)\,(\vec{d}) \wedge (Q/R_2)\,(\vec{d}))$

Negators and the pure negator in joined restrictors

$\forall \ldots (Q/(R_1 \,\&\, (R_2/N)))\,(d) \rightarrow (Q/(R_1 \,\&\, \sim R_2))\,(d)$

Commutativity of ∪

$\forall \ldots A(Q_1 \cup Q_2) \rightarrow A(Q_2 \cup Q_1)$

where $(Q_1 \cup Q_2)$ appears in A, and $(Q_2 \cup Q_1)$ replaces some but not necessarily all of those appearances.

Associativity of ∪

$\forall \ldots A((Q_1 \cup Q_2) \cup Q_3) \rightarrow A(Q_1 \cup (Q_2 \cup Q_3))$

where $(Q_1 \cup Q_2) \cup Q_3$ appears in A, and $Q_1 \cup (Q_2 \cup Q_3)$ replaces some but not necessarily all of those appearances.

Equivalence of ∪ and ∨
∀ ... (Q₁ ∪ Q₂) (d) ↔ (Q₁(d) ∨ Q₂(d))

∪ implies ∨ with restrictors
∀ ... ((Q₁ ∪ Q₂)/R) (d) → ((Q₁/R)) (d) ∨ (Q₂/R)) (d))

Restrictors and ∪
∀ ... (((Q₁ ∪ Q₂)/R) (d) ∧ Q₁(d)) → (Q₁/R) (d)

I'll let you prove that the axiomatization is sound.

The only changes from classical predicate logic in this formal theory are in the structure of atomic wffs and the semantic conditions on those. That is, we allow atomic wffs in the formal language to have more structure than they previously had, and we relate those semantically by their form. Because the conditions for satisfaction of compound wffs are the same as in classical predicate logic, we can use the same proof of strong completeness theorem as before in Appendix 7.

Strong completeness of the axiomatization of classical predicate logic with predicate modifiers and internal conjunctions

For any wffs Γ and any wff A, Γ⊢A iff Γ⊨A.

This does not mean we have all the consequences of our informal conception of how adverbs, adjectives, internal conjunctions, internal disjunctions, and transitive and intransitive verbs function in our ordinary reasoning. We can only axiomatize what we've assumed from our informal conception, and that's the collection of semantic conditions above.

In Appendix 5, I present a mathematical abstraction of the semantics of this system.

Predicates Used as Restrictors

32 Predicates Restricting Predicates

Consider:

(1) Suzy dances well for a cheerleader.

How are we to formalize this? We look to its consequences. From (1) we can conclude:

(2) Suzy dances.
(3) Suzy is a cheerleader.

But we can't conclude:

(4) Suzy dances well.

It may be that the standard for a cheerleader dancing well is lower than for the general population that includes ballet dancers and rap singers. So we can't formalize (1) as "((— dances)/well) (Suzy) ∧ (— is a cheerleader) (Suzy)". Nor can we use "((— dances + is a cheerleader)/well) (Suzy)", for there "well" modifies the conjoined predicates, while in the example "well" modifies only "dances".

In (1), the phrase "dances well" is relative to cheerleaders. That is, it is relative to "— is a cheerleader", for we use that predicate to pick out cheerleaders. So "dances well" is a restrictor of some sort. But it can't be a simple one, as we also have the predicate "— dances" and need to be able to infer the formalization of (2) from a formalization of (1). We need to consider "dances well" in the usual formalization we have of it as a predicate "— dances/well".

If we mark a predicate used as a restrictor with angle brackets, then we can formalize (1) as:

(5) (— is a cheerleader/<— dances/well>) (Suzy)

Since "<— dances/well>" is a restrictor, we can conclude the formalization of (3), "(— is a cheerleader) (Suzy)", from (5). But to ensure that our models respect the validity of the inference from (5) to the formalization of (2), we need a new semantic principle. It's not that if an object satisfies $Q_1/<Q_2>$, then it satisfies Q_2, for then the formalization of (4) would be a consequence of (5), while (4) is not a consequence of (1). Rather, we need:

   a. If o satisfies $(Q_1/<Q_2>) (x)$ and Q_2 is a simple predicate or conjunction of simple predicates, then o satisfies $Q_2 (x)$.
   b. If o satisfies $(Q/<P/R>) (x)$ and P is a simple predicate or conjunction of simple predicates and R is a restrictor, then o satisfies $P(x)$.

We need to allow for conjunctions of simple predicates in order to formalize propositions such as:

(6) Nancy is a good administrator and scholar, for someone who is obese.

From this, each of these follow:

Nancy is a scholar and administrator.
Nancy is (an) obese (person).

But "Nancy is a good scholar and administrator" does not follow. This is respected if we formalize (6) as:

((— is a person/obese)/<(— is a scholar + administrator)/good>) (Nancy)

Consider now:

(7) Suzy doesn't dance well for a cheerleader.

What is the role of "not" here? Again, we look to the consequences of the proposition. From (7) we can conclude:

(8) Suzy is a cheerleader.
(9) Suzy dances.

But we can't conclude:

(10) Suzy doesn't dance well.

Compared to all the people who can't even clap in rhythm she could be a very good dancer; it's just that most cheerleaders dance better. Because (8) is a consequence of (7), "not" shouldn't be formalized as a propositional connective: "Not: Suzy dances well for a cheerleader". Rather, "doesn't dance well" is a restrictor. But the "not" in that phrase doesn't govern the entire "dances well", since from (7) we can conclude (9). Rather, it negates the modifier "well". We can formalize (7) as:

(11) (— is a cheerleader/<— dances/~well>) (Suzy)

Then we can conclude the formalizations of (8) and (9), but the formalization of (10) is not a consequence. This is to read (7) as "Suzy dances not-well for a cheerleader".

It may be that sometimes we use predicates to modify relations or use relations to modify predicates, but I have no examples. So I won't formulate a theory for relations used as restrictors, nor for unary predicates used as restrictors of relations.

To extend our systems to allow for uses of predicates as restrictors we need to specify the formal syntax. The bracketing device "< >" has no meaning; it only marks the role of the predicate as a restrictor, and so it is punctuation.

It seems that all we need for the syntax of this theory is to allow for predicates to be enclosed in brackets, with a caution that a blank in an enclosed predicate is not one that ever is or needs to be filled. But it isn't that simple because now we have predicates used as restrictors that can then be used in predicates that can then be used as restrictors. We have to give a simultaneous inductive definition of formal

152   Chapter 32

atomic predicates and formal modifiers. It is because of this complication that I postponed this discussion to here.

The language of formal modifiers and formal atomic predicates
We begin as in Chapter 31 with a vocabulary, augmented now by the bracketing device, along with a definition of conjunctions of terms. Then we define formal modifiers and formal atomic predicates together in stages.

Stage 0
We use the definitions from Chapter 31 (pp. 138–140).

Stage n+ 1
Formal modifiers of stage $n + 1$

i. Every formal modifier of stage n is a formal modifier of stage $n + 1$ of degree 0.

ii. If Q is a unary formal atomic predicate of stage n, then $\langle Q \rangle$ is a formal restrictor of stage $n + 1$ of degree 0. It is a *predicate as restrictor*.

iii. If R is a formal restrictor of stage $n + 1$ of degree k, then (~R) is a formal restrictor of stage $n + 1$ of degree $k + 1$.

iv. If R is a formal restrictor of stage $n + 1$ of degree k and N is a formal negator, then (R/N) is a formal restrictor of stage $n + 1$ of degree $k + 1$.

v. If R and R´ are non-variable formal restrictors of stage $n + 1$ of degree k and degree j, respectively, then (R & R´) is a formal restrictor of degree $k + j$. It is a *conjunction of restrictors*.

vi. If R and R´ are formal restrictors of degree k and degree j respectively, then (R $\cup$ R´) is a formal restrictor of degree $k + j$. It is a *disjunction of restrictors*.

vii. A concatenation of symbols is a formal modifier of stage $n + 1$ iff it is a formal restrictor or formal negator of stage $n + 1$ of degree k for some k.

Formal atomic predicates of stage $n + 1$

i. Every formal atomic predicate of stage n is a formal atomic predicate of stage $n + 1$ of degree 0.

ii. If Q is a j-ary formal atomic predicate of stage $n + 1$ of degree k, and M is a formal modifier of stage $n + 1$ that is not a predicate as restrictor, then (Q/M) is a j-ary formal atomic predicate of stage $n + 1$ of degree $k + 1$.

iii. If Q_1 is a unary formal atomic predicate of stage $n + 1$ of degree k, and $\langle Q_2 \rangle$ is a predicate as restrictor of stage $n + 1$, then $(Q_1/\langle Q_2 \rangle)$ is a unary formal atomic predicate of stage $n + 1$ of degree $k + 1$.

iv. If Q_1 and B are unary formal atomic predicates of degrees k and j, then $(Q_1 + B)$ is a unary formal atomic predicate of stage $n + 1$ of degree $k + j + 1$. It is an *internally conjoined* formal predicate.

v. If $Q_1(-)$ and $Q_2(-)$ are unary formal atomic predicates of degrees k and j respectively, then $(Q_1 \cup Q_2)(-)$ is a unary formal atomic predicate of degree $k + j + 1$. It is an *internally disjoined* formal atomic predicate.

vi. A concatenation of symbols is a formal atomic predicate of stage $n + 1$ iff it is a formal atomic predicate formula of stage $n + 1$ of degree k for some k.

A concatenation of symbols is a *formal modifier* iff it is a formal modifier of stage n for some n.

A concatenation of symbols is a *formal atomic predicate* iff it is a formal atomic predicate of stage n for some n.

The definition of wffs for stage $n + 1$ is then as for wffs for the formal language on p. 140 except that any blank that appears within angle brackets requires no term to fill it.

For the semantics we add to the principles of our previous system (pp. 143–145) the following.

Predicates used as restrictors

i. If $\mathsf{v}_\sigma \vDash (Q_1/\langle Q_2 \rangle)(x)$ and Q_2 is a simple predicate or a conjunction of simple predicates, then $\mathsf{v}_\sigma \vDash Q_2(x)$.

ii. If $\mathsf{v}_\sigma \vDash (Q/\langle P/R \rangle)(x)$ where P is a simple unary predicate or conjunction of simple predicates and R is a restrictor, then $\mathsf{v}_\sigma \vDash P(x)$.

For a strongly complete axiomatization of this augmented system, we add to the axioms of our previous theory (pp. 146–148) the following.

Predicates used as restrictors

i. $\forall \ldots (P/\langle Q \rangle)(x) \to A(x)$
   if A is a simple unary predicate or conjunction of simple unary predicates.

ii. $\forall \ldots (Q/\langle P/R \rangle)(x) \to P(x)$
   if P is a simple unary predicate or conjunction of simple predicates and R is a restrictor.

33 Examples of Formalizing

Example 1   Ralph is a toy dog.

Analysis It seems here that "toy" is a negator: what is a toy dog isn't a dog; what is a toy car isn't a car. So we could formalize this as:

(— is a dog/toy) (Ralph)

But we also have a predicate "— is a toy". You might argue that this is not a predicate, that "Ralph is a toy" is not a proposition for the same reason that we excluded adjectives as predicates: a toy is a toy something, a toy car, or a toy dog, or . . . . But, no, there are some toys that are just toys, not meant to imitate any other kind of thing.

We can get "toy" used as a negator by formalizing the example as:

(a)   (— is a dog/⟨— is a toy⟩) (Ralph)

Alternatively, we could view "dog" in the example as the modifier, a restrictor, formalizing the example as:

(b)   (— is a toy/⟨— is a dog⟩) (Ralph)

Context alone can decide which of these is better. If someone asks, "Is Ralph a dog?" or "Is Ralph a real dog?", (a) is a better formalization of the example. If someone is answering "What kind of toy is Ralph?", (b) is better.

Example 2   Suzy is dancing well for a cheerleader.

   Not formalizable.

Analysis   It won't do to formalize this as:

(— is a cheerleader/⟨— is dancing/well⟩) (Suzy)

This says only that Suzy is dancing well now compared to other cheerleaders who are dancing right now. Yet the example asserts that Suzy is dancing well right now compared to how other cheerleaders dance generally (habitually). The problem here is the timelessness of classical predicate logic.

Example 3   Harold walks nearly normally for a parapalegic.

((— is a parapalegic)/⟨—walks/(normally/nearly)⟩) (Harold)

$(P_{19}(-))/\langle P_{20}(-)/(R_{43}/N_2)\rangle (c_{45})$

Analysis   Here we have a negator in the predicate used as restrictor. Though it may seem that this is an assertion that Harold walks nearly normally, it isn't. For this to be true, Harold need walk nearly normally compared only to parapalegics.

Example 4 Dick: *Suzy sings well for a cheerleader.*

Analysis In Example 8 of Chapter 12 we considered "Suzy is beautiful for a woman". That seems like a backhanded compliment to Suzy: she's not really beautiful, only beautiful compared to other women. But that's to assume there is a standard of beautiful that is absolute, not relative. If there is no such absolute standard, then that is the (logically) correct way to say "Suzy is beautiful".

In this example, however, there is clearly a standard of comparison that Dick is using: cheerleaders. Since Dick didn't say "Suzy sings well", perhaps we should conclude that he believes "Suzy doesn't sing well, but sings well only in comparison to cheerleaders".

All the examples we've seen of a predicate used as restrictor seem to suppose that the predicate without the comparison class does not apply. Perhaps we should add as a semantic principle:

(a) If σ satisfies $Q_1/\langle Q_2\rangle$, then σ does not satisfy Q_2.

In the examples we've seen, the predicate as restrictor is a compound, "dances well", "walks nearly normally", "is a good scholar and administrator". We use predicates as restrictors in English primarily to allow for a second comparison: first to a predicate within the predicate as restrictor, "dances", "walks", "is a scholar and administrator", and then to a wider predicate, "is a cheerleader", "is a parapalegic", "is obese". For those uses, I suspect (a) is correct: the wider comparison is asserted not to hold. But when there is no second comparison, when Q_2 is a simple atomic predicate or conjunction of simple ones, (a) is not correct. Though it is unusual to see that kind of construction in English, it is common in some other languages, as the next example illustrates.

Example 5 *Dick desceu a escada correndo.*

Analysis This example is in Portuguese. A literal translation would be "Dick descended the stairs running". But that's not good because in English we could rewrite that as "Dick descended the stairs while running", which is not equivalent to the example. In Portuguese the word "correndo" ("running") is used as an adverb, which to render in English we'd need something like:

(a) Dick descended the stairs runningly.
     Dick descended the stairs in a running manner.

In the next part of this volume we'll look at how to take account of the internal structure of "the stairs", but for now let's just give the stairs a name "c". Then we can formalize the example and (a):

(b) $((-\text{ desceu})/\text{obj}(c))/\langle -\text{ estava correndo}\rangle)$ (Dick)

$((-\text{ descended}/\text{obj}(c))/\langle -\text{ was running}\rangle)$ (Dick)

We can't take "running" or "runningly" as a simple restrictor because that would not

156   Chapter 33

respect how it is related to "— run" in inferences. The form of (b) is (Q/<P>) (a), where P is a simple predicate.[48] It does not seem to follow from (a) that Dick was not running, or at least that is not clearly a consequence.

Example 6   Spot is a dog that barks loudly.

(— is a dog)/<(—barks)/loudly> (Spot)

$(P_1(-)/<P_2(-)/R_5>)(c_3)$

Analysis   The phrase "barks loudly" is meant to characterize Spot relative to dogs. Hence, we can formalize the relative clause as a predicate used as restrictor.

Example 7   Suzy dances well even though she's a cheerleader.

Analysis   From this example we can conclude both "Suzy dances well" and "Suzy is a cheerleader". Just as we formalize "but" as $\wedge$ in propositional logic, arguing that the difference is only one of emphasis or an indication that it seems surprising that both parts are true, we can formalize the example using $\wedge$ for "even though":

((— dances)/well) (Suzy) $\wedge$ (— is a cheerleader) (Suzy)

We can also formalize:

Suzy danced well even though she's a cheerleader.

((— danced)/well) (Suzy) $\wedge$ (— is a cheerleader) (Suzy)

But the criterion of parity of form is violated with:

Suzy danced well even though she was a cheerleader.

We need that both "Suzy danced well" and "Suzy was a cheerleader" are true at the same time. With the resources we have we can formalize this as only:

(— danced/well + was a cheerleader) (Suzy)

Example 8   Mabel speaks well considering that she is deaf.

((— is a person/deaf)/<(—speaks)/well>) (Mabel)

$((P_{29}(-)/R_{63})/<P_{70}(-)/R_{21}>)(c_{806})$

Analysis   Here "considering that" is used to indicate a second comparison.

Example 9   Mark baas well considering that he is not a sheep.

Not formalizable.

---

[48] That "correndo" is used as an adverb becomes clearer when another adverb is used to modify it:

Dick desceu a escada correndo desajetadamente.

Dick descended the stairs in an awkward running manner.

This kind of construction is routine in French, too. The main example is adapted from one given by Letitia G. Naigles, Anne Fowler, and Atessa Helm in "Syntactic Bootstrapping from Start to Finish with Special Reference to Down Syndrome", p. 301: "Il descend l'escalier courant", which they translate as "He went down the stairs runningly".

Analysis In English "to baa" means to make a noise like a sheep. This example seems to have the same form as the previous one. But there is a big difference: we can't render "is not a sheep" as an atomic predicate. We would have to have something like:

(¬ (— is a sheep)/<— baas/well>) (Mark)

We do not allow a restrictor to apply to non-atomic predicates. We would have to use "not" as an internal predicate negator, so that "not-is a sheep" is atomic. We rejected using "not" in that way in Chapter 21 and we should reject it here, too. We don't know what the standard of comparison is if Mark is not a sheep. Mark could be a goat, or a lemming, or a person, or . . . . For each of those the standard of comparison is clear (enough), and we can formalize each of those. The example is too vague to formalize; the only reason it doesn't seems too vague is because we assume that "Mark" is the name of a person. Right, Mark? Come on boy, good dog.

Example 10 Tom is happy to be a friend of Dick.

   Not formalizable.

Analysis From the example we can conclude "Tom is (a) happy (person)" and also "Tom is a friend of Dick". But it's not equivalent to "Tom is happy and Tom is a friend of Dick". Nor does the example mean that Tom is happy in comparison to friends of Dick, with "— is a friend of Dick" used as a restrictor. Compare:

(a)   Tom is happy that he is a friend of Dick.

(b)   Tom is happy because he is a friend of Dick.

(c)   Tom is happy insofar as he is a friend of Dick.

   I see (a) as equivalent to the original example. Whether you agree that (b) and (c) are equivalent too, it is nonetheless clear that in each of these we are relating two propositions, not modifying a predicate. In (a) "that" can be read as "that it is true that". For (b) "because" indicates that an inferential relation holds between "Tom is a friend of Dick" and "Tom is happy". We will not be able to formalize the example or these two propositions in the systems we are developing because they involve further propositional operators, or connectives, or ways of saying "therefore".

Example 11 As a horse-trainer, Gerald has a lot of patience.

   Not formalizable.

Analysis In this example patience is treated as a mass, something one can have a lot of, and that seems to put the example outside the scope of predicate logic. But we can rewrite the example as "As a horse-trainer, Gerald is very patient". We needn't mass-ify the adjective.

   But the example is still not formalizable because it doesn't assert that Gerald is patient compared to other horse trainers but that when he is being a horse-trainer he

158   Chapter 33

is very patient. He may be curt, impatient, and generally irascible with everyone and everything other than horses. We need to take account of time with a connective for "while" in order to formalize this example.

Example 12   *Tom is a good football player but not as a professional.*

   Not formalizable.

Analysis   We can't conclude from this that Tom is a professional (football player). But neither can we conclude that Tom is not a professional. It doesn't seem that "as" is used here to mean "in the capacity of" but only to make a comparison. But how do we make a comparison to a class to which he does not belong?

Example 13   *Leo is well-adjusted for someone who has a cat.*

   Not formalizable.

Analysis   Here the comparison is to everyone who has a cat. To formalize the example we'd need to use "$\exists x\, ((x \text{ is a cat})/\text{of}\,(-))$" to pick out those people and then take "well-adjusted" as a restrictor of that. But we have not allowed for compound wffs to have blanks, and hence they cannot be modified. This example shows a need to allow for that.

Example 14   Suzy: *I love Zoe. I love Puff. I love Tom. I love Dick.*

Analysis   We scoff. She loves all of them? And perhaps she loves pizza, too. We think the word "loves" is being used so loosely by Suzy that it's lost all power to mean anything to us. But when Tom pushed her about this (since he wants to be her only love), she replied: "I love Zoe as a friend. And I love Puff as a cat. And I love you as a boyfriend. And I love Dick as a friend." There doesn't seem anything odd, vague, or too loose in that. We could formalize these as:

   [((− loves) / < − is a friend >) / obj (Zoe)] (Suzy)

   [((− loves) / < − is a cat >) / obj (Puff)] (Suzy)

   [((− loves) / < − is a boyfriend >) / obj (Tom)] (Suzy)

   [((− loves) / < − is a friend >) / obj (Dick)] (Suzy)

   This is to assume that, following Suzy's lead, "loves" has a single meaning. Zoe thinks that's still too loose. She says that there is so much difference between loving someone as a boyfriend and loving something as a cat that to use the same word "loves" for both is just silly. To formalize according to Zoe's standard, we should take each of "− loves as a friend", "− loves as a cat", and "− loves as a boyfriend" as a distinct simple predicate. If we were to use them in formalizations, we'd have to supply meaning axioms to relate them to the predicates "− is a friend", "− is a cat", and "− is a boyfriend".

Summary

Classical propositional logic is the simplest formal logic we can devise. We take into consideration about a proposition only its form relative to four connectives and the one semantic value any proposition must have: a truth-value. We can use it to formalize some of our ordinary reasoning. To be able to formalize more, we need to consider the internal structure of atomic propositions. And to do that, we need to make assumptions about how our language connects with the world.

We assume that the world is made up of things and that we have ways of referring to those things. Then classical predicate logic is the simplest formal logic based on classical propositional logic that we can devise relative to those assumptions. Though that logic is well-known, we improved the standard presentations by more clearly distinguishing the various roles of variables and by not allowing superfluous quantifications.

We can formalize and evaluate more of our ordinary reasoning in classical predicate logic relative to those assumptions. Doing so requires us to give criteria for what counts as a good formalization and then agree on how we will formalize many specific kinds of propositions and inferences.

But there is much that lies outside the scope of classical predicate logic. By taking account of further semantic values of predicates and names, we can formalize more. By adding to classical predicate logic a way to quantify over predicates, we can formalize more. By using a logic that allows for talk of masses rather than things, we can formalize more. All those methods have been developed, but only by adopting substantial semantic assumptions beyond what is needed for classical predicate logic.

In contrast, we can bring within the scope of classical predicate logic reasoning that takes account of the use of adverbs and relative adjectives without additional semantic assumptions. We need only parse the internal structure of what we previously took to be atomic predicates.

Some adverbs and relative adjectives are restrictors: restricting the application of a predicate to some of the things it applies to. Some adverbial phrases include names within them, and those can be formalized as variable restrictors requiring references for the (temporary) names in them in order to act as a restrictor. Some adverbs and relative adjectives act as negators, resulting in a new predicate whose application is incompatible with that of the predicate that's being modified. In our ordinary reasoning we apply adjectives and adverbs sequentially or to modify one another, and we can do that in our formalizations, too.

Inferential relations of many futher uses of "and" in our ordinary reasoning can be formalized by taking formal counterparts of "and" joining terms, joining modifiers, and joining predicates within what we previously took to be atomic predicates. Likewise, inferential relations of uses of "or" joining predicates can be formalized by taking a formal counterpart of that within atomic predicates. No new metaphysical assumptions are needed for such formalizations.

We did all this for unary predicates. Then we saw that we could formalize within that system much ordinary reasoning that involves relations by adopting a restrictor that indicates that a name or variable is being used as an object of a verb. We were justified in doing so by noting that there is no clear semantic distinction between transitive and intransitive verbs.

However, formalizing reasoning that involves classification predicates cannot always be reduced in an obvious way to reasoning with unary predicates, modifiers, internal conjunctions, and internal disjunctions. So we extended our system to allow for modifiers of relations, summarizing all that work in a formal system.

Some reasoning involves the use of predicates themselves as modifiers of other predicates. Because the formalization of a syntax for a formal system to model that is much more complicated, we left it to the last section.

Along the way, we investigated what we mean when we say that some part of speech or the use of some part of speech is extensional. And we adopted a principle of parsimony of formalizing for how much of ordinary reasoning we should take into account in a formal system of logic.

Through many examples we saw how much more we can now formalize from ordinary reasoning. We also saw examples of what we could not formalize in our work. Some of those require ways to take account of time in our formalizations, which we'll see in Volume 2, *Time and Space in Formal Logic*.

We've extended the scope of predicate logic by recognizing the internal structure of predicates. In the next part we'll see how to extend the scope of predicate logic by taking into account the internal structure of names.

The Internal Structure of Names

In order to better isolate the assumptions and methods for working with names, I don't use the methods of the previous part on the internal structure of predicates except in some examples. Only the background material in the first part of this text is assumed.

Functions and Descriptive Functions

34 Functions

In our ordinary speech, when we talk about a function we understand some kind of process or connection. We say that the volume of a gas is a function of the pressure and temperature, understanding it somehow as a physical or perhaps causal connection. We speak of addition of counting numbers as a function of two numbers, understanding that as a procedure to obtain a new number from two given ones. We speak of the tangent of an angle, understanding that as a ratio we calculate from co-ordinates of the point where the angle intersects a unit circle.

Mathematicians in the 19th century found that their notion of function as process did not help to resolve problems in reasoning with infinitesimals in the calculus. They found that the notion of a function as a procedure impeded deriving theorems about functions, for they needed to quantify over functions they might not be able to describe. So they abstracted from the notion of a function as process or procedure to view a function as just a correlation between things. The volume of a gas as a quantity is abstracted to be a number that is correlated to numbers giving the pressure and temperature of the gas; measurement and causal relations are ignored. Addition of counting numbers is abstracted to correlating a number to a pair of numbers, for example, 7 is correlated to 3 and 4); actual counting as the basis of addition is ignored. The tangent of an angle is a correlation of a real number to a real number; the procedure of thinking through how the angle intersects a unit circle yielding a ratio of two numbers is ignored. The procedures or processes are what establish the correlations, but once we have the correlations we ignore those procedures or processes. We simply have the correlations and take those to be the functions.

Abstracting more in order to fill out their theories that needed functions they could not describe, mathematicians took functions to be any relations between things such that given one (or several things), there is exactly one other thing correlated to that (or those). Processes and procedures were eliminated from the foundations of their reasoning in favor of only things and correlations of things. Functions became special kinds of predicates.

Functions in this abstraction became abstract, in the same way that predicates become abstract. They are assumed to exist independently of us and our powers, especially our linguistic powers. They simply are, and they can be discussed even when we cannot point to them.

In classical predicate logic we do not talk about predicates; we use predicates. We do not say, "No matter what predicate we have and what thing we have, either it is true of that or it isn't true of that". Such reasoning is a significant step beyond what we have done, taking predicates to be things we reason about not just use, as described in Chapter 10 of Volume 0. So in any model, in any semi-formal language in which we formalize reasoning, we do not need to agree on whether predicates are abstract or linguistic, real beyond the senses, or ways of talking that connect to our experience. We use predicates, and for that we need linguistic predicates such as "— is a dog" or "— is bigger than —". Predicate logic is thus open to many interpretations, available as a model for how to reason well regardless of one's metaphysics of predicates, for the metaphysics of predicates enters into the semantics only in determining the truth-values of atomic predications.

Similarly, in predicate logic we don't reason about functions; to do so would be to reason about certain kinds of predicates. Rather, we use functions in our reasoning. But that sounds odd, for we have grown accustomed to thinking of functions as distinct from any linguistic way of describing them.

Yet we do use names of functions in our reasoning. We use "$\tan(x)$" to stand for the tangent of a number, where that number is understood as a description of an angle. We write "$F = m \cdot a$" to assert that the value of the force is a function of the value of the mass times the value of the acceleration. We write "$x + y$" to stand for the addition of two numbers.

Because functions give a single output for given input(s), we use these linguistic function-names to give us terms. We take "$3 + 4$" to be a name, which designates exactly what "7" designates. We take "$x + 4$" to be a term, comparable to a variable in that it requires saying what x refers to for it to have a reference, but different from a variable in that it has structure. We take "$x + y$" to be a term, requiring references to be supplied for both x and y in order to have a reference.

In this way functions used in predicate logic are linguistic. But unlike predicates, no one takes a linguistic function plus its connection to our experience as all there is to a function. We would have to pack a lot into the notion of meaning to say that "$\tan(-)$" plus our understanding of that "word" is all there is to the tangent function. Rather, "$\tan(-)$" is a name, a name of a way to correlate certain things to certain other things. As with predicates, we do not need to resolve whether such a correlation is a way of proceeding in calculating or is an abstract thing: that's part of the metaphysics, and the metaphysics of functions enters into the semantics only in determining what objects are referred to by terms involving that function-name. Functions as used in predicate logic, then, are name-makers, ways we have to create terms in our language. Whatever notion of function as process, procedure, or abstraction that we have is confined to how we establish the references of such terms; it is absent from our logic.

Such terms can be quite complex as we iterate our name-making. We have "$\tan(x + \tan(y + (\pi \div 17)))$". As with predicates, and for the same reasons, we want to confine our choices via our metaphysics to only the simplest uses of function-names. For predicates, only the atomic predications need be given in order to have truth-values for all wffs. For functions, we want that only the references of the simplest use of function-names need be given, for example, "$\tan(x)$" and "$x + y$"

and "tan(π)". Then we want a way to use those to give references for all terms built from function-names, consonant, as with predicates, with an extensionality condition: how an object is named does not matter for what the reference of a term is. Thus, both "7" and "3 + 4" designate the same object in a universe, so the object designated by "tan(7)" must be the same as the object designated by "tan(3 + 4)", which is the same as the object designated by "tan(x)" when x designates the same object that "7" designates.

In the next chapter we'll see how to extend classical predicate logic to allow for reasoning with function-names. In that formal system, terms are names—perhaps temporary names—that have internal structure, and that internal structure is recognized in our inferences.

Classical predicate logic, though, has a strong restriction on names: every name must refer. So when reasoning with function-names, every term must yield a reference when references are supplied for whatever variables appear in it. That is not consonant with how we reason with functions in mathematics and science. The term "tan(x)" is not defined when x refers to $\pi/2$. It is quite common in mathematics and science to use partial functions: given any thing(s), there is either exactly one thing correlated to that (those) or else nothing at all is correlated to that (those). It is even more common in ordinary speech to use partial functions such as "the wife of" to pick out things. We'll turn to how to formalize that kind of reasoning after we see how to formalize reasoning with total functions.

35 Classical Predicate Logic with Function Names

Syntax
To incorporate talk of functions in our logic, we modify the formal language of classical predicate logic with equality to allow for function symbols and terms formed with those.

Vocabulary We add to the vocabulary:

   function symbols: f_i^n for $n \geq 0$ and $i \geq 1$

The subscript on f_i^n is the number of the symbol; the superscript is the arity.

Terms
   i. Every name symbol and every variable is a term of depth 0.

   ii. If $u_1, \ldots, u_m$ are terms of depth $\leq n$ and at least one of them has depth n, and f is an m-ary function symbol, then $f(-, \ldots, -)(u_1, \ldots, u_m)$ is a term of depth $n + 1$.

   iii. A concatenation of symbols is a term iff it is a term of depth n for some n.

Terms of depth 0 are *atomic*; all others are *complex*.
A term is *closed* if it neither is nor contains a variable; otherwise it is *open*.

I'll let you show that there is one and only one way to read each term.[49] The definition of "wff" then proceeds as usual with this more ample understanding of the word "term". However, we need to modify the definition of when one term is free to be substituted for another.

Terms free for a variable A term u is *free for an occurence* of a variable x in A iff both:

   i. The occurrence of x is free.

   ii. If u is or contains a variable y, then the occurrence of x does not lie within the scope of some occurrence of $\forall y$ or $\exists y$.

---

[49] The proof follows as in the proof of the unique readability of wffs in Appendix 2 of Volume 0 by letting γ be the following assignment of numbers to the symbols:

x_i	c_i	f_i^n	(	)	for each $i \geq 0$ and $n \geq 0$
1	1	$1-n$	2	-2	

Then:
   a. For every term u, $\gamma(u) = 1$.
   b. If β is an initial segment of a term other than the entire term, then $\gamma(\beta) < 1$.
   c. If β is a final segment of a term other than the entire term, then $\gamma(\beta) > 1$.
   d. No proper initial or final segment of a term is a term.
   e. There is one and only one way to parse each term.

A term u is *free for x* in A iff it is free for every free occurrence of x in A. We write $A(u/x)$ to mean the replacement of every free occurrence of x in A with u.

The definition of a realization of the formal language and of a semi-formal language are as before with the addition of the following.

Realizations of function symbols An n-ary function symbol can be realized as a function-name with n blanks, though no function symbol need be realized.

I'll continue to use $u, v, u_0, u_1, \ldots, v_0, v_1, \ldots$ for terms of the formal language or a semi-formal language, depending on context. I'll use the metavariables $f, f_0, f_1, \ldots$ to stand for function symbols or realizations of function symbols in a semi-formal language, depending on context. I'll speak of them loosely as functions, though they are really names of functions, such as "+" or "$\int_1^y \frac{\sin x}{x} dx$". In what follows I'll write informally, for example, $\tan(x_1)$ for $\tan(-)(x_1)$.

Semantics
Comparable to the application of predicates, we have applications of functions.

The value of a function Given an n-ary function f and terms $u_1, \ldots, u_n$ where the variables are consistently supplemented with indications of what each variable is to refer to, the object referred to by $f(u_1, \ldots, u_n)$ is the *value of the function applied to the objects* referred to by $u_1, \ldots, u_n$ in that order. If $u_1, \ldots, u_n$ are atomic, then $f(u_1, \ldots, u_n)$ is an *atomic application* of the function f.

For classical predicate logic we make the classical abstraction of functions, which is the classical abstraction of predicates for the special kinds of predicates that functions are.

The classical abstraction of functions The only properties of a function that matter to (this) logic are: (i) its arity and (ii) for any sequence of terms, if each variable in those terms is consistently supplemented with an indication of what object it is to refer to, the value of the function applied to those objects referred to by the terms.

Given a semi-formal language and universe we have, as before, assignments of references that assign a reference to each variable and to each simple name. We assume that the collection of assignments of references is *complete* (p. 21) and that all assignments agree on the names of the realization. We continue to write "$\tau \sim_x \sigma$" to mean that τ differs from σ at most in what it assigns x.

We wish to extend assignments of references to all terms. *We take as given the atomic applications of functions.* That is, if $u_1, \ldots, u_n$ are atomic terms,

Classical Predicate Logic with Function Names

we take as given $\sigma(f(u_1, \ldots, u_n))$. This must be what we do, since these are just atomic applications of special kinds of predicates, albeit predicates we have no access to in the semi-formal language except through their names. Since we are working in classical predicate logic where all names refer, this means that all atomic applications of functions are defined. Since an application of a function is really an application of a predicate, we require that applications of functions be extensional.

The extensionality condition for atomic applications of functions For any function f and atomic terms $u_1, \ldots, u_n$ and variables $y_1, \ldots, y_n$ not appearing in $u_1, \ldots, u_n$, and any σ and τ, if for all $i \le n$, $\sigma(u_i) = \tau(y_i)$, then:

$\sigma(f(u_1, \ldots, u_n)) = \tau(f(y_1, \ldots, y_n))$.

We want to extend the atomic applications of functions to all applications of functions in a way that will satisfy the same conditions we imposed on predicates:

   a. The extensionality condition with "atomic" deleted.

   b. The condition of *form and meaningfulness*: every term of the language is a name when the variables appearing in it are given reference.

   c. The *division of form and content*: if two terms have the same semantic values, they are indistinguishable in any semantic analysis, regardless of their form.

   d. The values of terms are *compositional*: the semantic value of a term is determined by its form and the semantic values of its parts.

Because in this system all names must refer, (b) requires that every function be total. To accomplish (a)–(d), we use the following definition.

The inductive extension of assignments of references to all terms
Terms of depth 0 and 1:

   For every term u of depth 0 or 1 and every assignment of references σ, $\sigma(u)$ is given.

Terms of depth $n + 1$:

   For any term $f(u_1, \ldots, u_m)$ of depth $n + 1$, let $z_1, \ldots, z_m$ be the first variables (ones with least index) that do not appear in it. Given any assignment of references σ, let τ be the assignment of references that differs from σ only in that $\tau(z_i) = \sigma(u_i)$. Then:

   $\sigma(f(u_1, \ldots, u_m)) = \tau(f(z_1, \ldots, z_n))$.

That there is an assignment τ as required in the second part of the definition is because the collection of assignments of references on atomic terms is complete.

I'll let you show that this definition yields a unique value for each application of a function and that the collection of those satisfies conditions (a)–(d). I'll also let you show that *extensionality for all terms* holds:

For any function f and terms $u_1, \ldots, u_n$ and $v_1, \ldots, v_n$, and assignments of references σ, τ, if for all $i \leq n$, $\sigma(u_i) = \tau(v_i)$, then $\sigma(f(u_1, \ldots, u_n)) = \tau(f(v_1, \ldots, v_n))$.

As before, we take as given the valuations of all atomic wffs subject to the condition on extensionality of predications with this more ample understanding of "term".

The extensionality of atomic predications Let A be an atomic wff and $u_1, \ldots, u_n$ all the names and variables in A. Let $v_1, \ldots, v_n$ be any terms, and σ, τ assignments of references such that for each i, $\sigma(u_i) = \tau(v_i)$. Then:

$$v_\sigma \vDash A(u_1, \ldots, u_n) \text{ iff } v_\tau \vDash A(v_1/u_1, \ldots, v_n/u_n).$$

The valuations on atomic wffs are extended to all wffs by the inductive definition given before (p. 25). We now have the extensionality of all predications (p. 26) with this more ample notion of term, using the same proof as before.

In order to ensure that our formalizations respect our informal notion of validity, we must also have enough models.

Sufficiency of the collection of models For any realization and any collection of things, any correlations satisfying the extensionality condition can serve as the assignments of references for atomic applications of functions and, relative to those, any assignment of truth-values to the atomic predications satisfying the extensionality condition can serve to define a model.

For an axiomatization of classical predicate logic with (total) functions and equality, we add to the axiomatization of classical predicate logic with equality a formalization of the condition that functions are extensional.

Axioms for functions

    7. $\forall \ldots \forall x \forall y (x \equiv y \rightarrow$ *extensionality of functions*

        $f(z_1, \ldots, z_k, x, z_{k+1}, \ldots, z_n) \equiv f(z_1, \ldots, z_k, y, z_{k+1}, \ldots, z_n))$

    for every $n + 1$-ary function symbol f

In Appendix 7, I prove the strong completeness of this axiomatization.

In *Classical Mathematical Logic* I present examples of the use of this system in formalizing reasoning in mathematics.

36 Functions and Descriptive Names

In classical predicate logic we use names of functions, not phrases from ordinary language that connect directly to our experience through our understanding of the words. We conceal the definition of the function, which cannot be reasoned about explicitly.

If we were to do the same with predicates, we might realize P_0 as "G" and evaluate "$G(x)$" as true if and only if x is indicated to refer to a cat. Predicates in the semi-formal language would have no internal structure or any direct connection with experience. We would be imposing one more level of language between the formal language and the semantics, for really we would be reasoning with the linguistic predicate "— is a cat", which does connect to the world via our experience and knowledge of our language.

In our ordinary reasoning, and even in mathematics, we don't reason with function-names: we reason with explicit definitions of functions. The mathematician invokes the definition of "tan (—)" in proving theorems in the calculus. We use "the wife of —" as a name-maker, and from "Gertrude is the wife of Sidney" we can conclude "Gertrude is a wife" and "there is one and only one wife of Sidney". We use "the cat that scratched —" as a name-maker, and from "Puff is the cat that scratched Zoe" we can conclude "Puff is a cat", "Puff scratched Zoe" and there is one and only one thing that is a cat that scratched Zoe. We use "the brother of — and —" as a name-maker, and from "Louis is the brother of Cindy Lou and Bertha" we can conclude that there is one and only one brother of Cindy Lou and Bertha. We take into account the internal structure of the phrases that define the function.

In our ordinary reasoning we use "the" to indicate that we are using a predicate to make names. But few of the phrases we use to define functions in our ordinary reasoning yield total functions. There is no object that satisfies "the wife of x" when x refers to Marilyn Monroe; there are several objects that satisfy "the cat that scratched x" when x refers to Zoe.

The problem of dealing with phrases that yield only partial functions and the complexity of iterating such name-makers led people to devise other ways of dealing with what I call *descriptive names*. Bertrand Russell's way of formalizing is widely known and used nowadays. To explain how that works, first recall from Volume 0, Chapter 9.A, that for any wff A with free variable x we define:

The unique existence quantifier

$\exists! x\, A(x) \equiv_{\text{Def}} \exists x\, A(x) \wedge \neg \exists y\, \exists z\, (y \neq z \wedge (A(y) \wedge A(z)))$

where y and z are the variables with least index that do not appear in $A(x)$.

If x is the only variable free in A, then $\exists! x\, A(x)$ is true in a model iff there is exactly one thing in the universe that satisfies $A(x)$.

172   Chapter 36

To formalize according to Russell's method:

(1)   The cat that scratched Zoe is male.

we use:

(2) $\exists ! x [(- \text{ is a cat}) (x) \land (- \text{ scratched } -) (x, \text{Zoe})] \land$
$\forall x [((- \text{ is a cat}) (x) \land (- \text{ scratched } -) (x, \text{Zoe})) \to (- \text{ is a male}) (x)]$

One problem with this method is that though Tom believes that "the cat that scratched Zoe" refers when he uses it, that phrase might not refer to a single object. In that case this method makes any predication in which it figures false. So "the cat that scratched Zoe is a cat" is false, which seems acceptable. But so, too, is:

(3)   The cat that scratched Zoe is a cat $\lor \neg$ (the cat that scratched Zoe is a cat)

So compositionality fails. We can adjust the formalization of (2) to make the scope of the existence quantifier as small as possible, which results in only atomic predications using non-referring descriptive names being deemed false while (3) is true. But determining the scope of the existential quantifier in such a formalization is not always obvious.

Another problem with using (2) to formalize (1) has to do with distinguishing what we assume from what we say. When Tom uttered (1), all he said was that the cat that scratched Zoe was male. He did not say that there is one and only one thing that is a cat and that scratched Zoe. We infer that from what he said and from what we know about how language works. But he did not say it. To use (2) is to import our assumptions about the use of a phrase used as a name into the formalization. They may be assumptions that Tom shares; they may not. But, as you can see in hundreds of examples in *Critical Thinking*, it is one thing to evaluate what someone says and quite another to set out further claims that are assumed or which we can infer from what was said. As emphasized in that book, in evaluating reasoning we should not put words in someone's mouth. We distinguish between formalization and analysis, between logic and metalogic.[50]

The grammar of (1) is a predicate and a (complicated) name, but the formalization eliminates the name entirely.[51] This violates criterion 7 of formalization, which requires that the grammar of the original be preserved by the formalization.

---

[50] P. F. Strawson proposed (roughly) that we maintain this distinction by following the form of (1) while using the descriptive name only in models in which there is a unique thing that is a cat that scratched Zoe; see Chapter VIII of *Predicate Logic* for a discussion.

[51] W.V.O. Quine in "On What There Is" went further and argued that we should get rid of all names, eliminating any need to work with non-referring names by changing every name into a predicate: instead of "Pegasus" we should use "— pegasizes". But we cannot get rid of all names. Essential to the foundations of predicate logic is the requirement that we can name and re-identify any object in the universe. That's what we summarize in our assignments of references. Even if we didn't have proper names, we would still have and need temporary names: variables with indications of what objects they refer to.

We know that this criterion can be violated in order to satisfy the other criteria of formalization, as we've seen in examples in this volume and Volume 0. Here, however, the formalization eliminates a name, and names and predicates are the basis of all we do in classical predicate logic. So there must be a very good reason to violate this criterion. Advocates of this approach have to argue not only that we have to use this method to correctly evaluate inferences in which the phrase "the cat that scratched Zoe" appears, but also that there is no other way to do that which respects the apparent grammar of (1).

These issues are motive enough to try to devise a method of formalizing "the" in our semi-formal languages to create names. Such a method will also allow us to make explicit our formulations of functions on a par with how we make explicit our formulations of predicates: we will have meaningful linguistic expressions for them in our semi-formal languages.

Aside: Other approaches to descriptive names
Here is a more general formulation of Russell's method:

> Given an atomic proposition B(a) where a is a descriptive phrase purporting to refer, we select a common noun phrase α using the same categorematic words as appear in a such that a refers to a unique object iff there is one and only one α. Then we rewrite B(a) as: *There is exactly one thing that is an α and* B(it). We then convert α into a predicate A(x) (where x does not appear in B(a)) to obtain a formalization of B(a) as: $\exists! x\, (A(x) \wedge B(x))$.

In some cases this is modified to vary the scope of the existential quantifier.

Russell defined contextually an *iota operator* that converts any (possibly complex) unary predicate A into a name via (with our methods):

$$A(\iota x\, B(x)) \equiv_{\text{Def}} \exists! x\, [B(x) \wedge \forall x\, (B(x) \to A(x))\,]$$

Such pseudo-names still replace naming by predication.

David Hilbert and Paul Bernays defined in context an ε-operator which allows for parity of form when formalizing "A dog barked" as "($\varepsilon x\, (-$ is a dog)) barked" with "The dog barked" as "($\iota x\, (-$ is a dog)) barked". That, however, makes the reverse confusion, replacing a predication with an "indefinite" name. See Chapter IX.E of *Predicate Logic* for a discussion.

Rudolf Carnap in *Meaning and Necessity*, pp. 32–39, gives a history and comparison of Hilbert and Bernays' approach, Russell's approach, and Gottlob Frege's analysis of descriptive names. Others, for example Dana Scott in "Existence and Predication in Formal Logic", have devised formal logics in which non-referring names are allowed, adding a "non-existent" to the universe to serve as reference of non-referring definite descriptions. See the review of Scott's paper by Alonzo Church.

37 The Syntax of Descriptive Names and Descriptive Functions

Before we can say how we'll understand descriptive names and functions, we need to be explicit about their syntax. I'll write "the" for a formal version of "the" and consider first how to form a name from an open wff.

Given any open wff A with exactly one free variable x, we want to be able to form a name "the x A(x)". For example, we'd like to formalize "the cat that scratched Zoe", as "the x (((— is a cat) (x) $\wedge$ ((— scratched)/obj(x) (Zoe))". Once we have such names we can use them in open wffs to create further names. For example, we could formalize "the dog that bit the cat that scratched Zoe".

With function-names we use an inductive definition of "term" to account for all iterations of terms within terms; then we use the usual definition of the formal language with that more ample notion of term. With "the" we are forming terms not from terms but from wffs that contain terms. To define the formal language we need to create levels of languages, not levels of just terms. At stage 0 we'll have the base language L, the language of classical predicate logic with equality. At stage 1 we can form "the x A(x)" for any wff A(x) of stage 0 that has exactly one free variable in it. With this expanded class of terms we use the usual definition of the formal language to get an expanded language L_1. At stage 2 we can form terms "the x A(x)" for wffs from L_1 and then use the usual definition of a formal language to get L_2 with this newly expanded notion of term. Continuing in this manner, we get a full language L* that has all terms and wffs that are defined at any stage. We separate syntax from semantics by making no assumption about the semantic values of A(x) when we form "the x A(x)".

The syntax of descriptive names

The formal language of descriptive names
Let L be the formal language of classical predicate logic with equality. This is the base language. We add to the vocabulary of L the logical operator "the". We define by simultaneous and repeated induction the collections of terms and wffs of a new formal language L* that extends L.

Stage 0 The terms and wffs of stage 0 are those of L. Call this language L_0.

Stage n +1
 Terms
   a. Every term of stage n is a term of stage $n + 1$.
   b. If A is a wff of stage n and not of stage m for any $m < n$, and there is exactly one variable x that has one or more free occurrences in A, then "the x A(x)" is a term of stage $n + 1$.

Every occurrence of x in "the x A(x)" is *bound*, and the term is *closed*.
The *scope* of the operator "the x" in "the x A(x)" is A(x).

Wffs

The definition of *wff at stage* $n + 1$ is then the usual one, taking this wider notion of term.

Terms and wffs of L*

A concatenation of symbols is a *term* iff it is a term of stage n for some n.

A concatenation of symbols is a *wff* iff it is a wff of stage n for some n.
It is *closed* iff it is closed at the first stage at which it is defined.

Note that we do not allow a superfluous use of "the x" before a formula in which x is not free, as in "the x ((— is a dog) (Ralph))".

Lemma 1 There is one and only one way to parse each wff of the language L*.

Proof At stage 0 we have the proof in Appendix 2 of Volume 0. If it's true at stage n, then each term of stage $n + 1$ has a unique reading because it is either already a term of stage n, or if it is not then it is of the form "the x A(x)" and by induction A(x) has a unique reading and hence there is one and only one x that is free in it. Hence, using the same proof as for stage 0 for this expanded class of terms, every wff of stage $n + 1$ has a unique reading. ∎

We define by induction the **height** of terms of the form "the x A(x)":

If no occurrence of the appears in A(x), the height of "the x A(x)" is 1.

Otherwise, let k be the largest height of any term "the y B(y)" that appears within A(x). Then the height of "the x A(x)" is $k + 1$.

I'll leave the proof of the following to you.

Lemma 2 ***a.*** The height of "the x A(x)" is n iff n is the first stage at which "the x A(x)" is defined.

b. If A is a wff that is first defined at stage $n + 1$, then there is a wff B($y_1, \ldots, y_m$) of stage 0 such that A is B($u_1/y_1, \ldots, u_m/y_m$) where $u_1, \ldots, u_m$ are terms of stage n and at least one of them has height n.

The syntax of descriptive functions

We want to formalize uses of descriptive functions in our reasoning, too. We'd like to formalize "the wife of y" as "the x ((— is a wife of —) (x, y))". To do this we need to allow for variables other than x to be free in A in "the x A(x)". Then "the x" will bind x in that formula and the other free variables in it will continue to be free, so we can have open the-terms. The only modification to the syntax for descriptive names is in the definition of "term" at stage $n + 1$ of the formal language.

Terms
    a. Every term of stage *n* is a term of stage *n* + 1.
       It is *closed* if it is closed at stage *n* ; otherwise it is open.

    b. If A is a wff of stage *n* and not of stage *m* for any *m* < *n*, and *x* is free in A, then "the *x* A" is a term of stage *n* + 1. Every occurrence of *x* in "the *x* A(*x*)" is *bound*. All free occurrences of other variables in A are *free* in "the *x* A". The term "the *x* A" is *closed* if there is no variable free in it; otherwise it is *open*. The *scope* of the operator "the *x*" in "the *x* A" is A(*x*).

A term *u* is *free for an occurence* of a variable *x* in A iff both:

i. The occurrence of *x* is free.

ii. If *y* is free in *u*, then the occurrence of *x* does not lie within the scope of some occurrence of $\forall y$ or $\exists y$ or the *y*.

In that case A(*u*/*x*) is A with every free occurrence of *x* replaced with *u*.

Aside: *Defining the language of descriptive names*
Donald Kalish and Richard Montague in *Logic: Techniques of Formal Reasoning* give a formal language for their iota-operator without such levels of languages. They say:

> The characterization of *terms* and *formulas* must be somewhat more involved than before, for the following reason. The grammatical function of descriptive phrases (as of their English counterparts) is to produce terms from formulas. Consequently, not only may terms occur within formulas, but also formulas within terms. The best way of introducing the present notions of term and formula is, it seems, to characterize them simultaneously. Like earlier characterizations the one below is to be regarded as exhaustive; that is, nothing is to be regarded as a term or formula unless it can be reached by successive applications of the following clauses. p. 235

Then to a list of the other ways to create terms and formulas they add (p. 236): "If φ is a formula and α is a variable, then ιαφ is a term". This is not a definition. We might construe it as characterizing the smallest class of concatenations of symbols closed under those operations. But that kind of definition has two defects. First, it introduces substantial metaphysical assumptions about the nature of sets, assumptions that are unneeded in the development of the theory. And second, it does not allow for proofs about the system by induction on the length of a formula, especially for the issue of stability of references and truth-values (p. 179 here). Similar comments apply to the more general treatment of variable binding term operators in John Corcoran, William Hatcher, and John Herring, "Variable Binding Term Operators".

    It may be that the work in this and the next two chapters is an example of some more general theory of "determiners" or "quantifiers" developed by others as surveyed in Johan van Benthem, *Essays in Logical Semantics* and Dag Westerståhl, "Quantifiers in Formal and Natural Languages". But I have not seen any application of those metalogical structural studies that are like the systems here.

38 Semantics for Classical Predicate Logic with Descriptive Names and Descriptive Functions

Descriptive names

We start with a model for the language of classical predicate with equality in which every name refers. Now we must decide what semantic values a descriptive name "the x A(x)" will have, where x is the only variable free in A.

If there is one and only one object in the universe that satisfies A(x), then the internal structure of that term, that is the description A(x), points us to that object, and the semantic value of "the x A(x)" is completely determined: what is true of it is what is true of that object.

If there is more than one object in the universe that satisfies A(x), then the description A(x) points ambiguously, so we can't use "the x A(x)" to refer. Nor is there reason to accept one rather than another of the things that satisfy A(x) as determining which predications "the x A(x)" satisfies. So for any atomic wff in which "the x A(x)" appears, it is not clear what it would mean for it to be true. So we treat it as we do all nonsense: atomic predications in which it appears are false.

If there is no object that satisfies A(x), then we can't use "the x A(x)" to refer. Is there any reason to accept as true a proposition in which it appears? We can't even assume that it satisfies its own description. After all, the formalizations of all the following would then be true:

> The square circle is a square.
> The square circle is a circle.
> $\forall x ((-\text{ is a square}) (x) \to \neg (-\text{ is a circle}) (x))$

The descriptive name "the square circle" is not referring because it's contradictory, so if it satisfied its own description, the whole system would be inconsistent. Yet if a descriptive name doesn't satisfy even its own description, what would count as an acceptable (much less good) reason for saying that any other predication using it should be true? So we'll treat any atomic wff in which a non-referring term "the x A(x)" appears as nonsense and hence false.

But then the following will be false in any model in which the universe contains just all living dogs:

> the x ((- is a dog) (x)) ≡ the x ((- is a dog) (x))

That seems acceptable. But the following will be false, too:

> $\forall x ((-\text{ is a dog}) (x))$

That's because "(- is a dog) (x)" is false when we substitute a non-referring descriptive name for x. Yet we don't want to falsify assertions about things that do exist by introducing descriptive names. We want to evaluate a wff $\forall x$ B(x) just as we did before: it's true iff B(x) is true of every object in the universe, the classical evaluation:

178   Chapter 38

$v_\sigma(\forall x \, B) = T$ iff for every assignment of references τ such that
$$\tau \sim_x \sigma, \; v_\tau(B) = T$$

If a descriptive name does refer, then the object it refers to is in the universe, and that is taken into account by this evaluation. Instead of universal instantiation, we'll have universal instantiation for referring terms only. Thus, when we add a term "the $x \, A(x)$", if the semantics determine that there is a unique object in the universe that satisfies $A(x)$, that object gives the semantic value of "the $x \, A(x)$". Otherwise, "the $x \, A(x)$" is nil.

Non-referring names are nil Every non-referring name is *nil*: any atomic predication in which it figures is false, and it has no effect on the evaluation of a universal quantifier.

Similarly, we evaluate $\exists x \, B$ as in classical predicate logic:

$v_\sigma(\exists x \, B) = T$ iff for some assignment of references τ such that
$$\tau \sim_x \sigma, \; v_\tau(B) = T$$

So everything in the semantics will be determined by the model we choose for the base language L.

The formal semantics

We start with a realization L of the language of classical logic with equality and a model M of L. We now define by simultaneous and repeated induction the assignments of references and valuations based on those for the extended language L* of the previous chapter.

Stage 0

We label L as L_0. With M we have a complete collection of assignments of references where every name refers. We also have a collection of valuations based on those that are extended to all wffs.

Stage n + 1

Assignments of references

We extend each assignment of references σ_n of stage n to all terms of the language of stage $n + 1$, denoting the new assignment as σ_{n+1}.

For every variable x, $\sigma_{n+1}(x) = \sigma_n(x) = \sigma_0(x)$.

For every atomic name c, $\sigma_{n+1}(c) = \sigma_n(c) = \sigma_0(x)$.

For every term of the form "the $x \, A(x)$":

σ_{n+1} (the $x \, A(x)$) = $\mathfrak{a}$ iff for all τ_n: $v_{\tau_n} \models A(x)$ iff $\tau_n(x) = \mathfrak{a}$.

In this case we say "the $x \, A(x)$" is *referring* and has *reference* $\mathfrak{a}$.

σ_{n+1} (the $x \, A(x)$) is not defined otherwise; it is *non-referring*.

Valuations We extend all valuations v_{σ_n} of stage n to all atomic wffs $A(u_1, \ldots, u_m)$ of the language of stage $n + 1$, including the equality predicate.

If for some i, $\sigma_{n+1}(u_i)$ is not defined, then $\mathsf{v}_{\sigma_{n+1}} \not\models A(u_1, \ldots, u_m)$.

Otherwise, proceeding from $i = 1$ to m, define v_i by:

If u_i is a variable or simple name, let v_i be u_i.

Then, proceeding from the left, if u_i is a the-term of height 1, let v_i be the least variable that does not appear in $A(u_1, \ldots, u_m)$ and is not v_j for any $j < i$. Then if all the-terms of height $k < n$ have been assigned a variable, proceeding from the left, if u_i is a the-term of height $k + 1$, let v_i be the least variable that does not appear in $A(u_1, \ldots, u_m)$ and is not v_j for any $j < i$.

Let τ_0 be an assignment of references of stage 0 such that for each i, $\tau_0(v_i) = \sigma_{n+1}(u_i)$ and τ_0 agrees with σ_{n+1} on all other variables. Then $\mathsf{v}_{\sigma_{n+1}} \models A(u_1, \ldots, u_m)$ iff $\mathsf{v}_{\tau_0} \models A(v_1/u_1, \ldots, v_m/u_m)$

These valuations are extended inductively to compound wffs of stage $n + 1$ by the usual definition for classical predicate logic (p. 25).

Hence, if A is a closed wff, then for all σ_n and τ_n, $\mathsf{v}_{\sigma_n} \models A$ iff $\mathsf{v}_{\tau_n} \models A$. So for any closed wff A we can use the notation $\models_n A$ to mean that for some σ_n, and hence for all σ_n, $\mathsf{v}_{\sigma_n} \models A$.

I'll adopt the following notation for assignments of references:

$\gamma(u)\!\downarrow$ means that γ assigns an object of the universe to u.

$\gamma(u)\!\updownarrow$ means no object is assigned to u by γ.

$\gamma(u) \approx \rho(v)$ means either $\gamma(u)\!\downarrow$ and $\rho(v)\!\downarrow$ and $\gamma(u) = \rho(v)$,
or both $\gamma(u)\!\updownarrow$ and $\rho(v)\!\updownarrow$.

We read "$\downarrow$" as "is defined" and "$\updownarrow$" as "is not defined".

Before we complete the definition of the model for L*, we need a lemma.

Lemma Stability of references and truth-values

a. If "the x B(x)" is a term of stage n, then:

$\sigma_{n+1}(\text{the } x\ B(x))\!\downarrow = \mathsf{a}$ iff $\sigma_n(\text{the } x\ B(x))\!\downarrow = \mathsf{a}$

b. For every wff A of stage n, for every σ_n, $\mathsf{v}_{\sigma_{n+1}} \models A$ iff $\mathsf{v}_{\sigma_n} \models A$.

Proof We induct on n. For $n = 0$, (a) is true because there are no such terms. We show (b) by induction on the length of A. It is true for atomic wffs because every term u in A is a variable or name, and for those $\sigma_1(u) = \sigma_0(u)$. Then it is true for compound wffs because the evaluation of them at stage 1 is the same as at stage 0.

Now suppose that $n \geq 1$ and B(x) is a wff of stage $m < n$, and "the x B(x)" is a term of stage n. We then have:

$\sigma_{n+1}(\underline{\text{the}}\ x\ B(x))\downarrow = \mathbf{o}$

iff for all τ_n, $\mathsf{v}_{\tau_n} \vDash B(x)$ iff $\tau_n(x) = \mathbf{o}$

iff (by induction on part (b)), for all τ_m, $\mathsf{v}_{\tau_m} \vDash B(x)$ iff $\tau_m(x) = \mathbf{o}$

iff $\sigma_{m+1}(\underline{\text{the}}\ x\ B(x))\downarrow = \mathbf{o}$

iff (by induction on part (a)) $\sigma_n(\underline{\text{the}}\ x\ B(x))\downarrow = \mathbf{o}$

This shows further that if u is non-referring at stage n, then u is non-referring at stage $n + 1$.

To show (b), we induct on the length of A. If A is atomic, by (a) the evaluation of A is the same at stage $n + 1$ as at stage n. Then it is true for compound wffs because the evaluation of them at stage $n + 1$ is the same as at stage n. ∎

Now we can complete the definition of the model M^* for L^*.

Assignments of references and valuations for the language L^*

By the stability of references and truth-values, we can define for each assignment of references σ_0,

$\sigma^*(u) \approx \sigma_n(u)$ for the least n such that u is defined at stage n.

u has *reference* $\mathbf{o}$ iff $\sigma^*(u)\downarrow = \mathbf{o}$.

u is *non-referring* iff $\sigma^*(u)\uparrow$.

$\mathsf{v}_{\sigma^*}(A) = \mathsf{v}_{\sigma_n}(A)$ for the least n such that A is defined at stage n.

For every closed wff A, $\mathsf{v}(A) = T$ iff for all σ^*, $\mathsf{v}_{\sigma^*}(A) = T$.

Note that M^* is completely determined by the model M of the base language L. Note also that in these models the equality predicate is evaluated as the identity on the universe: $\mathsf{v}_{\sigma^*} \vDash u \equiv v$ iff $\sigma^*(u)\downarrow = \sigma^*(v)\downarrow$.

Descriptive functions

Given "x is a son of y", we can form "$\underline{\text{the}}\ x\ (x\ \text{is a son of}\ y)$". This formalizes the function which for every object $\mathbf{o}$ in the universe yields the object that is the son of $\mathbf{o}$ if there is just one such object and otherwise is undefined. The discussion in the previous section carries over here by taking all talk of a term "$\underline{\text{the}}\ x\ A(x)$" having reference or being non-referring to be relative to particular assignments of references to the variables other than x in $A(x)$.

For the logic, we have the formal language of descriptive names and descriptive functions. For the formal semantics, the only modification is in the definition of assignments of references at stage $n + 1$.

Assignments of references

If u is a term of stage 0, then $\sigma_{n+1}(u) = \sigma_n(u)$.

If u is a term of the form "the x A(x)" then:

σ_{n+1}(the x A(x)) = ⊙ iff for every τ_n such that $\tau_n \sim_x \sigma_n$:
$$\vDash_{\tau_n} A \text{ iff } \tau_n(x) = ⊙.$$

In this case we say that "the x A(x)" is *referring with respect to* (the assignments made by) σ_{n+1} and that its reference is ⊙, or that ⊙ is *the value of* "the x A(x)" when the variables in "the x A(x)" are given references by σ_{n+1}.

σ_{n+1}(the A(x))↓ otherwise.

In this case we say that "the x A(x)" is *non-referring with respect to* σ_{n+1} or that σ_{n+1} assigns no value to "the x A(x)".

The proof of the stability of references and truth-values is as before with the insertion of the clause "such that $\tau_n \sim_x \sigma_n$" in the displayed equivalences.

In these models, too, the equality predicate is evaluated as the identity on the universe: $\vDash_{\sigma*} u \equiv v$ iff $\sigma*(u)\downarrow = \sigma*(v)\downarrow$.

Descriptive names and descriptive functions with predicate modifiers
The extension of this system to allow for predicate modifiers and internal conjunctions and disjunctions requires only taking a different base language and adding the semantic conditions on atomic predications for those.

To allow for internal conjunctions of terms requires a more complicated definition of the formal language, and I have not attempted that.

Aside: Free logics
A *free logic* is a logic in which the universal quantifier as well as the existential quantifier are interpreted as in classical predicate logic but some singular term(s) may fail to refer or refer to some object(s) outside of the universe.

A *negative free* logic is a free logic that classifies every atomic formula that contains a non-referring term as false. So the system presented here is a negative free logic. In contrast, a *postive free logic* has semantics that allow some atomic formulas that contain non-referring names to be true. And a *neutral free logic* is a free logic that takes every atomic formula in which a non-referring name appears to be truth-valueless. For a general discussion, see John Nolt, "Free Logic".

39 An Axiomatization of Classical Predicate Logic with Descriptive Names and Descriptive Functions

I. Propositional axioms

The axiom schemes of classical propositional logic in $L(\neg, \rightarrow, \wedge, \vee)$, where A, B, C are replaced by wffs of L* and the universal closure is taken.

II. Axioms governing $\forall$

1. a. $\forall \ldots (\forall x (A \rightarrow B) \rightarrow (\forall x A \rightarrow \forall x B))$ *distribution of $\forall$*
   if x is free in both A and B

   b. $\forall \ldots (\forall x (A \rightarrow B) \rightarrow (\forall x A \rightarrow B))$
   if x is free in A and not free in B

   c. $\forall \ldots (\forall x (A \rightarrow B) \rightarrow (A \rightarrow \forall x B))$
   if x is free in B and not free in A

2. $\forall \ldots (\forall x \forall y A \rightarrow \forall y \forall x A)$ *commutativity of $\forall$*

3.* $\forall \ldots (\forall x A(x) \wedge \exists x (x \equiv u)) \rightarrow A(u/x))$ *universal instantiation for referring terms*
   where u is free for x in A

III. Axioms governing the relation between $\forall$ and $\exists$

4. a. $\forall \ldots (\exists x A \rightarrow \neg \forall x \neg A)$

   b. $\forall \ldots (\neg \forall x \neg A \rightarrow \exists x A)$

Axioms for equality

5. a. $\forall x (x \equiv x)$ *identity*

   b.* $\exists x (x \equiv c)$ *atomic names are referring*
   for every atomic name symbol c

6. $\forall \ldots \forall x \forall y (x \equiv y \rightarrow (A(x) \rightarrow A(y/x)))$ *extensionality*
   where y replaces some but not necessarily all occurrences of x in A

Axioms for non-referring terms

8. $\forall \ldots ((A(u/x) \wedge \exists x (x \equiv u)) \rightarrow \exists x A(x))$ *existential generalization for referring terms*

9. $\forall \ldots (\neg \exists x (x \equiv u) \rightarrow \neg A(u_1, \ldots u, \ldots u_n))$ *non-referring descriptive names take falsity as default*
   for n-ary atomic wffs A and terms $u_1, \ldots, u, \ldots, u_n$

Axioms for the-terms

10. $\forall \ldots [\exists x\, A(x) \wedge \forall x\, \forall y\, (A(x) \wedge A(y/x) \to (x \equiv y))]$
    $\leftrightarrow \exists z\, (z \equiv \underline{\text{the}}\, x\, A(x))$ *referring descriptions yield referring terms*
    where y is the least variable not appearing in A

11. $\forall \ldots \exists z\, (z \equiv \underline{\text{the}}\, x\, A(x)) \to A(\underline{\text{the}}\, x\, A(x))$ *referring descriptive terms satisfy their own description*

Rule   *modus ponens* for closed wffs

In summary, the changes from the axiom system of classical predicate logic with equality are:

- Universal instantiation for referring terms replaces universal instantiaion.

- Axiom scheme 5b* is added to ensure that atomic names refer.

- Existential generalization for referring terms is added.

- An axiom scheme is added that nil terms use falsity as the default truth-value.

- Two schemes are added relating the-terms to their internal structure.

When we add function-names to classical predicate logic with equality, we need to add a restriction on the semantics that the application of function names is extensional and then add a corresponding axiom scheme. Those are not needed here because the extensionality of applications of descriptive functions is guaranteed by the extensionality of atomic predications.

The proof that classical predicate logic with descriptive functions is strongly complete is exactly the same as the proof that classical predicate logic with descriptive names is strongly complete, which is given in Appendix 7.

40 Examples of Formalizing

Example 1 *The cat that scratched Zoe is a male.*

(— is a male) (<u>the</u> *x* [(— is a cat) (*x*) ∧ (— scratched —) (*x*, Zoe)])

Analysis If there is no cat that scratched Zoe, the example is false. If, as is more likely, there is more than one cat that scratched Zoe, the example is also false.

Example 2 *The cat that belongs to some student and which scratched Zoe is a male.*

(— is a male) (<u>the</u> *x* [(— is a cat) (*x*) ∧ (— scratched —) (*x*, Zoe) ∧
∃*z* ((— belongs to —) (*x*, *z*) ∧ (— is a student) (*z*))]

Analysis Here the description used in the previous example is refined. There is no ambiguity about the scope of "some" in this formalization: it is part of the description and so falls within the scope of the <u>the</u>-operator.

Example 3 *Someone loves the cat that scratched Zoe.*

∃*z* (— loves —) (*z*, <u>the</u> *x* [(— is a cat) (*x*) ∧ (— scratched —) (*x*, Zoe)])

Analysis Here the existential quantifer is outside the scope of the <u>the</u>-operator.

Example 4 *The cat that scratched Zoe is a male.*
Therefore, *there is a cat that scratched Zoe.*

$$\frac{(-\text{ is a male}) (\underline{\text{the}}\ x\ [\ (-\text{ is a cat})\ (x)\ \wedge\ (-\text{ scratched }-)\ (x, \text{Zoe})\ ]\ )}{\exists\ x\ (\ (-\text{ is a cat})\ (x)\ \wedge\ (-\text{ scratched }-)\ (x, \text{Zoe})\ )}$$

Analysis The inference is valid. Though a <u>the</u>-term can be non-referring, on the assumption that an atomic predication in which it appears is true, it refers.

Example 5 *The cat that scratched Zoe is not a female.*
Therefore, *there is a cat that scratched Zoe.*

$$\frac{\neg(\ (-\text{ is a female}) (\underline{\text{the}}\ x\ [\ (-\text{ is a cat})\ (x)\ \wedge\ (-\text{ scratched }-)\ (x, \text{Zoe})\ ]\ )}{\exists\ x\ (\ (-\text{ is a cat})\ (x)\ \wedge\ (-\text{ scratched }-)\ (x, \text{Zoe})\ )}$$

Analysis The inference is invalid. It could be that the premise is true because the descriptive name does not refer.

If we were to read "not" in the example as negating only the predicate, as in Chapter 21, then we would have:

(~(— is a female) (<u>the</u> *x* [(— is a cat) (*x*) ∧ (— scratched —) (*x*, Zoe)])

Since "~(— is a female)" is atomic, the inference would be valid.

Example 6 *The cat that scratched Zoe is not a female.*
Something is not a female if and only if it is a male.
Therefore, *there is a cat that scratched Zoe.*

¬ (— is a female) (<u>the</u> *x* [(— is a cat) (*x*) ∧ (— scratched —) (*x*, Zoe)])
∀*x* (¬ (— is a female) (*x*) ↔ (— is a male) (*x*))
───
∃ *x* ((— is a cat) (*x*) ∧ (— scratched —) (*x*, Zoe))

Analysis Again the inference is invalid because the descriptive name might not refer. You might think that we could deduce from the premises:

(— is a male) (<u>the</u> *x* [(— is a cat) (*x*) ∧ (— scratched —) (*x*, Zoe)])

But universal instantiation applies only to referring terms, and the premises do not guarantee that "<u>the</u> *x* [(— is a cat) (*x*) ∧ (— scratched —) (*x*, Zoe)]" refers.

Example 7 *The wife of John is the wife of an American.*

(— is an American) (<u>the</u> *x* (— is a wife —) (*x*, John))

Analysis We cannot treat "is" here as the equality predicate because "The wife of John ≡ the wife of an American" could be false if "wife of an American" is non-referring, even were "the wife of John" referring and the example true.

Example 8 *There is only one dog that is loved by all friends of Dick.*

∃! *x* [(— is a dog) (*x*) ∧
    ∀*w* ((— is a friend of —) (*w*, Dick) → (— loves —) (*w*, *x*))]

Analysis Conventions on formalizing given in Volume 0 direct us to formalize the passive as active so that we don't have two unrelated predicates: "— loves —" and "— is loved by —".

Example 9 *Some dog is the one that's loved by all friends of Dick.*

Formalization as for the previous example.

Analysis The word "the" is not used in the example to form a name but only to indicate uniqueness.

Example 10 *The dog that is loved by all friends of Dick is Spot.*

<u>the</u> *x* [(— is a dog) (*x*) ∧ ∀*w* ((— is a friend of —) (*w*, Dick)
    → (— loves —) (*w*, *x*))] ≡ Spot

Analysis Here "the" is being used to create a name.

186   Chapter 40

Example 11 The person who hit the father of the cat that belongs to Suzy and which scratched him hates cats.

$\forall w \, (\, (- \text{ is a cat}) \, (w) \to (- \text{ hates } -) \, (c, w) \,)$

where c is:

the z [$(- \text{ is a person}) \, (z) \wedge (- \text{ hit } -) \, (z, \text{the } x \, (\, (- \text{ is a father of } -)$
  $(x, \text{the } y \, (\, (- \text{ is a cat}) \, (y) \wedge (- \text{ belongs to } -) \, (y, \text{Suzy})$
  $\wedge \, (- \text{ scratched } -) \, (y, z))))]$

Analysis I understand "him" to refer to the person who is asserted to have hit the father. I'll let you formalize that "him" is meant to indicate the person is male.

In the example "cats" is to be understood as "all cats", and we use the standard method of formalizing "hates all cats". The rest of the formalization is routine, just more complex because of the the-term embedded within a the-term. Using Russell's method we'd have a very much more complex formalization, assuming we could agree on the scope of the existential quantifiers in it.

Example 12 The nice cat is a nice cat.

$(\, (- \text{ is a cat}) / \text{nice}) \, (\text{the } x \, [\, (-\text{is a cat/nice}) \, (x) \,] \,)$

Analysis With universe all living creatures, "the x [$(-$is a cat/nice$) \, (x)$]" is non-referring, so the example is false. Even if we didn't make the simplifying assumption that falsity is the default truth-value for atomic predications, there's no reason we should accept that this claim, which has the form A(the x A(x)), is true because the the-term is non-referring.

Example 13 The nice cat is not a nice cat.

$\neg \, (\, (- \text{ is a cat}) / \text{nice}) \, (\text{the } x \, [\, (-\text{is a cat/nice}) \, (x) \,] \,)$

Analysis The example, which has the form $\neg$ A(the x A(x)), is true since the the-term is nil and atomic predications in which it appears are evaluated as false.

Because we know (or when you discover) that there is no nice cat, we won't reason with the descriptive name "the nice cat", so this example will have no place in our reasoning.[52] It and its evaluation are simply part of how we ensure that we can separate syntax from semantics.

Example 14 $\dfrac{(- \text{ is a dog}) \, (c) \vee \neg \, (- \text{ is a dog}) \, (c)}{\exists y \, (y \equiv c)}$

where c is "the x [$(- \text{ is a dog}) \, (x) \vee \neg \, (- \text{ is a dog}) \, (x)$]"

Analysis The premise also has the form A(the x A(x)) and is true, since A has the form of a tautology. But unlike Example 10, from the assumption of its truth we

---

[52] Some people mistakenly believe that the term is nil because there is more than one nice cat.

cannot conclude that "the x A(x)" refers because the premise is not atomic. The inference is invalid.

Example 15 *The morning star is the evening star.*

the morning star ≡ the evening star

$c_0 \equiv c_1$

Analysis This looks like an example of two descriptive names being used to pick out the same object, which we know is Venus. But we can't formalize this using:

the x [(— is a star/morning) (x)]

This does not refer: there are lots of stars in the morning, and even if there were only one, it wouldn't be Venus because Venus isn't a star. If we wish to consider "the morning star" as a descriptive name, it would have to be shorthand for something like "the thing that appears to be a star but is brighter than anything else in the sky at dawn", and it isn't clear that we could formalize that because "— appears to be" isn't extensional. The names "the morning star" and "the evening star" have to be taken as atomic, with meaning axioms used to circumscribe their use to respect appropriate inferences.

Example 16 *The victor at Jena was the loser at Waterloo.*

the victor at Jena ≡ the loser at Waterloo

$c_2 \equiv c_3$

Analysis This, too, appears to be an example of two descriptive names being used to pick out one object, Napoleon. But "the x ((— is a victor)/at Jena) (x)" is at best unclear. We'd have to understand "at Jena" to mean "at the battle of Jena" and then formalize the first name taking battles to be things.

Example 17 *The first cat that scratched Zoe was a female.*

Analysis Zoe has been working at the local animal shelter and has been scratched by many cats. So "the cat that scratched Zoe" is a non-referring descriptive name. However, "the first cat that scratched Zoe" does refer. How do we formalize it?

Here "first" means "first in time", so we should rewrite the example as "the cat that scratched Zoe before any other cat scratched Zoe is a female". Similarly, consider:

the first can on the shelf
— this is "first" in location

the second biggest dog at Arf's ranch
— this is second in size

the ninth smartest woman in Zoe's history class
— this is ninth in intelligence

These uses of ordinals are ways of counting, and as ways of counting they assume some relationship (temporal, spatial, perceptual, intellectual, ...) that we use to distinguish things with pointing. Each can be eliminated by taking any proposition in which they appear and rewriting it to take account of that relationship and the comparison, though for some we will need ways of formalizing temporal and spatial comparisons. To do that we need to be able to formalize cardinal uses of counting numbers in predicate logic. This we can do. With only the resources of classical predicate logic without modifiers we can formalize addition and subtraction and a great deal more of arithmetic with counting numbers, including defining quantifiers "$\exists!_n x$" such that when A is a unary predicate "$\exists!_n x\, A(x)$" is true iff there are exactly n things that satisfy A, as described in Chapter 9 of Volume 0. For example, we can formalize "the third tallest man" as:

the x [($-$ is a man) $(x) \land$
$\exists!_2 y\, ((-$ is a man$)\, (y) \land (-$ is taller than $-)\, (y, x)) $]

Until we come up with examples where ordinals are not eliminable in this way, we can treat ordinals not as adjectives but as shorthand for comparisons that can be expanded.

Example 18 *The man who is king is crazy.*

($-$ is crazy) [the x (($-$ is a man) $(x) \land (-$ is a king) (x))]

Analysis The example doesn't say "the king", so we can't import our usual understanding of "king" to require uniqueness of an object satisfying "$-$ is a king". There might also be a woman or a dog that is king.

Example 19 *Dick's apple tree is tall.*

Analysis The possessive here indicates uniqueness. We have two ways we can formalize such possessives.
One is to formalize "*a*'s X" as:

(a)   the x [($-$ is an X/of (a)) (x)]

Or we can use the binary predicate "$-$ belongs to $-$":

(b)   the x [($-$belongs to $-)\, (x, a) \land (-$ is an X) (a)]

The second will not work if instead of "$-$ is an X" we have "$-$ was an X" unless we have resources in our syntax and semantics to formalize a time-simultaneous "and". Moreover, it can be wrong to use "$-$ belongs to $-$" in some cases: "June is John's wife" means possession in only the most general sense, not that June is a wife that belongs to John. Even though (b) does not require predicate modifiers as (a) does, (a) seems better as a general approach. Using (a) we formalize the example as:

Chapter 40

(— is a tree / tall) (the *x* [((— is a tree) / apple) / of (Dick)) (*x*)])

It's tempting to think that the possessive is a function by itself. We have:

Dick's apple tree
Tom's friend (not a referring name because not unique)
Dick's elephant (not a referring name because there is no such object)

But if "—'s —" is a function, it's an odd one because the second blank isn't filled with a name but with a description.[53]

Example 20 *June is the gorgeous redheaded wife of John.*

June ≡ the *x* [((— is a woman) / (gorgeous & redheaded) &
(— is a wife) / of (John)) (*x*)]

Analysis Example 14 of Chapter 27 is:

June is a gorgeous redheaded Christian woman.

We said that the adjectives are meant as conjoined for a comparison to all women, not all Christian women, and formalized this as:

(((— is a woman) / (gorgeous & redheaded & Christian)) (June)

Here we have an equality being asserted:

(a)   June ≡ the gorgeous redheaded wife of John

As before, we want "gorgeous" and "redheaded" to be conjoined. And again they are used not for comparison to all wives, and certainly not to all wives of John, since if (a) is true, there is only one. The implicit comparison is to all women. As we've seen in previous examples, the criterion of formalizing that enjoins us to use no new categorematic words that do not appear in the original will have to be violated when formalizing propositions in which an adjective is used for comparison to a class that is clear, though implicit, in this case women. Allowing for that, and using the method of formalizing possessives of the last example, we have the formalization above.

Example 21 *Tom scaled the cliff.*

Analysis The phrase "the cliff" looks like a descriptive name. It might be if we are using it when we're talking about a particular cliff we all know about, which seems to be the case in the example. Then we could formalize the example as

(— scaled —) (Tom, the *x* [(— is a cliff) (*x*)])

Or "the cliff" might be used to refer because earlier in our conversation or our

---

[53] Some languages have two words for "has" or "belongs to". The *inalienable* "has" is used for that which one has in some integral sense, like you have your arm. The *alienable* "has" is used for that which you have but isn't integral to you, like you have your car. Our formalizations use "of (—)" for the two kinds of possession.

writing we'd already described the cliff, in which case that description should be incorporated into the formalization of "the cliff".

Or we might be standing in the mountains surrounded by many cliffs, and in our discussion we've been talking about one particular cliff that's right in front of us. Then we are using "the" as shorthand for the pointing we have implicitly accepted. In that case we can't take "the cliff" as a name unless it is supplemented in the language with a further predicate that makes explicit our method of pointing. Absent that, we can only coin a new name for that cliff, say, "Hergbut", and formalize the example as "Tom scaled Hergbut".

Rules concerning the use of "the" in English are very complicated. Explaining them to someone whose language has no such operator is next to impossible.[54] Criteria of formalization for the use of "the" will depend on the language of the reasoning that is being formalized.

Example 22   *There is a tree on the top of the cliff.*

Analysis   Suppose, as in the last example, we take "the cliff" as just semantic pointing, and we name that cliff as "Hergbut". Do we treat "the top of Hergbut" as a descriptive name, like "the dog of Dick"? We have to consider how we reason about parts of things, which is the subject of Appendix 6.

---

[54] A valiant effort is made by Rebecca E. Hayden, Dorothy W. Pilgrim, and Aurora Quiros Haggard in *Mastering American English*. See (the other) Richard Epstein, "The Definite Article, Accessibility, and the Construction of Referents" for a discussion of many uses of "the", some of which have no role in indicating a unique reference. That paper also discusses examples of uses of "the" where fiction and actual situations are considered in the same speech.

Non-Referring Simple Names

41 Names that Don't Refer

What is a name? It's a word we use to pick out some object. But that's not right, since we've seen descriptive names that don't pick out objects. Should they still be called names? Yes, for they are meant to pick out an object—it's just that the world (our model) is such that they don't. A name, it seems, is a word we use that is meant to pick out a single object.

But that's not right, for we use the name "Sherlock Holmes" and we know that there's no object in the world that it picks out. Yet "Sherlock Holmes" is meant to and does pick out a unique object in the stories we read that were written by Arthur Conan Doyle. In those stories there are people, and horses, and houses, and dogs, and rocks, and trees, and much else that we find in our everyday world. The stories talk about them as if they were real. All our reasoning about those stories can be done in classical predicate logic with equality, treating those objects as if they were real. Whatever methods we have for picking out people, horses, houses, dogs, and rocks can be supposed to hold in those stories, too. It could have been that way. We take as universe for the stories all the (kinds of) things that are mentioned in the stories as well as anything else that we suppose would have existed at the time of the stories if those stories had been true.

This is how we can reason about any possible way the world could be. We postulate what things or kinds of things are meant to exist, we postulate what is taken as true, and we use classical predicate logic with equality, so long as the assumptions of classical predicate logic hold in that "world": the world is made up at least in part of things; things can be distinguished for the purposes of indicating a reference for a name or temporary name; . . . . This is how we show that "Juney barks, therefore Juney is a dog" is not valid by postulating a way the world could be, a model, in which "Juney" picks out a seal. Sure, Juney neither was nor is a seal, but that doesn't matter so long as our description is consistent.

If our talk about fiction and our talk about possibilities makes any sense, then we can use classical predicate logic with equality plus descriptive names and descriptive functions to make deductions for those ways the world could be. Indeed, we could say that the talk makes sense just to the extent that we can provide models of it in classical predicate logic.

But it's not fiction when we ask whether there was a person called "Homer" who wrote *The Illiad*. We'd like to put down all we know about "him" in order to investigate whether "he" existed: Homer wrote the *Illiad*; Homer wrote the *Odyssey*; Homer spoke Greek; Homer was a man; Homer was not Achilles; . . . . We also put down what we know about ancient Greece and Troy and the history of the *Illiad* and the *Odyssey* as well as what we know about oral transmissions of sagas. Then we reason using these sentences to see if we can conclude that Homer did indeed exist.

In classical predicate logic the only way we can make existence assertions is by using the existence operator to say that there is something that satisfies a particular predicate. So the best we can do to formalize the pure existential claim that Homer exists is to use "$\exists x \, (x \equiv \text{Homer})$". But that's true in every model because of the assumption that names refer. We can't formalize "Homer doesn't exist" as a true proposition in classical predicate logic.

We could use "Homer" as an abbreviation for a descriptive name "the x H(x)" made out of the claims we believe are true of Homer. Then we can reason with that to try to deduce whether it refers, that is whether Homer existed, using the wff "$\exists z \, (z \equiv \text{the } x \, H(x))$". People who disagree with what we've assumed can make up their descriptive name based on what they believe.[55]

Or we could postulate a model of classical predicate logic in which "Homer" refers in order to see if a contradiction follows. This would be to treat "Homer existed" as a metalogical claim. The things in the universe of the model are the things and kinds of things we suppose existed at that time.

But sometimes we reason using both names that do refer alongside names that don't or might not refer, as when we talk of both Aristotle and Homer, or when we use both "Sherlock Holmes" and "Arthur Conan Doyle" in reasoning about how the stories were written. It would be odd at best to use classical predicate logic to reason in those situations, for we would have to accept models in which the universe contains both "real" things and "fictional" things. Perhaps that's not different from saying that Juney could have been a seal while "Richard L. Epstein" refers to me.

Or perhaps we could only mention the name "Sherlock Holmes" rather than using it, saying "Arthur Conan Doyle wrote a novel in which the name 'Sherlock Holmes' was used". But then we'd have to allow for a predicate "— is a name" and a universe for parts of speech, hoping to avoid self-referential paradoxes.

There is an easier way to formalize such reasoning that does not lead us into either metaphysical or syntactic complications. We treat "Sherlock Holmes" as a name, not worrying whether it refers, and, as in any model, say which atomic sentences using that name are true. Thus, we could postulate that "Sherlock Holmes was a detective" and "Sherlock Holmes was a man". Or with "Homer", we could take as true in our model "Homer was Greek" and "Homer wrote Greek", without worrying about whether the name actually refers. Then we see if we can deduce "$\exists z \, (z \equiv \text{Homer})$". We can use "Pegasus" as a name and postulate atomic sentences that use that name as true, such as "Pegasus was a horse" and "Pegasus had wings" while also postulating that "$\neg \exists z \, (z \equiv \text{Pegasus})$" is true.

This is what we'll do in the next chapter, allowing for non-referring simple names that do not refer yet which are not nil. Then we'll look at examples of formalizing using that system. After that, we'll see how mathematicians use non-referring names and extend our system to allow for formalizing their reasoning.

---

[55] See Fred Kroon's "Causal Descriptivism" for a history and analysis of this view.

42 Classical Predicate Logic with Non-Referring Simple Names

We need a way to incorporate in semi-formal languages names that might not refer yet are meaningful. We can do so in a minimal way without changing the requirement that existential assertions are made only with the existential operator by using "$\exists x\,(x \equiv c)$" to assert that there is something to which the name c refers.

We start with the language of classical predicate logic with equality.

For the semantics, we allow that an assignment of references can fail to give a reference to a name c of the semi-formal language. As before, we'll write:

$\sigma(u)\downarrow$ to mean that σ assigns an object of the universe to u

$\sigma(u)\not\downarrow$ to mean no object is assigned to u by σ

$\sigma(u) \approx \tau(v)$ to mean either $\sigma(u)\downarrow$ and $\tau(v)\downarrow$ and $\sigma(u) = \tau(v)$,
 or both $\sigma(u)\not\downarrow$ and $\tau(v)\not\downarrow$

Assignments of references An assignment of references σ assigns to each variable an object of the universe: for all x, $\sigma(x)\downarrow$. For each name c, for all σ and τ, $\sigma(c) \approx \tau(c)$. If $\sigma(c)\not\downarrow$, we say that c *does not refer* or is a *non-referring name*.

We require the collection of assignments to be complete as before (p. 21).

We want to take the valuations of atomic predications as primitive, where an atomic predication has an indication of what the variables refer to but the names in it might not refer. As before, we want that it doesn't matter in predications how we name an object. But what about non-referring names?

With referring names, we say that "Marilyn Monroe" and "Norma Jeane Baker" refer to the same thing. But since we might not know if a name we are using actually refers to anything, we should say that "Marilyn Monroe" and "Norma Jeane Baker" are meant to refer to the same thing. Similarly, in investigating whether there is an object named by "Zeus", we can say that "Zeus" and "Jove" are meant to refer to the same thing. For any terms u and v, we want "$u \equiv v$" to be true in a model to mean that the terms are meant to refer to the same thing. Whether they do refer or not, one can be used for the other in any assertion without changing truth-values. Our interpretation of the equality predicate will codify this.

We'll require that if $\sigma(u)\downarrow$ and $\sigma(v)\downarrow$, then $\vDash_\sigma u \equiv v$ iff $\sigma(u) = \tau(v)$. If just one of $\sigma(u)$ and $\sigma(v)$ is defined, then the terms can't refer to the same thing, so $\nvDash_\sigma u \equiv v$. Assignments of references are meant to give interpretations to the variables while the interpretation of the names remain the same, so for any assignments σ and τ and names c and d, $\vDash_\sigma c \equiv d$ iff $\vDash_\tau c \equiv d$. Any term u, referring or not, can be substituted for itself, so we want for every term u, $\vDash_\sigma u \equiv u$. We also want, for example, if Zeus is the same as Jove, then Jove is the same as Zeus, and if Zeus is the same as Jove, and Jove is the same as Thor, then Zeus is the same as Thor. That is, the interpretation of the equality predicate should be reflexive, symmetric, and transitive. These are all the conditions we'll assume.

Restrictions on the evaluation of the equality predicate with non-referring names

i. If $\sigma(u)\downarrow$ and $\sigma(v)\downarrow$, then $\vDash_\sigma u \equiv v$ iff $\sigma(u) = \sigma(v)$.

ii. If one and only one of $\sigma(u)$ and $\sigma(v)$ is defined, then $\nvDash_\sigma u \equiv v$.

iii. If u and v are names, then $\vDash_\sigma u \equiv v$ iff $\vDash_\tau u \equiv v$.

iv. For all u, $\vDash_\sigma u \equiv u$.

v. For all u and v, $\vDash_\sigma u \equiv v$ iff $\vDash_\sigma v \equiv u$.

vi. For all u, v, and w, if $\vDash_\sigma u \equiv v$ and $\vDash_\sigma v \equiv w$, then $\vDash_\sigma u \equiv w$.

Any assignment of truth-values to equality predications that satisfy these conditions is acceptable in a model. This means that for a given semi-formal language and universe, the interpretation of "$\equiv$" on the universe remains constant only on the universe. We can take "Zeus $\equiv$ Jove" as true or as false. So *with non-referring names the equality predicate $\equiv$ is not fully logical*, though we'll still take it to be part of the formal language since we'll want it in every semi-formal language.

Note that if both $\sigma(u)\updownarrow$ and $\sigma(v)\updownarrow$, then u and v are names, so by virtue of (iii) we can write $\vDash u \equiv v$ to mean that one and hence all assignments of references evaluate "$u \equiv v$" as true, understanding "$\vDash$" relative to the particular model.

Any assignment of truth-values to the other atomic predications is acceptable for a model so long as it satisfies the extensionality condition.

Extensionality of atomic predications If A is an atomic wff, σ and τ are assignments of references, $u_1, \ldots, u_n$ are all the terms in A, and $v_1, \ldots, v_n$ are terms such that for each i, $\sigma(v_i) = \tau(u_i)$ or $\vDash v_i \equiv u_i$, then

$\vDash_\sigma A(u_1, \ldots, u_n)$ iff $\vDash_\tau A(v_1/u_1 \ldots, v_n/u_n)$.

Now we have to decide how to extend the valuations on atomic wffs to all wffs. Nothing in what we've done affects how we understand the connectives, so we'll use the usual classical interpretation of them. The existential quantifier is meant to formalize "there exists", and so we should use the same interpretation as we did before: $\vDash_\sigma \exists x A(x)$ iff for some τ such that $\tau \sim_x \sigma$, $\vDash_\tau A(x)$. Then if x is the only variable free in $A(x)$, the proposition $\exists x A(x)$ is true in a model iff there is some object in the universe of which $A(x)$ is true.

We said previously that by the assumption that predicates apply to objects, "x is a dog" is true or is false whenever a reference is given to x or a name is substituted for x. We can use that understanding for universal quantification here: $\forall x\, A(x)$ is true iff $A(x)$ is true no matter what reference is given to x and no matter what name is substituted for x. When all names refer, the latter clause is superfluous. But here it does affect the evaluation: with universe all people who have ever lived, "$\forall x\, (x$ is a person)" is false if "Zeus" is a non-referring name in the semi-formal language and "(Zeus is a person)" is false.

Evaluation of the universal quantifier for classical predicate logic with non-referring simple names

$\mathsf{v}_\sigma \vDash \forall x\, A(x)$ iff for every assignment of references τ such that $\tau \sim_x \sigma$, $\mathsf{v}_\tau \vDash A(x)$, and for every name c, $\mathsf{v}_\sigma \vDash A(c/x)$

Now we can define models and truth in a model.

Models of classical predicate logic with non-referring simple names
A *model* is:
- a realization of the language of predicate logic with equality;
- a universe, denoted by U;
- a complete collection of assignments of references for the realization and universe, where a name need not have a reference;
- valuations relative to those assignments of references for all atomic wffs satisfying the conditions for the equality predicate and the extensionality condition for atomic predications;
- the extension of those valuations to all wffs by the classical tables for $\neg, \vee, \wedge, \vee$, the classical evaluation of $\exists$, and the evaluation of the universal quantifier for classical predicate logic with non-referring names;
- the valuation v, defined by $\mathsf{v}(A) = \mathsf{T}$ in a model iff for every σ, $\mathsf{v}_\sigma(A) = \mathsf{T}$.

Extensionality for all wffs Let $u_1, \ldots, u_n$ be a list of all names in A and variables free in A. Let $v_1, \ldots, v_n$ be any terms such that for each i, v_i is free for u_i in A. Let σ, τ be any assignments of references such that for each i, $\sigma(v_i) = \tau(u_i)$ or $\vDash v_i \equiv u_i$. Then

$\mathsf{v}_\sigma \vDash A(u_1, \ldots, u_n)$ iff $\mathsf{v}_\tau \vDash A(v_1/u_1 \ldots, v_n/u_n)$.

Proof We proceed by induction on the length of A. If A has length 0 this is the condition of extensionality for atomic predications. Suppose that the theorem is true for all wffs of length $\leq m$ and A is of length $m + 1$. I'll leave to you the cases when A is of the form $\neg B$, $B \wedge C$, $B \vee C$, or $B \rightarrow C$.

Suppose that A is $\forall x\, B$. Then:

$\nu_\sigma \vDash \forall x\, B(x, u_1, \ldots, u_n)$

    iff for every $\gamma \sim_x \sigma$, $\nu_\gamma \vDash B(x, u_1, \ldots, u_n)$
        and for every c, $\nu_\sigma \vDash B(c, u_1, \ldots, u_n)$

    iff for every $\delta \sim_x \tau$, $\nu_\delta \vDash B(x, v_1/u_1, \ldots, v_n/u_n)$
           (by induction, since x does not appear in any of
           $v_1, \ldots, v_n$ as these are free for $u_1, \ldots, u_n$ in A,
           so for each i, $\delta(v_i) = \tau(v_i) = \sigma(u_i)$)
        and for every c, $\nu_\tau \vDash B(c, u_1, \ldots, u_n)$
           (by induction)

    iff $\nu_\tau \vDash \forall x\, B(x, v_1/u_1, \ldots, v_n/u_n)$

The case when A is $\exists x\, B$ is done similarly. So by induction the theorem is true for wffs of all lengths. ∎

An axiomatization

To axiomatize classical predicate logic with non-referring names, we modify the axiom system of classical predicate logic with equality. Since we allow models in which every name does have a reference, the axioms are valid in classical predicate logic, too.

I.   **Propositional axioms**

    The axiom schemes of classical propositional logic (p. 10), where A, B, C are replaced by wffs of L and the universal closure is taken.

II.   **Axioms governing $\forall$**

    1. a. $\forall \ldots (\forall x\, (A \to B) \to (\forall x\, A \to \forall x\, B))$ *distribution of $\forall$*
         if x is free in both A and B

       b. $\forall \ldots (\forall x\, (A \to B) \to (\forall x\, A \to B))$
         if x is free in A and not free in B

       c. $\forall \ldots (\forall x\, (A \to B) \to (A \to \forall x\, B))$
         if x is free in B and not free in A

    2. $\forall \ldots (\forall x\, \forall y\, A \to \forall y\, \forall x\, A)$ *commutativity of $\forall$*

    3. $\forall \ldots (\forall x\, A(x) \to A(u/x))$ *universal instantiation*
       when u is free for x in A

Axioms for equality

    5. $\forall x\, (x \equiv x)$ *identity*

    6. $\forall \ldots \forall x\, \forall y\, (x \equiv y \to (A(x) \to A(y/x))$ *extensionality*
       where y replaces some but not necessarily all occurrences of x in A

Axioms for non-referring names

8. $\forall \ldots ((A(c/x) \wedge \exists y (y \equiv c)) \to \exists x A(x))$ *existential generalization*
   where c is a name symbol   *for referring terms*

12. $\forall \ldots (\forall y (\neg (\exists x (x \equiv y) \wedge A(y/x)) \to \neg \exists x A(x))$
    where y is free for x in A

Rule   *modus ponens* for closed wffs

In summary, the changes from the axiom system of classical predicate logic with equality are:

- The axioms governing the relation of $\forall$ and $\exists$ are deleted.
- Two axiom schemes for non-referring names are added.

I give a proof of the strong completeness theorem for this system in Appendix 7.

43 Examples of Formalizing

Example 1 *Everthing is a person or a god.*

$\forall x \,((- \text{ is a person})\,(x) \lor (- \text{ is a god})\,(x)\,)$

Analysis Suppose our universe is all living people, and in our semi-formal language we have just three names: "Zeus", "Neptune", and "Richard L. Epstein". Then the following is true:

$\forall x \,((- \text{ is a person})\,(x) \lor (- \text{ is a god})\,(x)\,) \leftrightarrow$

$\neg \exists x \neg \,((- \text{ is a person})\,(x) \lor (- \text{ is a god})\,(x))$

$\land \,((- \text{ is a person})\,(\text{Zeus}) \lor (- \text{ is a god})\,(\text{Zeus})\,)$

$\land \,((- \text{ is a person})\,(\text{Neptune}) \lor (- \text{ is a god})\,(\text{Neptune})\,)$

$\land \,((- \text{ is a person})\,(\text{Richard L. Epstein}) \lor (- \text{ is a god})\,(\text{Richard L. Epstein})\,)$

If $c_1, \ldots, c_n$ are the only names in a semi-formal language, then the following is true in every model of that language:

$\forall \ldots \forall x \, A(x) \leftrightarrow (\neg \exists x \neg A(x) \land A(c_1|x) \land \ldots \land A(c_n|x))$.

Example 2 *Pegasus is a winged horse.*
    Therefore, *something is a winged horse.*

$\dfrac{(- \text{ is a winged horse})\,(\text{Pegasus})}{\exists x \,(- \text{ is a winged horse})\,(x)}$

Analysis The inference is invalid: in any model in which "Pegasus" does not refer and the premise is true and the universe is all mammals that have ever lived, the conclusion is false. Existential generalization fails for non-referring names.

  Some say the example is valid. This seems to me a remnant of the idea that the use of any name entails existence of a reference. That view becomes more respectable, though, if we recognize a difference between "there exists" and "there is" (or "something"). The former requires existence, but the latter does not.

  Pegasus is a winged horse.   *invalid*
  Therefore, there exists a winged horse.

  Pegasus is a winged horse.   *valid*
  Therefore, there is a winged horse.

We can define within our logic of non-referring terms a quantifier to model this distinction.[56]

---

[56] See the issue of *The Monist*, vol. 97, no. 4, 2014, for a survey of how others have made a distinction between "there exists" and "there is".

The generous existence quantifier $\exists_G x\, A(x) \equiv_{Def} \neg \forall x \neg A(x)$

Then:

$$\frac{(-\text{ is a winged horse}) (\text{Pegasus})}{\exists_G x\, (-\text{ is a winged horse}) (x)} \quad valid$$

And generally, if c is a name and x is the only variable free in A:

$$\frac{A(c/x)}{\exists_G x\, A(x)} \quad valid$$

Example 3   *Everything that is a horse is a mammal.*
Pegasus is a horse.
Therefore, *Pegasus is a mammal.*

$$\frac{\forall x\, (\, (-\text{ is a horse}) (x) \to (-\text{ is a mammal}) (x)\,)}{(-\text{ is a mammal}) (\text{Pegasus})}$$
$$(-\text{ is a horse}) (\text{Pegasus})$$

Analysis   This is valid: it follows from universal instantiation and *modus ponens*.

Some say that the example is not valid. We could have a model in which the universe is all animals that ever lived and then the premises are true even though "Pegasus" does not refer, while the conclusion is false. On this view, "everything" is interpreted as meaning "every existing thing". We can model the view that "all" means "all that exists" with a defined quantifier.

The restricted universal quantifier $\forall_R x\, A(x) \equiv_{Def} \neg \exists x \neg A(x)$

Understanding "all" as "all that exists" we can then formalize this example as:

$$\frac{\forall_R x\, (\, (-\text{ is a horse}) (x) \to (-\text{ is a mammal}) (x)\,)}{(-\text{ is a mammal}) (\text{Pegasus})} \quad invalid$$
$$(-\text{ is a horse}) (\text{Pegasus})$$

The premises are true in the model just described, but the conclusion is false. Instantiation fails for the restricted universal quantifier.

Example 4   *Everything that is loved by Bellerophon is a winged horse.*
Pegasus is loved by Bellerophon.
Therefore, *something is a winged horse.*

$$\frac{\forall x\, (\, (-\text{ is loved by Bellerophon}) (x) \to (-\text{ is a winged horse}) (x)\,)}{\exists x\, (-\text{ is a winged horse}) (x)}$$
$$(-\text{ is loved by Bellerophon}) (\text{Pegasus})$$

Analysis This is invalid: the conclusion could be false in a model if there are no winged horses, yet the premises could be true.

Alternatively, we could formalize the example using the other interpretations of "all" and "some" from the previous two examples:

$\forall x\,((-\text{ is loved by Bellerophon})\,(x) \to (-\text{ is a winged horse})\,(x))$
Pegasus is loved by Bellerophon.   *valid*
―――――――――――――――――――――――――――――――――
    $\exists_G x\,(-\text{ is a winged horse})\,(x)$

$\forall_R x\,((-\text{ is loved by Bellerophon})\,(x) \to (-\text{ is a winged horse})\,(x))$
$(-\text{ is loved by Bellerophon})\,(\text{Pegasus})$ *invalid*
―――――――――――――――――――――――――――――――――
    $\exists x\,(-\text{ is a winged horse})\,(x)$

$\forall_R x\,((-\text{ is loved by Bellerophon})\,(x) \to (-\text{ is a winged horse})\,(x))$
$(-\text{ is loved by Bellerophon})\,(\text{Pegasus})$ *invalid*
―――――――――――――――――――――――――――――――――
    $\exists_G x\,(-\text{ is a winged horse})\,(x)$

Example 5 Pegasus is Pegasus.

    Pegasus ≡ Pegasus

Analysis This is a tautology. But some say the example is false because Pegasus does not exist. We can formalize that view using the following defined predicate.

The restricted equality predicate $x \equiv_R x \equiv_{\text{Def}} \exists y\,(y \equiv x \wedge x \equiv x)$
    where y is the least variable different from x

In any model in which there is a non-referring name, $\forall x\,(x \equiv_R x)$ is false. We can have "Pegasus ≡ Pegasus" is true, while "Pegasus $\equiv_R$ Pegasus" is false.

We can restrict any atomic predicate in the same way.

The restriction of an atomic wff A   If A is an atomic wff and the terms appearing in A are $u_1, \ldots, u_n$, and $y_1, \ldots, y_n$ are the least variables not appearing in A, then:
    $A_R \equiv_{\text{Def}} \exists y_1 \ldots \exists y_n\,(y_1 \equiv u_1 \wedge \ldots \wedge y_n \equiv u_n \wedge A)$

If x is the only variable free in A, $A_R\,(c/x)$ is false for any non-referring name c.

These examples show that though we based our formal system of classical logic with non-referring names on a particular motivation and understanding of "all", "exists", and "is the same as", the logic is flexible enough to model other views of how those words should be interpreted when using non-referring names.

Example 6 Helio is not barking.

Analysis In Chapter 21 we considered a reading of this in which the negation applies to only the predicate:

Helio is not-barking.

The truth-conditions for this are:

There is a thing referred to by the name "Helio", and it is not the case that it is barking.

We can now formalize this as:

$\exists x \, (x \equiv \text{Helio}) \land \neg (\text{Helio is barking})$

This is equivalent to "$\neg (— \text{ is barking}) (\text{Helio})$" when all names refer. More generally, we have the following if names need not refer.

Formalizing not-P We formalize an informal reading of a phrase not-P(u) as:

$\exists y \, (y \equiv u) \land \neg P(u)$ where y is distinct from u

---

Example 7 Dinosaurs are reptiles.

$\forall x \, (\, (— \text{ is a dinosaur}) (x) \rightarrow (— \text{ is a reptile}) (x) \,)$

Analysis The formalization of this is straightforward. But we know that the following is false:

(a) $\quad \exists x \, (— \text{ is a dinosaur}) (x)$

There aren't any dinosaurs. How can we make scientific generalizations about what doesn't exist?

Perhaps we should have all dinosaurs that ever existed in the universe, so that (a) is true. But the statement is meant as a general law, so it should apply to all future dinosaurs. If one were re-created using dinosaur DNA, it, too, would be a reptile. Perhaps our universe should contain all future dinosaurs, too. But that's getting pretty strange. What other non-existents should it contain?

The problem with this example is not one of non-referring names, since we don't have a name for any dinosaur (unless a skeleton of one has been dubbed by a curator). Rather, the problem is how to reason about things that did exist but do not exist, about the past and about the future, which we'll investigate in Volume 2, *Time and Space in Formal Logic*.

Example 8 Thor had a dog.

Analysis The formalization of this depends on what's meant by "a dog". If what's meant is a real dog, one that exists, we can formalize the example as:

$\exists x \, (\, (— \text{ had} —) (\text{Thor}, x) \land (— \text{ is a dog}) (x) \,)$

If by "a dog" what's meant is either a real dog or a named fictional one, we can formalize the example as:

$\exists_G x\, ((-\text{ had}-)(\text{Thor}, x) \wedge (-\text{ is a dog})(x))$

If by "a dog" only a named "fictional" one is meant, we can formalize the example:

$\exists_G x\, ((-\text{ had}-)(\text{Thor}, x) \wedge (-\text{ is a dog})(x))$
$\quad \wedge \neg \exists x\, ((-\text{ had}-)(\text{Thor}, x) \wedge (-\text{ is a dog})(x))$

But we have no way to assert that Thor had an unnamed fictional dog. In classical logic with non-referring names, we cannot talk about unnamed "things" that don't exist, which is why it is unsuitable for reasoning about fiction. Instead we use classical predicate logic with equality, as discussed in Chapter 41.

Example 9 *Vulcan orbits the sun.*

$(-\text{ orbits }-)(\text{Vulcan}, \text{the sun})$

Analysis In 1846 the mathematician Urbain Le Verrier predicted the existence of a planet that could account for the perturbations in the orbit of Uranus around the sun. Shortly thereafter astronomers located the planet, which we now call "Neptune".

In 1859 Le Verrier predicted the existence of a planet that could account for the perturbations in the orbit of Mercury. He said that the planet orbited between Mercury and the sun, which would make it very difficult to observe. Later that year Edmond Modeste Lescarbault announced that he had observed it passing in front of the sun.

Today we know that there is no such planet. Both Le Verrier and Lescarbault were wrong.

Vulcan was never conceived of as a fictional object like Sherlock Holmes. But there is a similarity: the claims about both of them are set out in a story. This and this and that are true. The difference is that we know that "Sherlock Holmes" does not refer to anything, whereas there was uncertainty whether "Vulcan" referrred to anything. To determine that there is no object satisfying what was asserted using the name "Vulcan", astronomers reasoned with claims using that name to devise experiments. Scientists, too, have need for a guide for how to reason with possibly non-referring names. But the system of classical logic with non-referring names won't work because we can't reason about whether, for example, there is a satellite of Vulcan: we can reason about "non-existent" things only if they are named. We use instead classical logic with equality, as discussed in Chapter 41.

44 Non-Referring Simple Names in Mathematics

Mathematicians want to build systems that are simple, elegant, and have lots of applications. To do so they often accept absurdities.

For example, the numeral "0" was first introduced as a placeholder into systems for representing numbers. This is what the Hindus did; this is what the Mayans did. But at some point, those doing calculations began to view it as a number, on a par with $1, 2, 3, \ldots$. That is, they said that zero is the number of nothing. On the face of it, this is incoherent. If it's nothing, it has no number. But accepting that "1", "2", "3" ... are symbols standing for things is pretty difficult to accept, too. Whatever things they are must be abstract, not the same as 2 dogs or 3 horses. And then we enter into a world of platonism, where we say that my dog Birta and my dog Chocolate together "participate" in 2.

One way to avoid such metaphysical complications is to view these numerals as adjectives: 1 dog, or 1 horse, or 1 cat; 2 dogs, or 2 horses, or 2 cats; .... Then "$1 + 1 = 2$" is not a truth about numbers but a summary of how our counting works. It is true only in application. Thus, 1 dog + 1 dog = 2 dogs. But 1 drop of water + 1 drop of water ≠ 2 drops of water. The "claims" of arithmetic and mathematics are not true or false but only true or false in application. Even then, "0" stands out, for it can hardly be a way of counting. Yet it is correct to say that there are no dogs in the yard and mark that "no" with "0". That analysis is compatible with what mathematicians do and actually represents their work better than other analyses.[57]

It's not just zero. Mathematicians accept that there are negative numbers: $-1, -2, -3, \ldots$. They accept that there is a number that is the square root of -1, which they call "i", even though a positive multiplied by a positive is positive, and a negative multiplied by a negative is positive. Here, too, the symbols were first introduced as merely placeholders that made calculations easier, simplifying the mathematics. The evident absurdity of accepting that they stood for actual things took a long time to overcome. By the time that set theory began to be developed, it was no longer hard for mathematicians to believe in absurdities, and they accepted that there is a set, denoted by "$\emptyset$", that is nothing. It seems, then, they accepted that nothing is something that has properties.[58]

One way to justify that view is to say that since science depends on mathematics, and since science is right, there must be such things. That "indispensability argument" is a variant on the method of inference to the best explanation, which is a fallacious form of argument that cannot be used to justify a claim.[59] In any case, applications do not prove that the premises of a scientific theory are true, only that they are useful.[60]

---

[57] See my "Mathematics as the Art of Abstraction".
[58] Compare "Nothing" by P. L. Heath.
[59] See "Explanations" in *Cause and Effect, Conditions, Explanations*.

A different justification of the existence of mathematical "objects", including zero, is to say that if our talk is consistent, then there are things that the talk is about.[61] But that leads to an even greater absurdity, for I can devise a consistent theory of unicorns, yet unicorns still don't exist. We can't create living things of blood and bone from our talk. If numbers are things, real things, we can't create them from our talk.

A platonist would say that we are not creating such abstract entities. Our talk leads us to "see" that such things exist. In the end, the platonists' story of abstract objects is the only serious alternative to seeing mathematical claims as true only in application. Even then, platonists have to explain in what way *nothing* exists as an abstract object.

But now our work on classical predicate logic with non-referring names allows for a third way to justify talk that involves symbols that it would be absurd to think refer to any things. We take "0", "–1", "–2", "–3", ... , "i", and "∅" as non-referring names, fictions that are useful to fill out our systems, leading to easier calculations and applications. To do that, we need to extend classical predicate logic with non-referring names to allow for names for partial functions, such as "tan (—)".

---

[60] See "Models and Theories" in *Reasoning in Science and Mathematics*.
[61] See, for example, "On the Infinite" by David Hilbert and the discussion in my "Mathematics as the Art of Abstraction".

45 Classical Predicate Logic with Non-Referring Simple Names and Names for Partial Functions

We have a logic for reasoning with non-referring simple names. But we also use functions that create non-referring names, such as "$\tan(x)$" when x is indicated to refer to $\pi/2$. We can extend our logic for non-referring names to allow for names for partial functions.

We start with the language of classical predicate logic with functions and equality. For the semantics, suppose we have a semi-formal language and universe. Since we are extending classical logic with non-referring names, we assume that we have a complete collection of assignments of references to variables and atomic names satisfying:

For all x, $\sigma(x)\downarrow$.

For each name c, for all σ and τ, $\sigma(c) \approx \tau(c)$.

We want to confine what we take as semantically primitive for functions to atomic applications, just as we confine to atomic predicates what we take as semantically primitive for predications. These will need to be linked by an extensionality condition.

The first issue to resolve is what to take as the value of an application of a function to a non-referring term. We have that "$\tan(\pi/2)$" does not refer. So what about "$\tan(\pi/2) + 1$"? The only place I know where function-names without any internal structure are used is in mathematics and applications of mathematics. The standard practice there is to take a term such as "$\tan(\pi/2) + 1$" as non-referring. So let's adopt the following simplification.

Non-referring is the default application of a function Any complex name that contains a non-referring term is non-referring. That is, for any term $f(u_1, \ldots, u_n)$ and assignment of references σ, if for some i, $\sigma(u_i)\updownarrow$, then $\sigma(f(u_1, \ldots, u_n))\updownarrow$.

The assignments we make for atomic applications of functions must satisfy an extensionality condition, which is easy to formulate because non-referring is the default application.

Extensionality condition for atomic applications of terms For any atomic terms $u_1, \ldots, u_n$ and $v_1, \ldots, v_n$, if for all i, $\sigma(u_i) \approx \tau(v_i)$, then

$\sigma(f(u_1, \ldots, u_n)) \approx \tau(f(v_1, \ldots, v_n))$.

To extend the atomic applications of function names to all applications of function names, we can use the same method as with total functions except that non-referring is the default application.

Applications of functions extended to all terms

Terms of depth 0: These are given.

Terms of depth 1: These are given, satisfying non-referring as default and the extensionality condition for atomic applications.

Terms of depth $m + 1$ for $m \geq 1$:

Applications of functions for terms of depth $\leq m$ are given.

For a term $f(u_1, \ldots, u_n)$ of depth $m + 1$:

If for some i, $\sigma(u_i)\updownarrow$, then $\sigma(f(u_1, \ldots, u_n))\updownarrow$.

If for all i, $\sigma(u_i)\downarrow$, let $z_1, \ldots, z_n$ be the first variables that do not appear in $f(u_1, \ldots, u_n)$. Let τ be the assignment of references that differs from σ only in that for all i, $\tau(z_i) = \sigma(u_i)$. Then:
$\sigma(f(u_1, \ldots, u_n)) \approx \tau(f(z_1, \ldots, z_n))$.

This definition ensures that the extensionality condition applies to all applications of terms, as you can show.

For an extensionality condition for atomic predications, we consider first the equality predicate. Recall the conditions for valuations of the equality predicate with non-referring simple names:

i. If $\sigma(u)\downarrow$ and $\sigma(v)\downarrow$, then $\mathsf{v}_\sigma \vDash u \equiv v$ iff $\sigma(u) = \sigma(v)$.

ii. If one and only one of $\sigma(u)$ and $\sigma(v)$ is defined, then $\mathsf{v}_\sigma \nvDash u \equiv v$.

iii. If u and v are names, then $\mathsf{v}_\sigma \vDash u \equiv v$ iff $\mathsf{v}_\tau \vDash u \equiv v$.

iv. For all u, $\mathsf{v}_\sigma \vDash u \equiv u$.

v. For all u and v, $\mathsf{v}_\sigma \vDash u \equiv v$ iff $\mathsf{v}_\sigma \vDash v \equiv u$.

vi. For all u, v, and w, if $\mathsf{v}_\sigma \vDash u \equiv v$ and $\mathsf{v}_\sigma \vDash v \equiv w$, then $\mathsf{v}_\sigma \vDash u \equiv w$.

In order to take account of complex terms, we replace condition (iii).

---

iii–functions If for every variable x appearing in u or v, $\sigma(x) = \tau(x)$, then $\mathsf{v}_\sigma \vDash u \equiv v$ iff $\mathsf{v}_\tau \vDash u \equiv v$.

Note that if u and v are closed terms, that is, ones in which no variable appears, then for every σ and τ, $\mathsf{v}_\sigma \vDash u \equiv v$ iff $\mathsf{v}_\tau \vDash u \equiv v$, so we can write $\vDash u \equiv v$ if for some σ, $\mathsf{v}_\sigma \vDash u \equiv v$, understanding "$\vDash$" to be relative to the particular model.

For the evaluations of atomic predicates we can use the same extensionality condition as for classical predicate logic with non-referring names:

If A is an atomic wff, σ and τ are assignments of references, $u_1, \ldots, u_n$ are all the names and variables in A, and $v_1, \ldots, v_n$ are terms such that for each i, $\sigma(v_i) = \tau(u_i)$ or $\vDash v_i \equiv u_i$, then

$$v_\sigma \vDash A(u_1, \ldots, u_n) \text{ iff } v_\tau \vDash A(v_1/u_1 \ldots, v_n/u_n).$$

To extend the atomic valuations to all wffs simultaneously by induction, we use the standard conditions for ¬, →, ∧, ∨, and ∃. For the evaluation of the universal quantifier, recall what we used with non-referring names: $\forall x\, A(x)$ is true iff $A(x)$ is true no matter what x refers to and no matter what name is substituted for x. But now we can have complex names.

For example, suppose we have a semi-formal language with simple names "0" and "π/2", the predicate "<", and the function-name "tan(−)", with universe all real numbers. Consider the wff:

(1) $\quad \forall x\, (x > 0 \lor x = 0 \lor x < 0)$

In evaluating this we have to consider:

(2) $\quad \tan(\pi/2) > 0 \lor \tan(\pi/2) = 0 \lor \tan(\pi/2) < 0$

But even if we have no simple names in the universe, the truth-value of (1) has to take into consideration:

(3) $\quad \tan(z) > 0 \lor \tan(z) = 0 \lor \tan(z) < 0$

When z is indicated to refer to π/2, this should have the same truth-value as (2). So let's take the evaluation of the universal quantifier to be the following, letting "$\tau \sim_u \sigma$" mean that τ differs from σ at most in what it assigns the variables that appear in the term u.

Evaluation of the universal quantifier with partial functions

$v_\sigma \vDash \forall x\, A(x)$ iff for every term u that is either x or contains no variable that appears in $A(x)$, for every τ such that $\tau \sim_u \sigma$, $v_\tau \vDash A(u/x)$

Now we can show that the extensionality condition holds for all predications.

The extensionality of all predications Let A be a wff, σ and τ assignments of references, and $u_1, \ldots, u_n$ all the atomic terms in A. Let $v_1, \ldots, v_n$ be any terms such that for each i, v_i is free for u_i in A, and either $\sigma(u_i) = \tau(v_i)$ or u_i and v_i are closed terms and $\vDash u_i \equiv v_i$. Then:

$$v_\sigma \vDash A(u_1, \ldots, u_n) \text{ iff } v_\tau \vDash A(v_1/u_1, \ldots, v_n/u_n).$$

Proof We proceed by induction on the length of A. We assumed the extensionality condition for the evalutaion of atomic wffs. Suppose now that the theorem is true for all wffs of length less than that of A. I'll leave to you the cases when A is B∧ C, B∨ C, B→ C, or ¬B.

Suppose A is $\forall x\, B(x, u_1, \ldots, u_n)$ and $\upsilon_\sigma \not\vDash A$. We need to show $\upsilon_\tau \not\vDash A$. First, there is a u with no variables except possibly x in $B(x, u_1, \ldots, u_n)$ and a $\gamma \sim_u \sigma$ such that $\upsilon_\gamma \not\vDash B(u, u_1, \ldots, u_n)$. If u is x, I'll leave the proof to you (compare the proof on p. 26). If u is not x, I'll show there is some λ and some u' with no variables that appear in $B(x, v_1/u_1 \ldots, v_n/u_n)$ and $\lambda \sim_{u'} \tau$ and $\upsilon_\lambda \not\vDash B(u', v_1, \ldots, v_n)$ so that $\upsilon_\tau \not\vDash A$. Let $y_1, \ldots, y_m$ be the variables in u. Let $z_1, \ldots, z_m$ be the first variables that do not appear in $B(u, u_1, \ldots, u_n)$ and do not appear in $B(x, v_1/u_1, \ldots, v_n/u_n)$. Let u' be $u(z_1/y_1 \ldots, z_m/y_m)$. Let δ be such that for each j, $\delta(z_j) = \gamma(y_j)$ and $\delta \sim_{u'} \sigma$. By induction, we have that $\upsilon_\delta \not\vDash B(u', u_1, \ldots, u_n)$. Let λ be such that for all j, $\lambda(z_j) = \delta(z_j) = \gamma(y_j)$ and $\lambda \sim_{u'} \tau$. Then by extensionality for terms, for each i, $\lambda(v_i) = \tau(v_i) = \sigma(u_i) = \delta(u_i)$ or $\upsilon_\lambda \vDash u_i \equiv v_i$. So by induction, $\upsilon_\lambda \not\vDash B(u', v_1/u_1 \ldots, v_n/u_n)$.

If A is $\forall x\, B(x, u_1, \ldots, u_n)$ and $\upsilon_\tau \not\vDash B(x, v_1/u_1 \ldots, v_n/u_n)$, the proof is similar, as is the case when A is $\exists x\, B$, so I will leave those to you. ∎

To complete the semantics, we assume that we have enough models to formalize validity.

Sufficiency of the collection of models For any realization and any collection of things, any correlations and undefined applications satisfying the extensionality condition can serve as the assignments of references for atomic applications of functions, and relative to those any assignment of truth-values to the atomic predications satisfying the extensionality condition can serve to define a model.

Axiomatization

We take the axiom system for classical predicate logic with non-referring names of the previous chapter and add the following two schemes governing function-names.

Axioms for partial functions

7. $\forall \ldots \forall x\, \forall y\, (x \equiv y \rightarrow$
   $f(z_1, \ldots, z_k, x, z_{k+1}, \ldots, z_n) \equiv f(z_1, \ldots, z_k, y, z_{k+1}, \ldots, z_n))$

   for every $n+1$-ary function symbol f   *extensionality of functions*

7.*b. $\forall \ldots (\neg \exists x\, (x \equiv u) \rightarrow \neg \exists y\, (y \equiv f(u_1, \ldots, u, \ldots, u_n)))$

   for every n-ary function symbol f and terms $u_1, \ldots u, \ldots, u_n$

   non-referring is the default application of functions

I give a proof of the strong completeness theorem for this system in Appendix 7.

46 Examples of Formalizing Mathematics

Example 1 $\tan(\pi/2) = \infty$

Analysis Mathematicians working in classical real analysis take "∞" as a name and designate certain atomic predications in which it appears as "given". But they aren't willing to say that there exists something that "∞" designates. Nor are they willing to say that "$\forall x\, (x \leq \infty)$" is true; they just take that as given, an assumption that allows them to flesh out their systems. We can use classical predicate logic with partial functions to formalize such reasoning, viewing "∞" and "$-\infty$" as non-referring names.

Example 2 $\aleph_0 + \aleph_0 \equiv \aleph_0$

Analysis Mathematicians working in set theory feel they must be platonists in order to justify this sentence as true. There really are infinite sets, completed infinities, and in particular "$\aleph_0$" refers to the cardinal number of the entire collection of natural numbers. We can relieve them of their burden of platonism by formalizing their reasoning in classical predicate logic with non-referring names and partial functions.

Example 3 $6 - 7 \equiv -1$

Analysis Rather than accepting that there are negative numbers, we can take "$-(\ )$" to be a partial function in classical predicate logic with non-referring names.

Example 4 $i^2 \equiv -1$

Analysis The acceptance of systems in which "i" was used were first justified by reducing every complex number to one of the form $a + bi$, where a and b are real numbers, and then giving rules for a special kind of multiplication of those as pairs of real numbers (a, b). This is compatible with taking i as a non-referring name, a fiction to aid in our calculations, a placeholder. It doesn't name a "non-existent" number. It doesn't name anything.

Example 5 (Non-standard numbers in arithmetic)

Analysis In the usual presentation of arithmetic with non-standard numbers, some name symbol is realized by a letter, say "c", and the following are taken as given (axioms): $\neg (c \equiv 0), \neg (c \equiv 1), \neg (c \equiv 1 + 1), \neg (c \equiv 1 + 1 + 1), \ldots$.[62] Logicians who use such systems do not point to a thing that "c" refers to. Rather, they add that symbol to the universe of natural numbers and get a new universe in which, for example, "c + 1 + 1" refers to c + 2. Either that is a subterfuge, for they do not

---

[62] See *Classical Mathematical Logic*, pp. 278–279.

accept that "c" really designates anything, or else if they do believe that such a thing exists, it indicates a commitment to a strong form of platonism, for such a thing would be abstract and there would be no way to distinguish one such thing from any other that we could take as the interpretation of "c". Using classical predicate logic with partial functions, we can model such reasoning without recourse to any such things as non-standard natural numbers. We need not augment the universe of natural numbers in order to have consistent reasoning.

Example 7 (Non-standard analysis)

Analysis Non-standard analysis builds the theory of the real numbers, integration, and differentiation not on the natural numbers but on a system of standard and non-standard natural numbers. If "c" is the name for a non-standard natural number that is added to the language of arithmetic, then "$\forall x \, (x \leq c)$" is taken as given, and "1/c" acts as the name of an infinitesimal, a number smaller than every standard positive real number but not equal to 0. Mathematicians do not think that such non-standard "numbers" exist: they consider the formal system as only a way to justify much intuitive reasoning with infinitesimals in calculating derivatives and integrals in the manner used in the 18th and 19th centuries. Infinitesimals are taken as useful fictions, and this kind of reasoning can be modeled in classical predicate logic with partial functions to the extent that it does not quantify over functions.

Example 8 $\mu \, y \, (y + y = 1) \simeq \mu \, z \, (z \cdot z = 3)$
the $y \, (y + y = 1 \wedge \forall x \, (x + x = 1 \rightarrow y \leq x)) \equiv$
the $z \, (z \cdot z = 3 \wedge \forall x \, (x \cdot x = 3 \rightarrow z \leq x))$

Analysis In the theory of computable functions, which deals with functions on only counting numbers, mathematicians write "$f(x) \simeq g(x)$" to mean "both $f(x)\downarrow$ and $g(x)\downarrow$ and they are equal, or both $f(x)\updownarrow$ and $g(x)\updownarrow$". They write "$\mu \, y$" to mean "the least y such that". A simple modification of classical predicate logic with descriptive names and descriptive functions will allow us to formalize such reasoning. All we need do is change the evaluation of the equality predicate to:

$\vDash_\sigma u \equiv v$ iff $\sigma(u)\downarrow$ and $\sigma(v)\downarrow$ and $\sigma(u) = \sigma(v)$
or $\sigma(u)\updownarrow$ and $\sigma(v)\updownarrow$

Example 9 $\{x : x > 1\} = \{y : y > 3\} \cup \{2\}$
the $w \, (\forall x \, (x \in w \leftrightarrow x > 1)) \equiv$
the $z \, (\forall y \, (y \in z \leftrightarrow y > 3)) \cup $ the $z \, (\forall y \, (y \in z \leftrightarrow y \equiv 2))$

Analysis The use of brackets to name sets in modern mathematics is often understood as an "abstraction operator". It can be seen as a use of the the-operator within classical predicate logic with descriptive functions.

The symbol "∅" is introduced as an abbreviation for:

the $w\ (\forall x\ (x \in w \leftrightarrow x \not\equiv x))$

We can take this as a non-referring descriptive name if we modify the evaluation of the equality predicate in classical predicate logic with descriptive names and descriptive functions as in the last example: all non-referring descriptions are counted as equal. Taking non-referring descriptions as nil is what we need for the "truths" that "∅" figures in. For example:

$\forall x\ (\emptyset \subseteq x)$
    is an abbreviation for "$\forall x\ (\forall z\ (z \in \emptyset \rightarrow z \in x))$"
    which is true because the antecedent is false for any value of z

$\{z : x > 2\} \cap \{z : y < 1\} \equiv \emptyset$
    this is true because the following is true:
    $\forall x\ (x \in (\{z : x > 2\} \cap \{z : z < 1\}) \leftrightarrow x \in \emptyset)$

Alternatively, we can take "∅" to be a non-referring atomic name that can be used with descriptive functions such as the abstraction operator, which is what we'll see in the next chapter.

47 Classical Predicate Logic with Non-Referring Simple Names, Descriptive Names, and Descriptive Functions

Consider:

The wife of the man who created Sherlock Holmes was rich.

This talks of both what is real and what is fictional together. But we have no way to formalize this, since we need to treat "the wife of —" and "the man who created —" as descriptive names, as in:

(— is rich) (the x (— is the wife/of ((the z (— created —) (z, Sherlock Homes)), x)

So in this chapter we'll add descriptive names and descriptive functions to the system of classical predicate logic with non-referring simple names of Chapter 42. This will be the most complicated system in this book.

Descriptive names

We start with a model of classical predicate logic with non-referring names (Chapter 42). I'll use c and d and subscripted versions of those to stand for atomic names. In this model, for every c, referring or not, "c ≡ c" is true.

Non-referring atomic names will affect how the descriptions in the-terms point to semantic values. Suppose we have a referring name "Rudy" in our semi-formal language along with the predicate "— is a brother of Rudy". In the logic of descriptive names (Chapter 38) if there is one and only one object in the universe satisfying that predicate, then the description in "the x (x is a brother of Rudy)" points to that object, which determines the semantic value of the term. However, here we might have in addition to that object a non-referring name "Zulgat" in the semi-formal language where "Zulgat is a brother of Rudy" is true. In that case, the description in "the x (x is a brother of Rudy)" does not point unambiguously to one semantic value. If on the other hand, no object in the universe satisfies "— is a brother of Rudy", and "Zulgat is a brother of Rudy" is true, then the description in "the x (x is a brother of Rudy)" points unambiguously to a semantic value if for any other name c for which "c is a brother of Rudy" is true, "c ≡ Zulgat" is true. In this case, though the term has no reference, it has *pseudo-reference*.

Thus, when we have non-referring names in our language that have non-nil semantic value, there are two ways in which a the-term can have a unique semantic value determined by the model of the base language:

the x A(x) is *referring*
There is one and only one object in the universe satisfying A(x),
and there is no non-referring name c such that A(c/x) is true.

the x A(x) is *pseudo-referring*
>There is no object in the universe satisfying A(x), and there is a non-referring name c such that A(c/x) is true and for any name d such that A(d/x) is true, "c ≡ d" is true.

In all other cases, "the x A(x)" does not point to a unique semantic value and so is *nil*.

Nil terms do not contribute to the evaluation of the quantifiers. Any the-term that is not nil contributes to the evaluation of quantifiers by way of its reference or pseudo-reference, which in the latter case is a name in the base language. So at every stage, the evaluation of the universal quantifier will be the same as in the model of the base language that takes account of non-referring simple names (p. 196).

$\nu_\sigma \vDash \forall x\, A(x)$ iff for every assignment of references τ such that $\tau \sim_x \sigma$, $\nu_\tau \vDash A(x)$ and for every atomic name c, $\nu_\sigma \vDash A(c)$

Some non-referring terms are now nil, and for those "$u \equiv u$" is false. Some non-referring names are not nil, and for those "$(u \equiv u)$" is true. So we can use "$(u \equiv u)$" to distinguish nil terms from those that play a role in the evaluation of the quantifiers.

Now we can set out this system explicitly.

Syntax
We start with the language L of classical predicate logic with equality and extend that to the language L* of descriptive names and descriptive functions (Chapter 37).

Semantics
We start with a model M of classical predicate logic with non-referring names. We define by simultaneous and repeated induction the assignments of references and valuations based on those for the extended language L*.

Stage 0 for L_0
In M we have a complete class of assignments of references for the terms of L satisfying:

>For all x, $\sigma(x)\downarrow$.

>For each name c, for all σ and τ, $\sigma(c) \approx \tau(c)$.

>The collection of such assignments is complete.

We then have valuations of the atomic wffs based on these assignments satisfying the extensionality condition for atomic predications and the following conditions on the equality predicate.

>i. If $\sigma(u)\downarrow$ and $\sigma(v)\downarrow$, then $\nu_\sigma \vDash u \equiv v$ iff $\sigma(u) = \sigma(v)$.

ii. If one and only one of $\sigma(u)$ and $\sigma(v)$ is defined, then $\nu_\sigma \not\models u \equiv v$.

iii. If u and v are closed terms, then $\nu_\sigma \models u \equiv v$ iff $\nu_\tau \models u \equiv v$.

iv. For all u, $\nu_\sigma \models u \equiv u$.

v. For all u and v, $\nu_\sigma \models u \equiv v$ iff $\nu_\sigma \models v \equiv u$.

vi. For all u, v, w, if $\nu_\sigma \models u \equiv v$ and $\nu_\sigma \models v \equiv w$, then $\nu_\sigma \models u \equiv w$.

The valuations are extended to all wffs by the conditions for the evaluations of the connectives and existential quantifer as for classical predicate logic and for the universal quantifier the same condition as for the base model with non-referring simple names (above).

We denote the assignments of references of stage 0 with a subscript, for example, σ_0, τ_0.

Stage $n + 1$ for L_{n+1}

Assignments of references

We extend each assignment of references σ_n of stage n to all terms of the language of stage $n + 1$, denoting the new assignment as σ_{n+1}.

If u is a term of stage 0, then $\sigma_{n+1}(u) \approx \sigma_n(u)$.

If u is a term of the form "the $x\, A(x)$", then:

$\sigma_{n+1}(\underline{\text{the}}\ x\, A(x)) = \mathbf{a}$ iff for all τ_n, $\nu_{\tau_n} \models A(x)$ iff $\tau_n(x) = \mathbf{a}$, and
for every atomic name c, $\nu_{\sigma_n} \not\models A(c/x)$.

In this case "$\underline{\text{the}}\ x\, A(x)$" is *referring* and has *reference* $\mathbf{a}$.

$\sigma_{n+1}(\underline{\text{the}}\ x\, A(x))\updownarrow$ otherwise.

If "$\underline{\text{the}}\ x\, A(x)$" is not referring and there is some atomic name c such that $\nu_{\sigma_n} \models A(c/x)$ and for any atomic name d such that

$\nu_{\sigma_n} \models A(d/x), \nu_{\sigma_n} \models c \equiv d$

then "$\underline{\text{the}}\ x\, A(x)$" is *pseudo-referring*; it has *pseudo-reference* the name c that realizes the name symbol with least index such that $\nu_{\sigma_n} \models A(c/x)$.

If "$(\underline{\text{the}}\ x\, A(x)$" is neither referring nor pseduo-referring, it is *nil*.

Valuations We extend all valuations ν_{σ_n} of stage n to all atomic wffs of the language of stage $n + 1$, including the equality predicate.

If for some i, u_i is nil, then $\nu_{\sigma_{n+1}} \not\models A(u_1, \ldots, u_m)$.

Otherwise, proceeding from $i = 1$ to n, define v_i by:

If u_i is a variable or atomic name, let v_i be u_i.

If u_i is pseudo-referring, let v_i be its pseudo-reference.

If u_i is a referring the-term, let v_i be the least variable that does not appear in $A(u_1, \ldots, u_m)$ and is not v_j for any $j < i$.

Let τ_0 be an assignment of references of stage 0 such that for each i such that u_i is a variable or is referring, $\tau_0(v_i) = \sigma_{n+1}(u_i)$, and τ_0 agrees with σ_{n+1} on all other variables. Then:

$$\vDash_{\sigma_{n+1}} A(u_1, \ldots, u_m) \text{ iff } \vDash_{\tau_0} A(v_1/u_1, \ldots, v_m/u_m)$$

In summary, for atomic wffs the presence of a nil term gives falsity as the default value. If all terms in the wff are not nil, then we replace pseudo-referring terms by their pseudo-references and all other terms are evaluated according to their references, ensuring the extensionality of atomic predications.

I'll let you show that these valuations satisfy the restrictions on the equality predicate of stage 0 with condition (iv) replaced by:

iv.* u is nil iff $\vDash_\sigma \neg u \equiv u$.

These valuations are then extended to all wffs in the same way as at stage 0.

Note that at each stage n, if A is a closed wff and for all σ_n and τ_n, then $\vDash_{\sigma_n} A$ iff $\vDash_{\tau_n} A$. So for any closed wff A we can use the notation "$\vDash_n A$" to mean that for some σ_n, and hence for all σ_n, $\vDash_{\sigma_n} A$.

Stability of references, pseudo-references, and truth-values

a. If "the x B(x)" is a term of stage n, then:

"the x B(x)" has reference σ at stage $n + 1$ iff
"the x B(x)" is has reference σ at stage n.

"the x B(x)" has pseudo-reference c at stage $n + 1$ iff
"the x B(x)" has pseudo-reference c at stage n.

"the x B(x)" is nil at stage $n + 1$ iff "the x B(x)" is nil at stage n.

b. For every wff A of stage n, for every σ_n, $\vDash_{\sigma_{n+1}} A$ iff $\vDash_{\sigma_n} A$.

Proof We induct on n. We start with $n = 0$. Then (a) is true because there are no such terms. We show (b) by induction on the length of A. It is true for atomic wffs because every term u in A is a variable or name, and for those $\sigma_1(u) \approx \sigma_0(u)$. Suppose it is true for all wffs shorter than A. I'll show the case when A is $\forall x\, B(x)$ and leave the other cases to you.

$\vDash_{\sigma_1} \forall x\, B(x)$ iff for all τ_1 such that $\tau_1 \sim_x \sigma_1$, $\vDash_{\tau_1} B(x)$,
    and for all c, $\vDash_1 B(c/x)$

iff (by induction on the length of A) for all τ_1 such that
    $\tau_1 \sim_x \sigma_1$, $\vDash_{\tau_0} B(x)$, and for all c, $\vDash_0 B(c/x)$

Non-Referring Simple Names and Descriptive Names 217

iff (by (a)) for all τ_0 such that $\tau_0 \sim_x \sigma_0$, $\nu_{\tau_0} \vDash B(x)$,
and for all c, $\vDash_0 B(c/x)$

iff $\nu_{\sigma_0} \vDash \forall x\, B(x)$

Suppose now that the theorem is true for stage $n \geq 1$. To show (a), suppose "the $x\, B(x)$" is a term of stage n, so that B is a wff of stage $m < n$. Then:

"the $x\, B(x)$" has reference $\mathfrak{a}$ at stage $n + 1$

  iff for all τ_n, $\nu_{\tau_n} \vDash B(x)$ iff $\tau_n(x) = \mathfrak{a}$, and for every c, $\nvDash_n B(c/x)$

  iff (by induction on n) for all τ_m, $\nu_{\tau_m} \vDash B(x)$ iff $\tau_m(x) = \mathfrak{a}$,
  and for every name c, $\nvDash_m B(c/x)$

  iff "the $x\, B(x)$" has reference $\mathfrak{a}$ at stage m

  iff (by induction) "the $x\, B(x)$" has reference $\mathfrak{a}$ at stage n

"the $x\, B(x)$" has pseudo-reference c at stage $n + 1$

  iff "the $x\, B(x)$" is not referring at stage $n + 1$ and there is some name c such that $\vDash_n B(c/x)$ and for any name d such that $\vDash_n B(d/x)$, $\vDash_n c \equiv d$

  iff (by induction and what we have just proved) "the $x\, B(x)$" is not referring at stage m and there is some name c such that $\vDash_m B(c/x)$ and for any name d such that $\vDash_m B(d/x)$, $\vDash_m c \equiv d$

  iff "the $x\, B(x)$" has pseudo-reference c at stage m

  iff (by induction) "the $x\, B(x)$" has pseudo-reference c at stage n

By process of elimination, u is nil at stage $n + 1$ iff u is nil at stage n.

To show (b), we induct on the length of A. If A is atomic, it follows by (a). The proof then follows as at stage 0. ∎

Now we can complete the definition of the model **M*** for **L***.

Assignments of references and valuations for the language **L***

For each assignment of references σ_0,

$\sigma^*(u) \approx \sigma_n(u)$ for the least n such that u is defined at stage n.

  u has *reference* $\mathfrak{a}$ iff $\sigma^*(u)\!\downarrow = \mathfrak{a}$.

  u has *pseudo-reference* c iff for the least n such that u is defined at stage n, u has pseudo-reference c at stage n.

  u is nil iff u is nil at the least stage n at which it is defined.

$\nu_{\sigma^*}(A) = \nu_{\sigma_n}(A)$ for the least n such that A is defined at stage n.

For every closed wff A, $\nu(A) = \mathsf{T}$ iff for all σ^*, $\nu_{\sigma^*}(A) = \mathsf{T}$.

The following are used to characterize the different classes of the-terms.

Uniqueness quantifiers

$Ux\, A(x) \equiv_{Def} \forall x\, \forall y\, (A(x) \wedge A(y) \rightarrow (x \equiv y))$

$Rx\, A(x) \equiv_{Def} \exists x\, A(x) \wedge Ux\, A(x)$

$Px\, A(x) \equiv_{Def} (\neg \exists x\, A(x) \wedge \neg \forall x\, \neg A(x)) \wedge Ux\, A(x)$

The definition of $Rx\, A(x)$ is equivalent to the definition of $\exists!\, x\, A(x)$ in classical predicate logic (p. 171), though its import is different here. I'll let you prove the following.

Characterizing kinds of the-terms

    a. $Rx\, A(x)$ is true in a model iff "the $x\, A(x)$" is referring.

    b. $Px\, A(x)$ is true in a model iff "the $x\, A(x)$" is pseudo-referring.

    c. For every term u, $\neg(u \equiv u)$ is true in a model iff u is nil.

Descriptive functions

We start with the language L of classical predicate logic with equality and then extend that to the language L* for descriptive names and descriptive functions (Chapter 37).

For the semantics, we modify the definition of assignments of references at stage $n + 1$ in the semantics above.

Assignments of references

If u is a term of stage 0, then $\sigma_{n+1}(u) \approx \sigma_n(u)$.

If u is a term of the form "the $x\, A(x)$" then:

$\sigma_{n+1}(\text{the } x\, A(x)) = \mathbf{o}$ iff for every τ_n such that $\tau_n \sim_x \sigma_n$,

$\mathbf{v}_{\tau_n} \models A$ iff $\tau_n(x) = \mathbf{o}$ and for every

non-referring name c, $\mathbf{v}_{\sigma_n} \not\models A(c/x)$.

In this case we say that "the $x\, A(x)$" is *referring* with respect to (the assignments made by) σ_{n+1}, and has reference $\mathbf{o}$.

$\sigma_{n+1}(\text{the } x\, A(x)) \updownarrow$ otherwise.

In this case we say that "the $x\, A(x)$" is not referring with respect to σ_{n+1}, or that σ_{n+1} assigns no value to "the $x\, A(x)$".

If "the $x\, A(x)$" is not referring with respect to σ_{n+1}, and there is some atomic name c such that $\mathbf{v}_{\sigma_n} \models A(c/x)$ and for any name d such that $\mathbf{v}_{\sigma_n} \models A(d/x)$, $\mathbf{v}_{\sigma_n} \models c \equiv d$, then "the $x\, A(x)$" is *pseudo-referring* with respect to σ_{n+1} with *pseudo-reference* the name c that realizes the least name symbol such that $\upsilon_{\sigma_n} \models A(c/x)$.

If "the $x\ A(x)$" is neither referring nor pseudo-referring with respect to σ_{n+1}, then it is *nil* with respect to σ_{n+1}.

The proof of the stability of references and truth-values is as before with the insertion of the clause "such that $\tau_n \sim_x \sigma_n$" in the displayed equivalences. The rest of the definition of the semantics then follows as before.

An axiomatization

I. Propositional axioms

The axiom schemes of classical propositional logic in $L(\neg, \to, \wedge, \vee)$, where A, B, C are replaced by wffs of L and the universal closure is taken.

II. Axioms governing $\forall$

1. a. $\forall \ldots (\forall x\ (A \to B) \to (\forall x\ A \to \forall x\ B))$ *distribution of* $\forall$
   if x is free in both A and B

   b. $\forall \ldots (\forall x\ (A \to B) \to (\forall x\ A \to B))$
   if x is free in A and not free in B

   c. $\forall \ldots (\forall x\ (A \to B) \to (A \to \forall x\ B))$
   if x is free in B and not free in A

2. $\forall \ldots (\forall x\ \forall y\ A \to \forall y\ \forall x\ A)$ *commutativity of* $\forall$

3†. a. $\forall \ldots ((\forall x\ A(x) \wedge (u \equiv u)) \to A(u/x))$ *universal instantiation*
   when u is free for x in A   *for non-nil terms*

Axioms governing the relation between $\forall$ and $\exists$

4. a. $\forall \ldots (\exists x\ A \to \neg \forall x \neg A)$

Axioms for equality

5. a. $\forall x\ (x \equiv x)$ *identity*

   b†. $\neg \forall x \neg (x \equiv u) \to (u \equiv u)$ *identity for non-nil terms*
   when u is a closed term

6. $\forall \ldots \forall x\ \forall y\ (x \equiv y \to (A(x) \to A(y/x))$ *extensionality*
   where y replaces some but not necessarily all occurrences of x in A

Axioms for non-referring terms

8. $\forall \ldots ((A\ (u/x) \wedge \exists y\ (y \equiv u)) \to \exists x\ A\ (x))$ *existential generalization for referring terms*

9.* $\forall \ldots (\neg (u \equiv u) \to \neg A(u_1, \ldots, u, \ldots, u_n))$ *nil terms use falsity*
   for n-ary atomic wffs A and terms $u_1, \ldots, u, \ldots, u_n$ *as default*

12. $\forall\ldots(\forall y\,(\neg\,(\exists x\,(x \equiv y) \wedge A(y/x)) \to \neg \exists x\, A(x))$
  where y is free for x in A

Axioms for "the"-terms

10.* a. $\forall\ldots\,(\mathsf{R}x\,A(x) \leftrightarrow \exists z\,(z \equiv \underline{\text{the}}\ x\,A(x)))$ *referring descriptions*
  where z is the least variable not appearing in A   *yield referring terms*

  b. $\forall\ldots\,(\mathsf{P}x\,A(x) \leftrightarrow \neg\,\mathsf{R}x\,A(x) \wedge \neg\,\forall z\,\neg\,(z \equiv \underline{\text{the}}\ x\,A(x)))$
  where z is the least variable not appearing in A
           pseudo-referring descriptions create pseudo-referring terms

11.* $\forall\ldots\,(\mathsf{R}x\,A(x) \vee \mathsf{P}x\,A(x)) \to A(\underline{\text{the}}\ x\,A(x))$
  referring and pseudo-referring descriptive terms satisfy their own description

13. $\forall\ldots\,\neg\,\mathsf{R}x\,A(x) \wedge \neg\,\mathsf{P}x\,A(x) \to \neg\,(\underline{\text{the}}\ x\,A(x) \equiv \underline{\text{the}}\ x\,A(x))$
           nil descriptions yield nil terms

Rule   *modus ponens* for closed wffs

I give a proof of the strong completeness theorem for this system in Appendix 7.

Summary

In this part of the book we investigated the internal structure of names.

We started by looking at functions. Functions as viewed by mathematicians and scientists are abstracted to just correlations. Though we come to know them by way of some process or procedure or description, we pay attention to only the relationships between input and output that they establish. In formal systems of predicate logic, a function is abstracted to a special kind of predicate.

Functions are different from other predicates in two ways. First, they can be used to pick out objects: given one or several things, the function picks out a single thing correlated to it or them. Picking out single things in the universe is what we do with names in our semi-formal languages, and we can use our representations of functions to create names. In Chapter 35 we saw how to extend classical predicate logic to incorporate function-names and complex names formed from them, names with internal structure that we recognize in our formal system.

The representations of functions are the other way that functions are treated differently from predicates. Predicates in our reasoning are or are represented as phrases from our ordinary language with one or more blanks such that when (possibly temporary) names for things in the universe fill in the blanks, a sentence results that is (or represents what is) true or false. Typically in modern logic, however, only names for functions are used in semi-formal languages, not linguistic expressions we understand in relation to our experience. Those function-names, such as "$\sin(-)$" or "$- + -$", are what we use to create names and open terms. But we do use descriptions of the process or procedure that establishes a correlation, such as "the least number x such that $x^2 + 9x + 3 = 0$" or "the wife of $-$". In our systems we have required that every name refers, yet if we use "the wife of $-$" as a function, it will be a partial one, for when "Marilyn Monroe" fills the blank, there is no thing that the phrase names.

The usual approach to resolving that problem eliminates such descriptions by formalizing propositions in which they appear as complex formulas that include a conjunct asserting that such a thing exists. That method misconstrues the role of such terms, for they are indeed terms and are treated as such in our ordinary reasoning. It is important to show how to reason with descriptions used as names or functions.

The assumption that every name refers was not a fundamental assumption about the nature of language, logic, and the world that we built into our systems. It was only a simplification. By dropping that assumption, we were able to build a formal logic of descriptive names and descriptive functions. In Chapter 37 we devised a syntax, adding to the logical vocabulary "<u>the</u>" to form terms "<u>the</u> x A(x)". In contrast to using function-names where a succession of stages are used in the definition of "term", for the-terms a succession of stages of languages are needed to build up a full formal language. In devising semantics for that language in Chapter 38 we found that there are serious impediments to ascribing a semantic value to non-referring the-terms, so we chose to treat them as nil: any atomic predication in which they appear is false, and they are not taken into account in evaluating the universal quantifier.

In Chapter 43 we saw examples of formalizing using that system of classical predicate logic with descriptive names and descriptive functions. We also saw that we had need of a way to formalize reasoning that involves non-referring simple names alongside names that do refer, and in Chapter 44 we found further motivation from mathematics for developing such a system, which we did in Chapter 45. In looking at examples in Chapter 46 of how to use that system, we found a need to allow for descriptive names and descriptive functions with non-referring simple names, which we did in Chapter 47.

Though these systems may prove useful and natural, I am not suggesting that we now understand how to reason with "the" or with non-referring simple names. Rather, we have devised systems throughout this book to guide us in our reasoning. Those systems are based on views about the nature of objects, truth, and inference that are taken as fundamental. To the extent that those views along with our criteria of formalization are accepted, we can agree that these systems provide a way to judge or improve our reasoning. When we encounter examples of reasoning that seem to be evaluated wrongly in these systems, we can go back to those fundamental views and criteria to see if there is some way we can adjust the path of abstraction to give better models of how to reason well or whether we should say that the intuition we had about those examples was wrong. In this way, we proceed in using and evaluating our formal models of how to reason well.

Appendices

Appendix 1 Minimal Metaphysics

We wish to use logic together to reason.[61] To do so, we must have some common background about how to reason to truths and, when that is not straightforward, how to determine if this were true, then that would follow. So here and in all my work, I look for minimal assumptions we need to develop a formal system or a method for evaluating reasoning. I assume:

- There are people in the world.
- We communicate and reason together using language.
- Our language connects in some way with the world so that we can classify some parts of our talk as true or false.

For specific kinds of reasoning I show that to have a theory or method we need to adopt further assumptions. Those might be about the nature of time, or the nature of individual things, or any number of different conceptions of the world.[62] Often I show how different assumptions about the nature of the world, language, and reasoning can lead to different theories or methods based on the minimal assumptions.

In this way I hope to develop formal systems and methods that are acceptable to people with very different assumptions about the nature of the world and how to reason. Here I'll point out how this approach begins with the notions of propositions and truth.

Propositions
On the first page of this volume I define:

A *proposition* is a written or uttered part of speech used in such a way that it is true or false, but not both.

Elsewhere, I have said that a proposition is a piece of language that we can *agree* to view as true or false, where that agreement may be tacit or implicit.[63]

Yet some say that what is true or false is not the sentence but the "meaning" or "thought" expressed by the sentence. Thus "Ralph is a dog" is not a proposition; it expresses one, the very same one expressed by "Ralph is a domestic canine" and by "Ralph es un perro".

Platonists take this one step further. A *platonist* is someone who believes that there are objects not perceptible to our senses that exist independently of us. Such abstract objects can be perceived by us only through our intellect. The independence and timeless existence of such objects account for objectivity in logic and mathematics. In particular, propositions are abstract objects, and a proposition is true or is false, though not both, independently of

---

[61] Some say that logic is an objective science whose objects of study are abstract propositions. That seems to remove logic from reasoning in our lives. I have explored this contrast in "Logic as the Art of Reasoning Well".

[62] See *Prescriptive Reasoning*; *The Fundamentals of Argument Analysis*; *Reasoning in Science and Mathematics*; *Cause and Effect, Conditionals, Explanations*.

[63] See *Propositional Logics*.

our even knowing of its existence. Thus each of the following, if uttered at the same time and place, expresses or stands for the same abstract proposition: "It is raining", "Pada deszcz", "Il pleut". Platonists say that the word "true" can be properly used only for things that cannot be seen, heard, or touched. Sentences are understood to "express" or "represent" or "participate in" such propositions. Linguistic types, too, are abstract objects, so that the assumption that words and propositions are types concerns which inscriptions and utterances represent or express or point to the same abstract proposition.

Those who take abstract propositions as the basis of logic argue that we cannot answer precisely the questions: What is a sentence? What constitutes a use of a sentence? When has one been used assertively or even put forward for discussion? These questions, they say, can and should be avoided by taking things inflexible, rigid, and timeless as propositions. But then we have the no less difficult questions: How do we use logic? What is the relation of these formal theories or methods to our arguments, discussions, and search for truth? How can we tell if this utterance is an instance of that abstract proposition? It's not that taking utterances and inscriptions as propositions raises questions that can be avoided.

Still, in the end, the platonist, as well as a person who thinks a proposition is the meaning of a sentence or a thought, reasons in language, using sentences that they call "representatives" or "expressions" of propositions. We can and do reason together using those, and to that extent my definition of "proposition" can serve those people, too.

Truth

There are many conceptions of what it means for a proposition to be true. Some say that the proposition must correspond to the way the world is. Some say that our mental understanding must correspond to the way the world is, perhaps mediated by concepts, which they say are things. Some go further and say that a way the world could be is a real thing, a possibility.

Here, and elsewhere, all that I assume is that we have some basis, some criteria for dividing propositions into two mutually exclusive kinds: those that are suitable to proceed on as the basis of reasoning and those that are not. This, I claim, is the underlying assumption of (virtually) all those who investigate reasoning, whether in formal or informal logic.[64] As long as the division functions structurally in a way that is compatible with the formalisms and methods we develop, we can supplement our work here with that method or criterion.

Similarly, a way the world could be, to the extent that we rely on it in our reasoning, either is or is expressed by a consistent collection of propositions.

My goal, then, is to develop formal and informal methods of how to reason well that require minimal metaphysics which, to the extent possible, are compatible with further metaphysical assumptions that could supplement or "ground" the theories. In this way we can see how those further metaphysical assumptions lead to different branchings of the same basic theory. This is particularly evident in the development of second-order logic and of how to reason with prescriptive claims.[65]

---

[64] See "Truth and Reasoning" in both *Prescriptive Reasoning* and *Reasoning and Formal Logic*.
[65] For second-order logic, see *Predicate Logic* and *Classical Mathematical Logic*. For prescriptive reasoning, see *Prescriptive Reasoning*.

Others have used this method, too. Compare what Ernest A. Moody says about William of Ockham's views:

> Insofar as Ockham is called a nominalist, his doctrine is not to be construed as a rejection of any ontological determination of meaning and truth, but rather as an extreme economy of ontological commitment in which abstract or intensional extralinguistic entities are systematically eliminated by a logical analysis of language.
>
> The principle of parsimony, whose frequent use by Ockham gained it the name "Ockham's razor," was employed as a methodological principle of economy in explanation. He invoked it most frequently under such forms as "Plurality is not to be assumed without necessity" and "What can be done with fewer [assumptions] is done in vain with more"; he seems not to have used the formulation "Entities are not to be multiplied without necessity." The principal use made by Ockham of the principle of parsimony was in the elimination of pseudo-explanatory entities, according to a criterion he expresses in the statement that nothing is to be assumed as necessary, in accounting for any fact, unless it is established by evident experience or evident reasoning, or is required by the articles of faith.[66]

This is similar to what I do. But I do not say that assuming more is in vain. My methodology grows from my being a pyrrhonist. I do not know what it would mean to say that it is true that abstract objects such as propositions and numbers exist. Unless those assumptions are necessary, I do not make them; I only note whether (it seems that) they are or are not compatible with the work here—or whether they are even internally coherent.

---

[66] p. 307 of "William of Ockham".

Appendix 2 Events in the Metaphysics of Predicate Logic

Some people have said that no new formalism is needed for formalizing inferences like:

(1) Juney is barking loudly.
    Therefore, Juney is barking.

We only need to recognize that events, like the burning of a flame in a fireplace, Caesar being stabbed, or Juney barking are things. Then we can formalize (1) as:

$\exists x$ (x is a barking $\wedge$ x is by Juney $\wedge$ x is loud)
Therefore, $\exists x$ (x is a barking $\wedge$ x is by Juney)

This is valid in classical predicate logic.

Formalizing in this manner, there is no need for an analysis of adverbs.[67] Indeed, there is no need for an analysis of verbs. Every verb is replaced by a gerund acting as a noun (or in some languages, like Italian, with an infinitive), so the only verb left is the copula of being: "to be" declined in all tenses and temporal locutions. Terence Parsons writes:[68]

> The basic assumption is that a sentence such as
>   Caesar died
> says something like the following:
>   For some event e,
>   e is a dying, *and*
>   the object of e is Caesar, *and*
>   e culminates before now.

If we formalize along these lines, propositions we previously viewed as atomic in predicate logic will be parsed as compound, requiring quantification with a variable that ranges over events. A logic with two sorts of variables would be needed to distinguish the use of such variables from variables used to refer to kinds of things that we previously took to be the universe of a realization.[69] Though "Juney barks" would seem to be atomic, we should understand it as having a hidden variable and quantifier:

$\exists e$ (e is a barking of Juney)

Advocates of this view have to argue that this is how we should understand such propositions, for there is no good evidence that we actually do understand them this way.[70]

---

[67] Event-talk accounts for adverbs by converting them into adjectives. So it would seem that a theory of predicate restrictors would still be needed to account for relative adjectives.

[68] *Events in the Semantics of English*, p. 6.

[69] The use of different kinds of variables is a standard part of the formalism of predicate logic; see Chapter XIV of *Classical Mathematical Logic*.

[70] When I asked one advocate of the use of events in formalizing why we should take events as basic, Donald Davidson replied that it's because we talk that way. Yes, we do talk about events sometimes, but not in the way that such a theory requires. We also talk about unicorns, but that doesn't mean we believe they exist as things. Roberto Casati and Achille Varzi in "Events" explain that view more carefully and review contemporary debates about whether events are things. In Davidson's comments and Casati and Varzi's article there is no acknowledgement that the talk they are considering is in English. At best they could be said to be discussing the implicit metaphysics of speakers of English.

228   *Appendix 2*

The justification offered for viewing events as things is that it allows us to formalize a great deal more in predicate logic than we could before. As Parsons says,

> I don't cite these results as evidence for the theory, or even as philosophically desirable consequences. The evidence for the theory lies in its ability to explain a wide range of data better than other existing theories. The existence and nature of events and states are by-products, in the same way that the symmetry of space and time are by-products of investigations in physics.[71]

This is no justification; it is an example of the fallacy of inference to the best explanation.[72] That good consequences come from particular metaphysical assumptions cannot justify those assumptions. In any case, Parson's comparison to physics is spurious: it isn't the symmetry of space and time that should be compared to whether events exist, but the existence of space-time.

In any case, in light of our work on predicate restrictors, which requires no metaphysical assumptions beyond those needed for predicate logic, it is hardly obvious that this method gives the best explanation of "the data". And there are many problems with adopting events as basic to our metaphysics.[73] One is so great that there seems to be no way to proceed in using events as things in predicate logic.

We have no way to distinguish events. We have no way to pick out one event rather than another when we wish to give a reference to a variable, and that is essential for the semantics of predicate logic. When we say that "x" is to refer to the stabbing of Caesar, is that the same event as the stabbing of Caesar with a knife? Is it the same event as the stabbing of Caesar with a knife by Brutus? When did the event start: with Brutus conceiving of the action? with Brutus lifting his hand? with Brutus pushing the knife into Caesar? If the last, how far into Caesar did the knife go in that event?

The only way anyone has been able to specify events is by using propositions that are meant to describe them. Thus, each of the above is a different event because each of the following is a different proposition: "Caesar was stabbed", "Caesar was stabbed with a knife", "Caesar was stabbed with a knife by Brutus", "Caesar was stabbed with a knife by Brutus only when Brutus lifted his hand with the knife", ...[74] No other way has been presented that is clear enough to use as the basis of naming in our models. Thus, to understand how to reason with events, we need to know how to parse and hence how to reason with the propositions that were supposed to be explicated by rewriting them by appeal to hidden variables ranging over events.[75]

---

[71] *Events in the Semantics of English*, p. 146.

[72] See "Explanations" in *Cause and Effect, Conditionals, Explanations* and Appendix 2 to "Prescriptive Theories?" in *Prescriptive Reasoning*. It also misconstrues the work of physicists because all that true (enough) consequences of a theory show us is the range of application of a theory, as explained in "Models and Theories" in *Reasoning in Science and Mathematics*.

[73] A general critique can be found in E. J. Borowski, "Adverbials in Action Sentences". I survey problems that arise in taking events as the basis for causal analyses in Appendix 1 of "Reasoning about Cause and Effect" in *Cause and Effect, Conditionals, Explanations*

[74] Compare Parsons in *Events in the Semantics of English*, pp. 145–146:

> Most events and states are concrete entities, not abstract ones. First, they are located in space. Since Brutus stabbed Caesar in the marketplace, the theory tells us that there was a stabbing, by Brutus, of Caesar, and the stabbing was in the marketplace.

Some disagree. Robin Le Poidevin in "Relatonism and Temporal Topology" says:

> Not only are events, on the face of it, less mysterious entities than instants, they are clearly things with which we can causally interact. p. 152

But instants are no more mysterious than points in geometry: we arrive at them through a process of abstraction. In any application of a theory of time in which instants play a role, we take as instants intervals of time so short that their duration is negligible relative to the rest of what we are paying attention to.[76] Events, on the other hand, are not obviously entities at all. As Benson Mates pointed out to me, "The cat is on the mat" is supposed to be made true by or describe an event. But what is included in that event? The cat is touching the mat? The cat is upon the mat? The mat is upon the earth, because up and down can only be determined relative to that? Where do we stop? Probably only at the entire universe. But simply, the event is that the cat is on the mat. We use "that" to restate the claim.

There is a further problem that I have not seen discussed elsewhere. Consider:

(‡) Juney is a dog.

If events are used in the foundations of predicate logic, then this should be converted into event talk as something like:

> There is an event and it is a dogging and it is by Juney.

But that is to convert "is a dog" into a process and then to convert that back to a thing. I've never seen anything like this. Rather, what is assumed is that (‡) is already in primitive form. But then we have an assumption that process verbs and classification verbs are quite distinct metaphysically so that every use of a non-copula verb is an implicit quantification while every use of a copula verb isn't. There seems to be no justification for this metaphysical distinction other than following the implicit metaphysics of some particular language, in this case English, which doesn't seem to be based on anything like an

---

[75] Nicholas Unwin in "The Individuation of Events" presents a survey of this problem. Arthur Prior in *Past, Present and Future*, p. 18, paraphrases talk of events in favor of talk of propositions.

Donald Davidson in "Causal Relations" says events are needed to clarify and to give the truth conditions of causal claims, since we apparently talk of events in our ordinary speech. He says that we need events as things, because otherwise we wouldn't be able to give the logical form of causal claims, meaning a predicate-logic form. But after surveying all the possibilities for criteria of individuating events, Davidson in "The Individuation of Events" comes to the conclusion that the best criterion we can muster is that events are different if and only if they differ in their causes and/or effects. That is, we need events to understand cause and effect, but first we need to understand causes and effects to be able to distinguish events. However, if we cast talk of events as talk of propositions we can analyze cause and effect quite well, as I show in "Reasoning about Cause and Effect".

It might seem that I, too, am committed to events and actions as things. In Example 16 of Chapter 12, I say "Spot was doing something". But that kind of speech is an artefact of English, which leads us to reify much that on reflection neither you nor I would consider to be a thing, for example, a huff, a snit, a hurry. When I say "Spot was doing something" I can be understood as meaning nothing more than "There is some verb such that 'Spot was (verb)ing'" or "There is some predicate P such that $P(\text{Spot})$".

[76] Compare the discussion of points and lines in geometry in "Mathematics as the Art of Abstraction" in *Reasoning in Science and Mathematics*.

understanding of the nature of the world, just accreted habits of speech crystallized in a grammar, as I discuss in Appendix 3 here.

Propositions are meant to describe the world at some place and time, at least if they are not meant to be about abstract objects. To reify the "part of the world" at that place and time and call it "an event" does not clarify, nor does it expand the scope of predicate logic; it only leads to confusions.

Appendix 3 The Dynamic and the Static

The view that predicates are to be divided into those that are dynamic and those that are static has a long history in formal logic. Peter Øhrstrøm and Per F.V. Hasle in *Temporal Logic* describe that view in medieval times:

> The general problem [of beginning and ending] had to do with the correct understanding of "incipit-statements" such as:
>
> (1) "Socrates begins to be white",
> (2) "Socrates begins to run",
>
> and analogously for statements containing the verb "desinit". The task of the logician was to give clear semantic definitions of "incipit" ("begins") and "desinit" ("ends"). The most common definition given in order to clarify the meaning of the above examples was the following:
>
> (1´) "Socrates is white and was not white immediately before"
> (2´) "Socrates does not run, but will run immediately after"
>
> This interpretation was for example defended by Peter of Spain (d. 1277). Obviously, the treatment offered by (1´) and (2´) does not fit the same pattern, or paradigm; "whiteness" and "running" are treated differently. This difference—inspired by Aristotle's treatment in the Physics—originates in a distinction between permanent things or states (whose parts appear simultaneously), and successive things or states (whose parts appear after one another). Medieval logicians considered the property of "running" to be successive and "whiteness" to be permanent. Hence the two kinds of predicates had to be treated differently. p. 52

But not all languages divide experience into what happens quickly as indicated with verbs versus what is static over time as indicated with nouns. Indeed, even in English that is not what we really do, as Benjamin Lee Whorf points out in "Science and Linguistics":

> In English we divide most of our words into two classes, which have different grammatical and logical properties. Class 1 we call nouns, e.g., "house, man"; class 2, verbs, e.g., "hit, run." Many words of one class can act secondarily as of the other class, e.g., "a hit, a run," or "to man (the boat)," but on the primary level, the division between the classes is absolute. Our language thus gives us a bipolar division of nature. But nature herself is not thus polarized. If it be said that "strike, turn, run," are verbs because they denote temporary or short-lasting events, i.e., actions, why then is "fist" a noun? It is also a temporary event. Why are "lightning, spark, wave, eddy, pulsation, flame, storm, phase, cycle, spasm, noise, emotion" nouns? They are temporary events. If "man" and "house" are nouns because they are long-lasting and stable events, i.e., things, what then are "keep, adhere, extend, project, continue, persist, grow, dwell," and so on doing among the verbs? If it be objected that "possess, adhere" are verbs because they are stable relationships rather than stable percepts, why then should "equilibrium, pressure, current, peace, group, nation, society, tribe, sister," or any kinship term be among the nouns? It will be found that an "event" to us means "what our language classes as a verb" or something analogized therefrom. And it will be found that it is not possible to define

> "event, thing, object, relationship," and so on, from nature, but that to define them always involves a circuitous return to the grammatical categories of the definer's language.
>
> In the Hopi language, "lightning, wave, flame, meteor, puff of smoke, pulsation" are verbs—events of necessarily brief duration cannot be anything but verbs. "Cloud" and "storm" are at about the lower limit of duration for nouns. Hopi, you see, actually has a classification of events (or language isolates) by duration type, something strange to our modes of thought. On the other hand, in Nootka, a language of Vancouver Island, all words seem to us to be verbs, but really there are no classes 1 and 2; we have, as it were, a monistic view of nature that gives us only one class of word for all kinds of events. "A house occurs" or "it houses" is the way of saying "house," exactly like "a flame occurs" or "it burns." These terms seem to us like verbs because they are inflected for duration and temporal nuances, so that the suffixes of the word for house event make it mean long-lasting house, temporary house, future house, house that used to be, what started out as a house, and so on.   pp. 215–216.

Otto Jespersen in *The Philosophy of Grammar* had previously noted that in English we could tense nouns:

> It is, of course, possible to imagine a language so constructed that we might see from the form of the word whether the sunset we are speaking about belongs to the past, to the present, or to the future. In such a language the words for "bride, wife, widow" would be three tense-forms of the same root. We may find a first feeble approximation to this in the prefix *ex-*, which in recent times has come into common use in several European languages: *ex-king*, *ex-roi*, etc. Otherwise we must have recourse to adjuncts of various kinds: the *late* Lord Mayor; a *future* Prime Minister; an owner, *present* or *prospective*, of property; he dreamt of home, or of *what was home once*; the life *to come*; she was already the *expected* mother of this child, etc. . . .
>
> In some far-off languages tense-distinctions of substantives are better represented. Thus, in the Alaska Eskimo we find that *ningla* "cold, frost," has a preterit *ninglithluk* and a future *ninglikak*, and from *puyok* "smoke" is formed a preterit *puyuthluk* "what has been smoke," and a future *puyoqkak* "what will become smoke," an ingenious name for gunpowder . . . Similarly in other American languages. Thus the prefix *-neen* in Athapascan (Hupa) denotes past time both in substantives and verbs . . .   pp. 282–283

The division between process predicates and classification predicates is not a difference that has a clear semantic basis and so is not a division that should be taken to be fundamental in our metaphysics. To place such a division into our formal logic would be only to try to track the vagaries of English or some other similar language. Moreover, the division gets in the way of incorporating tenses into our logical analyses, as I show in Volume 2, *Time and Space in Formal Logic*. And there is definitely no room for such a distinction in the logic of the world as process, as presented in Volume 3, *The World as Process*.

Appendix 4 Propositional Operators

Some see adverbs as modifiers not of predicates but of propositions. For example, in "Changes in Events and Changes in Things", p. 40, Arthur Prior says that in "I am allegedly having my breakfast", the adverb "allegedly" modifies the proposition "I am having my breakfast".

So consider:

(1)   John loves Mary.

This is not a proposition. In order to be true or false, references must be supplied for the words "John" and "Mary". But a lot more must be specified: the time which it is meant to describe, how we understand "loves", and more. To do so, at least in classical predicate logic, is to provide a model, a description of a way the world could be. Until we have done that, (1) is a scheme of propositions, not a proposition.

Suppose we have settled on how to convert the scheme (1) into a proposition. Let's label that:

(2)   <u>John loves Mary</u>.

Suppose now that under the same assumptions that convert the scheme (1) into (2), someone asserts:

(3)   John loves Mary passionately.

This, then, is a proposition. In what we've done, the adverb "passionately" is taken to be a modifier of "loves", part of the internal structure of a predicate. Then we relate the proposition (3) to the proposition (2) by noting that (2) is a consequence of (3).

To take "passionately" in (3) as a propositional operator means to view (3) as:

(4)   Passionately (John loves Mary).

In that case, the semantic value of (4), which in classical predicate logic is just its truth-value, must be a result of "passionately" applied to the semantic value of (2). But there are only four choices: "passionately" converts (i) a true proposition into a true one and a false one into a false one; (ii) a true one into a false one and a false one into a true one; (iii) a true one into a true one and a false one into a true one; or (iv) a true one into a true one and a false one into a false one. All these we can formalize using our propositional operators.

Those who advocate viewing adverbs as propositional operators say that such an analysis misses the point. To use a propositional operator such as "passionately" we must assume that propositions have more semantic value than just truth-value. What that value might be in this case is not clear to me. However, such advocates are explict about what semantic value is involved when they deal with the adverb "possibly".

Consider:

(5)   Possibly, John loves Mary.

The semantic value of (5), it is said, is determined by the truth-value of (2) and a further semantic value of (2): the ways in which (2) could be true. Thus, (5) is true just in case there is a way the world could be, that is, a possibility, in which "John loves Mary" is true. This is the standard analysis given in formal modal logic, as presented in my *Propositional Logics*. But there is only one way (2) could be true, the way that we chose in converting (1) into (2). What could be true in different ways and what could be false in different ways is (1). That is, "possibly" in (5) does not operate on (2) but on (1). The proposition (2) is not part of (5). To deny that is to confuse the scheme (1) with the proposition (2). That is what modal logicians do, and I know no way to rescue that misguided approach to logic.

It is not just "possibly" that gives rise to a scheme vs. proposition confusion but also "necessarily", "in the past", "in the future", "allegedly", and, I suspect, any adverb that someone might choose to treat as a propositional operator. Note that this scheme vs. proposition confusion does not arise with our propositional operators $\neg, \rightarrow, \wedge$, and $\vee$. For example, consider:

(6) $\neg$ (John loves Mary)

Under the same assumptions that convert the scheme (1) into (2), (6) is a proposition whose truth-value is determined by (2). That is, (2) is indeed a part of (1).

In "Reflections on Temporal and Modal Logic" I discuss this problem of confusing schemes with propositions in greater detail.

Appendix 5   A Mathematical Abstraction of the Semantics

The nature of formal semantics
Semantics is the study of meaning. The semantics we've given for our systems take as given the truth or falsity of each atomic predication and then use an inductive definition of truth in a model. The relation of the truth-values of some atomic predications to the truth-values of others, as codified in the semantic conditions on the model, are part of the semantics. We arrive at those conditions by reflecting on what we mean in asserting propositions of certain kinds and by reflecting on what follows from certain kinds of assertions involving various parts of language. This is the notion of meaning we have incorporated in our models.

We did not give an analysis of the meaning of each part of speech, such as predicates or restrictors, independently of that. We can't if we wish our semantics to be generally acceptable to people who hold very different views of the nature of language, truth, and the world. A platonist, a pragmatist, an idealist can all adopt our formal system, each giving a different explanation of the meaning of those parts of language. They need agree only that we will reason about things, that a (temporary) name is used to refer to one thing, and that an atomic predicate is true or false of each thing or sequence of things under discussion.

Some would say we have not given semantics for a formal system until we have supplemented what we have given with a fuller analysis or explanation of what it means for an atomic predicate to apply to an object or objects. That is part of a larger project, a metaphysics beyond that of assuming the world is made up at least in part of things. It can be a descriptive project for which the logician looks to the linguist and anthropologist: this is what people take as the meaning of such assertions. It can be a descriptive project for which the logician looks to the metaphysician: this is the underlying reality of the world that makes such assertions true or false. Or it can be a prescriptive project: this is what people should believe or mean when they make such assertions.

It has become common in modern formal logic to take one particular approach to giving a fuller analysis of meaning in formal semantics. Some variant of set theory is used as giving the meaning of atomic predications. In classical predicate logic a predicate is identified with its extension, those things or ordered n-tuples of things of which it is true. That extension is considered to be a set. A predicate is true of a thing or an n-tuple iff that thing or n-tuple is in the set that is the extension of the predicate.

This can be viewed as giving a fuller account of the meaning of the parts of speech and propositions of the formal system only if we accept that sets have an independent existence as abstract objects. Such semantics then would be either prescriptive for how we should understand our assertions or descriptive of an underlying reality of the nature of the world, language, and truth that give meaning to our assertions, a distinctly platonic reality. Those semantics are certainly not descriptive of how we actually do ascribe meaning to the various parts of speech.

The underlying reality of those sets is explicated in a formal set theory, a theory that is itself given in classical predicate logic. A circle of meaning dependence is present in such analyses, though it is not clearly vicious. Different set theories are proposed that are meant to give the meaning of atomic predications, leading to a proliferation of possible platonic interpretations of meaning in formal logic.

236   Appendix 5

There is a very different view of the role of set theory in formal semantics. Set theory is an abstraction of our notion of a predicate applying to an object or objects.[77] We devise it in the same way we devise other mathematics, through a process of abstraction.[78] If we abstract from meaning in the same way, identifying a predicate with its (informal) extension, then semantics formulated in terms of set theory give a mathematical analysis of meaning, as I show for classical predicate logic in Appendix 8 of Volume 0. We can then apply the methods of mathematics to derive structural analyses of our formal system.

Here I will present a mathematical abstraction of the semantics of classical predicate logic with predicate modifiers, internal conjunctions of predicates and modifiers, and internal disjunctions of predicates. After that I give mathematical semantics for conjunctions of terms.

I will let you choose what mathematical theory of sets you wish to adopt, whether constructive or nonconstructive, allowing for only finite sets or infinite ones, too, with strong cardinality axioms or not. However, such a theory must allow for ur-elements, that is, objects that are themselves not sets but can be elements of any set, such as dogs. Otherwise, we could not interpret the predicate "— is a dog" (or interpret a formal predicate symbol) as the collection of all dogs.

I assume familiarity with the usual notation of set theory. Sequences of elements of the universe are notated with angle brackets, viz., <a,b>.

Classical Predicate Logic with Predicate Modifers, Internal Conjunctions, and Internal Disjunctions

The universe
The universe of the realization is a non-empty set U.

Assignments of references
An assignment of references σ is any function:

$\sigma: \{u : u$ is a term of the semi-formal language$\} \to$ U

The collection of such functions is a set, and together they satisfy the condition:

If c is a name of the semi-formal language and σ, τ are assignments of references, then $\sigma(c) = \tau(c)$.

We assume that in, whatever set theory you are employing, the set of assignments of references is complete (p. 21).

Extensions of predicates
To define the extensions of all atomic predicates, we induct on the degee of atomic predicates of the semi-formal language.

Stage 0

$\mathsf{E}: \{P: P$ is a simple predicate$\} \to$ subsets of $\bigcup_n U^n$

where if P is n-ary, $\mathsf{E}(P) \subseteq$ subsets of U^n

---

[77] See Chapter XIV, "Second-Order Classical Predicate Logic" in *Classical Mathematical Logic*.
[78] See "Mathematics as the Art of Abstraction".

The set $\mathsf{E}(P)$ is the *extension of* P. Then for every assignment of references σ,

$$\mathsf{v}_\sigma \vDash (P)(u_1, \ldots, u_n) \text{ iff } \langle \sigma(u_1), \ldots, \sigma(u_n) \rangle \in \mathsf{E}(P)$$

Because the extension of an atomic wff is a subset of *n*-tuples of the universe, all predications are extensional.

The *extension of the equality predicate* is:

$$\langle \mathsf{a}, \mathsf{b} \rangle \in \mathsf{E}(\equiv) \text{ iff } \mathsf{a} = \mathsf{b}$$

Then for every assignment of references σ,

$$\mathsf{v}_\sigma \vDash (-\equiv-)(u_1, u_2) \text{ iff } \langle \sigma(u_1), \sigma(u_2) \rangle \in \mathsf{E}(\equiv)$$

Stage m + 1

For every atomic predicate B of degree $\leq m$, there is an extension **B** assigned to it. We now define the extension of every atomic predicate of degree $m + 1$ by defining (at stage 1) or extending (at stages $m + 1 \geq 2$) the following functions.

Non-variable Restrictors

To each simple non-variable restrictor R we associate a function **R** such that for each *n*:

$$\mathsf{R}: \{\mathsf{B}: \mathsf{B} \text{ is an } n\text{-ary atomic predicate of degree} \leq m\} \to \text{subsets of } \mathsf{U}^n$$

satisfying $\mathsf{R}(\mathsf{B}) \subseteq \mathsf{B}$

The *extension of* B/R is $\mathsf{R}(\mathsf{B})$. Then for every sequence of things of the universe that satisfy B/R:

$$\mathsf{v}_\sigma \vDash (B/R)(u_1, \ldots, u_n) \text{ iff } \langle \sigma(u_1), \ldots, \sigma(u_n) \rangle \in \mathsf{R}(\mathsf{B})$$

Note that **R** is a function from linguistic predicates to subsets of the set of *n*-tuples of the universe; it is not a function on extensions of predicates. See the discussion of the extensionality of restrictors in Chapter 13.

Variable restrictors

For each *k*-ary variable restrictor R we associate a function **R** such that for each *n*:

$$\mathsf{R}: \{\mathsf{B}: \mathsf{B} \text{ is an } k\text{-ary atomic predicate of degree} \leq m\} \times \mathsf{U}^k \to \text{subsets of } \mathsf{U}^k$$

satisfying $\mathsf{R}(\langle \mathsf{B}, \langle \mathsf{b}_1, \ldots, \mathsf{b}_k \rangle \rangle) \subseteq \mathsf{B}$

For each assignment of references σ, the set $\mathsf{R}(\langle \mathsf{B}, \langle \mathsf{b}_1, \ldots, \mathsf{b}_k \rangle \rangle)$ is the *extension* of $(B/R)(u_1, \ldots, u_k)$ *relative to* σ, and

$$\mathsf{v}_\sigma \vDash ((B/R)(v_1, \ldots, u_k))(u_1, \ldots, u_k) \text{ iff}$$

$$\langle \sigma(u_1), \ldots, \sigma(u_n) \rangle \in \mathsf{R}(\langle \mathsf{B}, \langle \sigma(v_1), \ldots, \sigma(v_n) \rangle \rangle)$$

Negators

For each negator N other than $\sim$ we associate a function **N** such that for each *n*:

$$\mathsf{N}: \{\mathsf{B}: \mathsf{B} \text{ is an } n\text{-ary atomic wff of degree} \leq m\} \to \text{subsets of } \mathsf{U}^n$$

satisfying $\mathsf{N}(\mathsf{B}) \cap \mathsf{B} = \emptyset$

The set $\mathsf{N}(\mathsf{B})$ is the *extension* of B/N and

$$\mathsf{v}_\sigma \vDash (B/N)(u_1, \ldots, u_n) \text{ iff } \langle \sigma(u_1), \ldots, \sigma(u_n) \rangle \in \mathsf{N}(\mathsf{B})$$

The pure predicate negator

For the pure negator $\sim$ there is a function $\sim$ such that for each n:

$\sim$: {B : B is an n-ary atomic wff of degree $\leq m$} $\rightarrow$ subsets of U^n

satisfying $\sim$ (B) = the complement of B in U^n

Modifiers of modifiers

In addition to the conditions above:

If R is a non-variable restrictor and N is a negator, the function F associated with the restrictor R/N satisfies:

$F(B) \cap R(B) = \emptyset$

If R is a n-ary variable restrictor and N is a negator, then the function F associated with the restrictor $R(u_1, \ldots, u_n)/N$ relative to σ satisfies:

$F(B) \cap R(B) = \emptyset$

For pairs of negators N, N' the function F associated with the restrictor N/N' satisfies:

$F(B) \cap N(B) = \emptyset$

For each restrictor R the function F associated with the restrictor $\sim$R satisfies:

$F(B) = B \cap$ the complement of $R(B)$

For each restrictor R the function F associated with the restrictor $\sim$R and the function G associated with R/N satisfy:

$G(B) \subseteq F(B)$

The predicate conjoiner

For the predicate conjoiner + there is a function + such that:

+ : {(B_1, B_2) : B_1 and B_2 unary atomic predicates of degree $\leq m$} $\rightarrow$ subsets of U

and $+((B_1, B_2)) \subseteq B_1 \cap B$

and $+((B_1, B_2 + B_3)) = +((B_1 + B_2, B_3))$

and $+((B_1, B_2/R)) \subseteq +((B_1, B_2))$

and $+((B_1/R_1 \& R_2N)) \subseteq +((B_1/R_1 \& \sim R_2))$

The set $+((B_1, B_2))$ is the *extension* of $B_1 + B_2$ and

$v_\sigma \vDash (B_1 + B_2)(u)$ iff $\sigma(u) \in +((B_1, B_2))$

Since this function is on unordered pairs, we have $+((B_1, B_2)) = +((B_2, B_1))$.

The restrictor conjoiner

For the restrictor conjoiner & there is a function & such that:

& (R, R') = the function associated with the restrictor $R + R'$

and & $((R, R'))(B) \subseteq R(B) \cap R'(B)$

and & $((R_1, R_2 \& R_3)) = $ & $((R_1 \& R_2, R_2))$

and & $((R_1, R_2/N)) = $ & $((R_1, \sim R_3))$

Since this function is on unordered pairs, & $((R, R')) = $ & $((R', R))$

The predicate disjoiner
For the predicate disjoiner $\cup$ there is a function $\cup$ such that:

$\cup : \{(B_1, B_2) : B_1 \text{ and } B_2 \text{ are unary atomic predicates of degree } \leq m+1\} \to$ subsets of U

and $\cup((B_1, B_2)) = B_1 \cup B_2$

and $\cup((B_1, B_2 \cup B_3)) = \cup((B_1 \cup B_2, B_3))$

and $\cup((B_1 \cup B_2)/R)) \subseteq \cup((B_1/R)) \cup \cup((B_2/R))$

and $\cup((B_1 \cup B_2)/R)) \cap B_1 \subseteq \cup((B_1/R))$

The set $\cup((B_1, B_2))$ is the *extension* of $B_1 \cup B_2$ and

$v_\sigma \vDash (B_1 \cup B_2)(u)$ iff $\sigma(u) \in \cup((B_1, B_2))$

Since this function is on unordered pairs, we have $\cup((B_1, B_2)) = \cup((B_2, B_1))$.

In this way we define for every atomic wff B:

$v_\sigma \vDash B(u_1, \ldots, u_n)$ iff $\langle \sigma(u_1), \ldots, \sigma(u_n) \rangle \in B$

These valuations relative to assignments of references are then extended to all wffs in the usual way (p. 25).

I'll let you show that relative to the set theory you adopt all the semantic assumptions of the original theory are satisfied.

Classical Predicate Logic with Conjunctions of Terms
To each simple unary predicate we can assign not only its extension in the usual way but also an extension of unordered pairs of things, an extension of unordered triplets of things, and an extension of unordered n-tuples of things for every n. This is to push the n-ary aspect of a unary predicate into the semantics rather than the syntax.

Formally, to each unary predicate P we associate a sequence of extensions:

$\langle P, P_2, \ldots, P_n, \ldots \rangle$ where $P_n \subseteq U^n$

For an atomic wff $P(d)$ where the terms appearing in d are $u_1, \ldots, u_n$ in order reading from the left with repetitions:

$v_\sigma \vDash P(d)$ iff $\langle \sigma(u_1), \ldots, \sigma(u_n) \rangle \in P_n$

These extensions must satisfy the conditions:

$\langle \sigma(u_1), \ldots, \sigma(u_n) \rangle \in P_n$ iff every permutation of that sequence is also an element of P_n.

If $\langle \sigma(u_1), \ldots, \sigma(u_n) \rangle \in P_n$, then for every i, $\sigma(u_i) \in P$.

A mathematical abstraction for the theory with modifiers is more complicated, and I'll leave that to you.

It might be argued that the mathematical abstraction of the semantics requires the same metaphysics as enlarging a base universe U to $U+ = U \cup U^2 \cup U^3 \cup \ldots$. Formally that is not so. In any case, to mathematize the semantics of any of the systems, we have to adopt substantial metaphysical assumptions beyond those needed to establish the logic, as I discuss in *Classical Mathematical Logic*.

Appendix 6 Parts of Things

Predicate logic is a logic for reasoning about things. Some things have parts. My car has four wheels, and a motor, and a steering wheel. My dog Birta has a tail, four paws, and lots of teeth. We can reason about those as we reason about any other things. Can we take into account in our formal analyses that they are parts?

Suppose we want to talk about all the parts of my dog Birta. How many are there? A tail, a head, a tongue, four paws, ... How do we continue? Do we include the toenail on the left-most toe of her right front paw? Do we include each hair? Do we include the top half of each hair? Do we include each molecule of each hair?

What we take to be a part of a thing depends on what we are paying attention to in our reasoning. Along with a particular notion of part of a thing comes a particular notion of naming. With the notion of part including molecules, naming will be substantially different from the ways we point in order to give names to the hairs of Birta. There is not one notion of naming or any simple disjunction of ways of naming that fits all the ways we could parcel Birta into parts. If we want to talk of all parts of things, we have the same problem we have with a universe of all things: there is too much diversity to assume we can specify a notion of naming.[79]

We can reason about things and particular kinds of parts of those. We use specific predicates in the semi-formal language to distinguish those kinds of parts. We can use a specific predicate "— is a detachable mechanical part", a specific predicate "— is a paw", a specific predicate "— is a molecule". Then pointing-naming can be accomplished, for to use that predicate is to assume that we can identify whether a thing satisfies it. *A predicate is not just true or false; it is a part of how we point to a thing. Predicates are part of our basis of pointing as much as they are part of our notion of truth.*

Parts of things compared to elements of sets
Some logicians have given axiom systems to serve as a guide for how to reason about things and their parts.[80] They add a formal predicate symbol "$P(-,-)$" to the language, which is meant to be an abstraction of "— is a part of —". How does that compare to how logicians and mathematicians have given theories of sets and their elements?

We have an informal notion of a collection of things. We abstract from that and get a theory of sets.[81] But we find that if we use our daily assumptions about collections we get an inconsistent theory. In ordinary reasoning and daily life, any things we encounter we can talk about as a collection, yet the assumption that any things together constitute a set leads to a contradiction—for example, the set of all things that are not elements of themselves. But really we talk of things as constituting a collection only in restricted circumstances when we can "collect" those things under a common description. No one in ordinary speech or

---

[79] In Volume 0, *An Introduction to Formal Logic*, pp. 75–76, I explain why assuming that there is reference without any connection to human understanding and capabilities is an unsatisfactory basis for the semantics of predicate logic.

[80] See "Mereology" by Achille Varzi for a short survey of such work. See Roberto Casati and Achille Varzi, *Parts and Places* for a fuller presentation.

[81] See "Mathematics as the Art of Absraction" for abstracting to create mathematical theories.

reasoning talks about the collection composed of Ralph, the Eiffel Tower, and all canaries. So we jettison the assumption that any things together can comprise a set. Instead, we can collect together things built up from things we already have in a prescribed manner. Depending on what we mean by "a prescribed manner" we get one of many different set theories. Each, it turns out, is incomplete: there is at least one proposition of the semi-formal language such that neither it nor its negation is a consequence of the axioms. So set theorists add more axioms, trying to focus better on that intuitive notion. But quickly they run out of assumptions from our ordinary speech and reasoning. So they turn to assumptions used in or suggested by work in mathematics. Different set theories arise. The question then is whether they are talking about different things or formalizing different aspects of our (more or less) ordinary notion of collection.

With parts of things, if we suppose that any things together can comprise a whole, we get a contradiction: "The thing that is the sum of all things that are not parts of themselves is not a part of itself" is true if it is false, false if it is true. One way to avoid this is to assume that the relation "— is a part of —" is reflexive. But then we can reconstruct the paradox using the relation "— is a proper part of itself —". Yet our ordinary notion of "— is a part of —" does not allow for any things together to count as all the parts of one thing: we do not think that there is a thing made up of exactly Ralph, the Eiffel Tower, and all canaries. So we restrict the ways in which things together can constitute another thing.[82]

One way is to assume we have certain *ur*–things, things that are not parts of anything else. This is compatible with and perhaps even the basis of our usual talk about things. My dog Birta is a thing, but she is not a part of anything. This is like what some set theorists do when they allow ur-elements to be in the universe: elements that have no elements in them. The difference is that with set theory we are, conceptually at least, building up sets from other things in prescribed manners, whereas with a theory of parts of things we are breaking down things into other things, again in prescribed manners if we wish to be consistent.

Using predicate logic to reason about sets, we cannot take as universe all sets. The usual reason given is that to do so generates a contradiction, for the universe, too, would be a set and every set has "fewer things" than the set of its subsets, which are also things. But an equally important reason is that we have no notion of naming and pointing for all sets. The platonist denies that: sets, to a platonist, are abstract things, and we point to all of them in the same way through our intellect. Alternatively, the nominalist identifies sets with predicates, which if understood as pieces of language can be quantified over.

With parts of things, we cannot take as universe some ur-things and all their parts. That's not because we get a contradiction, or at least it doesn't seem to be. Rather, we have no notion of naming and pointing for all parts of things. The platonist response is not available here, for most certainly with a universe whose ur-things are dogs, neither a dog nor any part of it is abstract. Nor is the nominalist approach possible, for we cannot identify Birta's leg with a piece of language.

---

[82] See Casati and Varzi, *Parts and Places*. In "Wholes and Parts: The Limits of Composition", D. H. Mellor argues against what he calls the "principle of unrestricted composition" on the basis of the incongruity of putting different kinds of things into the same notion of part-whole:

> As a rule, part-whole relations relate entities of the same kind. The best way to explain both the rule and the exception to it is to allow a multiplicity of part-whole relations. p. 140

Appendix 7 Completeness Proofs

Classical Propositional Logic (PC) 243

Classical Predicate Logic 246

Classical Predicate Logic with Equality 251

Classical Predicate Logic with Function Names 253

Classical Predicate Logic with Descriptive Names
   and Descriptive Functions 254

Classical Predicate Logic with Non-Referring Simple Names 258

Classical Predicate Logic with Non-Referring Simple Names
   and Names for Partial Functions 263

Classical Predicate Logic with Non-Referring Simple Names,
   Descriptive Names and Descriptive Functions 265

The letter L stands for the formal language of the system under discussion.

I assume that for each language considered here we can number the wffs; see, for example, Walter Carnielli's and my *Computability*.

When no proof is appended to a lemma or theorem I've left the proof to you.

I write "Axiom" for "axiom scheme".

Classical Propositional Logic, PC

The language is $L(\neg, \rightarrow, \wedge, \vee, p_0, p_1, \dots)$. Every wff that is an instance of one of the following schemes is an axiom.

1. $\neg A \rightarrow (A \rightarrow B)$
2. $B \rightarrow (A \rightarrow B)$
3. $(A \rightarrow B) \rightarrow ((\neg A \rightarrow B) \rightarrow B)$
4. $(A \rightarrow (B \rightarrow C)) \rightarrow ((A \rightarrow B) \rightarrow (A \rightarrow C))$
5. $A \rightarrow (B \rightarrow (A \wedge B))$
6. $(A \wedge B) \rightarrow A$
7. $(A \wedge B) \rightarrow B$
8. $A \rightarrow (A \vee B)$
9. $B \rightarrow (A \vee B)$
10. $(A \rightarrow C) \rightarrow ((B \rightarrow C) \rightarrow ((A \vee B) \rightarrow C))$

rule $\dfrac{A, A \rightarrow B}{B}$ *modus ponens*

Lemma 1 Soundness If $\Gamma \vdash A$, then $\Gamma \vDash A$.

Proof I'll let you show that every wff that has the form of one of the axiom schemes is a tautology. Then soundness follows, because if the premises of an instance of *modus ponens* are true in a model, so, too, is the conclusion.

Lemma 2 a. $\vdash A \rightarrow A$
         b. $\{A, \neg A\} \vdash B$

Proof
(a) 1. $\vdash A \rightarrow ((A \rightarrow A) \rightarrow A)$ by Axiom 2
    2. $\vdash A \rightarrow (A \rightarrow A)$ by Axiom 2
    3. $\vdash (A \rightarrow ((A \rightarrow A) \rightarrow A)) \rightarrow ((A \rightarrow (A \rightarrow A)) \rightarrow (A \rightarrow A))$ by Axiom 4
    4. $\vdash (A \rightarrow (A \rightarrow A)) \rightarrow (A \rightarrow A)$ *modus ponens* using (1) and (3)
    5. $\vdash A \rightarrow A$ *modus ponens* using (2) and (4)

(b) 1. $\vdash \neg A \rightarrow (A \rightarrow B)$ by Axiom 1
    2. $\neg A$ premise
    3. $(A \rightarrow B)$ by *modus ponens* using (1) and (2)
    4. A premise
    5. B by *modus ponens* on (3) and (4) ∎

Lemma 3 The Syntactic Deduction Theorem
    a. $\Gamma, A \vdash B$ iff $\Gamma \vdash A \rightarrow B$
    b. $\Gamma \cup \{A_1, \dots, A_n\} \vdash B$ iff $\Gamma \vdash A_1 \rightarrow (A_2 \rightarrow (\cdots \rightarrow (A_n \rightarrow B) \cdots))$

Proof (a) From right to left is immediate, since *modus ponens* is our rule. To show that if $\Gamma, A \vdash B$, then $\Gamma \vdash A \rightarrow B$, suppose that $B_1, \dots, B_n$ is a proof of B from $\Gamma \cup \{A\}$.

I'll show by induction that for each i with $1 \le i \le n$, $\Gamma \vdash A \to B_i$. Either $B_1 \in \Gamma$ or B_1 is an axiom, or B_1 is A. In the first two cases the result follows by using Axiom 2. If B is A, it follows by Lemma 2.a.

Now suppose for all $k < i$, $\vdash A \to B_k$. If B_i is an axiom, or $B_i \in \Gamma$, or B_i is A, we have $\vdash A \to B_i$ as before. The only other case is when B_i is a consequence by *modus ponens* of B_m and $B_j = B_m \to B_i$ for some $m, j < i$. By induction we have both $\Gamma \vdash A \to (B_m \to B_i)$ and $\Gamma \vdash A \to B_m$, so by Axiom 4, $\Gamma \vdash A \to B_i$. ∎

Lemma 4   *a.* Γ is consistent iff there is some B such that $\Gamma \nvdash B$.

         b. $\Gamma \cup \{A\}$ is consistent iff $\Gamma \nvdash \neg A$.

         c. $\Gamma \cup \{\neg A\}$ is consistent iff $\Gamma \nvdash A$.

         d.   If Γ is consistent, then $\Gamma \cup \{A\}$ or $\Gamma \cup \{\neg A\}$ is consistent.

         e.   If Γ is consistent and complete, then Γ is a theory.

         f. Γ is consistent iff every finite subset of Γ is consistent.

Proof (a) From left to right is immediate. So suppose $\Gamma \cup \{A\}$ is not consistent. Then for some A, $\Gamma \vdash A$ and $\Gamma \vdash \neg A$. So by Lemma 2.b, for every B, $\Gamma \vdash B$.

(b) We proceed by proving the contrapositive in each direction. Suppose $\Gamma \vdash \neg A$. So $\Gamma \cup \{A\} \vdash \neg A$. But also $\Gamma \cup \{A\} \vdash A$. So $\Gamma \cup \{A\}$ is inconsistent. Now suppose that $\Gamma \cup \{A\}$ is inconsistent. By part (a), $\Gamma \cup \{A\} \vdash \neg A$. Hence by Lemma 3, $\Gamma \vdash A \to \neg A$. By Lemma 2.a, $\Gamma \vdash \neg A \to \neg A$. Hence by Axiom 3, $\Gamma \vdash \neg A$.

(c) The proof is as for (b).

(d) Suppose both $\Gamma \cup \{A\}$ and $\Gamma \cup \{\neg A\}$ are inconsistent. Then by (b) and (c), $\Gamma \vdash A$ and $\Gamma \vdash \neg A$, and hence Γ is inconsistent.

(e) Suppose that Γ is complete and consistent, and $\Gamma \vdash A$. If A is not in Γ, then $\neg A$ is in Γ, and hence $\Gamma \vdash \neg A$, so that Γ would be inconsistent. So A is in Γ.

(f) If Γ is inconsistent, then for some A, $\Gamma \vdash A$ and $\Gamma \vdash \neg A$. Let $B_1, \ldots, B_n$ be a proof of A from Γ, and let $C_1, \ldots, C_m$ be a proof of $\neg A$ from Γ. Then we have that $\{B_1, \ldots, B_n, C_1, \ldots, C_m\}$ is a finite subset of Γ that is not consistent. On the other hand, if some finite subset $\Delta \subseteq \Gamma$ is inconsistent, then for some A, $\Delta \vdash A$ and $\Delta \vdash \neg A$. But the same proofs are proofs from Γ, too. So Γ is inconsistent. ∎

Lemma 5 Γ is a complete and consistent theory iff there is a model with valuation υ such that $\Gamma = \{A: \upsilon(A) = T\}$.

Proof I'll let you show that the set of wffs true in a model is a complete and consistent theory.

Suppose now that Γ is a complete and consistent theory. Define a valuation on all wffs by $\upsilon(A) = T$ iff $A \in \Gamma$. To show that υ is a model we need to show that it evaluates the connectives correctly.

If $\upsilon(\neg A) = T$, then $\neg A \in \Gamma$, so by consistency $A \notin \Gamma$, so $\upsilon(A) = F$. If $\upsilon(A) = F$, then $A \notin \Gamma$, so by completeness $\neg A \in \Gamma$, so $\upsilon(\neg A) = T$.

Suppose $\upsilon(A \to B) = T$. Then $A \to B \in \Gamma$. If $\upsilon(A) = T$, then $A \in \Gamma$, so $\Gamma \vdash B$, and since Γ is a theory, $B \in \Gamma$, so $\upsilon(B) = T$. Suppose now that $\upsilon(A) = F$ or $\upsilon(B) = T$. If the former then $A \notin \Gamma$, so $\neg A \in \Gamma$, and by Axiom 1, $A \to B \in \Gamma$; so $\upsilon(A \to B) = T$. If the latter, then $B \in \Gamma$, and as Γ is a theory, by Axiom 2, $A \to B \in \Gamma$; so $\upsilon(A \to B) = T$.

For conjunction,

$v(A \wedge B) = T$ iff $v(A) = T$ and $v(B) = T$
iff $A \in \Gamma$ and $B \in \Gamma$
iff $(A \wedge B) \in \Gamma$ using Axioms 5, 6 and 7

For disjunction, if $A \in \Gamma$ or $B \in \Gamma$, then $(A \vee B) \in \Gamma$ by Axioms 8 and 9. So if $v(A) = T$ or $v(B) = T$, then $v(A \vee B) = T$. In the other direction, if $v(A \vee B) = T$, then $(A \vee B) \in \Gamma$. Suppose that $A \notin \Gamma$. Since Γ is complete, $\neg A \in \Gamma$. Hence, $\Gamma \cup \{A\}$ is inconsistent. So by Lemma 4.a, for any C we have $\Gamma \cup \{A\} \vdash C$. Similarly, if $B \notin \Gamma$, then for any C we have $\Gamma \cup \{B\} \vdash C$. So by the Syntactic Deduction Theorem (Lemma 3), for any C, $\Gamma \vdash A \rightarrow C$ and $\Gamma \vdash B \rightarrow C$. Hence by Axiom 10, $\Gamma \vdash (A \vee B) \rightarrow C$. As $(A \vee B) \in \Gamma$, this means that for every C, $\Gamma \vdash C$, which is a contradiction on the consistency of Γ. Hence, either $A \in \Gamma$ or $B \in \Gamma$, so $v(A) = T$ or $v(B) = T$. ■

Lemma 6 If $\nvdash D$, then there is some complete and consistent theory Γ such that $D \notin \Gamma$.

Proof Let $A_0, A_1, \ldots$ be a numbering of the wffs of the formal language. Define:

$\Gamma_0 = \{\neg D\}$

$\Gamma_{n+1} = \begin{cases} \Gamma_n \cup \{A_n\} & \text{if this is consistent} \\ \Gamma_n & \text{otherwise} \end{cases}$

$\Gamma = \bigcup_n \Gamma_n$

Γ_0 is consistent by Lemma 4.b. So by construction, each Γ_n is consistent. Hence Γ is consistent, for if not some finite $\Delta \subseteq \Gamma$ is inconsistent by Lemma 4.f, and Δ being finite, $\Delta \subseteq \Gamma_n$ for some n, so Γ_n would be inconsistent.

Γ is complete because if $\Gamma \nvdash A$, then by Lemma 4, $\Gamma \cup \{\neg A\}$ is consistent, and hence by construction, $\neg A \in \Gamma$, and so $\Gamma \vdash \neg A$.

Finally, Γ is a theory, since if $\Gamma \vdash A$, then $\Gamma \cup \{A\}$ is consistent, and hence by construction, $A \in \Gamma$. ■

Theorem 7

    a. *Completeness* $\Gamma \vdash A$ iff $\Gamma \vDash A$.

    b. *Compactness* Γ has a model iff every finite subset of Γ has a model.

    c. If $\vdash A$, then there is a proof of A in which the only propositional variables that appear in the proof are those that appear in A.

Proof a. By Lemma 1, we need only show that if $\Gamma \vDash A$ then $\Gamma \vdash A$. If $\Gamma \vDash A$, suppose that $\Gamma \nvdash A$. Then by Lemma 4, $\Gamma \cup \{\neg A\}$ is consistent, and so by Lemmas 5 and 6 it has a model. So $\Gamma \nvDash A$, a contradiction. Hence, $\Gamma \vdash A$.

b. Γ has a model iff Γ is consistent (Lemmas 5 and 6). Γ is consistent iff every finite subset of Γ is consistent (Lemma 4). Every finite subset of Γ is consistent iff every finite subset of Γ has a model (Lemmas 5 and 6).

c. All the proofs here apply regardless of the collection of propositional variables in the formal language. If $\vdash A$, then $\vDash A$. Hence, A is valid also for the language whose only propositional variables are those that appear in A. Hence, by part (a), A is a theorem of the language whose only propositional variables are those that appear in A. ■

Classical Predicate Logic

The language L is $L(\neg, \rightarrow, \wedge, \vee, \forall, \exists; P_0, P_1, \ldots, c_0, c_1, \ldots)$.

A *propositional form* of a wff in this language is a wff B of the language of classical propositional logic, $L(\neg, \rightarrow, \wedge, \vee, p_0, p_1, \ldots)$, such that there is a way to assign wffs of L, possibly open, to the propositional variables in B that results in A, where the *substitution (replacement) is uniform*: the same variable is assigned the same wff throughout B.

By "PC" I mean classical propositional logic.

Recall that only closed wffs can appear in a proof sequence.

I. *Propositional axioms*

The axiom schemes of classical propositional logic, where wffs are substituted uniformly for A, B, C and the universal closure is taken.

II. *Axioms governing* $\forall$

1. a. $\forall \ldots (\forall x (A \rightarrow B) \rightarrow (\forall x A \rightarrow \forall x B))$ *distribution of* $\forall$
      if x is free in both A and B
   b. $\forall \ldots (\forall x (A \rightarrow B) \rightarrow (\forall x A \rightarrow B))$
      if x is free in A and not free in B
   c. $\forall \ldots (\forall x (A \rightarrow B) \rightarrow (A \rightarrow \forall x B))$
      if x is free in B and not free in A

2. $\forall \ldots (\forall x \forall y A \rightarrow \forall y \forall x A)$ *commutativity of* $\forall$

3. $\forall \ldots (\forall x A(x) \rightarrow A(u/x))$ *universal instantiation*
   when u is free for x in A

III. *Axioms governing the relation between* $\forall$ *and* $\exists$

4. a. $\forall \ldots (\exists x A \rightarrow \neg \forall x \neg A)$
   b. $\forall \ldots (\neg \forall x \neg A \rightarrow \exists x A)$

rule $\dfrac{A, A \rightarrow B}{B}$ for A, B closed wffs

Lemma 8 *Soundness of the axiomatization* If $\Gamma \vdash A$, then $\Gamma \vDash A$.

Proof See pp. 84–85 of Volume 0.

Lemma 9 *The Syntactic Deduction Theorem*
   a. $\Gamma, A \vdash B$ iff $\Gamma \vdash A \rightarrow B$.
   b. $\Gamma \cup \{A_1, \ldots, A_n\} \vdash B$ iff $\Gamma \vdash A_1 \rightarrow (A_2 \rightarrow (\cdots \rightarrow (A_n \rightarrow B) \cdots))$.

Proof Since A, B, and all wffs in Γ are closed, the proof is as for PC. ∎

Lemma 10 If $\vdash A \rightarrow B$ and $\vdash B \rightarrow C$, then $\vdash A \rightarrow C$.

Proof If $\vdash A \rightarrow B$ and $\vdash B \rightarrow C$, then $A \vdash B$ and $B \vdash C$. Combining those proofs we have a proof of C from A. So by the Syntactic Deduction Theorem, $\vdash A \rightarrow C$. ∎

Lemma 11 a. $\vdash \forall \ldots (A \rightarrow B) \rightarrow (\forall \ldots A \rightarrow \forall \ldots B)$
   b. Generalized *modus ponens* $\{\forall \ldots (A \rightarrow B), \forall \ldots A\} \vdash \forall \ldots B$

Proof a. We proceed by induction on the number of variables in the universal closure for $(A \rightarrow B)$. If $n = 0$, this is just $\vdash (A \rightarrow B) \rightarrow (A \rightarrow B)$, which we have by the PC axioms as in Lemma 2. If $n = 1$, this is one of the schemes of Axiom 1. Suppose the lemma is true for n. Let x be the last variable (in alphabetical order) that appears free in $(A \rightarrow B)$. We have three cases, depending on whether x appears free in A, B, or both. I will do one case and leave the others to you. An instance of Axiom 1 is:

$$\forall \ldots (\forall x (A \rightarrow B) \rightarrow (\forall x A \rightarrow B))$$

Since the universal closure of this formula has only n variables, we have (a) by induction. Part (b) then follows from (a). ∎

Lemma 12 **PC in predicate logic** If A has the form of a PC-tautology, then $\vdash \forall \ldots A$.

Proof Suppose that one form of A is the PC-tautology B. By the completeness theorem for PC, there is a proof $B_1, \ldots, B_n = B$ in PC. By Theorem 7.c, we can assume there is no propositional variable appearing in any of $B_1, \ldots, B_n$ that does not also appear in B. Let B_i^* be B_i with propositional variables replaced by predicate wffs just as they are replaced in B to obtain A. I'll show by induction on i that $\vdash \forall \ldots B_i^*$. The lemma will then follow for $i = n$.

For $i = 1$, B_1 is a PC-axiom. Suppose now that for all $j < i$, $\vdash \forall \ldots B_j^*$. If B_i is a PC-axiom, we are done. If not, then for some $j, k < i$, B_j is $B_k \rightarrow B_i$. Since $(B_k \rightarrow B_i)^*$ is $B_k^* \rightarrow B_i^*$, by induction we have $\vdash \forall \ldots B_k^*$ and $\vdash \forall \ldots (B_k^* \rightarrow B_i^*)$. Hence by generalized *modus ponens*, $\vdash \forall \ldots B_i^*$. ∎

When invoking Lemma 11 or Lemma 12, I'll just say "by PC". Here is an example.

The transitivity of $\rightarrow$ $\forall \ldots (A \rightarrow B), \forall \ldots (B \rightarrow C) \vdash \forall \ldots (A \rightarrow C)$

By PC, we have $\vdash \forall \ldots [(A \rightarrow B) \rightarrow ((B \rightarrow C) \rightarrow (A \rightarrow C))]$. So by Lemma 11, we have $\forall \ldots (A \rightarrow B) \vdash \forall \ldots (B \rightarrow C) \rightarrow (A \rightarrow C)$, and using Lemma 1 again, the transitivity of $\rightarrow$ follows.

Lemma 13 If $y_1 \ldots y_n$ are the variables free in A in alphabetic order, then:

$$\vdash \forall \ldots A \rightarrow \forall y_k \forall y_1 \ldots \forall y_{k-1} \forall y_{k+1} \ldots \forall y_n A.$$

Proof We induct on n. For $n = 0$ or 1, this is by PC. For $n = 2$ this is an instance of Axiom 2. Suppose now the lemma is true for fewer than n variables. If $k \neq n$, we are done by induction (replacing A by $\forall y_n A$). If $k = n$, then by Axiom 2:

$$\vdash \forall \ldots ((\forall y_{n-1} \forall y_n A) \rightarrow (\forall y_n \forall y_{n-1} A))$$

By induction, since there are less than n variables in the prefix $\forall \ldots$ here, we can permute them to obtain: $\vdash \forall y_1 \ldots \forall y_{n-2} (\forall y_{n-1} \forall y_n A) \rightarrow \forall y_1 \ldots \forall y_{n-2} (\forall y_n \forall y_{n-1} A)$.
By induction we have:

$$\vdash \forall y_1 \ldots \forall y_{n-2} \forall y_n (\forall y_{n-1} A) \rightarrow \forall y_n \forall y_1 \ldots \forall y_{n-2} (\forall y_{n-1} A)$$

Hence by Lemma 10, we are done. ∎

Lemma 14 Let $B(x)$ be a formula with one free variable x.
  a. If $\vdash B(c/x)$, then $\vdash \forall x B(x)$.
  b. If $\Gamma \vdash B(c/x)$ and c does not appear in any wff in Γ, then $\Gamma \vdash \forall x B(x)$.

Proof a. We proceed by induction on the length of a proof of $B(c/x)$. If the proof has length 1, then $B(c/x)$ is an axiom. I will show that (a) holds for instances of Axiom 1.a. Instances of the other axiom schemes follow similarly.

One instance of the scheme is:

$$\vdash (\forall \ldots)_1 (\forall y (C(c/x) \to D(c/x))) \to (\forall y\, C(c/x) \to \forall y\, D(c/x))$$

But another instance of Axiom 1 is: $\vdash (\forall \ldots)_2 (\forall y (C(x) \to D(x))) \to (\forall y\, C(x) \to \forall y\, D(x))$ where the only difference between $(\forall \ldots)_1$ and $(\forall \ldots)_2$ is that $\forall x$ appears in the latter. Hence, by Lemma 13, we are done.

Suppose now that (a) is true for theorems with proofs of length m, $1 \le m < n$, and the shortest proof of $B(c/x)$ has length n. Then for some closed A, $\vdash A$ and $\vdash A \to B(c/x)$, both of which have proofs shorter than length n. By induction, $\vdash \forall x\, (A \to B(x))$, so by Axiom 1.c and PC, $\vdash A \to \forall x\, B(x)$. Hence, $\vdash \forall x\, B(x)$.

b. Suppose $\Gamma \vdash B(c/x)$. Then for some closed $D_1, \ldots, D_n \in \Gamma$, we have that $\{D_1, \ldots, D_n\} \vdash B(c/x)$. Hence by the Syntactic Deduction Theorem:

$$\vdash D_1 \to (D_2 \to \cdots \to (D_n \to B(c/x)) \ldots)$$

Since c does not appear in any of $D_1, \ldots, D_n$, we have by (a):

$$\vdash \forall x\, (D_1 \to (D_2 \to \cdots \to (D_n \to B(x)) \ldots))$$

So by Axiom 1, $\vdash D_1 \to (D_2 \to \cdots \to (D_n \to \forall x\, B(x)) \ldots)$. By repeated use of *modus ponens*, $\{D_1, \ldots, D_n\} \vdash \forall x\, B(x)$. So $\Gamma \vdash \forall x\, B(x)$. ∎

Theorem 15 Let Γ be a consistent collection of closed wffs of L. Let $L(w_0, w_1, \ldots)$ be L with the addition of name symbols $w_0, w_1, \ldots$ that do not appear in L. Then there is a collection of closed wffs Σ in $L(w_0, w_1, \ldots)$ such that:

    a. $\Gamma \subseteq \Sigma$.

    b. Σ is a complete and consistent theory.

    c. If $\exists x B \in \Sigma$ and x is free in B, then for some m, $B(w_m/x) \in \Sigma$.

    d. For every wff $B(x)$ in $L(w_0, w_1, \ldots)$ with one free variable,
       if for each i, $B(w_i/x) \in \Sigma$, then $\forall x\, B(x) \in \Sigma$.

Proof Let $A_0, A_1, \ldots$ be a numbering of the closed wffs of the expanded language $L(w_0, w_1, \ldots)$. Let $\vdash$ stand for derivations in this language. Define Σ by stages:

$\Sigma_0 = \Gamma$

Σ_{n+1} is defined by cases:

    i. If $\Sigma_n \vdash \neg A_n$, then $\Sigma_{n+1} = \Sigma_n \cup \{\neg A_n\}$.

    If $\Sigma_n \nvdash \neg A_n$, then:

       ii. If A_n is not $\exists x\, B$, then $\Sigma_{n+1} = \Sigma_n \cup \{A_n\}$.

       iii. If A_n is $\exists x\, B$ and w_m is the least w_i that does not appear in Σ_n, then $\Sigma_{n+1} = \Sigma_n \cup \{\exists x\, B, B(w_m/x)\}$.

$\Sigma = \bigcup_n \Sigma_n$

Part (a) follows by construction.

For (b), I'll first show by induction that for each n, Σ_n is consistent. We have $n = 0$ by hypothesis. So suppose that Σ_n is consistent. If Σ_{n+1} is defined by (i), it's immediate that Σ_{n+1} is consistent. If Σ_n is defined by (ii), Σ_{n+1} is consistent follows by induction and Lemma 4. So suppose Σ_{n+1} is defined by (iii). Then $\Delta = \Sigma_n \cup \{\exists x B(x)\}$ is consistent by Lemma 4. Suppose now that Σ_{n+1} is not consistent. Then by Lemma 4, $\Delta \vdash \neg B(w_m/x)$. So by Lemma 13, $\Delta \vdash \forall x \neg B(x)$. Hence, by Axiom 4.a and PC, $\Delta \vdash \neg \exists x B(x)$. But then Δ is not consistent, which is a contradiction. So Σ_{n+1} is consistent. It then follows that Σ is consistent, for if it were not, then some finite subset of it would be inconsistent, and hence some Σ_n would be inconsistent.

For every A, by construction either $A \in \Sigma$ or $\neg A \in \Sigma$. So Σ is complete, and hence by Lemma 4, Σ is a theory, so (b) is proved.

For (c), suppose $\exists x B(x) \in \Sigma$. Then for some n and m,

$$\Sigma_{n+1} = \Sigma_n \cup \{\exists x B, B(w_m/x)\} \subseteq \Sigma$$

For (d), I'll show the contrapositive. Suppose $\forall x B(x) \notin \Sigma$. Then by (b), $\neg \forall x B(x) \in \Sigma$. Hence by Axiom 4.b and PC, $\exists x \neg B(x) \in \Sigma$. So by (c), for some m, $\neg B(w_m/x) \in \Sigma$. So by the consistency of Σ, $B(w_m/x) \notin \Sigma$. ∎

In the proof of Theorem 15, the definition of Σ requires viewing the collection of consequences of a collection of wffs as a completed infinity that we can survey at one time or else assuming that we can complete an infinite search.

Lemma 16 Existential generalization $\vdash \forall \ldots (A(c/x) \rightarrow \exists x A(x))$

Proof By Axiom 3, $\vdash \forall \ldots (\forall x \neg A(x) \rightarrow \neg A(c/x))$. So by PC, $\vdash \forall \ldots (A(c/x) \rightarrow \neg \forall x \neg A(x))$. So by Axiom 4.b and PC, $\vdash \forall \ldots (A(c/x) \rightarrow \exists x A(x))$.

Theorem 17 Every consistent collection of closed wffs in L has a countable model.

Proof Let Γ be a consistent collection of closed wffs of L.

Let $\Sigma \supseteq \Gamma$ in $L(w_0, w_1, \ldots)$ be as in Theorem 15. We define a model M^* of $L(w_0, w_1, \ldots)$. The realization is the formal language itself. Set:

$$U = \{w_i, c_i : i \geq 0\}$$

We take a complete collection of assignments of references such that for every σ,

$$\sigma(c_i) = c_i \text{ and } \sigma(w_i) = w_i.$$

We evaluate the atomic wffs by:

$$\mathsf{v}_\sigma \models P_i^n(v_1, \ldots, v_n) \text{ iff } P_i^n(\sigma(v_1), \ldots, \sigma(v_n)) \in \Sigma$$

Lemma α Suppose x is free in B and $d \in U$. Then for any σ,
   If $\sigma(x) = d$, then $\mathsf{v}_\sigma \models B(x)$ iff $\mathsf{v}_\sigma \models B(d/x)$.

Proof We proceed by induction on the length of wffs. If B has length 1, the lemma follows by definition.

So suppose the lemma is true for all wffs of length $\leq n$ and B has length $n + 1$. I'll leave the cases when B has the form $\neg C$, $C \rightarrow D$, $C \wedge D$, or $C \vee B$ to you. So suppose that B has the form $\forall y C(x)$. Note that y is not x, for x is free in B. So we have the following.

250 *Appendix 7*

$v_\sigma \vDash \forall y\, C(x,y)$ iff for every τ such that $\tau \sim_y \sigma$, $v_\tau \vDash C(x,y)$

iff for every τ such that $\tau \sim_y \sigma$, $v_\tau \vDash C(d/x, y)$
(by induction, since τ agrees with σ on x)

iff $v_\sigma \vDash \forall y\, C(d/x, y)$

I'll leave to you the case when B has the form $\exists y\, C(y)$. □

That the valuations satisfy the extensionality condition now follows from this lemma and the definitions of the valuations.

Now we'll show by induction on the length of wffs that for every closed wff A in $L(w_0, w_1, \ldots)$, $M \vDash A$ iff $A \in \Sigma$.

Suppose A is atomic. Then all terms in A are names, so we are done by the definition of the evaluation of atomic wffs. Now suppose it is true for wffs shorter than A. I'll do the cases when A is $\exists x\, B$ or $\forall x\, B$ and leave the others to you as in the proof for PC.

Suppose A is $\exists x\, B$ and $\exists x\, B(x) \in \Sigma$. Then x is the only variable free in $B(x)$. Since Σ satisfies the conditions in Theorem 15, for some m, $B(w_m/x) \in \Sigma$. Hence by induction, for any σ, $v_\sigma \vDash B(w_m/x)$, and so by Lemma α, for any σ, if $\sigma(x) = w_m$, then $v_\sigma \vDash B(x)$. So $M \vDash \exists x\, B(x)$.

Suppose A is $\exists x\, B$ and $M \vDash \exists x\, B(x)$. Then for some σ, $v_\sigma \vDash B(x)$. Take one where $\sigma(x) = d$. Then by Lemma α, $v_\sigma \vDash B(d/x)$. Since $B(d/x)$ is closed, $M \vDash B(d/x)$, so by induction $B(d/x) \in \Sigma$. By Lemma 16, $\vdash B(d/x) \rightarrow \exists x\, B(x)$, so $\exists x\, B(x) \in \Sigma$.

Suppose A is $\forall x\, B$ and $\forall x\, B(x) \in \Sigma$. Since Σ is a theory, by Axiom 3, for every name d in the language, and hence for all $d \in U$, $B(d/x) \in \Sigma$. Hence by induction, for all $d \in U$, $M \vDash B(d/x)$. Hence by Lemma α, for every σ, $v_\sigma \vDash B(x)$, and hence $M \vDash \forall x\, B(x)$.

Suppose A is $\forall x\, B$ and $M \vDash \forall x\, B(x)$. So for every $i \geq 0$, if $\sigma(x) = w_i$, then $v_\sigma \vDash B(x)$. So by Lemma α, for every i, for every σ, $v_\sigma \vDash B(w_i/x)$. So by induction, for every i, $B(w_i/x) \in \Sigma$. Since Σ satisfies condition (d) of Theorem 15, $\forall x\, B(x) \in \Sigma$.

To complete the proof of the theorem, define a model N for L by taking M* and deleting the interpretation of each w_i (the universes are the same). Then for any closed wff A in L, $M \vDash A$ iff $N \vDash A$, as you can show. So $N \vDash \Gamma$. And N is countable. ∎

Theorem 18

    a. For any collection of closed wffs Σ in L, Σ is a complete and consistent theory iff there is a model M such that $M \vDash A$ iff $A \in \Sigma$.

    b. For any model M of L, there is a countable model M* such that $M^* \vDash A$ iff $M \vDash A$.

    c. Completeness $\Gamma \vdash A$ iff $\Gamma \vDash A$.

    d. Compactness Γ has a model iff every finite subset of Γ has a model.

Proof a. If $\Sigma = \{A : M \vDash A\}$, then Σ is a complete and consistent theory. The other direction follows by Theorem 17.

    b. If M is a model, then $\{A : M \vDash A\}$ is complete and consistent, so by Theorem 17, there is a countable model M* such that $\{A : M \vDash A\} = \{A : M^* \vDash A\}$.

    Parts (c) and (d) follow as for Theorem 7. ∎

Classical Predicate Logic with Equality

The following axioms are added to those for classical predicate logic.

Axioms for equality

5. $\forall x \, (x \equiv x)$ *identity*
6. $\forall \ldots \forall x \, \forall y \, (x \equiv y \rightarrow (A(x) \rightarrow A(y/x)))$ *extensionality*
   where y replaces some but not necessarily all occurrences of x in A

Lemma 19
   a. $\vdash \forall x \, \forall y \, (x \equiv y \rightarrow y \equiv x)$ *symmetry*
   b. $\vdash \forall x \, \forall y \, \forall z \, (x \equiv y \rightarrow (y \equiv z \rightarrow x \equiv z))$ *transitivity*

Proof
   a. 1. $\vdash \forall x \, (x \equiv x)$ identity axiom
      2. $\vdash \forall x \, \forall y \, (x \equiv y \rightarrow (x \equiv x \rightarrow y \equiv x))$ extensionality axiom
      3. $\vdash \forall x \, \forall y \, (x \equiv x \rightarrow (x \equiv y \rightarrow y \equiv x))$ (2) and PC
      4. $\vdash \forall x \, \forall y \, (x \equiv y \rightarrow y \equiv x)$ (1), (3), and Axiom 1
   b. 1. $\vdash \forall z \, \forall y \, \forall x \, (y \equiv x \rightarrow (y \equiv z \rightarrow x \equiv z))$ extensionality axiom
      2. $\vdash \forall x \, \forall y \, (x \equiv y \rightarrow y \equiv x)$ part (a)
      3. $\vdash \forall x \, \forall y \, \forall z \, (x \equiv y \rightarrow (y \equiv z \rightarrow x \equiv z))$ (1), (2), PC, Lemma 12 ■

To prove the strong completeness of this axiomatization, the lemmas and theorems through Theorem 17, along with their proofs, are the same as for classical predicate logic without equality.

Theorem 20   Every consistent set of closed wffs of L has a countable model in which "$\equiv$" is interpreted as the identity of the universe.

Proof   Let Γ be a consistent collection of closed wffs of L. Let $\Sigma \supseteq \Gamma$ be constructed as in the proof of Theorem 17. By Theorem 18, there is a countable model M of Σ and hence of Γ. In that model, write "$\simeq$" for the interpretation of "$\equiv$":

$$v_\sigma \vDash v \equiv u \text{ iff } (\sigma(v) \equiv \sigma(u)) \in \Sigma$$

This need not be the identity on the universe of M. However, as you can show, $\simeq$ is an equivalence relation (see Exercise 1, p. 123 of Volume 0) by virtue of Axiom 5, Lemma 19, and Axiom 3. That is, for every c, d, and e in U:

   $c \simeq c$
   If $c \simeq d$, then $d \simeq c$.
   If $c \simeq d$, and $d \simeq e$, then $c \simeq e$.

Denote by [d] the equivalence class of d for $\simeq$:

   $[d] = \{c : c \simeq d\}$

We have that $[d] = \{c : (c \equiv d) \in \Sigma\}$. Given an equivalence class c, we say that d is a *representative* of c if $\mathsf{c} = [d]$.

   We'll now define a model $\mathsf{M}_{/\simeq}$ in which "$\equiv$" is interpreted as the identity on the universe such that $\mathsf{M}_{/\simeq}$ validates exactly the same wffs as M.

The semi-formal language of $M_{/\simeq}$ is the same as for M. The universe of $M_{/\simeq}$ is:

$\{[d] : d$ is in the universe of $M\}$

For each assignment of references σ of M, define an assignment of references $\sigma_{/\simeq}(v)$ by setting for every term v,

$\sigma_{/\simeq}(v) = [\sigma(v)]$

Since the collection for M is complete, the collection of these assignments is complete.

For each assignment of references, define the valuation on atomic wffs:

$\upsilon_{\sigma_{/\simeq}} \vDash P(v_1, \ldots, v_n)$ iff $\upsilon_\sigma \vDash P(v_1, \ldots, v_n)$

$\upsilon_{\sigma_{/\simeq}} \vDash u \equiv v$ iff $\upsilon_\sigma \vDash u \equiv v$

Hence, by the definition of M,

$\upsilon_{\sigma_{/\simeq}} \vDash P(v_1, \ldots, v_n)$ iff $P(\sigma(v_1), \ldots, \sigma(v_n)) \in \Sigma$

$\upsilon_{\sigma_{/\simeq}} \vDash u \equiv v$ iff $(\sigma(u) \equiv \sigma(v)) \in \Sigma$

Now we show that for every closed formal wff A and every σ for M,

$\upsilon_{\sigma_{/\simeq}} \vDash A$ iff $\upsilon_\sigma \vDash A$

If A has length 1, it is immediate. Suppose now that it is true for all closed formal wffs of length n, and A has length $n + 1$. I will leave the cases when A has the form $\neg C, C \to D, C \wedge D$, or $C \vee B$ to you. Now note that the choice of representative of the equivalence class does not matter:

($\ddagger$) For any assignments of references τ, σ, if for all z, $\tau(z) \simeq \sigma(z)$, then by Axiom 6 (extensionality) for every wff A, $\upsilon_\tau \vDash A$ iff $\upsilon_\sigma \vDash A$.

Now suppose that A has the form $\forall x\, B(x)$. We have:

$\upsilon_{\sigma_{/\simeq}} \vDash \forall x\, B(x)$ iff for every assignment $\tau_{/\simeq} \sim_x \sigma_{/\simeq}$, $\upsilon_{\tau_{/\simeq}} \vDash B(x)$
  iff for every assignment $\tau \sim_x \sigma$, if $\tau(x) = d$,
    then $\upsilon_\tau \vDash B(d/x)$ (by induction and Lemma α and ($\ddagger$))
  iff $\upsilon_\sigma \vDash B(x)$ (by Lemma α)

Now suppose that A has the form $\exists x\, B(x)$. We have:

$\upsilon_{\sigma_{/\simeq}} \vDash \exists x\, B(x)$ iff for some assignment $\tau_{/\simeq} \sim_x \sigma_{/\simeq}$, $\upsilon_{\tau_{/\simeq}} \vDash B(x)$
  iff for some assignment $\tau \sim_x \sigma$ where $\tau(x) = d$, $\upsilon_\tau \vDash B(d/x)$
    (by induction and Lemma α and ($\ddagger$))
  iff $\upsilon_\sigma \vDash B(x)$ (by Lemma α)

Hence, for every A, $M \vDash A$ iff $M_{/\simeq} \vDash A$. And in $M_{/\simeq}$ we have:

$\upsilon_{\sigma_{/\simeq}} \vDash v \equiv u$ iff $(\sigma(v) \equiv \sigma(u)) \in \Sigma$
  iff $\sigma(v) \simeq \sigma(u)$
  iff $[\sigma(v)] = [\sigma(u)]$

To complete the proof of the theorem, define a model N for L by taking $M_{/\simeq}$ and deleting the interpretation of each w_i (the universes are the same). Then for any closed wff A in L, $M_{/\simeq} \vDash A$ iff $N \vDash A$, as you can show. So $N \vDash \Gamma$. And N is countable. ∎

The completeness and compactness of this axiom system is proved as in Theorem 18.

Classical Predicate Logic with Function Names

The following axioms are added to those for classical predicate logic with equality.

Axioms for functions   *extensionality of functions*

7. $\forall \ldots \forall x \, \forall y \, (x \equiv y \rightarrow$
$f(z_1, \ldots, z_k, x, z_{k+1}, \ldots, z_n) \equiv f(z_1, \ldots, z_k, y, z_{k+1}, \ldots, z_n))$
for every $n + 1$-ary function symbol f

The proof of strong completeness is just as for classical predicate logic with equality, noting only that in the proof of Theorem 20, by the extensionality axiom for functions, we can define: $\sigma/{\simeq}(f(u_1, \ldots, u_n)) = [\sigma(f(u_1, \ldots, u_n))]$.

Classical Predicate Logic with Descriptive Names and Descriptive Functions

I. *Propositional axioms*

The axiom schemes of classical propositional logic, where wffs of L are substituted uniformly for A, B, C and the universal closure is taken.

II. *Axioms governing* $\forall$

1. a. $\forall\ldots(\forall x\,(A\rightarrow B)\rightarrow(\forall x\,A\rightarrow\forall x\,B))$ *distribution of* $\forall$
   if x is free in both A and B
   b. $\forall\ldots(\forall x\,(A\rightarrow B)\rightarrow(\forall x\,A\rightarrow B))$
   if x is free in A and not free in B
   c. $\forall\ldots(\forall x\,(A\rightarrow B)\rightarrow(A\rightarrow\forall x\,B))$
   if x is free in B and not free in A

2. $\forall\ldots(\forall x\,\forall y\,A\rightarrow\forall y\,\forall x\,A)$ *commutativity of* $\forall$

3.* $\forall\ldots(\forall x\,(A(x)\wedge\exists x\,(x\equiv u))\rightarrow A(u/x))$ *universal instantiation*
   when u is free for x in A   *for referring terms*

III. *Axioms governing the relation between* $\forall$ *and* $\exists$

4. a. $\forall\ldots(\exists x\,A\rightarrow\neg\forall x\,\neg A)$
   b. $\forall\ldots(\neg\forall x\,\neg A\rightarrow\exists x\,A)$

Axioms for equality

5. a. $\forall x\,(x\equiv x)$ *identity*
   b.* $\exists x\,(x\equiv c)$ *atomic names are referring*
   for every atomic name symbol c

6. $\forall\ldots\forall x\,\forall y\,(x\equiv y\rightarrow(A(x)\rightarrow A(y/x)))$ *extensionality*
   where y replaces some but not necessarily all occurrences of x in A

Axioms for non-referring terms

8. $\forall\ldots((A(u/x)\wedge\exists x\,(x\equiv u))\rightarrow\exists x\,A(x))$ *existential generalization*
        for referring terms

9. $\forall\ldots(\neg\exists x\,(x\equiv u)\rightarrow\neg A(u_1,\ldots,u,\ldots u_n))$ *non-referring*
   for n-ary atomic wffs A and terms $u_1,\ldots,u,\ldots,u_n$ *descriptive names use falsity as default*

Axioms for the-terms

10. $\forall\ldots\,[\exists x\,A(x)\wedge\forall x\,\forall y\,(A(x)\wedge A(y/x)\rightarrow(x\equiv y))]$ *referring descriptions*
    $\leftrightarrow\exists z\,(z\equiv\underline{\text{the}}\,x\,A(x))$ *create referring terms*
    where y is the least variable not appearing in A

11. $\forall\ldots\,\exists z\,(z\equiv\underline{\text{the}}\,x\,A(x))\rightarrow A(\underline{\text{the}}\,x\,A(x))$ *referring descriptive terms satisfy their own description*

rule   *modus ponens* for closed wffs

Completeness Proofs 255

I'll let you prove that this system is sound. Lemmas 2–13 for classical predicate logic hold for this system because the axiom schemes used in their proofs are included here.

Theorem 21 Let Γ be a consistent set of closed wffs of L*. Then there is a collection of closed wffs Σ in $L^*(w_0, w_1, \dots)$ such that:

  a. $\Gamma \subseteq \Sigma$.
  b. Σ is a complete and consistent theory.
  c. If $\exists x B \in \Sigma$, then for some m, $B(w_m/x) \in \Sigma$ and $\exists x (x \equiv w_m) \in \Sigma$.
  d. For every wff $B(x)$ in $L^*(w_0, w_1, \dots)$ with one free variable,
     if for each i, $B(w_i/x) \in \Sigma$, then $\forall x B(x) \in \Sigma$.

Proof This is the same as for classical predicate logic (Theorem 15) because Axioms 1, 2, 4.a, 4.b, and the propositional Axioms are the same here.

Lemma 22 a. $\vdash \forall x \forall y (x \equiv y \rightarrow y \equiv x)$
           b. $\vdash \forall x \forall y \forall z (x \equiv y \rightarrow (y \equiv z \rightarrow x \equiv z))$

Proof This is the same as the proof for Lemma 19 for classical logic with equality because the identity axioms (Axiom 5.a) and the extensionality axioms (Axiom 6) are in our system.

Theorem 23 Every consistent collection of closed wffs in L has a countable model.

Proof Let Γ be a consistent collection of closed wffs of L*. Let $\Sigma \supseteq \Gamma$ in $L^*(w_0, w_1, \dots)$ be as in Theorem 21.

We first define a model M* of $L^*(w_0, w_1, \dots)$ except that the equality predicate might not be evaluated as the identity on the universe.

For the model M of classical predicate logic with equality for stage 0 we take:

$$U = \{c_i : i \geq 0\} \cup \{w_i : i \geq 0\}$$

We take a complete collection of assignments of references where for every name symbol d and assignment of references σ, $\sigma_0(d) = d$. For valuations of atomic wffs, including equality, we set:

$$v_{\sigma_0} \models A(u_1, \dots, u_n) \text{ iff } A(\sigma_0(u_1), \dots, \sigma_0(u_n)) \in \Sigma$$

This determines a model for stage 0 and hence for each stage $n \geq 0$ and hence M*, as noted on p. 180.

Lemma β For every $d \in U$, both $\exists x (x \equiv d) \in \Sigma$ and $(d \equiv d) \in \Sigma$.

Proof By Axiom 5.b*, for all i, $\exists x (x \equiv c_i) \in \Sigma$. By construction (Theorem 21), $\exists x (x \equiv w_i) \in \Sigma$. Hence by Axiom 5.a and 3*, for every i, $(c_i \equiv c_i) \in \Sigma$ and $(w_i \equiv w_i) \in \Sigma$. ∎

Lemma α' Suppose x is free in B and $d \in U$. Then for any σ:
If $\sigma_n(x) = d$, then $v_\sigma \models B(x)$ iff $v_\sigma \models B(d/x)$.

Proof We proceed by induction on n to show that if $\sigma_n(x) = d$, then $v_{\sigma_n} \models B(x)$ iff $v_{\sigma_n} \models B(d/x)$. The Lemma will then follow by the lemma on the stability of references and truth-values (p. 179). For $n = 0$ the proof is as for Lemma α (p. 249).

So suppose it is true for n. Then to show it for $n + 1$, we induct on the length of wffs. It holds for atomic wffs because the evaluation of the wff goes back to stage 0. Then the proof continues as for Lemma α (p. 249). □

Now I'll induct on the length of A to show that $M^* \models A$ iff $A \in \Sigma$. To begin, assume that A is an atomic closed wff. By virtue of the stability of references and truth-values, it suffices to show that if A is first defined at stage n, then:

(a) $\models_n A$ iff $A \in \Sigma$

Here "$\models_n A$" to means that for every σ, $\vee_{\sigma_n} \models A$. To do so, we will need to show at the same time:

(b) v is a closed referring term at stage n iff $\exists z\, (z \equiv v) \in \Sigma$.

Suppose $n = 0$. We have (b) as noted above because the only closed terms are atomic names. For (a), I'll repeat here the proof of Theorem 17 for classical predicate logic, replacing α with α´ and two modifications enclosed in double brakcets:

Suppose A is atomic. Then all terms in A are names, so we're done by the definition of the evaluation of atomic wffs. Now suppose it is true for wffs shorter than A. I'll do the cases when A is $\exists x\, B$ or $\forall x\, B$ and leave the others to you.

Suppose A is $\exists x\, B$ and $\exists x\, B(x) \in \Sigma$. Then x is the only variable free in $B(x)$. Since Σ satisfies the conditions in Theorem 14, for some m, $B(w_m/x) \in \Sigma$. Hence by induction, for any σ, $\vee_\sigma \models B(w_m/x)$, and so by Lemma α´, for any σ, if $\sigma(x) = w_m$, then $\vee_\sigma \models B(x)$. So $M \models \exists x\, B(x)$.

Suppose A is $\exists x\, B$ and $M \models \exists x\, B(x)$. Then for some σ, $\vee_\sigma \models B(x)$. Take one where $\sigma(x) = d$. Then by Lemma α´, $\vee_\sigma \models B(d/x)$. Since $B(d/x)$ is closed, $M \models B(d/x)$, so by induction $B(d/x) \in \Sigma$. [[By Lemma β, $\exists x\, (x \equiv d) \in \Sigma$. So by Axiom 8, $\exists x\, B(x) \in \Sigma$.]]

Suppose A is $\forall x\, B$ and $\forall x\, B(x) \in \Sigma$. Since Σ is a theory, by [[Axiom 3* and Lemma α´,]] for every $d \in U$, $B(d/x) \in \Sigma$. Hence by induction, for all $d \in U$, $M \models B(d/x)$. Hence by Lemma α, for every σ, $\vee_\sigma \models B(x)$, and hence $M \models \forall x\, B(x)$.

Suppose A is $\forall x\, B$ and $M \models \forall x\, B(x)$. So for every $i \geq 0$, if $\sigma(x) = w_i$, then $\vee_\sigma \models B(x)$. So by Lemma α´, for every i, for every σ, $\vee_\sigma \models B(w_i/x)$. So by induction, for every i, $B(w_i/x) \in \Sigma$. Since Σ satisfies condition (d) of Theorem 21, $\forall x\, B(x) \in \Sigma$.

Suppose now that (a) and (b) are true for all stages $\leq n$. I'll show that first (b) and then (a) are true for stage $n + 1$.

(b) The only new cases are when v is a closed term of the form "the $x\, B(x)$" where B is a wff of stage n and not of any earlier stage.

$\exists z\, (z \equiv \text{the } x\, B(x)) \in \Sigma$

iff (by Axiom 10) $\exists x\, B(x) \wedge \forall x\, \forall y\, (B(x) \wedge B(y) \to (x \equiv y)) \in \Sigma$

iff (by induction on n and PC) $\models_n \exists x\, B(x)$ and
$\models_n \forall x\, \forall y\, (B(x) \wedge B(y)) \to (x \equiv y))$

iff there is a unique d in U that satisfies $B(x)$

iff "the $x\, B(x)$" is a referring term at stage $n + 1$.

(a) I'll this show first for atomic wffs.

Suppose that $A(v_1, \ldots, v_m)$ is an atomic closed wff of stage $n + 1$. Then each v_i is closed.

(i) Suppose that $\vDash_{n+1} A(v_1, \ldots, v_m)$. Then every v_i is referring. Further, $\vDash_0 A(u_1/v_1, \ldots, u_m/v_m)$, where if v_i is an atomic name c, then u_i is c, and if v_i is "the $x\ B(x)$", u_i is the reference d of v_i. By induction, $A(u_1/v_1, \ldots, u_m/v_m) \in \Sigma$. By Lemma β, $(c \equiv c) \in \Sigma$. If we can show that $(d \equiv \underline{\text{the}}\ x\ B(x)) \in \Sigma$, then by Axiom 6 (extensionality), we will have that $A(v_1, \ldots, v_m) \in \Sigma$.

So if $\sigma_{n+1}(\underline{\text{the}}\ x\ B(x)) = d$, then d is the unique object satisfying $B(x)$ at stage n. So $\vDash_n \forall x\ (B(x) \rightarrow (x \equiv d))$. So by induction, $\forall x\ (B(x) \rightarrow (x \equiv d)) \in \Sigma$, and by (b), $\exists z\ (z \equiv \underline{\text{the}}\ x\ B(x)) \in \Sigma$. Hence by Axiom 11, $B(\underline{\text{the}}\ x\ B(x)) \in \Sigma$, and by Axiom 3* (universal instantiation for referring terms), we have $(\underline{\text{the}}\ x\ B(x) \equiv d) \in \Sigma$. Hence by Lemma 22 and Axiom 3*, $(d \equiv \underline{\text{the}}\ x\ B(x)) \in \Sigma$, which was to be proved.

(ii) Now suppose that $A(v_1, \ldots, v_m) \in \Sigma$. Then by Axiom 9 (non-referring names use falsity as default) and PC, for every i, for some x, $\exists x\ (x \equiv v_i) \in \Sigma$. If v_i is "the $x\ B(x)$", then by Axiom 10 and PC, $\exists x\ B(x) \in \Sigma$ and $\forall x\ \forall y\ (B(x) \wedge B(y/x) \rightarrow (x \equiv y)) \in \Sigma$. So by induction, $\vDash_n \exists x\ B(x)$ and $\vDash_n \forall x\ \forall y\ (B(x) \wedge B(y/x) \rightarrow (x \equiv y))$. So there is a unique d that satisfies $B(x)$ and hence is the reference of "the $x\ B(x)$" at stage $n + 1$. So by Lemma α, $\vDash_n B(d/x)$ and so by induction $B(d/x) \in \Sigma$. By Axiom 11, $B(\underline{\text{the}}\ x\ B(x)) \in \Sigma$. So by Axiom 3*, $(\underline{\text{the}}\ x\ B(x) \equiv d) \in \Sigma$. Hence, by Axiom 3*, $A(d_1, \ldots, d_m) \in \Sigma$, where for each i, d is either v_i itself or else is the reference of the the-term that is v_i. So by induction, $\vDash_0 A(d_1, \ldots, d_m)$. Hence, by definition $\vDash_{n+1} A(v_1, \ldots, v_m)$.

The proof for compound wffs then follows as before.

Hence, we have established (a) and (b). Hence, for all closed A, by the lemma on the stability of truth (p. 179), $\mathbf{M}^* \vDash A$ iff $A \in \Sigma$.

Now proceed exactly as in Theorem 20 to obtain a model of $\mathbf{L}^*$ from $\mathbf{M}^*$ in which the equality predicate is interpreted as the identity on the universe. ∎

Strong completeness is then proved for this axiom system exactly as in Theorem 18.

258 Appendix 7

Classical Predicate Logic with Non-Referring Simple Names

I. *Propositional axioms*
The axiom schemes of classical propositional logic, where wffs of L are substituted uniformly for A, B, C, and the universal closure is taken.

II. *Axioms governing* $\forall$

1. a. $\forall \ldots (\forall x (A \rightarrow B) \rightarrow (\forall x A \rightarrow \forall x B))$ *distribution of* $\forall$
    if x is free in both A and B

    b. $\forall \ldots (\forall x (A \rightarrow B) \rightarrow (\forall x A \rightarrow B))$
    if x is free in A and not free in B

    c. $\forall \ldots (\forall x (A \rightarrow B) \rightarrow (A \rightarrow \forall x B))$
    if x is free in B and not free in A

2. $\forall \ldots (\forall x \forall y A \rightarrow \forall y \forall x A)$ *commutativity of* $\forall$

3. $\forall \ldots (\forall x A(x) \rightarrow A(u/x))$ *universal instantiation*
   when u is free for x in A

Axioms for equality

5. $\forall x (x \equiv x)$ *identity*

6. $\forall \ldots \forall x \forall y (x \equiv y \rightarrow (A(x) \rightarrow A(y/x)))$ *extensionality*
   where y replaces some but not necessarily all occurrences of x in A

Axioms for non-referring terms

8.* $\forall \ldots ((A(c/x) \wedge \exists y (y \equiv c)) \rightarrow \exists x A(x))$ *existential generalization*
   where c is a name symbol   *for referring names*

12. $\forall \ldots (\forall y (\neg (\exists x (x \equiv y) \wedge A(y/x)) \rightarrow \neg \exists x A(x))$
    where y is free for x in A

rule   *modus ponens* for closed wffs

I'll let you prove that this system is sound.

Lemmas 2–14 and Lemma 19 for classical predicate logic hold for this system because the axiom schemes used in their proofs are included here.

Theorem 24   Let Γ be a consistent set of closed wffs of L. Let $L(w_0, w_1, \ldots)$ be L with the addition of name symbols $w_0, w_1, \ldots$ that do not appear in L. Then there is a collection of closed wffs Σ in $L(w_0, w_1, \ldots)$ such that:

a. $\Gamma \subseteq \Sigma$.

b. Σ is a complete and consistent theory.

c. If $\exists x B \in \Sigma$, then for some m, $B(w_m/x) \in \Sigma$ and $\exists x (x \equiv w_m) \in \Sigma$.

d. If $\neg \forall x B \in \Sigma$, then for some m, $\neg B(w_m/x) \in \Sigma$.

e. For every wff $B(x)$ in $L(w_0, w_1, \ldots)$ with one free variable,
   if for each i, $B(w_i/x) \in \Sigma$, then $\forall x B(x) \in \Sigma$.

Proof Let $A_0, A_1, \ldots$ be a numbering of the closed wffs of the expanded language $L(w_0, w_1, \ldots)$. Let '⊢' refer to derivations in this language. Define Σ by stages:

$\Sigma_0 = \Gamma$

Σ_{n+1} is defined by cases:

  i. If $\Sigma_n \vdash \neg A_n$, then $\Sigma_{n+1} = \Sigma_n \cup \{\neg A_n\}$.

  If $\Sigma_n \nvdash \neg A_n$, then:

  ii. If A_n is not $\exists x\, B$ or $\neg \forall x\, B$, then $\Sigma_{n+1} = \Sigma_n \cup \{A_n\}$.

  iii. If A_n is $\exists x\, B$, and w_m is the least w_i that does not appear in Σ_n, then $\Sigma_{n+1} = \Sigma_n \cup \{\exists x\, B, B(w_m/x), \exists x\, (x \equiv w_m)\}$.

  iv. If A_n is $\neg \forall x\, B$, and w_m is the least w_i that does not appear in Σ_n, then $\Sigma_{n+1} = \Sigma_n \cup \{\neg \forall x\, B, \neg B(w_m/x)\}$.

$\Sigma = \bigcup_n \Sigma_n$

We need to show that Σ satisfies (a)–(e). Part (a) follows by construction.

For part (b) we first show by induction that for each n, Σ_n is consistent. For $n = 0$ it's true by hypothesis. If it's true for n and Σ_{n+1} is defined by (i), it's immediate. If Σ_{n+1} is defined by (ii), it follows by induction and Lemma 4.

Suppose Σ_{n+1} is defined by (iii). Then $\Delta = \Sigma_n \cup \{\exists x\, B(x)\}$ is consistent by induction and Lemma 4. Suppose that $\Sigma_{n+1} = \Delta \cup \{B(w_m/x), \exists x\,(x \equiv w_m)\}$ is not consistent. Then by PC, $\Delta \cup \{B(w_m/x) \wedge \exists x\,(x \equiv w_m)\}$ is not consistent, so by Lemma 4, $\Delta \vdash \neg(\exists x\,(x \equiv w_m) \wedge B(w_m/x))$. So by Lemma 14, since w_m is not in Δ, $\Delta \vdash \forall y \neg(\exists x\,(x \equiv y) \wedge B(y/x))$ where y is the first variable that does not appear in B. So by Axiom 12, $\Delta \vdash \neg \exists x\, B(x)$, which contradicts that Δ is consistent. So Σ_{n+1} is consistent.

Suppose Σ_{n+1} is defined by (iv). Then $\Delta = \Sigma_n \cup \{\neg \forall x\, B(x)\}$ is consistent by Lemma 4 and PC. Suppose that Σ_{n+1} is not consistent. Then by PC, $\Delta \vdash B(w_m/x)$. So by Lemma 14, $\Delta \vdash \forall x\, B(x)$, which contradicts that Δ is consistent. So Σ_{n+1} is consistent.

It then follows that Σ is consistent, for if it were not then some finite subset of it would be inconsistent, and hence some Σ_n would be inconsistent. By construction, for every A, either $A \in \Sigma$ or $\neg A \in \Sigma$, so Σ is complete. By Lemma 4, Σ is a theory.

Parts (c) and (d) follow by construction, since if $A \in \Sigma$, then for some n, A is A_n and the appropriate formulas are put into Σ at stage $n + 1$.

For part (e) we'll show the contrapositive. Suppose $\forall x\, B(x) \notin \Sigma$. Then by (b), $\neg \forall x\, B(x) \in \Sigma$. Hence by (d), for some m, $\neg B(w_m/x) \in \Sigma$. So $B(w_m/x) \notin \Sigma$. ∎

Recall the conditions that the interpretation of "≡" must satisfy in a model.

  i. If $\sigma(u)\downarrow$ and $\sigma(v)\downarrow$, then $\mathbf{v}_\sigma \vDash u \equiv v$ iff $\sigma(u) = \sigma(v)$.

  ii. If one and only one of $\sigma(u)$ and $\sigma(v)$ is defined, then $\mathbf{v}_\sigma \nvDash u \equiv v$.

  iii. If u and v are names, then $\mathbf{v}_\sigma \vDash u \equiv v$ iff $\mathbf{v}_\tau \vDash u \equiv v$.

  iv. For all u, $\mathbf{v}_\sigma \vDash u \equiv u$.

  v. For all u and v, $\mathbf{v}_\sigma \vDash u \equiv v$ iff $\mathbf{v}_\sigma \vDash v \equiv u$.

  vi. For all u, v, and w, if $\mathbf{v}_\sigma \vDash u \equiv v$ and $\mathbf{v}_\sigma \vDash v \equiv w$, then $\mathbf{v}_\sigma \vDash u \equiv w$.

Theorem 25 Every consistent collection of closed wffs in L has a countable model.

Proof Let Γ be a consistent collection of closed wffs of L. Let $\Sigma \supseteq \Gamma$ in $L(w_0, w_1, \ldots)$ be as in Theorem 24. We define a model M of $L(w_0, w_1, \ldots)$ except that the evaluation of the equality predicate might not satisfy condition (i).

For the universe of M we take:

$$U = \{c_i : \text{for some } x, \exists x\, (x \equiv c_i) \in \Sigma\} \cup \{w_i : \text{for some } x, \exists x\, (x \equiv w_i) \in \Sigma\}$$

Assignments of references:

For every σ,
  for every x, $\sigma(x)\downarrow$
  and for every atomic name d, if $d \in U$ then $\sigma(d)\downarrow = d$, and if $d \notin U$, then $\sigma(d)\updownarrow$.

The collection of such σ is complete.

Evaluation of the equality predicate:

$v_\sigma \vDash v \equiv u$ iff $\sigma(v)\downarrow = c$ and $\sigma(u)\downarrow = d$, and $(c \equiv d) \in \Sigma$
or $\sigma(v)\updownarrow$ and $\sigma(v)\updownarrow$ and $(v \equiv u) \in \Sigma$

Conditions (ii) and (iii) of the restrictions on interpretations of the equality predicate follow by definition. Condition (iv) follows by Axiom 5 (identity) and Axiom 3 (universal instantiation). Conditions (v) and (vi) follow by Lemma 19.

For the valuations of atomic wffs other than the equality predicate we take:

$v_\sigma \vDash P(v_1, \ldots, v_n)$ iff $P(d_1, \ldots, d_n) \in \Sigma$
where if v_i is a variable, then $d_i = \sigma(v_i)$
  if v_i is a name c, then $d_i = c$

Using Axiom 6 (extensionality) you can show that these valuations satisfy the extensionality condition. We now have a model M of the language except that the interpretation of "$\equiv$" might not satisfy condition (i). We proceed to show that M is a model of Γ and then, as in the case for classical predicate logic with equality, proceed to a model that does satisfy condition (i) by taking equivalence classes.

Lemma α'' Suppose x is free in B and $d \in U$. Then for any σ:
If $\sigma(x) = d$, then $v_\sigma \vDash B(x)$ iff $v_\sigma \vDash B(d/x)$.

Proof We proceed by induction on the length of wffs. If B has length 1, the lemma follows by definition.

So suppose the lemma is true for all wffs of length $\leq n$ and B has length $n + 1$. I'll leave the cases when B has the form $\neg C, C \to D, C \wedge D$, or $C \vee B$ to you. So suppose that B has the form $\forall y\, C(x,y)$, and leave to you the case when B has the form $\exists y\, C(x,y)$.

$v_\sigma \vDash \forall y\, C(x,y)$ iff   for every τ such that $\tau \sim_y \sigma$, $v_\tau \vDash C(x,y)$
                              and for every name c, $v_\sigma \vDash C(c/x, y)$
                    iff   for every τ such that $\tau \sim_y \sigma$, $v_\tau \vDash C(d/x, y)$
                              and for every name c, $v_\tau \vDash C(c/x, y)$
                              (by induction, since τ agrees with σ on x)
                    iff $v_\sigma \vDash \forall y\, C(d/x, y)$ □

Now we show by induction on the length of A that for every closed wff A in $L(w_0, w_1, \ldots)$, $M \vDash A$ iff $A \in \Sigma$. It is true for wffs of length 1 by definition. Suppose that the lemma is true for all wffs of length n, and let A be a wff of length $n + 1$. I'll leave to you the cases when A is $\neg B, B \rightarrow C, B \wedge C$, and $B \wedge C$.

Suppose that A is $\exists x\, B(x)$ and $M \vDash \exists x\, B(x)$. Then for some σ, $\mathsf{v}_\sigma \vDash B(x)$. Take one such σ, where $\sigma(x) = d$. By Lemma α'', $\mathsf{v}_\sigma \vDash B(d/x)$. Since $d \in U$, for some y, $\exists y\, (y \equiv d) \in \Sigma$. Since $B(d/x)$ is closed, $M \vDash B(d/x)$, so by induction $B(d/x) \in \Sigma$. Hence, using Axiom 8* (existential generalization for referring terms), $\exists x\, B(x) \in \Sigma$.

Suppose A is $\exists x\, B(x)$ and $\exists x\, B(x) \in \Sigma$. Then x is the only variable free in $B(x)$. Since Σ satisfies condition (c) of Theorem 24, for some m, $B(w_m/x) \in \Sigma$ and $\exists x\, (x \equiv w_m) \in \Sigma$. So $w_m \in U$. And by induction, $M \vDash B(w_m/x)$. So for any σ, if $\sigma(x) = w_m$, then $\mathsf{v}_\sigma \vDash B(x)$. So $M \vDash \exists x\, B(x)$.

Suppose that A is $\forall x\, B(x)$ and $M \vDash \forall x B$. Then for each i, $M \vDash B(w_i/x)$. Hence by induction, for each i, $B(w_i/x) \in \Sigma$. Since Σ satisfies condition (e) of Theorem 24, $\forall x\, B \in \Sigma$.

Suppose that A is $\forall x\, B(x)$ and $\forall x\, B \in \Sigma$. Then by Axiom 3 (universal instantiation), for every d, $B(d/x) \in \Sigma$. Hence by induction, $M \vDash B(d/x)$. Hence, for all σ, for all $d \in U$, $\mathsf{v}_\sigma \vDash B(d/x)$ as $B(d/x)$ is closed. So by Lemma α'', for each σ, $\mathsf{v}_\sigma \vDash B(x)$. So $M \vDash \forall x\, B(x)$.

Write '$\simeq$' for the interpretation of '$\equiv$' in M, which might not satisfy condition (i). However, by virtue of Axiom 5, Lemma 19, and Axiom 3, for all names c, d, and e :

$c \simeq c$
If $c \simeq d$, then $d \simeq c$.
If $c \simeq d$, and $d \simeq e$, then $c \simeq e$.

So $\simeq$ is an equivalence relation on the names. Denote by $[d]$ the equivalence class of d:

$[d] = \{c : c \simeq d\}$

We have that $[d] = \{c : (c \equiv d) \in \Sigma\}$.

Lemma γ If $(c \equiv d) \in \Sigma$ and $\sigma(c)\downarrow$, then $\sigma(d)\downarrow$.

Proof If $(c \equiv d) \in \Sigma$ and $\sigma(c)\downarrow$, then $c \in U$. So for some x, we have $\exists x\, (x \equiv c) \in \Sigma$. So by the Axiom 6 (extensionality), since Σ is a theory, $\exists x\, (x \equiv d) \in \Sigma$, so $d \in U$ and $\sigma(d)\downarrow$. □

Define a model $M/_\simeq$ by:

$U/_\simeq = \{[d] : d \in U\}$

If $\sigma(v)\downarrow$, then $\sigma/_\simeq(v) = [\sigma(v)]$.
If $\sigma(v)\updownarrow$, then $\sigma/_\simeq(v)\updownarrow$.

For each assignment of references define the valuation:

$\mathsf{v}_{\sigma/_\simeq} \vDash P(v_1, \ldots, v_n)$ iff $\mathsf{v}_\sigma \vDash P(v_1, \ldots, v_n)$
$\mathsf{v}_{\sigma/_\simeq} \vDash u \equiv v$ iff $\mathsf{v}_\sigma \vDash u \equiv v$

262   *Appendix 7*

Hence, by the definition of M,

$\nu_{\sigma/\simeq} \vDash P(v_1, \ldots, v_n)$ iff $P(d_1, \ldots, d_n) \in \Sigma$
    where if v_i is a variable, then $d_i = \sigma(v_i)$
        if v_i is a name c, then $d_i = c$

$\nu_{\sigma/\simeq} \vDash u \equiv v$ iff $\sigma(u){\downarrow} \equiv \sigma(v){\downarrow}$ and $\sigma(u) \equiv \sigma(v) \in \Sigma$
    or $\sigma(u){\updownarrow}$ and $\sigma(v){\updownarrow}$ and $(v \equiv u) \in \Sigma$
    iff by Lemma γ, $\sigma(u) \equiv \sigma(v) \in \Sigma$ or $(v \equiv u) \in \Sigma$

Now we show that for every closed formal wff A and every σ of M,

$\nu_{\sigma/\simeq} \vDash A$ iff $\nu_\sigma \vDash A$

If A has length 1, it is immediate. Suppose now that it is true for all closed formal wffs of length n, and A has length $n + 1$. I'll leave the cases when A has the form $\neg C, C \to D, C \wedge D, C \vee B$ to you. First note that for any assignments of references τ, σ, if for all v, $\tau(v) \simeq \sigma(v)$, then by Axiom 6 (extensionality) for every wff A, $\nu_\tau \vDash A$ iff $\nu_\sigma \vDash A$. Now suppose that A has the form $\forall x\, B(x)$. We have:

$\nu_{\sigma/\simeq} \vDash \forall x\, B(x)$ iff for every assignment $\tau/\simeq\, \sim_x \sigma/\simeq$, $\nu_{\tau/\simeq} \vDash B(x)$
        and for every name c, $\nu_{\sigma/\simeq} \vDash C(c)$
    iff for every assignment $\tau \sim_x \sigma$, if $\tau(x) = d$,
        then $\nu_\tau \vDash B(d/x)$ (by induction and Lemma α'')
    iff $\nu_\sigma \vDash B(x)$ by Lemma α''

Hence, for every A, $M \vDash A$ iff $M_{/\simeq} \vDash A$. The case when A has the form $\exists x\, B(x)$ is done similarly.

In $M_{/\simeq}$ we have:

$\nu_{\sigma/\simeq} \vDash u \equiv v$ iff $\sigma(u) \equiv \sigma(v) \in \Sigma$ or $(v \equiv u) \in \Sigma$
    iff $[\sigma(u)] = [\sigma(v)]$ or $[u] = [v]$

It then follows that $M_{/\simeq}$ is a model of Σ in which the interpretation of "$\equiv$" satisfies all the conditions on the equality predicate.

Now define a model N for L by taking $M_{/\simeq}$ and deleting the interpretations of the w_i's (the universes are the same). For any closed wff A in L, $N \vDash A$ iff $M_{/\simeq} \vDash A$, as you can show. So $N \vDash \Gamma$. ∎

The strong completeness theorem then follows as in Theorem 18.

Classical Predicate Logic with Non-Referring Simple Names and Names for Partial Functions

The following axioms are added to those for classical predicate logic with equality.

Axioms for partial functions

7. $\forall \ldots \forall x \, \forall y \, (x \equiv y \rightarrow$
   $f(z_1, \ldots, z_k, x, z_{k+1}, \ldots, z_n) \equiv f(z_1, \ldots, z_k, y, z_{k+1}, \ldots, z_n))$
   for every $n+1$-ary function symbol f   *extensionality of functions*

7.*b. $\forall \ldots (\neg \exists x \, (x \equiv u) \rightarrow \neg \exists y \, (y \equiv f(u_1, \ldots, u, \ldots, u_n)))$
   for every n-ary function symbol f and terms $u_1, \ldots u, \ldots, u_n$
   non-referring is the default application of functions

Everything follows as for classical predicate logic with non-referring names until we get to the following.

Theorem 26 Every consistent collection of closed wffs in L has a countable model.

Proof Let Γ be a consistent collection of closed wffs of L. Let $\Sigma \supseteq \Gamma$ in $L(w_0, w_1, \ldots)$ be as in Theorem 24. We define a model M of $L(w_0, w_1, \ldots)$. Set:

$U = \{c_i : \text{for some } x, \exists x \, (x \equiv c_i) \in \Sigma\} \cup \{w_i : \text{for some } x, \exists x \, (x \equiv w_i) \in \Sigma\}$

We order the elements of U by taking $c_i < c_j$ iff $i < j$, and $w_i < w_j$ iff $i < j$, and for every i and j, $c_i < w_j$. I'll use $d, d_0, d_1 \ldots$ and $e, e_0, e_1 \ldots$ as metavariables ranging over elements of U.

Assignments of references:

For every σ and every x, $\sigma(x)\downarrow$, and the collection of such σ is complete.

For every atomic name c: If $c \in U$, then $\sigma(c)\downarrow = c$.

If $c \notin U$, then $\sigma(c)\updownarrow$.

For terms $f(v_1, \ldots, v_n)$ of depth 1:

If for some v, $\sigma(v_i)\updownarrow$, then $\sigma(f(v_1, \ldots, v_n))\updownarrow$.

If for all i, $\sigma(v_i)\downarrow$, let $\sigma(v_i) = d_i$.

Let d be the least atomic name such that $(f(d_1, \ldots, d_n) \equiv d) \in \Sigma$ if there is one, and set $\sigma(f(v_1, \ldots, v_n))\downarrow = d$.
If there is none, $\sigma(f(v_1, \ldots, v_n))\updownarrow$.

For terms $f(v_1, \ldots, v_n)$ of depth > 1 :

If for some i, $\sigma(v_i)\updownarrow$, then $\sigma(f(v_1, \ldots, v_n))\updownarrow$.

If for all i, $\sigma(v_i)\downarrow$, let $z_1, \ldots, z_n$ be the first variables not appearing in $f(v_1, \ldots, v_n)$. Let τ be an assignment of references that differs from σ only in that $\tau(z_i) = \sigma(v_i)$. Then $\sigma(f(v_1, \ldots, v_n)) \approx \tau(f(z_1, \ldots, z_n))$.

Appendix 7

I'll let you show that this definition of assignments gives a unique value for each term and satisfies the extensionality condition for atomic values of functions.

Evaluation of the equality predicate:

$\mathsf{v}_\sigma \vDash v \equiv u$ iff $\sigma(v)\downarrow$ and $\sigma(u)\downarrow$, and $(\sigma(v) \equiv \sigma(u)) \in \Sigma$
or $\sigma(v)\updownarrow$ and $\sigma(u)\updownarrow$ and
$y_1, \ldots, y_n$ is a list of all the variables appearing in v
$z_1, \ldots, z_n$ is a list of all the variables appearing in u
and $\sigma(y_i)\downarrow = d_i$ and $\sigma(z_i)\downarrow = e_i$ and, denoting by
$v \ll d_i/y_i \gg$ the result of substituting d_i for y_i for all i,
and by $u \ll e_i/z_i \gg$ the result of substituting e_i for z_i for all i,
$(v \ll d_i/y_i \gg \equiv u \ll e_i/z_i \gg) \in \Sigma$

I'll let you show that all of the conditions on the equality predicate in a model are satisfied by this interpretation of the equality predicate except possibly

(i) If $\sigma(u)\downarrow$ and $\sigma(v)\downarrow$, then $\mathsf{v}_\sigma \vDash u \equiv v$ iff $\sigma(u) = \sigma(v)$.

For the valuations of atomic wffs other than the equality predicate we use the following:

Let $y_1, \ldots, y_n$ be a list of all the variables appearing in $v_1, \ldots, v_n$, and let d_i be such that $\sigma(y)_i = d_i$. Denote by $P(v_1, \ldots, v_n) \ll d_i/y_i \gg$ the result, for all i, of substituting d_i for y_i in $P(v_1, \ldots, v_n)$, set

$\mathsf{v}_\sigma \vDash P(v_1, \ldots, v_n)$ iff $P(v_1, \ldots, v_n) \ll d_i/y_i \gg \in \Sigma$

I'll let you now modify the proof of Theorem 25 to apply here, using Axiom 7 (extensionality of functions) to show that the interpretation of "≡" in U is an equivalence relation that respects predication. ∎

Classical Predicate Logic with Non-Referring Simple Names, Descriptive Names, and Descriptive Functions

I. *Propositional axioms*

The axiom schemes of classical propositional logic, where wffs are substituted uniformly for A, B, C and the universal closure is taken.

II. *Axioms governing* $\forall$

1. a. $\forall \ldots (\forall x (A \to B) \to (\forall x A \to \forall x B))$ *distribution of* $\forall$
    if x is free in both A and B

   b. $\forall \ldots (\forall x (A \to B) \to (\forall x A \to B))$
    if x is free in A and not free in B

   c. $\forall \ldots (\forall x (A \to B) \to (A \to \forall x B))$
    if x is free in B and not free in A

2. $\forall \ldots (\forall x \forall y A \to \forall y \forall x A)$ *commutativity of* $\forall$

3.a† $\forall \ldots ((\forall x A(x) \land (u \equiv u)) \to A(u/x))$ *universal instantiation*
    when u is free for x in A   *for non-nil terms*

III. *Axioms governing the relation between* $\forall$ *and* $\exists$

4. a. $\forall \ldots (\exists x A \to \neg \forall x \neg A)$

Axioms for equality

5. a. $\forall x (x \equiv x)$ *identity*

   b.† $\neg \forall x \neg (x \equiv u) \to (u \equiv u)$ *identity for non-nil terms*
    when u is a closed term

6. $\forall \ldots \forall x \forall y (x \equiv y \to (A(x) \to A(y/x))$ *extensionality*
    where y replaces some but not necessarily all occurrences of x in A

Axioms for non-referring terms

8. $\forall \ldots ((A(u/x) \land \exists y (y \equiv u)) \to \exists x A(x))$ *existential generalization*
         for referring terms

9.* $\forall \ldots (\neg (u \equiv u) \to \neg A(u_1, \ldots, u, \ldots, u_n))$ *nil terms use*
    for n-ary atomic wffs A and terms $u_1, \ldots, u, \ldots, u_n$ *falsity as default*

12. $\forall \ldots (\forall y (\neg (\exists x (x \equiv y) \land A(y/x)) \to \neg \exists x A(x))$
    where y is free for x in A

Axioms for "the"-terms

10.* a. $\forall \ldots (\mathsf{R}x A(x) \leftrightarrow \exists z (z \equiv \underline{\text{the}}\, x\, A(x)))$ *referring descriptions*
    where z is the least variable not appearing in A   *create referring terms*

   b. $\forall \ldots (\mathsf{P}x A(x) \leftrightarrow \neg \mathsf{R}x A(x) \land \neg \forall z \neg (z \equiv \underline{\text{the}}\, x\, A(x)))$
    where z is the least variable not appearing in A   *pseudo-referring descriptions*
         yield pseudo-referring terms

11.* $\forall\ldots$ (Rx A(x) $\vee$ Px A(x)) $\rightarrow$ A(the x A(x))   *referring and pseudo-referring descriptive terms satisfy their own description*

13. $\forall\ldots$ ¬Rx A(x) $\wedge$ ¬Px A(x) $\rightarrow$ ¬(the x A(x) $\equiv$ the x A(x))   *nil descriptions yield nil terms*

Rule *modus ponens* for closed wffs

I'll let you prove that this system is sound. Lemmas 2–14 hold because the axiom schemes used in their proofs are the same here.

The proof of the following is the same as for Theorem 24 for non-referring names because of Axiom 12 here.

Theorem 27 Let Γ be a consistent set of closed wffs of L*. Let L*($w_0, w_1, \ldots$) be L* with the addition of name symbols $w_0, w_1, \ldots$ that do not appear in L. Then there is a collection of closed wffs Σ in L($w_0, w_1, \ldots$) such that:

a. $\Gamma \subseteq \Sigma$.
b. Σ is a complete and consistent theory.
c. If $\exists x\, B \in \Sigma$, then for some m, $B(w_m/x) \in \Sigma$ and $\exists x\, (x \equiv w_m) \in \Sigma$.
d. If ¬$\forall x\, B \in \Sigma$, then for some m, ¬$B(w_m/x) \in \Sigma$.
e. For every wff $B(x)$ in L($w_0, w_1, \ldots$) with one free variable, if for each i, $B(w_i/x) \in \Sigma$, then $\forall x\, B(x) \in \Sigma$.

The proof of the following is the same as the proof for Lemma 19 for classical logic with equality because Axioms 5.a and 6 for equality are in this system.

Lemma 28 a. $\vdash \forall x \forall y\, (x \equiv y \rightarrow y \equiv x)$
b. $\vdash \forall x \forall y \forall z\, (x \equiv y \rightarrow (y \equiv z \rightarrow x \equiv z))$

Theorem 29 Every consistent collection of closed wffs in L* has a countable model.

Proof Let Γ be a consistent collection of closed wffs of L*. Let $\Sigma \supseteq \Gamma$ in L*($w_0, w_1, \ldots$) be constructed as in Theorem 27. We define a model M* of L*($w_0, w_1, \ldots$) except that the evaluation of the equality predicate might not satisfy that if $\sigma(u)\downarrow$ and $\sigma(v)\downarrow$, then $\vDash_\sigma u \equiv v$ iff $\sigma(u) = \sigma(v)$.

We take as universe:

$U = \{c_i : \text{for some } x, \exists x\, (x \equiv c_i) \in \Sigma\} \cup \{w_i : \text{for some } x, \exists x\, (x \equiv w_i) \in \Sigma\}$

Lemma β For every $d \in U$, both $\exists x\, (x \equiv d) \in \Sigma$ and $(d \equiv d) \in \Sigma$.

Proof By construction and definition, using Axioms 4.a and 5.b†. □

Stage 0
Assignments of references:

For every σ_0 and every x, $\sigma_0(x)\downarrow$.
For every atomic name c: $c \in U$ iff $\sigma_0(c)\downarrow$, and if $\sigma_0(c)\downarrow$, then $\sigma_0(c) = c$.
The collection of such assignments is complete.

For valuations of the equality predicate:

$\vDash_\sigma v \equiv u$ iff $\sigma(v){\downarrow} = c$ and $\sigma(u){\downarrow} = d$, and $(c \equiv d) \in \Sigma$
or both are undefined and $(v \equiv u) \in \Sigma$

For valuations of atomic wffs other than the equality predicate:

$\vDash_\sigma P(v_1, \ldots, v_n)$ iff $P(d_1, \ldots, d_n) \in \Sigma$
where if v_i is a variable, then $d_i = \sigma(v_i)$
if v_i is a name c, then $d_i = c$

This determines all stages $n \geq 0$ and hence M^*.

Lemma α''' Suppose x is free in B and $d \in \mathsf{U}$. Then for any σ:
If $\sigma_n(x) = d$, then $\vDash_{\sigma_n} B(x)$ iff $\vDash_{\sigma_n} B(d/x)$.

Proof For stage 0, this is Lemma α' (p. 255). For stage $n + 1$, for atomic wffs it follows because the evaluation comes from stage 0. For compound wffs, it's as for Lemma α''. ∎

Now we'll induct on the length of A to show that $\mathsf{M}^* \vDash A$ iff $A \in \Sigma$. By virtue of the stability of references and truth-values, it suffices to show that if A is first defined at stage n, then:

(a) $\vDash_n A$ iff $A \in \Sigma$

To do so, we will need to show at the same time:

(b) At stage n, for every closed u, u is referring or pseudo-referring iff $(u \equiv u) \in \Sigma$.

I'll write "$\vDash_n A$" to mean that for every σ_n, $\vDash_{\sigma_n} A$.

Suppose $n = 0$. We have (b) as noted above because the only closed terms are atomic names. For (a), the proof is the same as for classical logic with descriptive names and descriptive functions (p. 256) except that Axiom 3† is used in place of Axiom 3*.

Suppose (a) and (b) are true for all stages $\leq n$.

(b) At stage $n + 1$, the only new cases are when u is "the x A(x)" where A is a wff of stage n and not of any earlier stage.

Suppose (the x A(x) $\equiv$ the x A(x)) $\in \Sigma$. By Axiom 13 and PC, (Rx A(x) $\vee$ Px A(x)) $\in \Sigma$. This wff is of stage n. Hence by induction, $\mathsf{M} \vDash$ Rx A(x) $\vee$ Px A(x). Hence by Lemma B of Chapter 47 (p. 218), "the x A(x)" is referring or pseudo-referring.

Now suppose that "the x A(x)" is referring or pseudo-referring. So by Lemma B of Chapter 47, $\mathsf{M} \vDash$ Rx A(x) $\vee$ Px A(x). So by induction (Rx A(x) $\vee$ Px A(x)) $\in \Sigma$. So by Axiom 11*, A(the x A(x)) $\in \Sigma$. So by Axiom 9 and PC, the x A(x) $\equiv$ the x A(x) $\in \Sigma$.

We can use (b) to show something more:

(c) If σ_{n+1}(the x B(x)) $= d$, or if d is the pseudo-reference of "the x B(x)",
then $(d \equiv$ the x B(x)) $\in \Sigma$.

Proof If σ_{n+1}(the x B(x)) $= d$ then d is the unique object satisfying B(x). So by Lemma α''', $\vDash_n B(d/x)$. If d is the pseudo-reference of "the x B(x)", then $\vDash_n B(d/x)$. If the x B(x) has reference or pseudo-reference, then by Lemma B of

Chapter 47 and induction, $\vDash_n Rx\, A(x) \vee Px\, A(x)$. So $\vDash_n Ux\, A(x)$, that is, $\vDash_n \forall x\, \forall y\, (B(x) \wedge B(y) \rightarrow (x \equiv y))$. Hence by induction, $B(d/x) \in \Sigma$ and $\forall x\, \forall y\, (B(x) \wedge B(y) \rightarrow (x \equiv y)) \in \Sigma$. By Axiom 11*, $B(\underline{\text{the }} x\, B(x)) \in \Sigma$. By (b), $(\underline{\text{the }} x\, B(x) \equiv \underline{\text{the }} x\, B(x)) \in \Sigma$. So by Axiom 3†, $(d \equiv \underline{\text{the }} x\, B(x)) \in \Sigma$. Hence, (c) holds at stage $n + 1$. □

(a) We'll show this at stage $n + 1$ by induction on the length of A.

Suppose that $A(v_1, \ldots, v_m)$ is atomic and $\vDash_{n+1} A(v_1, \ldots, v_m)$. Since A is closed, each v_i is closed. So each v_i is referring or pseudo-referring, where if v_i is an atomic name then u_i is v_i; if v_i is a pseudo-referring term, then u_i is its pseudo-reference; and if v_i is referring, u_i is its reference. Since this is a wff of stage 0, we have by induction $A(u_1/v_1, \ldots, u_m/v_m) \in \Sigma$. Hence by (c) and Axiom 6, $A(v_1, \ldots, v_m) \in \Sigma$.

Now suppose that A is atomic and $A(v_1, \ldots, v_m) \in \Sigma$. By Axiom 9* and PC, for each i, $(v_i \equiv v_i) \in \Sigma$. So for each i, by Axiom 13 and PC, $Rx\, A(x) \vee Px\, A(x) \in \Sigma$. So by induction, $M \vDash Rx\, A(x) \vee Px\, A(x)$. So by Lemma B of Chapter 47, for each i, v_i is a referring or pseudo-referring term. For each i, if v_i is an atomic name, let d_i be v_i; if v_i is referring or pseudo-referring, let d_i be its reference or pseudo-reference. Hence for all i, by (c) and Lemma β, for every i, $(d_i \equiv v_i) \in \Sigma$. So by Axiom 6, $A(d_1, \ldots, d_m) \in \Sigma$. Since $A(d_1, \ldots, d_m)$ is a wff of stage 0, we have by induction $\vDash_0 A(d_1, \ldots, d_m)$. Hence by the definition of satisfaction, $\vDash_{n+1} A(v_1, \ldots, v_m)$. Hence, (a) is true at stage $n + 1$ for atomic wffs.

Suppose now that (a) is true for all wffs of length k, and let A be a wff of length $k + 1$. I'll leave to you the cases when A is ¬B, B→C, B∧C, and B∧C.

Suppose that A is $\exists x\, B$ and $\vDash_{n+1} \exists x\, B(x)$. Then for some σ_{n+1}, $\nu_{\sigma_{n+1}} \vDash B(x)$. Take one such, where $\sigma_{n+1}(x) = d$. By Lemma α''', $\nu_{\sigma_{n+1}} \vDash B(d/x)$. Since d is in the universe, for some y, $\exists y\, (y \equiv d) \in \Sigma$. Since $B(d/x)$ is closed, $\vDash_{n+1} B(d/x)$, so by induction, $B(d/x) \in \Sigma$. Hence, using Axiom 8, $\exists x\, B(x) \in \Sigma$.

Suppose that A is $\exists x\, B$ and $\exists x\, B(x) \in \Sigma$. Since Σ satisfies (c) of Theorem 27, for some m, $w_m \in U$ and $B(w_m/x) \in \Sigma$. Hence by induction, $\vDash_{n+1} B(w_m/x)$. So by Lemma α''', for any σ_{n+1}, if $\sigma_{n+1}(x) = w_m$, then $\nu_{\sigma_{n+1}} \vDash B(x)$. So $\vDash_{n+1} \exists x\, B(x)$.

Suppose A is $\forall x\, B$ and $\vDash_{n+1} \forall x\, B$. Then by Lemma α''', for each i, $\vDash_{n+1} B(w_i/x)$. Hence by induction, for each i, $B(w_i/x) \in \Sigma$. Since Σ satisfies condition (e) of Theorem 27, $\forall x\, B \in \Sigma$.

Finally, suppose that A is $\forall x\, B$ and $\forall x\, B \in \Sigma$. Then by Axiom 3† and Lemma β, for every d, $B(d/x) \in \Sigma$. Hence by induction, $\vDash_{n+1} B(d/x)$. Hence, for all σ_{n+1}, for all d, $\nu_{\sigma_{n+1}} \vDash B(d/x)$ as $B(d/x)$ is closed. So by Lemma α''', for each σ_{n+1}, $\nu_{\sigma_{n+1}} \vDash B(x)$, so $\vDash_{n+1} B(x)$.

Recall the conditions on the equality predicate:

i. If $\sigma(u)\!\downarrow$ and $\sigma(v)\!\downarrow$, then $\nu_\sigma \vDash u \equiv v$ iff $\sigma(u) = \sigma(v)$.

ii. If one and only one of $\sigma(u)$ and $\sigma(v)$ is defined, then $\nu_\sigma \not\vDash u \equiv v$.

iii. If u and v are closed terms, then $\nu_\sigma \vDash u \equiv v$ iff $\nu_\tau \vDash u \equiv v$.

iv.* u is nil iff $\mathsf{v}_\sigma \not\models u \equiv u$.

v. For all u and v, $\mathsf{v}_\sigma \models u \equiv v$ iff $\mathsf{v}_\sigma \models v \equiv u$.

vi. For all u, v, w, if $\mathsf{v}_\sigma \models u \equiv v$ and $\mathsf{v}_\sigma \models v \equiv w$, then $\mathsf{v}_\sigma \models u \equiv w$.

We will show that in M^* the evaluation satisfies conditions (ii)–(vi).

We proceed by induction on the stages of construction of the model. We start with $n = 0$. Conditions (ii) and (iii) follow by definition. Condition (iv*) follows by Lemma β as there are no nil terms. Conditions (v) and (vi) follow by Lemma 28.

Suppose that the conditions are fulfilled at stage n. For condition (iv*), if u is nil, then $\mathsf{v}_\sigma \not\models u \equiv u$ by definition of how the valuations are extended. If u is not nil, then let c be the reference or pseudo-reference of it. Then by definition, $\mathsf{v}_{\sigma_n} \models u \equiv u$ iff $\mathsf{v}_{\sigma_0} \models c \equiv c$. Hence, by Lemma β, condition (iv*) is satisfied. Conditions (ii), (iii), (v), and (vi) follow because they hold at stage 0.

To create a model N that validates the same wffs as M^* and in which the equality predicate is evaluated as the identity on the universe, that is, satisfies conditon (i), we can proceed as in the proof of Theorem 25. ∎

The strong completeness theorem then follows in as in Theorem 18.

BIBLIOGRAPHY

Citations are to the most recent English reference listed unless otherwise noted.
Works cited in the text without attribution are by the author of this book, Richard L. Epstein.

BENTHEM, Johan Van. See VAN BENTHEM.
BOROWSKI, E. J.
    1974   Adverbials in Action Sentences
                Synthese, vol. 28, pp. 483–512.
BUNT, Harry C.
    1985   *Mass Terms and Model Theoretic Semantics*
                Cambridge University Press.
BURIDAN, Jean
    2001   *Summulae de Dialectica*
                Translated and with an introduction by Gyula Klima. Yale University Press.
CARNAP, Rudolf
    1947   *Meaning and Necessity*
                University of Chicago Press. 2nd edtion, 1956.
CASATI, Roberto and Achille VARZI
    1999   *Parts and Places*: *The Structure of Spatial Representation*
                MIT Press.
CHENEY, Dorothy L. and Robert M. SEYFARTH
    2007   *Baboon Metaphysics*
                University of Chicago Press.
CHURCH, Alonzo
    1973   Review of SCOTT, 1967
                Journal of Symbolic Logic, vol. 38, pp. 166–169.
CLARK, Romane
    1970   Concerning the Logic of Predicate Modifiers
                Noûs, vol. 4, pp. 311–335.
    1989   Deeds, Doings and What Is Done: The Non-Extensionality of Modifiers
                Noûs, vol. 23, pp. 199–210.
CORCORAN, John, William HATCHER, and John HERRING
    1972   Variable Binding Term Operators
                Zeitschrift f. math. und Grundlagen d. Math., vol. 18, pp. 177–182.
DAVIDSON, Donald
    1966   The Logical Form of Action Sentences
                In *The Logic of Decision and Action*, ed. Nicholas Rescher, University of Pittsburgh Press, pp. 81–120.
    1967   Causal Relations
                Journal of Philosophy, vol. 64, pp. 691–703. Reprinted in Davidson, *Essays on Actions and Events*, Oxford University Press, 1980.
    1969   The Individuation of Events
                In *Essays in Honor of Carl G. Hempel,* ed. Nicholas Rescher, D. Reidel. Reprinted in Davidson, *Essays on Actions and Events*, Oxford University Press, 1980.

EDWARDS, Paul, ed.
    1967   *The Encyclopedia of Philosophy*
              Macmillan and The Free Press.

ELLIS, John M.
    1993   *Language, Thought, and Logic*
              Northwestern University Press.

EPSTEIN, Richard (not the author of this book)
    2001   The Definite Article, Accessibility, and the Construction of Referents
              Cognitive Linguistics, vol. 12, pp. 333–378.

EPSTEIN, Richard L.
    1990   *Propositional Logics (The Semantic Foundations of Logic)*
              Kluwer. 2nd edition, Oxford University Press, 1995. 2nd edition with
              corrections, Wadsworth, 2000. 3rd edition, Advanced Reasoning Forum, 2012.
    1994   *Predicate Logic (The Semantic Foundations of Logic)*
              Oxford University Press. Reprinted, Advanced Reasoning Forum, 2012.
    1998   *Critical Thinking*
              Wadsworth. 5th edition with Michael Rooney, Advanced Reasoning Forum, 2017.
    2004   On Models and Theories with Applications to Economics
              Bulletin of Advanced Reasoning and Knowledge, vol. 2, pp. 77–98. Revised in
              EPSTEIN, 2012B, as "Models and Theories", pp. 67–109.
    2005   Paraconsistent Logics with Simple Semantics
              Logique et Analyse, vol. 189–192, pp. 189–207.
    2006   *Classical Mathematical Logic (The Semantic Foundations of Logic)*
              Princeton University Press.
    2011   *Cause and Effect, Conditionals, Explanations*
              Advanced Reasoning Forum. This includes:
                  Explanations, pp. 127–175.
                  Reasoning about Cause and Effect, pp. 13–93.
                  The Directedness of Emotions, pp. 95–100.
    2012A   *Reasoning in Science and Mathematics*
              Advanced Reasoning Forum.
    2012B   Mathematics as the Art of Abstraction
              In *The Argument of Mathematics*, eds. Andrew Aberdein and Ian Dove,
              Springer-Verlag. Reprinted in EPSTEIN, 2012A.
    2013A   *The Fundamentals of Argument Analysis*
              Advanced Reasoning Forum.
    2013B   *Prescriptive Reasoning*
              Advanced Reasoning Forum. This includes:
                  Truth and Reasoning, pp. 101–127. Also in EPSTEIN, 2015, pp. 133–159.
                  Prescriptive Theories?, pp. 129–163.
                  Reasoning with Prescriptive Claims, pp. 1–99.
    2014   Reflections on Temporal and Modal Logic
              Logic and Logical Philosophy, DOI 10.12775/LLP.2014.020. Reprinted in
              EPSTEIN, 2015, pp. 73–102.
    2015   *Reasoning and Formal Logic*.
              Advanced Reasoning Forum. This includes:
                  Postscript: Logic as the Art of Reasoning Well, pp. 156–161.

2016   *An Introduction to Formal Logic*
Advanced Reasoning Forum.

201?   "Language-Thought-Meaning"
Typescript. To appear in *Essays on Language and the World*.

EPSTEIN, Richard L. and Walter A. CARNIELLI
1989   *Computability*
Wadsworth. 3rd edition, Advanced Reasoning Forum, 2008.

EPSTEIN, Richard L. and Stanisław KRAJEWSKI
2004   Relatedness Predicate Logic
Bulletin of Advanced Reasoning and Knowledge, vol. 2, 2004, pp. 19–38.

HAYDEN, Rebecca E., Dorothy W. PILGRIM, and Aurora Quiros HAGGARD
1956   *Mastering American English*
Prentice-Hall.

HEATH, P. L.
1967   Nothing
EDWARDS, vol. 5, pp. 524–525.

HILBERT, David
1925   On the Infinite
A translation of "Über das Unendliche", *Mathematische Annalen,* vol. 95, pp. 161–190 by E. Putnam and G. Massey, in *Philosophy of Mathematics*, 2nd ed., eds. P. Benacerraf and H. Putnam, pp. 183–201.

JACKSON, Frank
1977   *Perception*
Cambridge University Press.

JESPERSEN, Otto
1924   *The Philosophy of Grammar*
Henry Holt and Company.

KALISH, Donald and Richard MONTAGUE
1964   *Logic: Techniques of Formal Reasoning*
Harcourt, Brace & World, Inc.

KAMP, J. A. W.
1975   Two Theories about Adjectives
In *Formal Semantics of Natural Language*, ed. E. Keenan, Cambridge University Press, pp. 123–155.

KLIMA, Gyula. *see* BURIDAN.

KRAJEWSKI, Stranisław. See EPSTEIN and KRAJEWSKI.

KROON, Fred
1987   Causal Descriptivism
Australasian Journal of Philosophy, vol. 65, pp. 1–17.

Le POIDEVIN, Robin
1990   Relatonism and Temporal Topology
Philosophical Quarterly, vol. 40, pp. 419–432. Reprinted in *The Philosophy of Time*, eds. Le Poidevin and Murray MacBeath, Oxford University Press, 1993, pp. 149–167.

MELLOR, D. H.
2006   Wholes and Parts: The Limits of Composition
South African Journal of Philosophy, vol. 25, pp. 138–145.

MONTAGUE, Richard. *See* KALISH and MONTAGUE.

MOODY, Ernest A.
   1967   William of Ockham
             In EDWARDS, Vol. 8, pp. 306–317.
MORTON, Adam
   1975   Complex Individuals and Multigrade Relations
             Noûs, vol. 9, pp. 309–318.
NAIGLES, Letitia, Anne FOWLER, and Atessa HELM
   1995   Syntactic Bootstrapping from Start to Finish with Special Reference to Down Syndrome
             In *Beyond Names for Things*; *Young Children's Acquisition of Verbs*, eds. Michael Tomasello and William E. Merriman, Lawrence Erlbaum Associates, pp. 299–330.
NOLT, John   Free Logic
             The Stanford Encyclopedia of Philosophy, online at <http://plato.standford.edu>.
ØHRSTRØM, Peter and Per F.V. HASLE
   1995   *Temporal Logic: From Ancient Ideas to Artificial Intelligence*
             Kluwer.
PARSONS, Terence
   1970   The Logic of Grammatical Modifiers
             Synthese, vol. 21, pp. 320–334.
   1990   *Events in the Semantics of English*
             MIT Press.
POIDEVIN. *See* Le POIDEVIN.
PORN, Ingmar
   1983   On the Logic of Adverbs
             Studia Logica, vol. XLII, pp. 293–298.
PRIOR, Arthur
   1962   Changes in Events and Changes in Things
             Preprint. Reprinted in *The Philosophy of Time*, eds. Robin Le Poidevin and Murray MacBeath, Oxford University Press, 1993, pp. 35-46. Also reprinted in *Papers on Time and Tense* by Arthur Prior, Oxford University Press, 2003, pp. 7–19.
QUINE, Willard van Orman
   1953   On What There Is
             In Quine, *From a Logical Point of View*, Harvard University Press, 2nd ed., 1961, pp. 1–19.
RENNIE, M.K.
   1974   *Some Uses of Type Theory in the Analysis of Language*
             Monograph Series, No. 1, Department of Philosophy, Research School of Sciences, Australian National University.
SAPIR, Edward
   1921   *Language: An Introduction to the Study of Speech*
             Harcourt Brace.
SCHWARZ, Thomas
   1975   The Logic of Modifiers
             Journal of Philosophical Logic, vol. 4, pp. 361–380.
SCOTT, Dana
   1967   Existence and Description in Formal Logic
             In *Bertrand Russell*, ed. Ralph Shoenman, Little Brown and Company, pp. 181–200. Reprinted with additions in *Philosophical Application of Free Logic*, ed. K. Lambert, Oxford University Press, 1991, pp. 28–48. See also CHURCH.

STRAWSON, P. F.
- 1959 *Individuals*
  Routledge.

SVENONIUS, Peter
- 2008 The Physiology of P
  In *Syntax and Semantics of Spatial P*, ed. A. Asbury, J. Dotlacil, B. Gehrke, and R. Nouwen, *Linguistik Aktuell/Linguistics Today*, vol. 120, pp. 63–84.

THOMASON, Richmond
- 1971 Logic and Adverbs
  Journal of Philosophy, vol. 68, pp. 715–716.

THOMASON, Richmond and Robert C. STALNAKER
- 1973 A Semantic Theory of Adverbs
  Linguistic Inquiry, vol. 4, pp. 195–220.

UNWIN, Nicholas
- 1996 The Individuation of Events
  Mind, vol. 105, pp. 315–330.

VAN BENTHEM, Johan F. A. K.
- 1986 *Essays in Logical Semantics*
  Kluwer.

VARZI, Achille
- 2003 Mereology
  Stanford Encyclopedia of Philosophy, online at <http://plato.standford.edu>.
  See also CASATI and VARZI.

WESTERSTÅHL, Dag
- 1989 Quantifiers in Formal and Natural Languages
  In *Handbook of Philosophical Logic*, eds. D. Gabbay and F. Guenther, Vol. 4, pp.1–131.

WHITE, Alan R.
- 1970 *Truth*
  Anchor Books, Doubleday & Company.

WHORF, Benjamin Lee
- 1940 Science and Linguistics
  Technology Review vol. 42, 1940 pp. 229–231, 247–248. Reprinted in *Language, Thought, and Reality: Selected Writings of Benjamin Lee Whorf*, ed. John B. Carroll, MIT Press, pp. 233–245.

WILLIAM of SHERWOOD
- 1966 *William of Sherwood's Introduction to Logic*
  Translated by Norman Kretzmann, University of Minnesota Press, 1966.

Index of Notation

¬, →, ∧, ∨   5
$p_0, p_1, p_2, \ldots$ 5
$A, B, C, A_0, A_1, \ldots$ 5, 15, 17
$L(\neg, \rightarrow, \wedge, \vee, p_0, p_1, \ldots)$ 5
T   8
F   8
v   8, 25
$v \models A$ 8
$v \not\models A$ 8
$\Gamma \models A$ 8
$\Gamma \not\models A$ 8
⊢   9
⊬   9
$\Gamma \vdash A$ 8
$\Gamma \not\vdash A$ 8
$c_0, c_1, \ldots$ 14
∀   14
∃   14
$x_0, x_1, \ldots$ 14
$P_0^1, P_0^2, P_0^3, \ldots, P_1^1, P_1^2, P_1^3, \ldots$ 15
$i, j, k, m, n, i_0, i_1, \ldots$ 15
$u, v, u_0, u_1, \ldots$ 15, 168
c   15
$P, Q, Q_0, Q_1, \ldots$ 15
—   15
x 15
$y, z, w, y_0, y_1, \ldots$ 15
$A(x)$ 16
$A(u/x)$ 16, 167
∀ . . .   19
$\sigma, \tau, \gamma, \sigma_0, \sigma_1, \ldots$ 21
$\mathfrak{a}, \mathfrak{a}_1, \ldots, \mathfrak{a}_n$ 21, 23
$\tau \sim_x \sigma$ 21
$v_\sigma \models A$ 24, 25

$v_\sigma \not\models A$ 24
$\sigma \models A$ 24
$M, N, M_0, M_1, \ldots$ 25
$M \models A$ 25
$M \models \Gamma$ 25
≡   29
/   39
$R_0, R_1, \ldots$ 44
$N_0, N_1, \ldots$ 77
$M, M', M_1, M_2, \ldots$ 83
R, R' 83
N, N' 83
∧   95
$d, d', d_1, d_2, \ldots$ 98, 99
e 143
$A(d)$ 100
+   104
&   108
∪   113
obj( )   125
< >   151
f_i^n 167
∃!   171
the   174
↓   179
↡   179
≈   179
$\exists_G$ 200
$\forall_R$ 200
$\equiv_R$ 201
A_R 201
$\tau \sim_u \sigma$ 208
Ux, Rx, Px 218
$<\mathfrak{a}, \mathfrak{b}>$ 236

Index of Examples

underlined page numbers indicate an example in the example-analysis format

A big man or dog is barking loudly. <u>121</u>
All dogs are loyal. <u>52</u>
All the men conspired. <u>118</u>
Anubis is a big wild big dog. <u>71</u>
Anubis is a big wild dog. 61
Any person who is tall is not short. <u>55</u>
As a horse-trainer, Gerald has a lot of patience. <u>157</u>
Bidú is a large mammal. Bidú is a dog. Every dog is a mammal. Therefore, Bidú is a large dog. <u>55</u>
Birta and Buddy are chasing and sniffing. <u>120</u>
Birta barked very loudly. <u>89</u>
Birta is a female. So Birta is not a male. <u>48</u>
Birta is a large cute dog. 81
Birta is a loveable large and not-cute dog. <u>119</u>
Birta is a not-fake dog. 84
Birta is a not-small dog. 84
Birta is a small and cute dog. 107
Birta is almost barking fakily. 80
Bon Bon and Gladys are matched donkeys. Therefore, Bon Bon is one of
    a matched pair of donkeys. <u>117</u>
Brutus stabbed with a knife with a knife. <u>71</u>
Buddy and Birta barked loudly at a stranger. <u>117</u>
Buster is a small elephant. Therefore, Buster is an elephant. 41
Caesar died. 227
Dick and Tom and Harry sang in three-part harmony. Therefore, Dick and Tom
    sang in three-part harmony. <u>116</u>
Dick and Tom lifted the table and tablecloth. 128
Dick and Tom sang. 94
Dick and Tom sang in harmony. 96
Dick and Tom wheeled Manuel in a wheelchair up a ramp into a gym. <u>130</u>
Dick and Zoe are a happy couple. <u>134</u>
Dick and Zoe are living together. <u>131</u>
Dick danced with Suzy and Zoe. Therefore, Dick danced with Suzy. <u>116</u>
Dick desceu a escada correndo. <u>155</u>
Dick doesn't like Zeke. Dick dislikes Zeke. <u>91</u>
Dick está esperando pacientemente. <u>121</u>
Dick has a dog. <u>130</u>
Dick has two dogs. <u>51</u>
Dick is a brother of Jane. Therefore, Dick is a brother. <u>129</u>
Dick is a brother. Therefore, Dick is a brother of someone. <u>129</u>
Dick is a bachelor. Therefore, Dick is not married. 32
Dick is awake. <u>49</u>
Dick is standing nearly next to Zoe. 80

Dick was dancing with Suzy and Zoe. 96
Dick was quickly irritated and chased Spot. 132
Dick's apple tree is tall. 188
Dinosaurs are reptiles. 202
Dward is a good scholar and administrator. 102
Every faithful and obedient dog is house-trained. 118
Every rabid cat is killed. 72
Everthing is a person or a god. 199
Everything is blond. 47
Everything that barks is a dog. Juney barks loudly. Therefore, Juney is a dog. 53
Everything that breathes also senses, and vice versa. Tom breathes slowly.
    Therefore, Tom senses slowly. 56
Everything that is a horse is a mammal. Pegasus is a horse. Therefore, Pegasus is a mammal. 200
Everything that is loved by Bellerophon is a winged horse. Pegasus is loved by Bellerophon.
    Therefore, something is a winged horse. 200
Example 1 is an example of ordinary speech. 72
Flo slid down a hill on the snow in a sled. 72, 119
Foo-Foo is a nearly purebred dog. 79
Harold walks nearly normally for a parapalegic. 154
Helen is strong. 111
Helga and Leopoldo are fraternal twins. 127
Helga and Leopoldo are twins. 134
Helio is not barking. 85, 202
I love Zoe. I love Puff. I love Tom. I love Dick. 158
If everything breathes, then Tom and Dick breathe. 116

$$\frac{(- \text{ is a dog})(c) \lor \neg (- \text{ is a dog})(c) \qquad 186}{\exists y\,(y \equiv c)} \qquad c \text{ is "\underline{the}\ } x\,[\,(- \text{ is a dog})(x) \lor \neg (- \text{ is a dog})(x)\,]"$$

John loves Mary. 234
June is a gorgeous redheaded Christian woman. 118
June is the gorgeous redheaded wife of John. 189
Juney barked almost loudly. 79
Juney is a dog. 229
Juney is a not-ugly black-and-white dog. 119
Juney is barking loudly and quietly. Therefore, Juney is barking. 118
Juney is barking loudly. Therefore, Juney is barking. 33, 38, 227
Juney is barking loudly. Therefore, Juney is not barking softly. 52
Juney is barking not-loudly. 84
Juney is loud. 52
Juney is running and barking. 102
Leo is well-adjusted for someone who has a cat. 158
Louis and Lorelei are neighbors of John and Sue. Therefore, Lorelei is a neighbor of John. 129
Mabel speaks well considering that she is deaf. 156
Manuel almost walked. 76
Manuel almost walked. Therefore, Manuel walked. 38
Manuel is emotional. 51
Manuel's singing is emotional. 51
Marilyn Monroe and Norma Jeane Baker sang. 98
Mark baas well considering that he is not a sheep. 156

Nancy is a good administrator and scholar, for someone who is obese. 151
(Non-standard analysis) 211
(Non-standard numbers in arithmetic) 210
Otto is an alleged thief. 78
Pegasus is a winged horse. Therefore, something is a winged horse. 199
Pegasus is Pegasus. 201
Peter left in a car. Therefore, there is something Peter left in. 69
Peter left in a huff. Therefore, there is something Peter left in. 69
Puff barely jumped. 88
Puff is an unattractive cat. 90
Puff is not even a nearly cute cat. 88
Ralph is a dog. All dogs bark. Therefore, Ralph barks. 2, 11
Ralph is a small and toy dog. 108
Ralph is a toy dog. 154
Ralph is a very fake dog. 89
Ralph is purple. Therefore, Ralph is not a dog. 47
Roger and Clara are happily married. 115
Slowly, Tom escorted Zoe and Dick pushed Manuel. 132
Slowly with Dick Spot stalked Puff. 131
Snakes are bad. 51
Socrates begins to be white. 231
Socrates begins to run. 221
Socrates died Xantippe. 130
Some dog is the one that's loved by all friends of Dick. 185
Some dogs are loyal. 54
Someone loves the cat that scratched Zoe. 184
Spot barked loudly at Puff. So Spot barked at Puff. 64
Spot belongs only to Dick. Therefore, Spot belongs only. 70
Spot chased a ball. 124
Spot chased Puff. 125
Spot is a dog that barks loudly. 156
Spot is a male. 47
Spot is a not-fierce large and cute dog. 119
Spot is afraid. 48
Spot is barking loudly rapidly. 71, 119
Spot is Dick's dog. 70
Spot is fearless. 90
Spot is nearly a cute dog. So Spot is a dog, but not a cute dog. 88
Spot ran towards Suzy and Zoe. 97
Spot was barking at 47. Therefore, Spot was barking. 70
Spot was barking at Suzy. 63
Spot was doing something loudly. 53
Spot was running from Dick. 64
Suzy carefully carried and petted Puff. 132
Suzy dances well even though she's a cheerleader. 156
Suzy dances well for a cheerleader. 150
Suzy is (a) too naive (person). 90

Suzy is beautiful. 49
Suzy is dancing well for a cheerleader. 154
Suzy nonchalantly stood between Tom and Dick and next to Zoe. 120
Suzy passionately loves Tom. 131
Suzy sings well for a cheerleader. 155
tan(π/2) = ∞   210
That is a big rabbit or hare. 112
That's an obviously fake Rodin. 81
The cat that belongs to some student and which scratched Zoe is a male. 184
The cat that scratched Zoe is a male. Therefore, there is a cat that scratched Zoe. 184
The cat that scratched Zoe is male. 172, 184
The cat that scratched Zoe is not a female. Something is not a female if and only it is a male. Therefore, there is a cat that scratched Zoe. 185
The cat that scratched Zoe is not a female. Therefore, there is a cat that scratched Zoe. 184
The dog that is loved by all friends of Dick is Spot. 185
The first cat that scratched Zoe was a female. 187
The man who is king is crazy. 188
The morning star is the evening star. 187
The nice cat is a nice cat. 186
The nice cat is not a nice cat. 186
The one lecturing and disputing is a master or bachelor. 121
The person who hit the father of the cat that belongs to Suzy and which scratched him hates cats. 186
The square circle is a square. 177
The victor at Jena was the loser at Waterloo. 187
The wife of John is the wife of an American. 185
The wife of the man who created Sherlock Holmes was rich. 213
There is a tree on the top of the cliff. 190
There is only one dog that is loved by all friends of Dick. 185
This is a pair of shiny shoes. So that one is a shiny shoe. 117
This is a nearly counterfeit dollar bill. 80
This towel is drier than that towel. 133
Thor had a dog. 202
Those are really sheep. 78
Three men conspired. 118
Tom almost sang and danced. 103
Tom and Suzy are lovers. 130
Tom is a good football player but not as a professional. 158
Tom is almost a college graduate. Therefore, someone is a college graduate. 88
Tom is almost speaking clearly. 89
Tom is happy to be a friend of Dick. 157
Tom is in Dick's house. 69
Tom is speaking almost clearly. 89
Tom is speaking, too. 90
Tom is speaking too loudly. Therefore, Tom is speaking loudly. 90
Tom is standing between Zoe and Suzy. 64, 116
Tom is walking from somewhere. 115
Tom ran a marathon. 124
Tom scaled the cliff. 189

Tom walked faster than Wanda ran. 134
Tom will telephone in a day. 70
Vulcan orbits the sun. 203
Wanda and Suzy very loudly and merrily danced and sang, though not with abandon, with all of their friends. 120
Wanda and Suzy very loudly and merrily danced and sang with all of their friends. 120
Wanda was fired. 51
Yoshikawa is a Japanese pilot. Therefore, Yoshikawa is a pilot and Yoshikawa is Japanese. 54
Zoe is blond. Therefore, Zoe is a person. 47
Zoe is running from something. 73
Zoe packed a bag. So Zoe packed. 129

$\aleph_0 + \aleph_0 \equiv \aleph_0$ 210

$6 - 7 \equiv -1$ 210

$i^2 \equiv -1$ 210

$\mu y (y + y = 1) \simeq \mu z (z \cdot z = 3)$ 211

$\{x : x > 1\} = \{y : y > 3\} \cup \{2\}$ 211

(x_1, x_2) is between (x_3, x_4) and (x_5, x_6) 134

$\forall x (\emptyset \subseteq x)$ 212

Index

Italicized page numbers indicate a definition, statement of principle, or a quotation.

n indicates a footnote

The Introduction and the Summaries are not indexed.

abstract objects, 1–2, 14, 40, 57–58, 60, 164–165, 204–205, 211, 224–226, 230, 235, 241
abstraction operator in set theory, 211
abstracting, 7, 11, 164, 236, 240
adjectives, 41–43
    order of, 61–62
    relative, *42*, 47–52
    relativizing quantifiers with, *54*
adverbs, 38–40
    adjectives vs., 41
    event-talk eliminates, 227
"all", 14
analysis vs. formalization, *32*, 47, 91, 134, 172
"and" joining modifiers, 107–110
"and" joining predicates, 102–106, 128
"and" joining terms, 94–101
application of a predicate. *See* predicate applies to an object or objects.
arguments, 2
Aristotle, 231
arithmetic, 204, 210
arity of a predicate, 15
assignment(s) of references, *21*, *141*
    complete collection of, *21*, *141*, 168, 194, 196, 206
    extended to all descriptive terms, *178–181*
    extended to all terms with functions, *169*
    with non-referring simple names, *194*
    with non-referring simple names and descriptive names, *217*
associativity of
    ∧, *100*, *101*, *143*, *146*
    +, *105*, *106*, *144*, 146, *147*
    &, *109*, *144*, 146, *147*
    ∪, *113*, *114*, *145*, 146, *147*
Athapascan, 232

atomic application of a function, *168*, *207*
atomic names are referring, *182*
atomic predicate, formal, *66–67*, *105*, *113*, *139–140*, *152–153*
    degree of, *66–67*, *105*, *113*, *140*
atomic predications, extensionality condition for, *24*, *143*
    with function names, *170*
    with non-referring simple names, *195*
atomic term, *167*
atomic wff,
    predicate logic, *16*, *17*, *23*, *44*
    propositional logic, *6*
Axelrod, Melissa, 125n
axiom, *9*
axiom system, *9*. *See also name of logic*, e.g. classical propositional logic, axiom system.

"beautiful", 49–51
Bernays, Paul, 173
binary predicate, *14*
binding of a variable, *16*, *141*, *176*
blanks in a predicate, 13–14, 19, 106
    variable fills a blank, *15*, 19
Borowski, E. J., 34n, 228n
Bunt, Harry C., 33n
Buridan, *1n*, *42n*, 85n, 121

Carnap, Rudolph, 173
Casati, Robert, 227n, 240n, 241n
categorematic vocabulary, *17*
    ∧ is — ?, 96
    formalizing and, 31–32, 48
    obj ( ) is, 126
cause and effect, 2, 229n
Cheney, Dorothy L., 127n

Church, Alonzo, 173
Clark, Romane, 34n, 42n, 54, 71, 78n
classical abstraction of,
    functions, *168*
    names, *20*
    predicates, *23*
    propositions, *7*
classical evaluation of ∀, *25*
classical evaluation of ∃, *25*
classical predicate logic, *27*
    axiom system, *28*
    completeness theorem, 246–250
    with equality, *29–30*
        completeness theorem 251–252
classical propositional logic, *9*
    axiom system, *10*
    completeness theorem, 243–245
classification predicate, 42–43, 76, 94, 126–127, 128, 129, 160, 229, 231–232. *See also* process predicate.
closed term, *176*
closed wff, *16, 140–141*
collections, 33
commutativity of
    ∀, *28*
    ∧, *100, 101, 143, 146*
    +, *105, 106, 144,* 146, *147*
    &, *109, 110, 144,* 146, *147*
    ∪, *113, 114, 144,* 146, *147*
compactness theorem, *245, 250*
comparatives, 133–134
complementing object, 125
complete collection of wffs, *9*
completeness of collection of assignments of references, *21, 141,* 168, 194, 196, 206
complex term, *176*
compositionality,
    functions and, 169
    predicate logic, *24*
    propositional logic, *7*
compound wff,
    full theory of modifiers and internal conjunctions and disjunctions, *140*
    predicate, *6*
    propositional logic, *16*
computable functions, 211
conditional, the, *5*
conjunction, *5*

conjunction (internal),
    of unary predicates, *104*
    of restrictors, *108, 139*
    of terms, 96, *139*
        formal —, *98–99*
        mathematical semantics for, 239
    not of relations, 128
    See also disjunction of predicates.
connectives, *5–6*
consequence, formal vs. material, *33*
consistent collection of wffs, *9*
contradiction, 3
copula, 229
Corcoran, John, 176
cross-referencing, 14

Davidson, Donald, *11*, 227n, 229n
declarative sentence, 1n
degree,
    of atomic predicate, *66–67, 105, 113, 140*
    of conjunction of terms, *98–99, 139*
    of formal modifier, *82, 139*
degrees, comparisons formalized with, 133–134
depth of a term, *167*
derivation, formal, *9*
descriptive functions,
    axiom system, *182–183*
        completeness theorem, 254–257
    extensionality of, 183
    semantics of, *180–181*
    syntax of, *175–176*
    with non-referring simple names, 218–220
        axioms for, *219–220*
        completeness theorem, 265–269
    See also term.
descriptive names, 171–173
    axiom system, *182–183*
        completeness theorem, 254–257
    extensionality of, 183
    in mathematics, 211–212
    non-referring simple names are —?, 193
    semantics of, *177–180*
    syntax of, *174–175*
    use falsity as the default truth-value, *182,* 186
    with non-referring simple names, 213–218
        axioms, *219–220*
        completeness theorem, 265–269
    See also term.

direct object, 125–127
disjunction, *5*
disjunction (internal). *See* disjunction of predicates.
disjunction of predicates, *113*
    not relations, 128
distribution of ∀, *28*
division of form and content,
    extensionality and, 57, 59–60
    functions and, 169
    predicate logic, *24*
    propositional logic, *7*
duplicated reference in a conjunction of terms, *100*, *101*, *144*, *147*

Ellis, John M., 51
emphasizer, *78*
Epstein, Richard (not the author of this book), 190n
equality predicate, *29–30*
    descriptive names and, 180
    descriptive functions and, 181
    restricted, *201*
    with non-referring simple names, *194–195*
        not fully logical, 195
        with partial functions, *207*
    with non-referring simple names and descriptive functions, *214–215*
equivalence of ∪ and ∨, *114*, *145*, *148*
equivalence relation, *251*
events, 52, 227–230
existence and ∃, *18*
existential generalization, *64*, *249*
    for referring terms, *182*, *198*, *219*
existential quantifier, *14*
    descriptive names and, 178
    generous, *199*–201
    unique, *171*
    with non-referring simple names, 195
"exists", 18, 69, 192–193
    vs. "something" or "there is", 199
explanations, 2
extension of a predicate, *58*, 235–237
extensionality axiom, *29*
extensionality condition for atomic predicates, *24*, *143*
    with function names, *170*
    with non-referring simple names, *195*

extensionality condition for functions, *169*, 183
    axiom for, *170*
    for partial functions, *206*
extensionality for descriptive names, 183
extensionality of all predications, *26*
    with non-referring simple names, *196*
    with partial functions, *208*
extensionality of functions, 165–166
    axiom, *170*
extensionality of names, *57*
extensionality of predicate restrictors, 56, 58–60
extensionality of predicates, *23*, 57–58
    atomic predicates, 68.
    See also extensionality of all predications.
external logical symbols, 138

falsity is the default truth-value, 22, 177, *182*, 186, 216, *219*. *See also* non-referring is default for terms; nil terms use falsity as the default truth-value.
fiction, 192–193, 202–203. *See also* non-referring simple names.
form and meaningfulness,
    functions and, 169
    predicate logic, *22*
    propositional logic, *6*
form of a proposition, 27
formal atomic predicate, *66–67*, *105*, *113*, *139–140*, *152–153*
formal conjunction of terms, *98–99*
formal consequence, *33*, *124–125*
formal language, 5
    full theory of modifiers and internal conjunctions and disjunctions, *138–141*
    of descriptive names and descriptive functions, *174–176*
    with function names, *167*
    with predicates as modifiers, *152–153*
formal logic, *3*
formal modifier(s), *82*, *139*, *152–153*
formal semantics for natural language, 62
formalization vs. analysis, *32*, 47, 91, 134, 172
formalizing,
    avoiding *ad hoc* assumptions, 32, 50
    conventions for, 32
    criteria of, *31–32*, 33
    general view of, 11–12
    grammar, 31, 131, 172–173

formalizing (*continued*)
    meaning axioms and, 32
    parsimony of, *43*
Fowler, Anne, 156n
free logic, *181*
Frege, Gottlob, 173
function(s), 164–166
    as predicates, 164
    atomic application of, *168*
        extended to all terms, *169, 207*
        non-referring is default, *206*
    axioms for, *170*
        completeness theorem, 253
    extensionality of, 165–166, *169*, 183
        partial functions, *206*
    linguistic?, 165
    names of, 165
    partial, 166, 205, 206–209
        axioms for, *209*
        extensionality of, *206*
    total, 166
    value of a —, *168*
    See also descriptive function.

generalized *modus ponens*, 246
generous existence quantifier, *199–201*
geometry, Euclidean, 135
grammar, formalizing, 31, 131, 172–173

Haggard, Aurora Quiros, 190n
"has". *See* "possesses".
Hasle, Per F.V., *231*
Hatcher, William, 176
Hayden, Rebecca E., 190n
height of a term, *175*
Helm, Atessa, 156n
Herring, John, 176
Hilbert, David, 173
"Homer", 192–193
Hopi, 232

identity axiom, *29, 182, 197*
    for non-nil terms, *219*
indirect object, 126
individual. *See* thing.
inducting on experience is not a justification
    for semantics, *65*
inference, *2*. *See also* valid inference.

inference to the best explanation, 204, 228
intension of a predicate, 59, 60
intensive, an, *78*
intentions, 2
internal logical symbol, *138*
iota operator, *173*, 176
"is" as equality, 185, 187, 189
"is" as "remains", 69–70

Jackson, Frank, *58*, 62
Jespersen, Otto, *232*

Kalish, David, *176*
Kamp, J. A. W., 39n, *58–59*, 62
Krajewski, Stanisław, 33n
Kroon, Fred, 193

language, ordinary, *passim*. *See also* formal
    language.
length of wff,
    in full theory of modifiers and internal
        conjunctions and disjunctions, *140*
    in predicate logic, *15–16*
    in propositional logic, *5*
Le Verrier, Urbain, 203
Lescarbault, Edmond Modeste, 203
liar paradox, *18*
logic. *See kind of logic*, e.g., propositional
    logic.
logic and reasoning, *passim*
logical vocabulary. *See* syncategorematic
    vocabulary.
"loves", 158

many-valued logic, 22n
masses, 33
material consequence, *33*, 124–125
mathematical reasoning, 2
mathematics, 164–166
    non-referring names in —, 204–205, 210–212
    objectivity of, 224
meaning,
    axioms, *32*
    calculus of, 11
    formal semantics and, 235
    of a predicate restrictor, 46
medieval logic, 1n, 42n, 77n, 85n, 121, 226, 231
Mellor, D. H., 241n

metalogic, *18*
  vs. logic, *18*
metaphysics, *passim*
  minimal, 224–226
modal logic, 233–234
model,
  predicate logic, *25*
  propositional logic, *8*
  See also sufficiency of collection of models.
modified atomic predicate, formal.
  See atomic predicate, formal.
modifier, formal, *82*
modus ponens, *10*
Montague, Richard, *176*
Moody, Ernest A., *226*

n-ary predicate, *15*
n-tuples and conjunctions of terms, 95
Naigles, Letitia G., 156n
name, *14*, 20, 192–193.
  See also descriptive function; descriptive name; non-referring name.
name symbol, *14*
names refer, *20*, 166, 169
Neg, 77, *143*, *146*
negated modifiers, *83*
negation, *5*
negator, *76*
  pure, 84–87
negators and pure negators in joined restrictors, *109*, *110*, *144*, *147*
negators of restrictors and pure negated restrictors, 87, *143*, *146*
neutralizer, 78n
nil descriptions yield nil terms, *220*
nil name, *178*, *214*, *215*
nil terms use falsity as the default truth-value, 216, *219*
NN′, *83*, *143*, *146*
Nolt, John, 181
nominalism, 226, 241
non-referring is default application of a function, *206*
  axiom, *209*
non-referring names take falsity as default, *182*
non-referring simple name, *194*
  axiom system, *197–198*

completeness theorems, 258–262, 263–264, 265–269
descriptive names, names for partial functions, and —, 213–220
nonsense, 19, 22, 42, 70, 98, 114, 177
Nootka, 232
"not" as modifier, 84–87, 184, 201–202
nothing, 204–205, 212
numbers, 204–205
  as adjectives, 51

Ockham, William of, 226
Øhrstrøm, Peter, *231*
"of", 69–70, 188. *See also* "possesses".
open term, *176*, 188
open wff, *16*
  full theory of modifiers and internal conjunctions and disjunctions, *140–141*
  is a proposition?, 18
"or" joining predicates, 111–114
ordinals, 187–188

paraconsistent logic, 3n
parentheses, deleting, 16
parity of form, *31*, 118–119, 156, 173
parsimony of formalizing, *43*
Parsons, Terence, 34n, *227*, *228*
partial functions. *See* function, partial.
parts of things, 190, 240–241
passive tense, formalizing, 51, 185
PC, *246*
Peter of Spain, 231
picking out an object. *See* referring.
Pilgrim, Dorothy W., 190n
platonist (platonism), 23, 49, 58, 204–205, 210–211, *224–225*, 235, 241
Porn, Ingmar, 34n
"possesses" ("has"), 51, 69–70, 130, 188–189, 202–203.
possibility, *3*, 225, 233–234
predication, *23*. *See also* atomic predications.
predicate(s), *14*, 57–60
  as restrictor, *149–153*
  extension of, *58*, 235
  formal atomic. *See* atomic predicate, formal.
  intension of, 59, 60
  linguistic?, 57–60, 164–165, 171
  modified atomic. *See* atomic predicate, formal.

predicate (*continued*)
  modified atomic. *See* atomic predicate, formal.
  quantifying over, 33
  vagueness and, 21–22
predicate applies to an object or objects (satisfaction), *23*, *142–143*
  meaning of, 235
predicate conjoiner, *104*
predicate disjoiner, *113*
predicate negator. *See* negator.
predicate restrictor(s), *39–40*, *43*
  extensionality of, 56, 58–60
  meaning of, 46
  multiple, 61–62
  repeated, 71–72
  variable, *64*
prepositions, 63
prescriptive claims, 85n
prescriptive nature of logic, 65
process predicate, 42–43, 76, 124, 126, 128, 229, 231–232
proof, formal, *9*
proposition, *1*, 224–226, 230
propositional form of a wff, *246*
propositional logic, 5
propositional modifier, 40
propositional operators, 40, 46, 106, 132, 159, 233–234
propositional symbols, 5
propositional variables, 5
pseudo-reference, *213*–214, *215*, *218*
pseudo-referring descriptions yield pseudo-referring terms, *220*
punctuation, *17*
pure negated predicate, *139*
pure negated predicates, *86*, *87*
pure negated restrictors, *86*, *87*, *143*, *146*
pure negator, 84–87, *86*

quantification in atomic predicates?, 115
quantifier,
  binds a variable, *16*, *143*
  existential, *14*
  superfluous, 19
  universal, *14*
Quine, W. V. O., 172n

realization,
  full theory of modifiers and internal conjunctions and disjunctions, *141–142*
  of a function symbol, *168*
  predicate logic, *17*
  propositional logic, *6*
reasoning, *passim*
relation, *124*
relative adjective, *42*, 47–52
relativizing quantifiers with adjectives, *54*
referring (designating, picking out), 20
referring and pseudo-referring descriptions satisfy their own descriptions, *220*
referring descriptions yield referring terms, *183*, *220*
referring descriptive terms satisfy their own description, *183*
Rennie, M. K., 34n
RES, *143*, *146*
Res$_1$, *45*
RES$_1$, *68*
restricted equality predicate, *201*
restricted universal quantifier, *200*–201
restriction of an atomic wff, *201*
restrictor, predicate. *See* predicate restrictor.
restrictors and +, *106*, *144*, *147*
restrictors and ∪, *114*, *145*, *148*
RN, *83*, *143*, *146*
Russell, Bertrand, 171–173

Sapir, Edward *1n*
satisfaction of a predicate. *See* predicate applies to an object or objects.
Schwarz, Thomas, 34n, 134n
scope of a quantifier, *16*, *141*
scope of a <u>the</u>-term, *175*, *176*
scope of an informal quantifier, 172, 173, 184, 186
Scott, Dana, 173, 181
second-order logic, 33n, 53
semantic consequence, *8*
semi-formal language,
  predicate logic, 27
  propositional logic, 6
set theory, 235–236
  compared to theory of parts of things, 240–241
Seyforth, Robert M., 127n

"Sherlock Holmes", 192–193, 203, 213
simple name, *17, 141–142*
simple predicate, *17*, 67, *141–142*
simple restrictor, *67, 141–142*
"some", 14
sound axiom system, 9
stability of references and truth-values, 176, *179*
stability of references, pseudo-references, and truth-values, *216*
Stalnaker, Robert, 34n
Strawson, P. F., *22n*, 172n
strongly complete axiom system, 9
sufficiency of collection of models,
    full theory of modifiers and internal conjunctions and disjunctions, *145*
    predicate logic, 27
    propositional logic, *8*
    with functions, *170*
    with non-referring names and partial functions, *209*
superfluous quantifier, 19
Svenonius, Peter, 126n
syncategorematic vocabulary, *17*
    ^ is —, 96
syntactic consequence, 9
syntactic deduction theorem, *243, 246*

tautology,
    predicate logic, *26*
    propositional logic, *8–9*
tenses. *See* time.
term(s), *15, 99, 139*
    atomic, *167*
    closed, *176*
    complex, *167*
    depth of, *167*
    descriptive names and functions and, *174–176*
    free for a variable, *16, 167, 176*
    height of a, *175*
    open, *176*
    See also conjunction (internal) of terms.
the, 174–175
    scope of, *175, 176*
"the" not used for a name, 185, 190n
theorem, formal, *9*
theory, *9*

things, 13
    all —, 20, 47, 240
    distinguishability of, 13, 21
    events are?, 227–230
    fictional, 192–193
    masses aren't, 33, 72
    parts of, 190, 240–241
    processes aren't, 73
    See also abstract objects; universe of a realization.
Things, the World, and Propositions, *13*
Thomason, Richmond, 34n
time, 52, 70, 72, 84, 86, 94, 102–103, 111, 128, 132, 154, 156, 158, 187, 188, 192, 202, 231, 232, 233.
    See also process predicate.
"too", 90
transitive verb, 124–127
transitivity of →, *247*
truth, 2, 224–226
type *1*, 225

unary predicate, *14*
universal closure of a wff, *19*
universal instantiation, *28*
    for conjunction of terms, 98, 100, 116
    for non-nil terms, *219*
    for referring terms, 178, *182*
"un-" (prefix), 90
unique existential quantifier, *171*
uniqueness quantifiers, *218*
universal quantifier, *14*
    descriptive names and, 177–178
    restricted —, *200*–201
    with non-referring simple names, *196*
    with partial functions, *208*
universe of a realization, *20, 142*
Unwin, Nicolas, 229n

vagueness, 21–22, 42, 47, 48, 53, 55–56, 71, 86, 157, 158
valid inference, *2*
    predicate logic, *26*–27
    propositional logic, *8*
valuation,
    based on σ, *24*
    propositional logic, *8*
    predicate logic, *25*

value of a function, *168*
van Benthem, Johan, 176
variable(s), *14*
    consistently supplemented with references, *23*
    different roles in logic, 19
    essential for predicate logic, 172n
    fills a blank, *15*
    free, *15–16*
    term is free for —, *16*.
    See also blanks in a predicate.
variable formal modifier, *82*
variable predicate restrictor, *63–64*
Varzi, Achille, 227n, 240n, 241n
Venn diagrams, 62
verbs,
    eliminated by event-talk, 227
    transitive, 124–127.
    See also process predicate; transitive verb.
"very", 89

well-formed formula,
    full theory of modifiers and internal conjunctions and disjunctions, *140*
    predicate logic, *15–16*
    propositional logic, *5*
Westerståhl, Dag, 176
wff. *See* well-formed formula.
White, Alan R., 22n
Whorf, Benjamin Lee, *231–232*
William of Sherwood, *77n*

www.ingramcontent.com/pod-product-compliance
Lightning Source LLC
Chambersburg PA
CBHW082032300426
44117CB00015B/2450